Andrea Mantegna

and the Italian Renaissance

Joseph Manca

Author: Joseph Manca

Layout: Baseline Co. Ltd.
127-129A Nguyen Hue
Fiditourist, 3rd floor
District 1, Ho Chi Minh-City
Vietnam

ISBN 10: 1-85995-012-4
ISBN 13: 978-1-85995-012-8

Printed in Singapore

Andrea Mantegna

and the Italian Renaissance

Joseph Manca

Contents

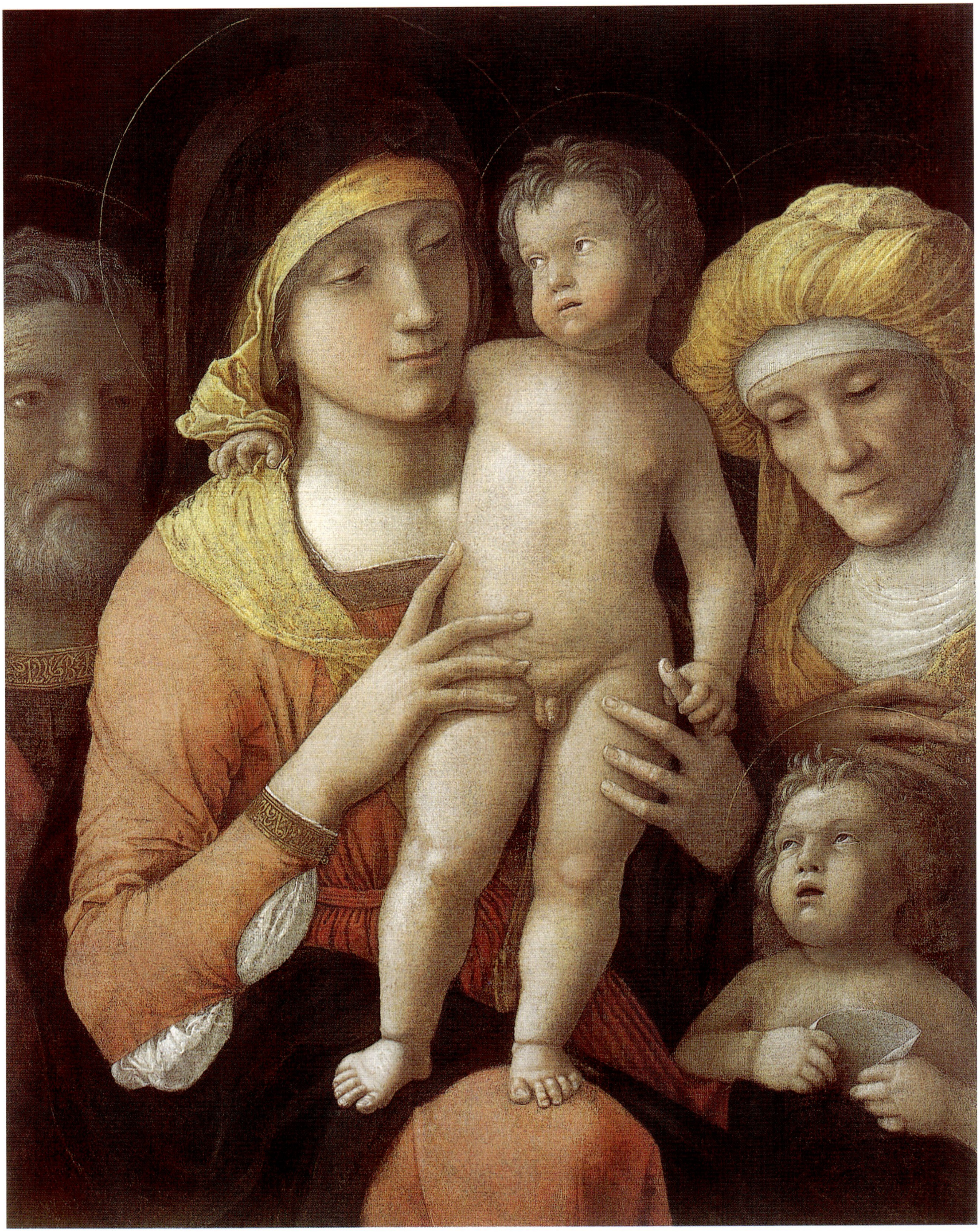

Mantegna as Artistic Revolutionary

The art of Andrea Mantegna (born c.1431, died 1506) has long maintained a broad and deep appeal. From the impressive illusionism of his earliest works (Fig. 4) to the narrative power of his mature paintings (Fig. 2), Mantegna's art remained vivid and heroic, dramatic and emotional. They are also painted in stunning detail: pebbles, blades of grass, veins, and hair are rendered with excruciating care, and he depicted even in his great narrative works the mundane particulars of earthly existence, showing laundry hanging out to dry and buildings fallen into disrepair. He had a deep interest in human nature and issues of moral character. Perhaps most strikingly, Mantegna's pictures are filled with references to classical antiquity. No other painter of the fifteenth century so thoroughly understood and abundantly included in his art the costumes, drapery folds, inscriptions, architecture, subject matter, ethical attitude, and other aspects of ancient classical civilisation. And instead of the cool classicism of later centuries, his vision of Greco-Roman civilisation is lively and has a familiar and nostalgic air about it. For him, antiquity was a near, palpable presence, one which he sought constantly to bring to colourful existence in his pictures. It is this thirst for a vanished classical past that places Mantegna most firmly in the context of his time, as his art was favoured most warmly by Renaissance contemporaries who shared his visionary quest to revive the moral strength and naturalism which marked the art of antiquity.

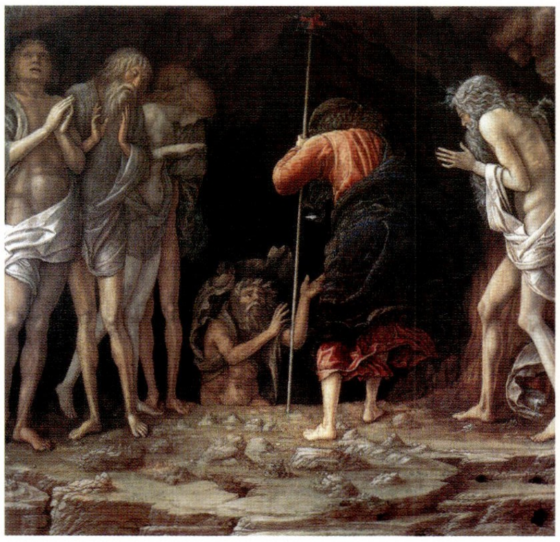

Mantegna was a leader in the renewal of culture occurring during his time, a movement we call the Renaissance, or "rebirth." In the fifteenth century, classical civilisation was a whole universe open to rediscovery. It offered an alternative to the confining, medieval world of scholastic thought and Christian theology. Classicism meant the liberation of the mind and the joys of literary study. The writers and artists of antiquity indulged freely in the delights of the material world, an attitude shared by Mantegna and many of his contemporaries. Renaissance men found spiritual ancestors from centuries past who had similar ideas about virtue and vice, and whose secular sensibility embraced a naturalistic art that was idealised in its formal perfection and its harmonious proportions. Mantegna painted his classical visions for enthusiasts, men and women who were dilettantes in the original sense of the word, delighting in their new discoveries. His life and works contributed to the air of celebration and self-congratulation characterising much of Renaissance culture. Some modern scholars avoid using the word "Renaissance" and, rather than see the period as being an age of confidence and a glorious rebirth of values, they describe Italian culture from 1400 to 1600 as one of conflicting interests, a hesitant and contradictory world in which the men and women cautiously "negotiated" their places in society. Period texts, however, reveal a mentality not as tentative and fearful as modern scholarship would have us believe. To be sure, the Renaissance had its political crises and social dislocations. It is important to bear in mind the larger picture: leading patrons, intellectuals, and artists in Italy felt they were living in a period of rebirth, and were forcibly helping to shape a new order of things. In the visual sphere, Renaissance writers about art – Lorenzo Ghiberti, Leon Battista Alberti, and Giorgio Vasari, for example – were quite clear in seeing the Middle Ages as a dark period, and their own age as one of enlightenment and human improvement. They looked back with admiration towards the achievement of the Greeks and Romans, and called for, not a bland imitation of antiquity, but an embracing of the ideals and values which made ancient societies superior to the cultural decline that followed: reason, an acceptance of natural law, and ethical moderation.

1. *The Holy Family with St Elizabeth and the young St John*, c. 1485-1488. Tempera and gold on canvas, 62.9 x 51.3 cm. Kimbell Art Museum, Fort Worth.

2. *The Descent into Limbo*, c. 1490. Tempera on panel, 38.2 x 42.3 cm. Private collection.

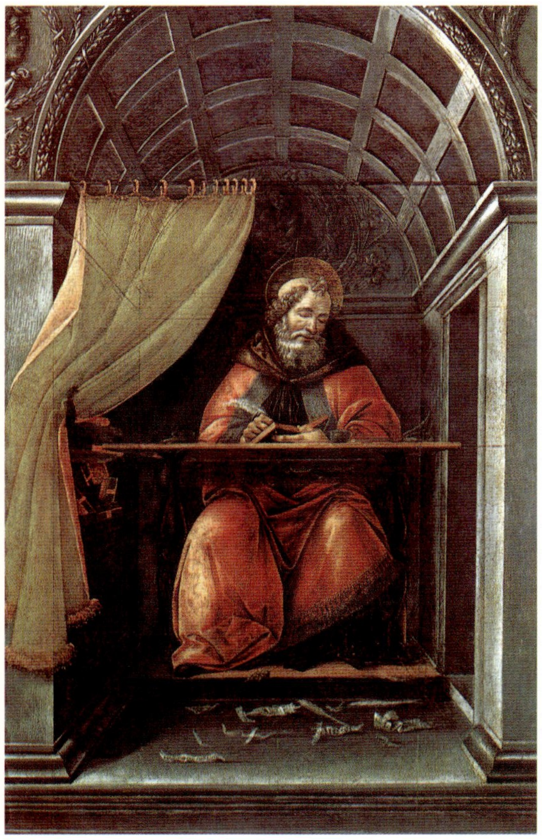

3. Sandro Botticelli, *St Augustine in his Cell*, 1494.
Tempera on panel, 41 x 27 cm.
Galleria degli Uffizi, Florence.

The rebirth of the art of painting was one of the major aspects of the Renaissance period. Mantegna's pictures – embracing a vivid realism and a learned antiquarianism – epitomised the art of the Early Renaissance period perhaps better than the works of any other artist of the fifteenth century. This is an extraordinary claim to make for a painter who was born, trained, and lived in the relatively provincial cities of Padua and Mantua, removed from the flourishing cultural centres of Florence, Venice, and Rome. But somehow Mantegna managed to seize on the avant-garde intellectual ideas of his time and forge a style which set him apart from his contemporaries. His greatest achievement was that he did not accommodate medieval tradition in his art; he fought against it. The older Gothic painters, active in the early fifteenth century, clung to the dreamy, soft, gentle vision we associate with the late medieval world. Moreover, many of the so-called Renaissance painters of the fifteenth century chose not to eradicate this idyllic and elegant tradition. Painters such as Fra Angelico, Alessandro Botticelli, Pietro Perugino, and even Leonardo da Vinci continued to incorporate some of the elegant and decorative aspects of the Gothic manner in their artistry. But Mantegna confronted the medieval style, and he set out already at an early age to destroy an older tradition and create a new one. Soft surfaces and languorous movement gave way to sharp definition and virile action.

Mantegna had other painters in his camp who were revolutionaries, some of whom preceded him. Masaccio, Piero della Francesca, and Andrea del Castagno are among the central Italian artists who first turned to a new tough and monumental style. These painters also reacted against the sweet Gothic manner, and Mantegna was greatly indebted to several older masters for blazing a trail. Yet, Mantegna was more thoroughly engaged than any previous painter of the *Quattrocento* (1400s) in archaeological study and a conscious revival of Greco-Roman civilisation. The result of this historical attitude made Mantegna's art striking for his contemporaries, as it is for us. Mantegna neglected no detail in his art, and his works are based on intense and enthusiastic study. The young painter from Padua created a manner which epitomised the Early Renaissance, combining a plausible realism and cogent narrative style with a thoughtful attempt to re-create the visual world of antiquity. His special achievement as an antiquarian-painter was recognised by many observers, including Giovanni Santi, the father of the painter Raphael, who said observantly of Mantegna: "No man ever took or used the brush or other pencil, who was a clear successor of ancient times, as he is, with such truth."[1]

Why was Mantegna among the revolutionaries of his time, so intent on establishing a new artistic vision? For many Renaissance artists it would be difficult to guess the origins of their style, because we lack sufficient biographical information or documentation. Yet, we do know a great deal about Mantegna's personality, artistic training, and social relations; it is possible to hypothesise why Mantegna's art looks the way it does. For example, it is telling that he was known to have been argumentative, territorial, and sometimes cruel; surely the stony, incisive, and at times violent world he created as an artist is appropriate for one with such a temperament. It is difficult to imagine Mantegna having embraced the languid narrative and sweet lyricism that remained in vogue throughout the fifteenth century in many quarters. On the whole, both his personality and his art were hard-edged and aggressive. Renaissance viewers who wanted prettier, less detailed, or less historical pictures could have found them elsewhere, and there were surely many who disliked Mantegna's art. He was not interested in painting slender angels with pink cheeks, long blonde hair, and pious, vapid expressions. His art is rarely charming, and those who favoured the suave elegance of Alessandro Botticelli or the gentle piety of Pietro Perugino perhaps found little to enjoy in Mantegna. Nor did he, like some of the painters in the northern Italian court at Ferrara, establish an extravagant and self-conscious manner; his paintings are more straightforward and naturalistic than that. Avoiding both the pedestrian naturalism of a Domenico Ghirlandaio and the sweet or fantastic style, Mantegna – strong willed and tough minded – developed a manner based on incisive narrative and classical revivalism.

It is also clear from the beginning that Mantegna was an intellectual artist, if not in an academic way at least in the sense that he was curious about literary as well as visual ideas. He associated with scholars and other writers, and the results appear in his poetic and well researched art. Indeed, he was drawn to words during his whole lifetime, enjoying the study of Roman inscriptions and depicting Greek and Hebrew lettering in his works. His timely art found a ready following in *Quattrocento* Italy, and he drew support from contemporaries who favoured the revival of classical culture. Importantly, he had a ready affinity for allegory and historical accounts, and was able to follow literary programs and illustrate stories successfully, avoiding the awkwardness plaguing many Renaissance artists who based their art on detailed verbal programs. Mantegna bridged the gap between the written and the pictorial worlds.

Finally, in seeking the source of his artistry in his personality, it is worth pointing out Mantegna was extraordinarily ambitious and he worked hard. His dedication to his craft and his physical energy led him to study, learn, and borrow ideas from other artists, whether from antiquity or from around the Europe of his time. He can hardly be called an eclectic artist, but he did absorb different styles and forge them together to create a distinct style of his own. Mantegna had the drive to get ahead and the will to create a striking artistic style which would catch the attention of his contemporaries. As it turns out, he had a teacher of note who himself was attracted to antiquity, and who imparted to his students progressive ideas.

The Renaissance period, with its ever-waxing secularism, presented a challenge to traditional Christian civilisation. Yet there was apparently no contradiction in Mantegna's mind between Christian and secular thought. Most of Mantegna's oeuvre consisted of sacred works, and in them he applied his keen observation of the natural world and his interest in pagan antiquity, the sculpture, architecture, clothing, and figural types of which fill his religious pictures as part of his historical approach. There were varying attitudes in fifteenth-century Italy, and some clerics and laymen too were puzzled as to why anyone would want a painting of Mars and Venus or would be vain enough to desire a self-portrait. Mantegna worked for a range of clients, and each had different expectations and needs. Some shunned the revival of classical culture and the expansion of the secular spirit, but for his part Mantegna moved freely from the sacred to the worldly. His liberal attitude won out, and by the end of Mantegna's long life a peaceful coexistence held sway. A nearly seamless fusion of the sacred and profane came to form a chief aspect of Italian Renaissance culture.

In the following pages, we will look at Mantegna's life and art. While only scattered documents exist for his earliest period, Mantegna's mature years are better recorded, and we know more about him than any other Italian Renaissance artist before Leonardo da Vinci. We can trace his associations with patrons and public, friends and foes, teachers and colleagues in a way not possible with most other painters of the fifteenth century. We can explore the context of his artistry and establish the historical background and the nature of an art that has endured.

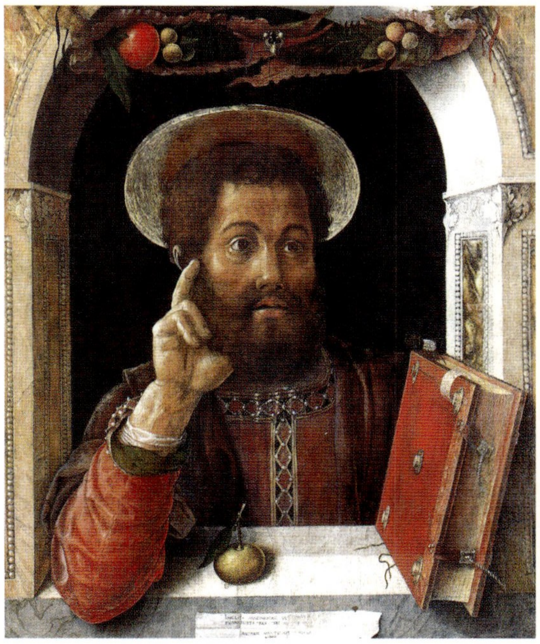

4. *St Mark*, c. 1448-1449.
Casein on canvas, 82 x 63.7 cm.
Städelsches Kunstinstitut, Frankfurt.

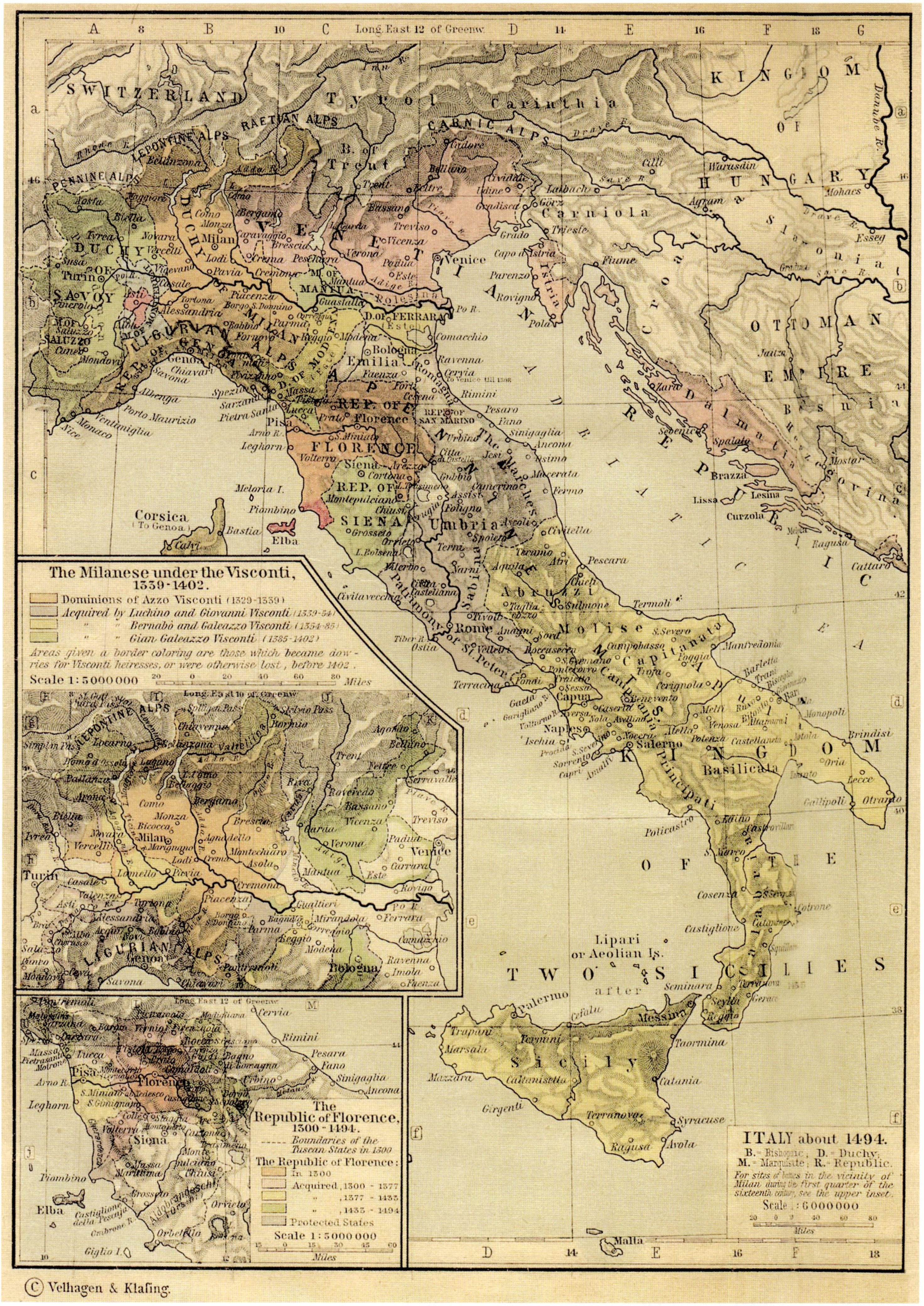
ITALY about 1494.
B. = Bishopric; D. = Duchy; M. = Marquisate; R. = Republic.
For sites of battles in the vicinity of Milan during the first quarter of the sixteenth century, see the upper inset.
Scale 1 : 6 000 000
Miles
The Milanese under the Visconti, 1339-1402.
Dominions of Azzo Visconti (1329-1339)
Acquired by Luchino and Giovanni Visconti (1339-54)
" " Bernabò and Galeazzo Visconti (1354-85)
" " Gian Galeazzo Visconti (1385-1402)
Areas given a border coloring are those which became dowries for Visconti heiresses, or were otherwise lost, before 1402.
Scale 1 : 3 000 000
Miles
The Republic of Florence, 1300-1494.
Boundaries of the Tuscan States in 1300
The Republic of Florence:
In 1300
Acquired, 1300 - 1377
" ,1377 - 1433
" ,1433 - 1494
Protected States
Scale 1 : 3 000 000
Miles
Long. East 12 of Greenw.
SWITZERLAND
Tyrol
Carinthia
KINGDOM OF HUNGARY
Carniola
Slavonia
OTTOMAN EMPIRE
Bosnia
Dalmatia
Herzegovina
DUCHY OF SAVOY
DUCHY OF MILAN
VENICE
REP. OF FLORENCE
REP. OF SIENA
Umbria
The Marches
Abruzzi
Molise
Capitanata
Campania
Basilicata
KINGDOM OF THE TWO SICILIES
Sicily
Corsica
(To Genoa)
Elba
Lipari or Aeolian Is.
ADRIATIC SEA
Malta
© Velhagen & Klafing.

The Debut of a Prodigy: Mantegna's Early years in Padua

Andrea Mantegna lived during a time of social and cultural change in Italy. The continuity of institutions – government, church, family – masks the social and cultural changes which occurred in Italy over several centuries leading up to Mantegna's time. By the *Quattrocento*, in place of static, agrarian society there had developed flourishing, urban economies based on trade and small manufacturing. Fifteenth-century Italy had become evermore dominated by bankers, manufacturers, traders and lawyers rather than landholders. A dynamic social structure resulted from this shift toward mercantile, city life, leading to more head-to-head competition between individuals and families, and one had to get along in a constantly changing world which promised few people automatic status or continued prosperity. This shift was readily apparent in larger urban centres such as Florence and Venice, but was also felt in smaller cities and city-states where political control remained held by a single family, who had to operate in the framework of a dynamic balance of political power and had to survive in a fragmented world.

This competitive and changing atmosphere gave rise to a new, pragmatic attitude among Italians. People came more and more to observe, measure, describe, and admire the world around them; a new culture took root based increasingly on science, commerce, and exploration. Indeed, this worldly attitude would lead to the discovery of new lands and peoples in Africa, Asia, and the Americas. The nineteenth-century historian Jacob Burckhardt aptly called the Renaissance the era of the "rediscovery of the world and of man." This entailed broad intellectual changes, and affected all aspects of the sciences and the humanities. Italians became more keenly interested in what we would call psychology, analysis of family life and societal roles, and an incipient fascination with anthropological issues. There was even a new realistic approach taken in the social science of political philosophy; we recognise the pragmatic and sometimes cynical advice on statecraft of Niccolò Machiavelli as a sign of the times, a tough-minded response to the vicissitudes of ever-changing fortune. The new naturalism encompassed a growing focus on the personal experience, and this gave rise to a new kind of individualism. Renaissance literature, letters, and other records indicate a level of self-reflection and self-consciousness not seen since antiquity.

Fifteenth-century artists such as Mantegna responded to the growing interest in the real world with an increasing naturalism in their paintings and sculpture. The development of convincing perspective, the representation of cityscape and landscape views, and the growth of portraiture all progressed during the fifteenth century. Many painters consciously sought to imitate Nature, although some artists still indulged in unnatural effects and fantastic idealism in their art. Mantegna belonged to a group of artists known among contemporaries for their striking realism.

In addition to this ever-increasing engagement with material existence, another major aspect of the new, comprehensive investigation of the secular world was the rediscovery of antiquity, especially ancient Roman civilisation, which had left in Italy so many monuments and surviving literary texts

5. *Map of Italy*, c. 1450.
The University of Texas Libraries, Austin.

in its wake. There developed an almost obsessive preoccupation in early *Quattrocento* Italy with all things classical: statues, poetry, inscriptions, and coins were collected, treasured, and studied, and ancient buildings were admired as never before since the time of the collapse of the Roman Empire nearly a thousand years before. These two focal points of Renaissance culture – a fascination with the real world (both human and natural) and a powerful attraction to classical art and civilisation – formed the central focal points of Andrea Mantegna's art.

During the Middle Ages there remained only a lukewarm interest in the visual arts of Greek and Roman antiquity. Ancient Roman art was only known to a minor extent even in Italy, and there was little inclination to excavate the remains of a fallen, pagan civilisation. An incident that occurred in the central Italian city of Siena in the 1340s will serve to indicate the ambivalent attitude held toward the classical past in medieval Italy. A marble statue of the Roman goddess Venus was unearthed by chance and was placed in the central square of the city. The public was interested at first, and at least one painter even drew copies of it. But after a while the Sienese became worried, and some claimed it would bring disaster on the city if they continued to pay attention to this nude, heathen idol. The Sienese, who were at war with the Florentines at the time, smashed the sculpture into bits and crossed over one night into Florentine territory to bury the fragments, believing their enemies would come to suffer misfortune just by having these pieces in their lands!

This superstitious attitude changed rapidly in the early years of the fifteenth century. How different it was in the year of Mantegna's death when the *Laocoön* was rediscovered near Rome. This ancient Greek sculpture, representing a high priest of Troy and his sons being strangled by a serpent sent by a punishing god, was universally admired when it was dug out of the ground in 1506. It was brought to the city in a grand parade as flowers were strewn in its path and church bells tolled, despite the pagan subject matter and the nudity of the figures. The Italian people had come to worship all things classical, and Mantegna – with his vividly painted representations of the ancient world – was an active player in the rebirth of Greek and Roman culture which has come to be called the Renaissance.

An important development in intellectual culture of the early fifteenth century was the remarkable rise in humanistic learning. Today there are several meanings and connotations for the word "humanist." In the context of Renaissance history, a humanist is one whose chief field of study was literature, especially that of classical Greece and Rome. Some ancient literature was known throughout the Middle Ages, but it was studied largely for its value as way of improving one's grammar, logic, and vocabulary, though its underlying paganism caused it to be held in suspicion. In the fourteenth- and, increasingly, the fifteenth century classical writings were avidly being sought by scholars and wealthy patrons. The Florentine humanist Poggio Bracciolini (d. 1454) scoured the libraries in medieval monasteries in Switzerland and rediscovered manuscripts of works by Cicero and Tertullian; valuable texts which had been left rotting in piles of parchment, neglected and unknown for centuries. The scholar Niccolò Niccoli (d. 1437) rediscovered several classical texts, and he formed his own small collection of Roman statuary and cameos. By the time of Mantegna's birth, the revival of classical literature and ideals was in full swing, the interest in antiquity fuelled by a tenacious and passionate group of humanists. The interest in classical culture spread quickly to a larger public in fifteenth-century Italy, well beyond the narrow ranks of humanist scholars. A whole new secular world opened that had hitherto been largely ignored, and people of all ages and

6. Francesco Squarcione, *San Lazara Altarpiece,* 1449-1452.
Tempera on panel.
Musei Civici, Padua.

7. *Martyrdom of St Christopher,* c. 1448-1457.
Fresco. Ovetari Chapel,
Church of the Eremitani, Padua.

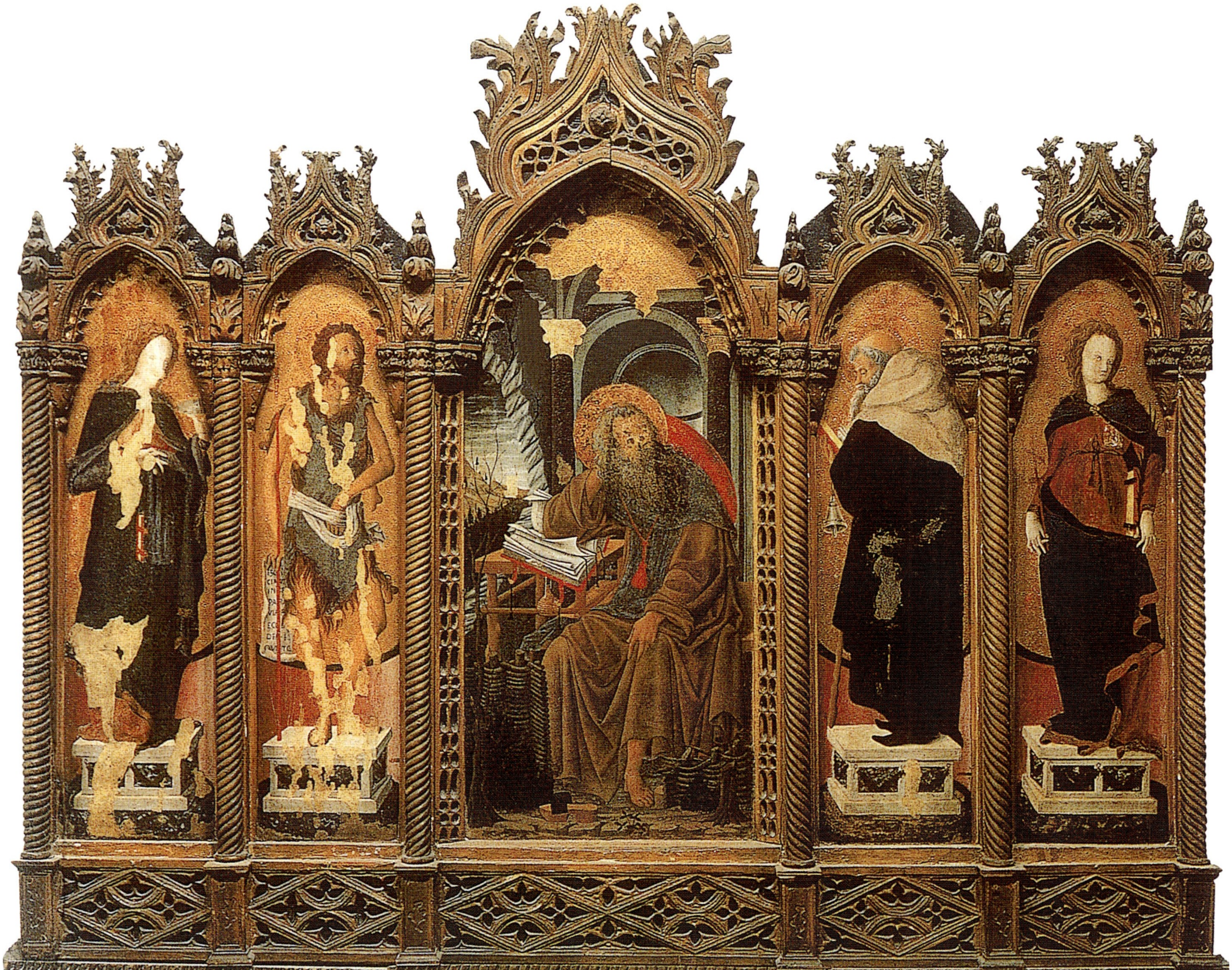

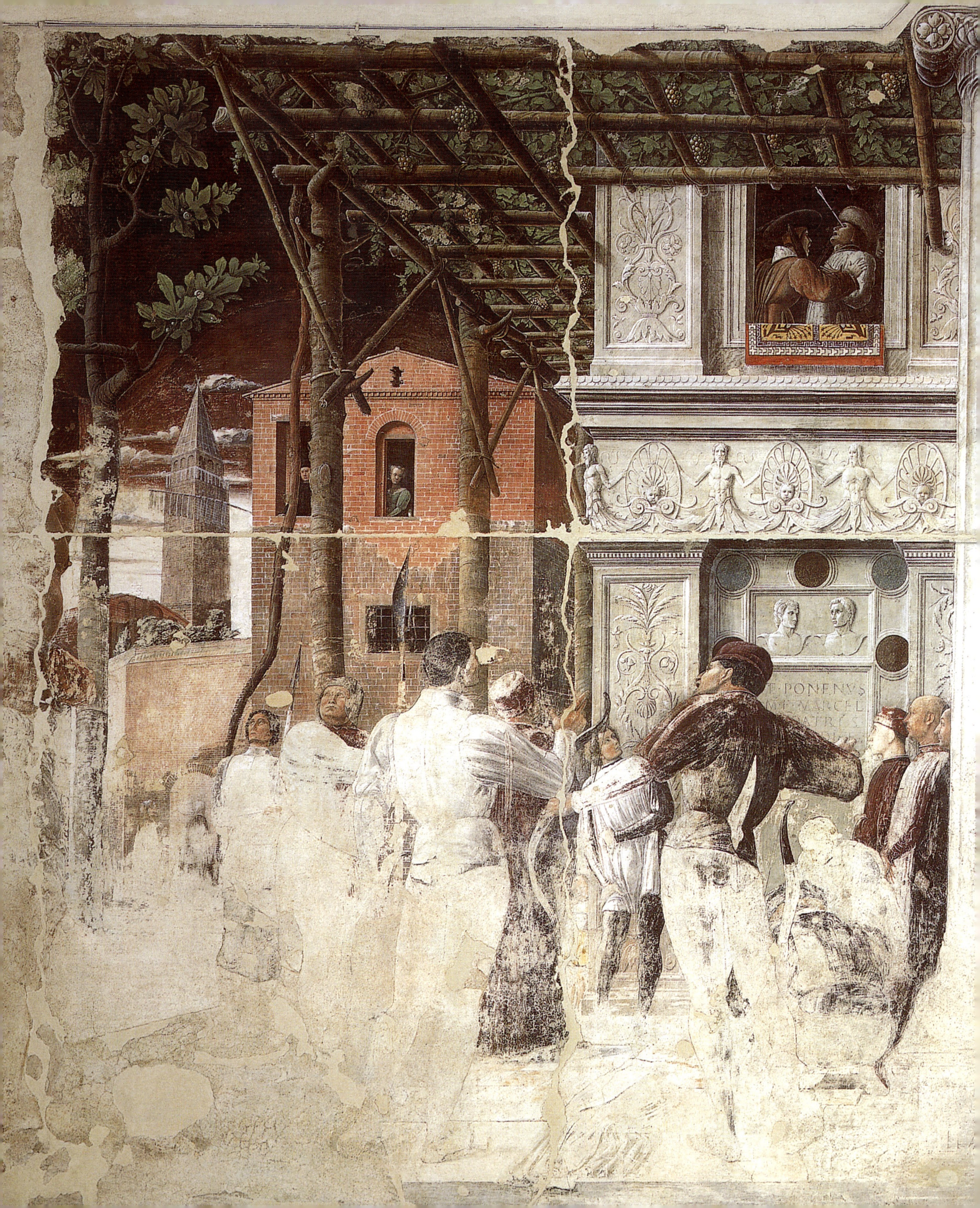

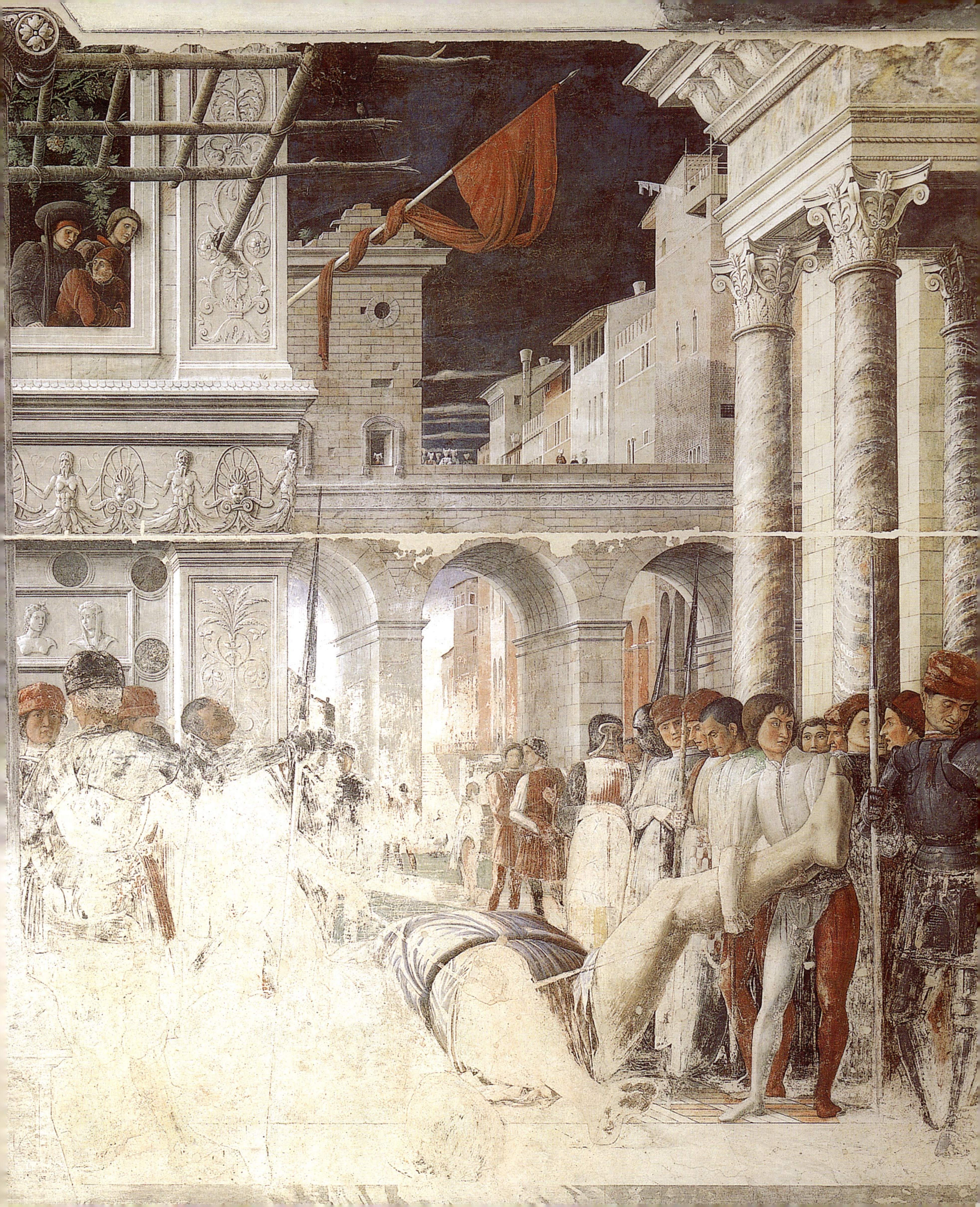

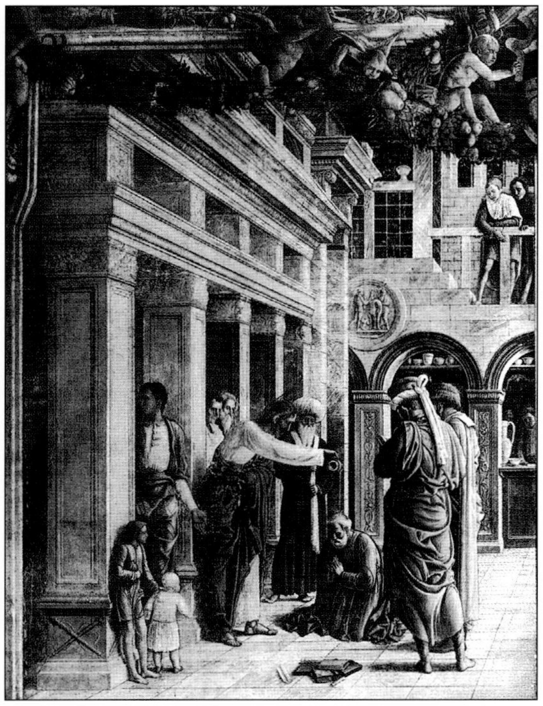

social backgrounds came to embrace this great rediscovery. As a painter, Mantegna would cater to the demands of a public thirsting for art, both sacred and secular, which imitated the distant but laudable civilisations of classical antiquity.

The northern Italian city of Padua (Fig. 5), where Mantegna would begin his artistic career, had been the ancient Roman city of Patavium and in the fifteenth century as today still contained some classical ruins. In addition to these physical remains of Roman civilisation, it was a city redolent with the spirit of antiquity because of the intellectual interests there in ancient literature. Padua was one of the main centres in Renaissance Italy of humanist scholarship; its university was the chief institution of higher learning in the Venetian Republic (to which Padua was subjected in 1405 and thereafter), and a number of professors were leaders of their fields in the study of ancient Greek and Latin literature.

Many of the humanists in Padua were passionate recorders of ancient inscriptions, and throughout his life Mantegna maintained a strong interest in classical Roman lettering. Some humanists became admirers and counsellors of Mantegna, including the artist's friend Ulisse degli Aleotti and the scholar Giovanni Marcanova, the latter a professor at the University of Padua. Mantegna maintained friendly relations throughout his life with learned advisers, and his early conversion to the spirit of classical revivalism was owed in large part to the humanistic atmosphere in Padua, where patrons as well as local scholars shared a taste for Greek and Roman culture.

The world of humanist scholars and classically minded patrons was an elite realm. Mantegna's parents, who were of humble stock and living in a provincial village, certainly knew little of this exciting literary revival or of the new Renaissance artistic style. Mantegna's father was a country carpenter from Isola di Cartura, a small town a few miles outside of Padua. Andrea spent some of his early years herding cattle near the family's village, yet he must have shown some early interest or talent in drawing, for by 1442, probably at about the age of ten or eleven (the standard age at the time to begin an apprenticeship), Andrea's father took him to the thriving city of Padua to a certain master painter named Francesco Squarcione (c. 1394-1468) and asked he give the boy room and board and teach him to be a professional painter.

Francesco Squarcione is not exactly a household name today, but he was an important figure in Italian painting of the period. The records of his professional activity as an artist and teacher constitute some of the most colourful episodes of Renaissance art history. Squarcione started his career as a tailor and embroiderer, and only turned to painting later on in life. The extent of his own artistic output is in dispute, but it is generally agreed that at least two of his paintings have survived, a small altarpiece (Fig. 6) and a panel painting of the *Madonna and Child*. These works, although carried out with a lively sense of design and an attention to detail, demonstrate he was a competent but not extraordinary painter.

Yet his workshop, which he kept filled with apprentices and pupils over the years, was a novel institution. Although guild regulations classified his school as a workshop, Squarcione called it a *studium*, or what we might call an art studio. It was arguably the first professional art school in Italy and in Europe. Beginning in 1431 and continuing until his death in 1468, Squarcione trained over 130 young artists in his school, among them Andrea Mantegna.

8. *St James Baptising Hermogenes* (destroyed), c. 1448-1457. Fresco. Ovetari Chapel, Church of the Eremitani, Padua.

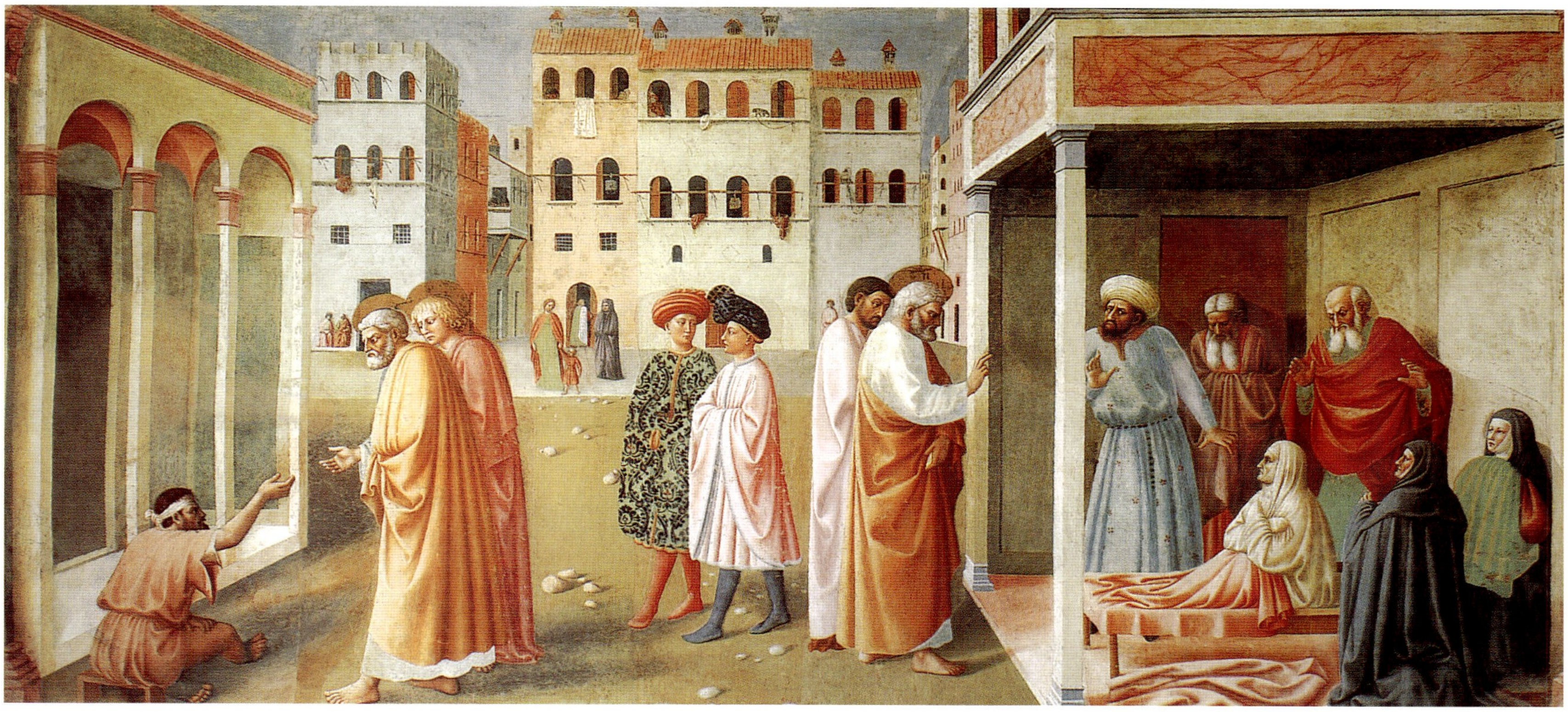

Boys came not just to help turn out works in the master's style but to learn more broadly about the art of painting and design by studying plaster casts of ancient Greek and Roman statues and by copying some of the hundreds of drawings of works of art Squarcione had collected during his wide travels. Squarcione is said to have been to Greece (a rare experience for an artist of this period), making drawings of remarkable works of art, which he used in his courses of instruction. He would sometimes take boys in solely to teach them one aspect of painting, such as perspective. Thus, Squarcione introduced a novel idea into the art world: pupils could be more than mere apprentices. He treated them as students in a broader sense and taught them a variety of skills necessary to become independent masters.

Since a master painter could avoid paying some guild fees by collaborating with family members, Squarcione legally adopted several of his students as his own sons. Andrea Mantegna was one of these adoptees, and he called himself "Andrea Squarcione" as late as 1466, when he was a mature and accomplished artist. Mantegna lived with Squarcione as a pupil and collaborator from about 1441 until 1448, and Squarcione was undoubtedly an important influence on the boy's artistic formation. Indeed, Squarcione bragged in a legal document he had "made Mantegna what he was".

Despite the close relations and the legal adoption, Mantegna had to sue Squarcione to receive a greater payment for his collaboration with him. Indeed, many others working under Squarcione felt he was benefiting unduly from their work as pupils. They helped him complete commissions and he gave them room, board, instruction, and some payment, but sometimes they felt their remuneration was insufficient. One pupil sued Squarcione for not being capable of teaching what he promised. Still, it is clear Squarcione's proto-academy for the arts was a new type of institution, and there were bound to be disputes about the conditions of one's course of study and the contracts under which one gave assistance to the master-teacher. For his part, Mantegna perhaps settled his dispute with Squarcione amicably, for the two were in occasional professional relations with each other until Mantegna left Padua permanently in the late 1450s.

9. Masolino, *Healing of the Cripple and Raising of Tabatha*, 1426-1427. Fresco, 255 x 588 cm (full fresco). Brancacci Chapel, Santa Maria del Carmine, Florence.

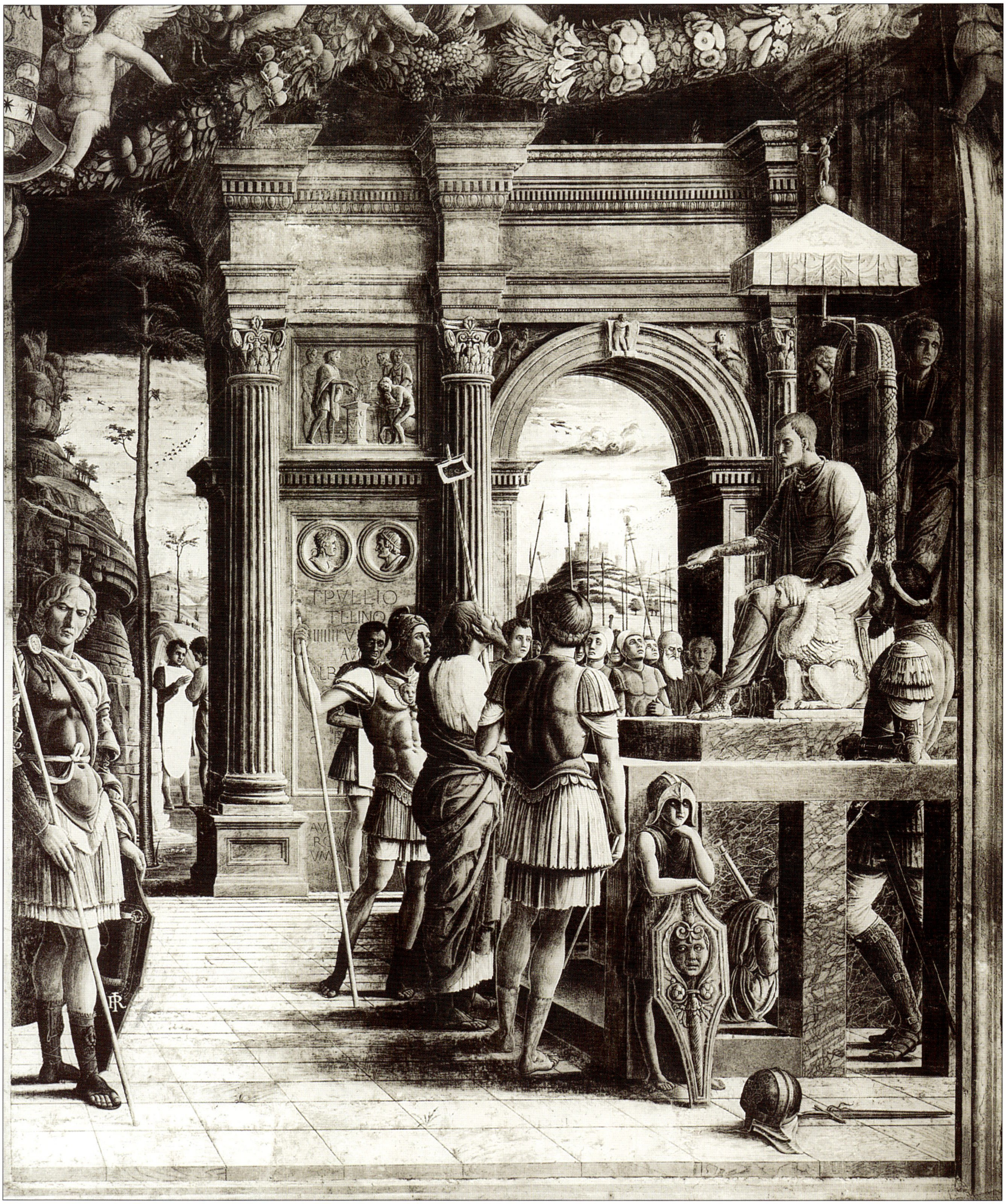

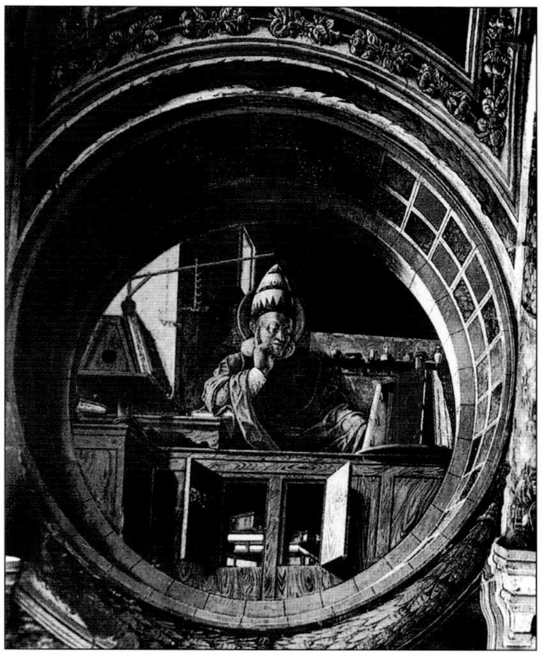

Squarcione's use of plaster casts of ancient Roman and Greek sculpture for teaching is of great importance, and surely Mantegna's attraction to classical statuary and civilisation derived in a significant part from such instruction. Many Paduan scholars during the early fifteenth century fostered the rediscovery of classical culture, and the intellectual fascination with antiquity was shared by a broad public in Padua, as a growing number of prominent citizens were beginning to form collections of ancient Roman statuary, cameos, and coins; it is no wonder his *studium* for training painters gained the approval of Paduan scholars. One prominent Paduan humanist, Michele Savonarola, praised the Paduan school of painting, pointing out its learned character and praising its artists for their ability to represent perspective.

Mantegna's lifelong utilisation of strong, and at times jumpy, perspective springs from his training in Squarcione's studio. Mantegna went on to surpass Squarcione in depicting spatial depth and three-dimensionality, and he came to learn more about antiquity than Squarcione ever knew. He paid particular attention to the abundant remains of Roman architecture in northern Italy, so when he later went to Rome for the first time as a middle-aged man he had already had significant contact with the ruins of classical civilisation. In short, everything conspired to make Mantegna passionate about the ancient past and classical art: his artistic training with Squarcione, an educated public yearning for visual revivals of the ancient world, and his opportunity in northern Italy to study ancient art and architecture first-hand. We will see that his paintings included convincing and well-researched recreations of ancient Roman costumes, architecture, and sculpture.

Many of Squarcione's pupils, including Mantegna, Giorgio Schiavone, and Marco Zoppo came to have certain features in common in their art: clear colouring, sharp, lively contours, profuse details, a certain restless energy, and a liberal use of classical elements such as swags of vegetation and architectural components. Mantegna surely learned the essence of his art in Squarcione's *studium*. Yet, Mantegna was highly independent and precocious, and his art swiftly progressed beyond the training Squarcione gave him. In addition to the master's in-house instruction, Squarcione must also have pointed him in the right direction in a search for sources of inspiration. Squarcione was not the most progressive artist in the area, and Mantegna would certainly have profited from seeing the works of several Florentine masters whose works were in Padua or in nearby Venice.

It was in Florence in the early fifteenth century that many of the aspects of the Early Renaissance style first developed, including vivid realism, use of linear perspective, clear storytelling, and the convincing representation of emotional expression. This style challenged the sweet, elegant Gothic manner, which continued to flourish in northern Italy until Mantegna's time.

One of the characteristic exponents of the late Gothic style was Stefano da Zevio, whose *Madonna and Child with God the Father in a Garden* serves as an example of this graceful, decorative style: with its flowery background, elegant, ethereal figures, inexpressive faces, and delicate lighting running like quicksilver across the surfaces, it is characteristic of the traditional medieval fashion that was beginning to be replaced by the new tough and worldly manner which came to prevail in the early fifteenth century. In contrast to such a work, Mantegna would have been able to study Florentine Renaissance works in Venice, such as the saints by Andrea del Castagno in San Zaccaria, which convey a blunt, naturalistic, and monumental ideal of the human figure. Some bronze reliefs and freestanding figures by the Florentine sculptor Donatello

10. *The Trial of St James* (destroyed), c. 1448-1457.
Fresco. Ovetari Chapel, Church of the Eremitani, Padua.

11. Niccolò Pizzolo, *St Gregory in his Study* (destroyed), c. 1448-1453.
Fresco. Ovetari Chapel, Church of the Eremitani, Padua.

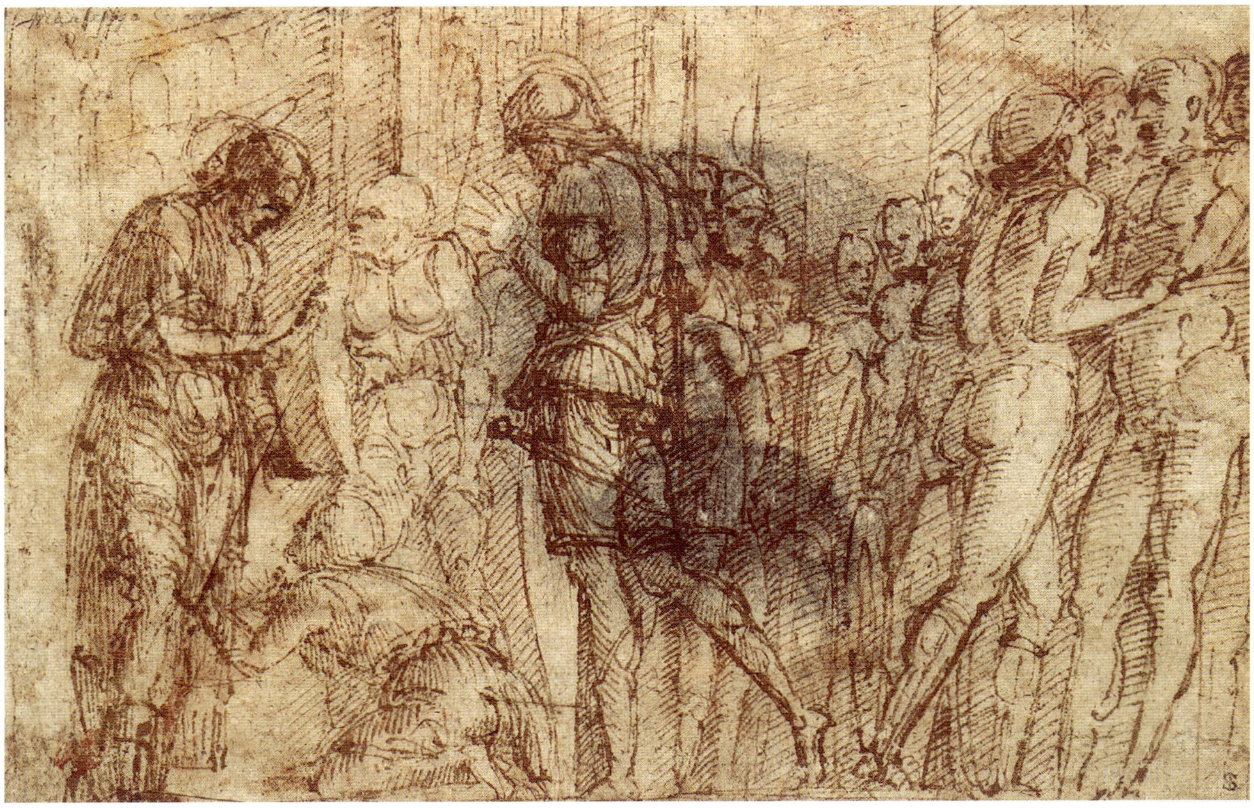

were designed for the Paduan church of Sant'Antonio soon after 1443. These reliefs show the kind of deep space and dramatic narrative Mantegna would later echo in his own art. Donatello was mostly in Padua for the eleven years prior to 1453, and Mantegna is likely to have known him personally. Inspiration from Florentine art helped to propel art in northern Italy, including Mantegna's, away from dreamy legacy of the late Middle Ages towards a brittle, dry, and more classicised style.

Blessed with a progressive training in the craft of painting and enviable talents, Mantegna was ready to start his professional career at an early age. In 1448, Mantegna painted an altarpiece in Padua for the high altar of the church of Santa Sophia. He was only seventeen years old, and even so this work was received with critical acclaim. Unfortunately this altarpiece is now lost. His next great commission came when he began, at the age of eighteen or so, to paint murals in a chapel in the Church of the Eremitani in Padua. The frescoes were commissioned by Antonio degli Ovetari, a member of a wealthy and established family of Padua.

12. Preparatory drawing for the *St James Led to Execution*, c. 1448-1457. Pen and ink and black chalk on paper, 15.5 x 23.4 cm. British Museum, London.

13. *St James Led to Execution* (destroyed), c. 1448-1457. Fresco. Ovetari Chapel, Church of the Eremitani, Padua.

After he died in 1448, his wife, Imperatrice, used the funds left in his will to have the project brought to completion. The chapel, a small section of the much larger church, was to be filled with frescoes depicting the lives of Saints James and Christopher. It is impossible to separate the religious from the secular motives of patrons of such grand projects, but clearly there was – in addition to the religious devotion of Antonio – a desire on his part to bring glory to himself and his whole family by causing such a great artwork to come into being. Indeed, murals in private chapels were essentially public monuments, symbols of the refinement and devotion of the local citizens; visitors to Padua from other parts of Italy and the rest of Europe would come to see the great frescoed walls of the Eremitani church. Today the family chapels of Italy form living museums, legacies of the religious spirit of the age as well as evidence of the personal pride of the patrons.

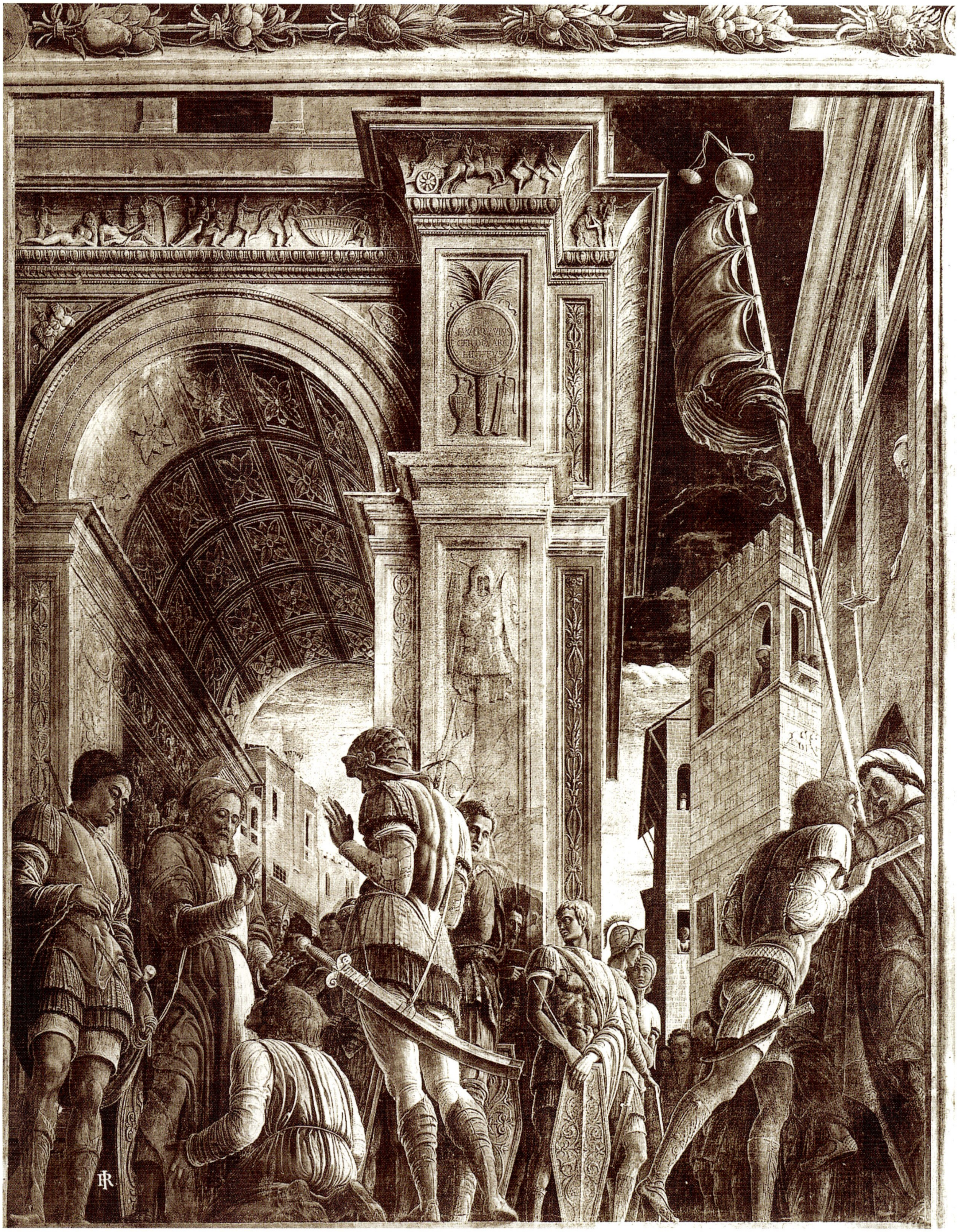

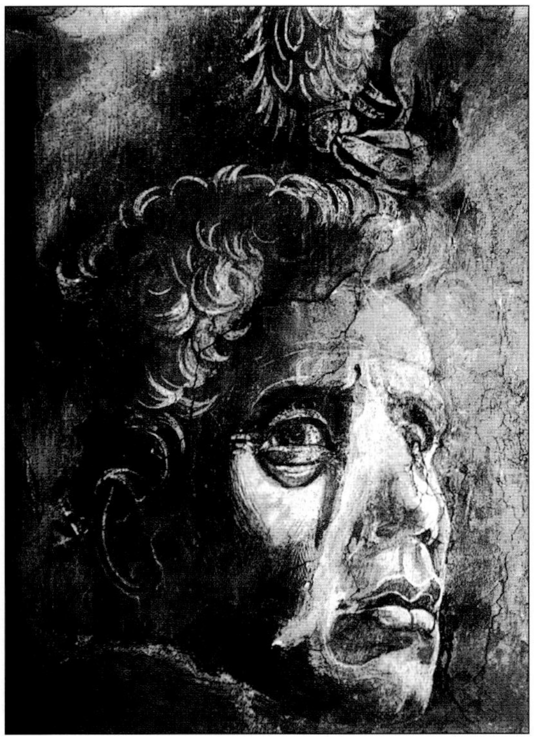

14. *Self-Portrait* (destroyed), c. 1448-1457. Fresco. Ovetari Chapel, Church of the Eremitani, Padua.

Since Antonio degli Ovetari and his wife Imperatrice had friends and associates who were learned and scholarly citizens of Padua, it is not surprising they would wish to have paintings done in the new Renaissance style, with strong classical overtones. And indeed, although some older, more conservative artists from Venice were for a brief time intended to share in the project (they eventually painted only some lesser parts of the chapel), it was the new generation of Renaissance painters who were destined to paint the great narrative scenes. The patrons perhaps turned first to the locally famous Squarcione, who then passed along the work largely to his talented student Mantegna. Other painters were involved as well. Another pupil of Squarcione, Niccolò Pizzolo, was now a practicing painter and sculptor, and he got a large part of the commission. Pizzolo died in a sword fight at the age of thirty-three, before he could paint anything but a few figures around the perimeter and on the vault of the chapel; he also made the sculptured altar showing the *Madonna and Saints*, its wiry figures inspired by the style of Donatello.

Pizzolo was about ten years older than Mantegna, and he must have impressed upon the young artist the importance of studying the new Tuscan Renaissance manner, which he had so thoroughly imbibed. Indeed, the Ovetari Chapel is a microcosm of the pattern of change which brought about the change toward the new style in art. Older masters did not respond favourably to the Tuscan Renaissance style, but the younger generation, including Mantegna and Pizzolo, took the lead in ushering the novel manner in to their local setting. This shift occurred in city after city during the fifteenth century – including Ferrara, Milan, Venice, Urbino – as the central Italian style was adopted, interpreted, and varied by a wide range of artists. Compared to Mantegna and Pizzolo, even the work of Squarcione was rather conservative and unadventurous (cf. Fig. 6); it was the master's training and open attitude to the study of various styles that was progressive. The Ovetari Chapel was a showpiece of artistic revolution, and Mantegna, thanks partly due to the early death of Pizzolo, was responsible for the greatest part of the work.

The Ovetari Chapel was almost completely destroyed during an aerial raid in 1944 when a cluster of bombs meant for the nearby railroad yards fell wide of the mark. Fortunately, colour illustrations of the works were taken shortly before the destruction. Some of the works were removed from the wall for restoration before the raid, notably Mantegna's *Assumption of the Virgin* (Fig. 19) and his *Martyrdom of Saint Christopher* (Fig. 7); these survive and have been reinstalled in the chapel, giving us an idea of Mantegna's great achievement.

Some of the more extraordinary works of art of the fifteenth century resulted from the application of Renaissance ideals of lively and detailed narrative to the illustration of fantastic medieval accounts of saints. Most of Mantegna's scenes in the Ovetari Chapel were drawn from the *Golden Legend* of Jacobus de Voragine, a thirteenth-century Dominican priest from northern Italy. His colourful stories of the lives of saints are often lacking in historical authenticity or Biblical authority, but for centuries they moved and inspired the faithful to worship Christian martyrs and heroes. In Mantegna's time, despite new secular trends in culture, the religious fervour of the Middle Ages had not passed. Men and women still saw visions, went on long pilgrimages, believed in miracles, and feared the intervention of the devil in human affairs. The frescoes of the Ovetari Chapel were painted for people who still passionately believed in the power of God and even in the veracity of the most far-fetched Christian legends. On the left wall of the Ovetari Chapel Mantegna represented scenes from the life of Saint James the Greater. Niccolò Pizzolo was originally to have painted part of the left wall, but his slowness and his early death meant Mantegna ended up painting this wall, working off and on between 1449 and 1455 (Fig. 16).

Already at this early stage in his life Mantegna proved he was one of the great illustrators of the Renaissance, for he could take a simple text and present a clear and faithful narrative while also painting in his own unique style, based on a dry realism and a thoughtful attempt to re-create the style, costumes, and architecture of antiquity. Mantegna began painting at the top of the wall with a scene from the Bible (*Matthew 3:21* and *Mark 1:19*), representing Christ calling the fishermen James and John to join him in his cause (Fig. 18). That these are specimens of the new style in painting would have been instantly obvious to contemporaries; instead of the sweet, decorative, soft style of Gothic painting, here we see a simple composition, and a sweeping landscape of heroic grandeur. Mantegna's stocky, tough figures have the substance and blunt realism reminiscent of Roman sculpture.

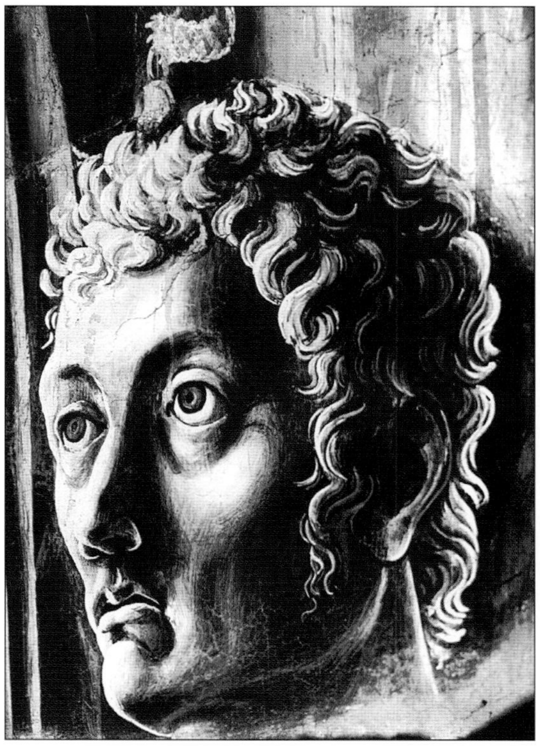

The rest of Mantegna's scenes follow the narrative of James' life as told by Jacobus de Voragine, whose *Golden Legend* included some especially dramatic, if improbable, details of the life of James. The legendary account is lively enough, but young Mantegna fleshed out the details of the story even further in his mural, adding his own particular narrative clarity and classical features. In one panel, Saint James is shown preaching to a crowd in the Holy Land. However, a certain magician named Hermogenes, intent on rooting out Christianity, had demons come and try to cast a spell on the saint. Here is Mantegna's vivid realism and dramatic narrative; the crowd includes a variety of emotional attitudes, from frightened contemplation to outright terror, and the scene is presented by Mantegna with economy and force. Even his bits of classical sculpture add to the drama, as a carved dolphin leaps above the lintel to the door on the right, and a very realistic stone head in a roundel seems to cry out in fright. To further enliven the work, Mantegna shows various chubby little boys (called *putti* in Italian), climbing about on swags of fruit, and one of them is even falling off! This kind of busy, witty detail would remain characteristic of his artistic style. Certainly, nothing in the legendary account by Voragine helped the young artist to invent such a striking and eye-catching motif.

In the next scene, James forced the demons to bring Hermogenes before him, and in this scene James is shown baptising the magician, the water splashing off of his bald head (Fig. 8). This section marks a breakthrough for Mantegna in its representation of space, for it is the first time he employed the rigorous, single-point perspective system that was a hallmark of Early Renaissance painting in Florence. Increasingly, fifteenth-century viewers wanted the precision of a carefully constructed perspective system offering the convincing illusion that a window to another world has been opened up beyond the picture frame. In single-point perspective, a grid of orthogonal and transversal lines marks the apparent diminution of space, with the orthogonals leading back to a single vanishing point.

Perspective, an important aspect of Renaissance visual culture, was a way to organise the chaos of visual experience, using an orderly, mathematical system. Artistic perspective is an objective and scientific method of spatial organisation, but it is also intensely subjective, showing the world as if seen by an individual spectator who occupies a particular position in the world. Medieval artists, with their otherworldly vision, were not interested in such a rigorous organisation of picture space.

15. Niccolò Pizzolo, *Self-Portrait* (destroyed), c. 1448-1457. Fresco. Ovetari Chapel, Church of the Eremitani, Padua.

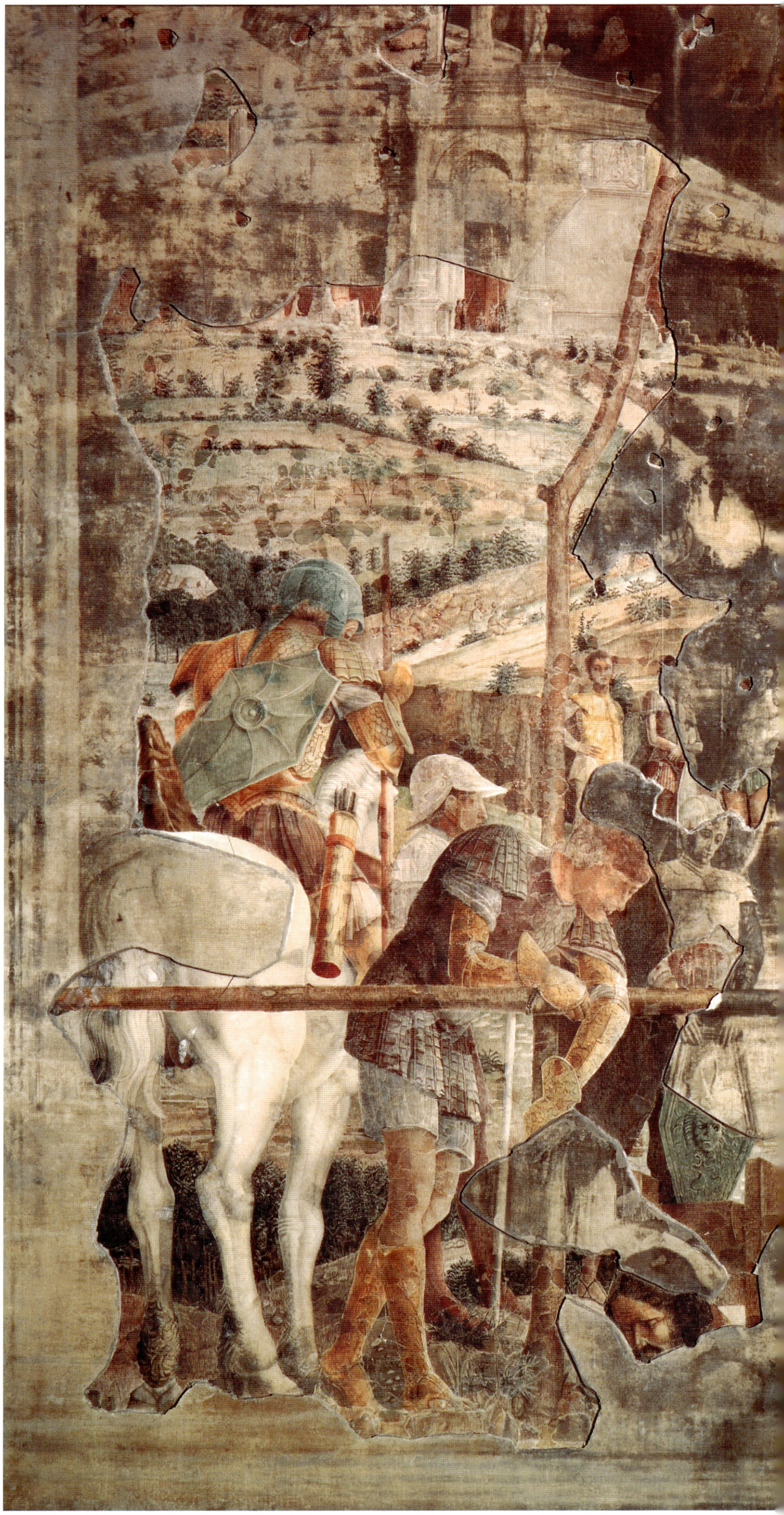

16. *The Excecution of St James,*
c. 1448-1457.
Fresco. Ovetari Chapel,
Church of the Eremitani, Padua.

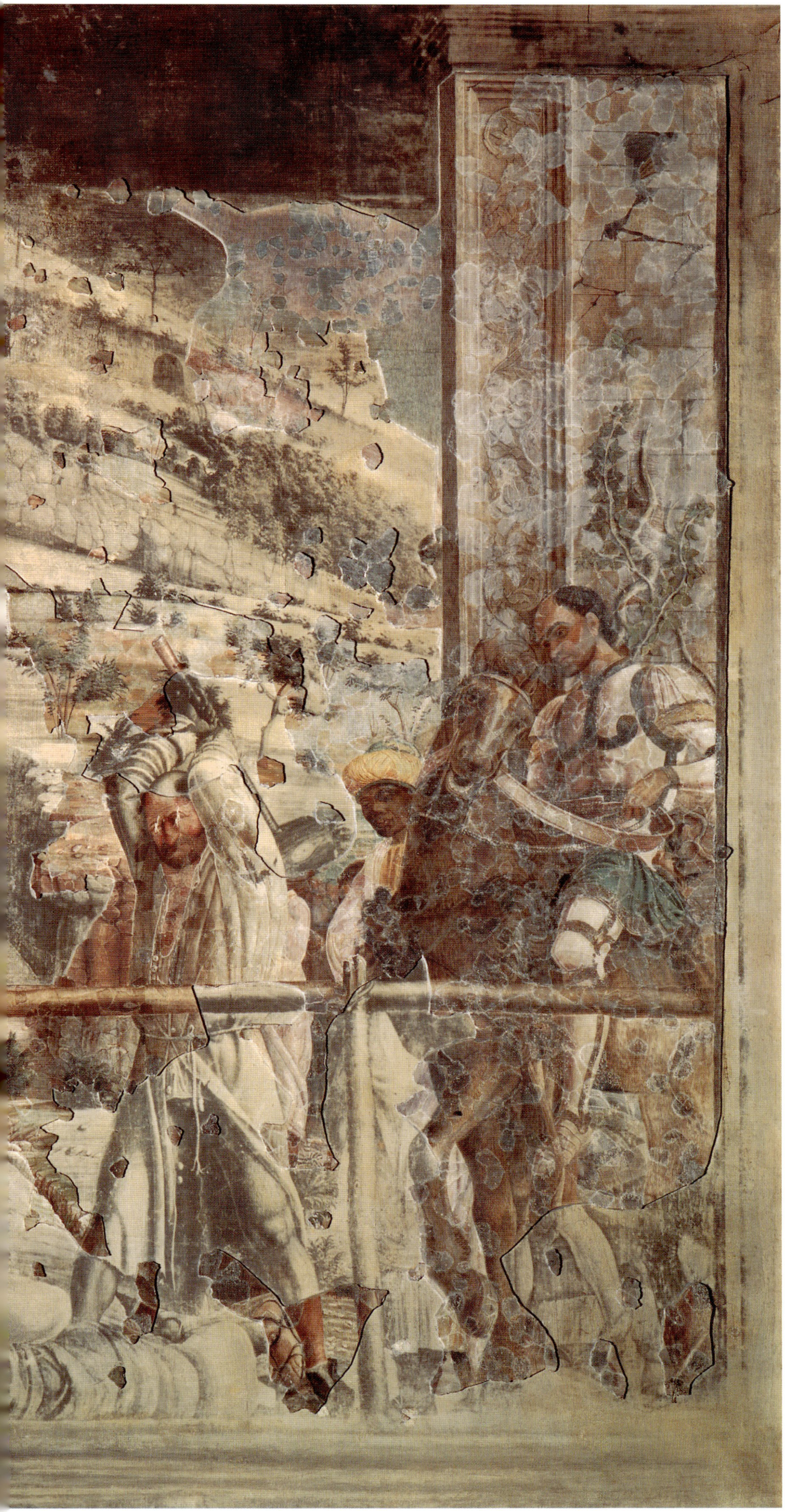

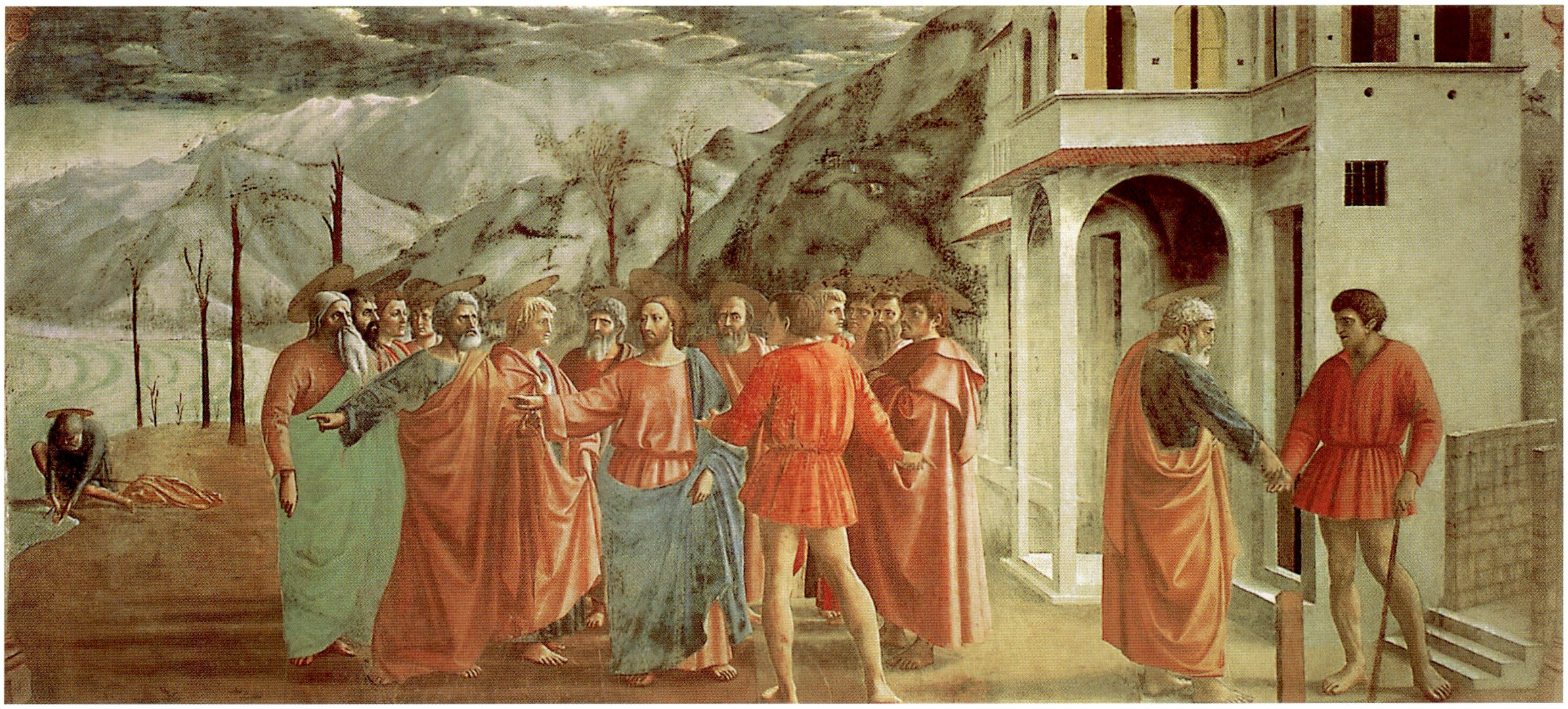

The system did contain two appealing aspects for Italians of the fifteenth century, for it is timelessly mathematical on the one hand and very personal on the other. It became the standard system of spatial organisation in Italian painting, although, as with other innovations, its adoption happened over the course of two generations, occurring one city and one artist at a time.

In his *Saint James Baptising Hermogenes*, all the lines in the pavement, on the entablature at the left, the lines of the roof and so forth converge on a single point on the right, giving the little city square in Jerusalem where the action takes place plausible depth on the chapel wall. This system was not used in the *Preaching of Saint James*, where one can sense even without measuring it that the space was cramped and inaccurately drawn. Clearly, during the time between the making of these works, Mantegna had learned about the new perspective system. Squarcione did not seem to comprehend single-point perspective until later in his life, so Mantegna must have learned the system elsewhere. Perhaps Mantegna had seen the book *On Painting* by the theorist Leon Battista Alberti (l435), in which the author set out in simple terms the rules for making paintings in perspective (Fig. 8). Or maybe Mantegna received a perspective drawing or instructions from the Florentine sculptor Donatello, who was making reliefs for the nearby church in Padua at this time using convincing spatial recession in elaborate settings.

In addition to using single-point perspective and filling his works with reminiscences of antiquity, Mantegna linked his art to classical thought and humanism through its very simplicity and economy. A widespread belief in antiquity, revived by fifteenth-century theorists like Leon Battista Alberti, was that art should be direct, simple, and without unnecessary elements and affectation; some pictorial variety is good, but overabundance is distracting and unworthy of the best artistic minds. A good painting, like a good person, it was thought, is without excess and without superfluous finery. In this spirit, Mantegna's story-telling is economical and vivid. Thus, the young artist managed to convey the moral quality of classical culture as well as including in his murals specific details borrowed from Greco-Roman art. Included throughout these murals is Mantegna's adaptation of Roman drapery

17. Masaccio, *The Tribute Money*, c. 1428. Fresco, 255 x 598 cm. Brancacci Chapel, Santa Maria del Camine, Florence.

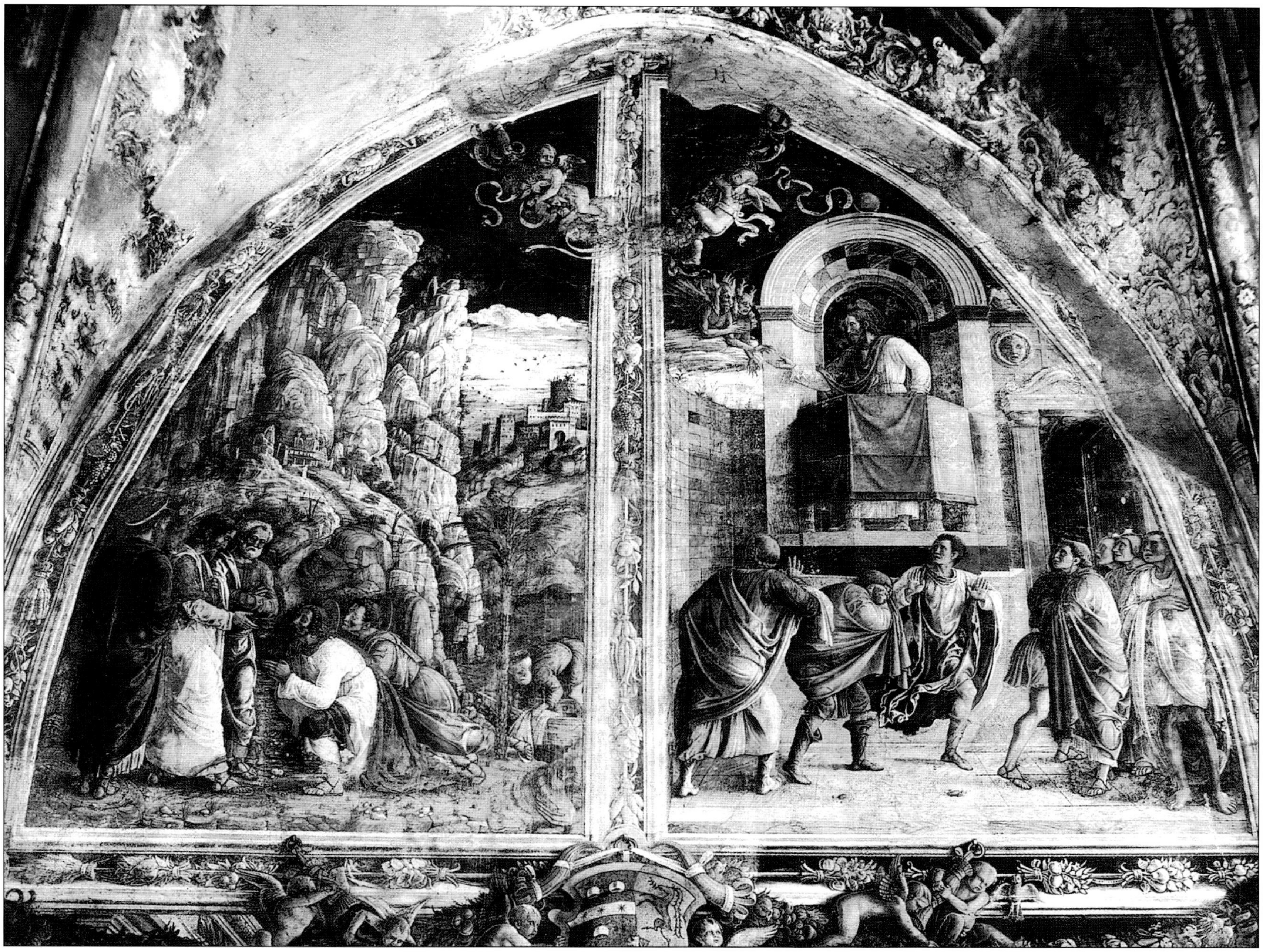

style. Avoiding the gentle, curvilinearity of late Gothic painting, Mantegna depicts garments that are folded, bent, and weighty, resembling the heavy and simplified garment style found in Roman relief sculpture and in the works of Donatello, who was also indebted to the ancients. It is possible that in arriving at this manner Mantegna used small wooden models of figures cloaked in wet cloth. Thus, in his drapery folds, as elsewhere in his art, Mantegna turned away from Gothic tradition, basing his art instead on Roman antiquity, the Tuscan Renaissance and real models.

Mantegna's inclination to draw inspiration from classical art is brought to a dramatic climax in the *Trial of Saint James* (Fig. 10). Having been denounced for his aggressive efforts to spread the word of Christ, James is brought before the ruler Herod Agrippa, who is dressed in a carefully researched version of a Roman costume. The triumphal arch behind is a variant on those found throughout the Roman Empire, several of which survived in the fifteenth century in northern Italy. It is replete with inscriptions, only partly legible, written in beautiful, clear Roman lettering typical of thousands of surviving examples of Roman writing on stone. Even Squarcione had written in his paintings with a cursive, decorative Gothic script, but Mantegna adopted the humanistic practice of imitating the blockier, simpler Roman style of lettering.

18. *The Calling of James and John* (destroyed), c. 1448-1457. Fresco. Ovetari Chapel, Church of the Eremitani, Padua.

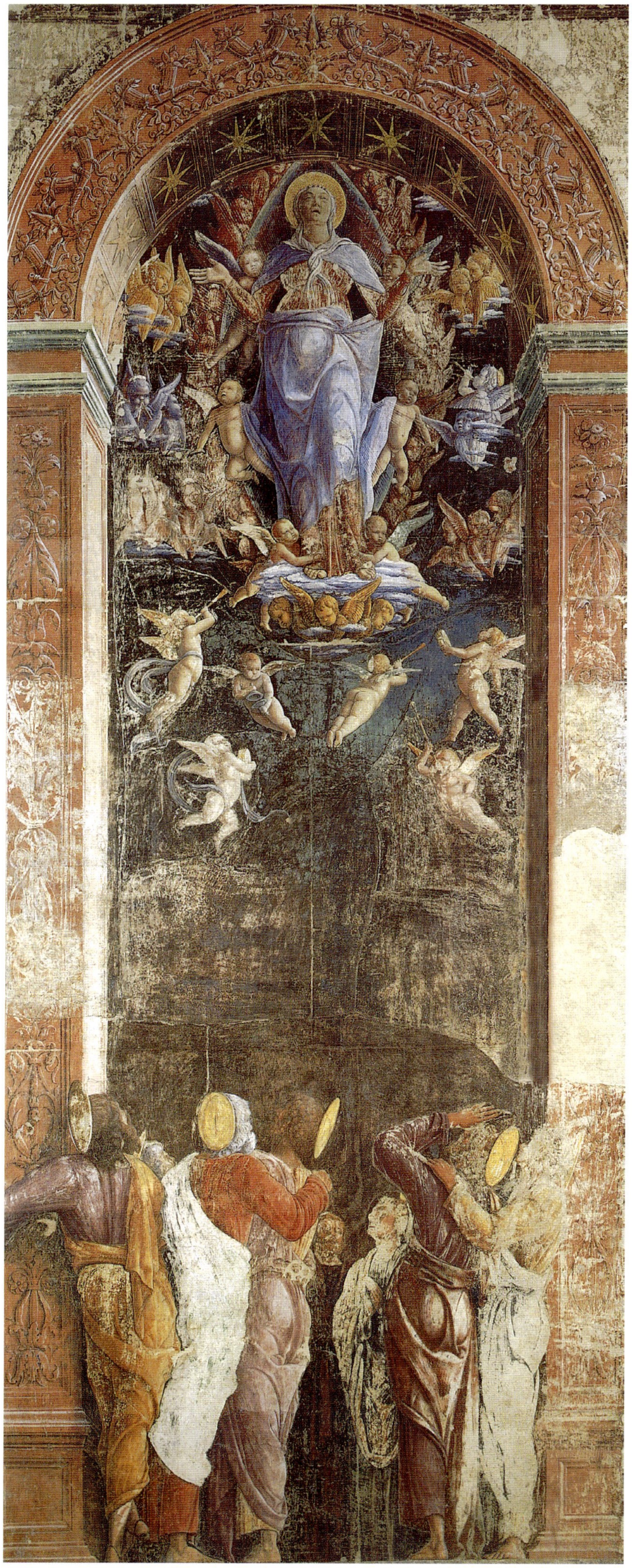

19. *Assumption of the Virgin,*
c. 1448-1457.
Fresco. Ovetari Chapel,
Church of the Eremitani, Padua.

Among the reliefs in the *Trial of Saint James* (Fig. 10) are portraits of two Roman emperors, probably Augustus and Nero, and above the emperors is a rectangular panel representing a pagan sacrifice. This last relief is evidence of the ambivalent attitude held in the fifteenth century toward the classical past: Renaissance men admired its artistic forms and certain aspects of its thought, but they lamented the opposition of Roman paganism to Christianity. Mantegna's depiction of a pagan sacrifice was a reminder to fifteenth-century viewers that the Romans practised, not the ritual sacrifice of Christ's own flesh and blood, but the sacrificial slaughter of animals. In another part of the picture, Mantegna adumbrates the victory of Christianity over paganism: the ancients celebrated their victories, as seen by the presence of female allegorical Victory figures on the spandrels just atop the arch, but the inclusion of those allegories here would have been interpreted by Renaissance viewers as an indication that Christianity would triumph over pagan religion and secular power.

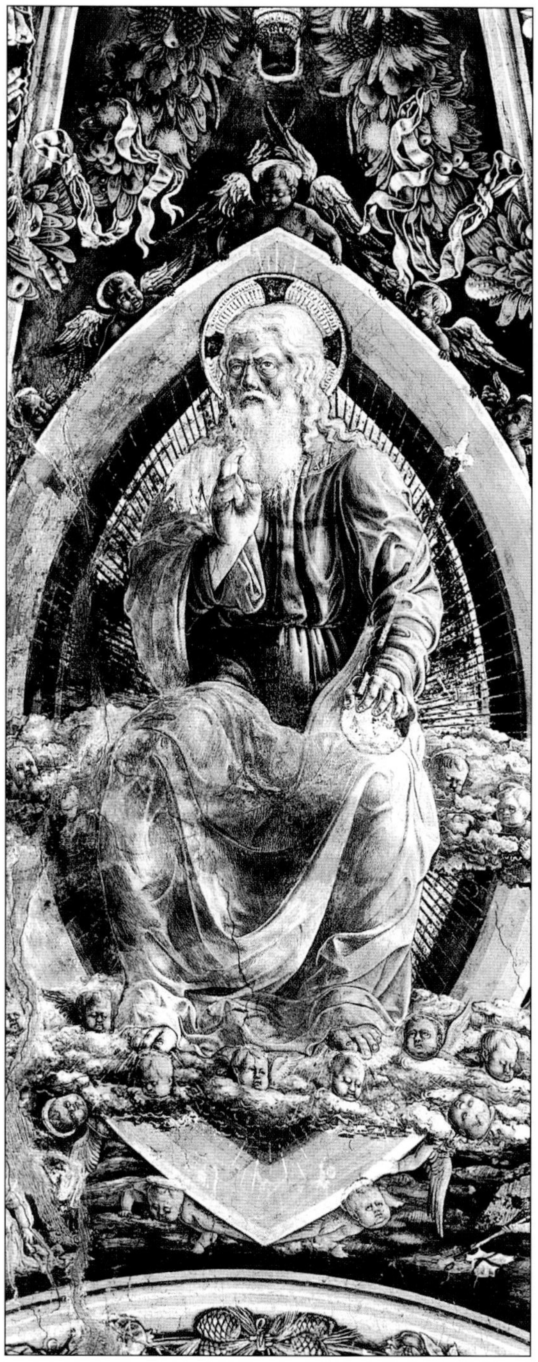

Mantegna's mastery of space and illusionism grew as he worked in the chapel, and the *Saint James Led to Execution* surpasses all his earlier efforts (Fig. 13). Here the figures and the massive triumphal arch – roughly based on the now-lost Arch of the Gavi in Verona – are shown in worm's-eye view, foreshortened from below as one would see them from the very floor of the chapel. All this echoes the miraculous event taking place. According to the account in the *Golden Legend* of Jacobus de Voragine, on the way to his execution James cured a scribe, who is kneeling on the road. The soldier on the far left holding the rope was inspired by this miracle and looks on with quiet sympathy. A well-armed centurion toward the centre gestures in amazement. On the far right, in the kind of gripping motif that helped to establish his reputation as an exciting painter, Mantegna shows one onlooker trying to push his way into the area where the saint stands. A Roman soldier forces him away and they shout at each other, their anger echoed by the flapping banner above and the turning of the corner of a crenellated building toward the viewer. Space rushes back to the left of this pair, the eye drawn to a soldier with a shield anchoring his body position, the motif drawn from Donatello's marble *Saint George* at Orsanmichele in Florence, a work Mantegna must have known through a copy. Mantegna wanted to make his painting as vigorous and vivid as possible, qualities which come out also in the boldly executed sketch he made in preparation for painting this remarkable composition (Fig. 12).

The climax of Mantegna's work on this wall is the *Execution of Saint James*, his youthful masterpiece and indeed one of the great paintings of the Early Renaissance (Fig. 16). The saint is lying on the ground, and is about to be beheaded by an executioner who will strike a sharpened board with a mallet, a clumsy system lacking the humane precision of the later guillotine. Mantegna's clever invention comes through in his use of the tearing motif: as the neck of the saint is about to be severed, one sees overhead a snapped branch, a split building in the upper left, a fissure in the upper part of the wall on the right, and a tear in the cloak on the arm of the executioner. The illusionism Mantegna had been developing in all the earlier scenes finally results in the ultimate, explosive spatial device: the viewer might expect that in a moment the head of Saint James will fall at his feet in the chapel of the Ovetari. The *Execution of Saint James* vividly makes it appear that the scene depicted and the world of the viewer are coterminous.

20. Niccolò Pizzolo, *God the Father* (destroyed), c. 1448-1453. Fresco. Ovetari Chapel, Church of the Eremitani, Padua.

Antonio degli Ovetari was not alive to see Mantegna's work progress in his family chapel, but his wife was, and she had occasion to question the artist's execution of the next scene, the *Assumption of the Virgin*, which still survives on the far wall of the chapel (Fig. 19). Imperatrice filed a complaint and a minor civil suit against Mantegna because he did not include all twelve Apostles. Renaissance

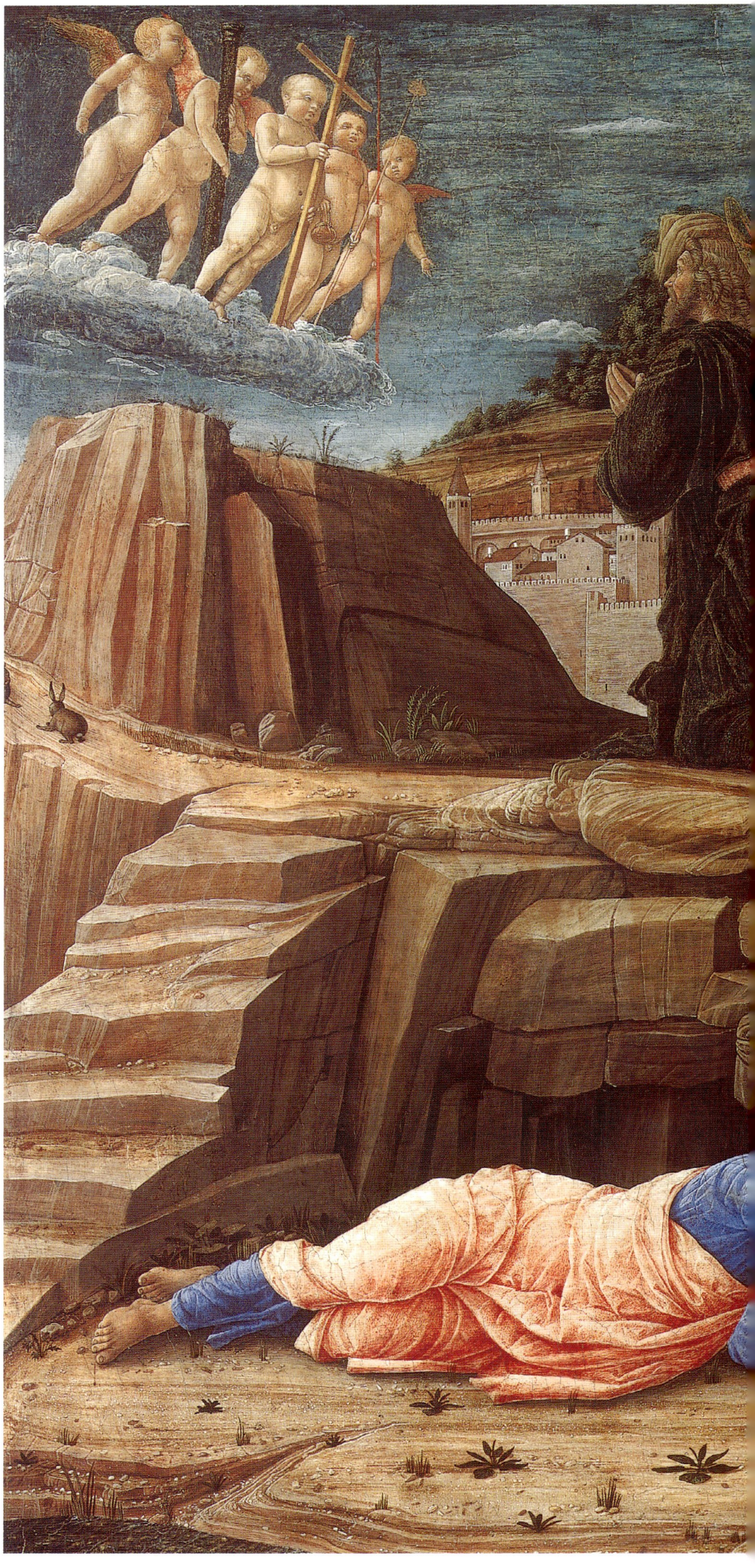

21. *The Agony in the Garden,*
c. 1455.
Tempera on panel, 63 x 80 cm.
The National Gallery, London.

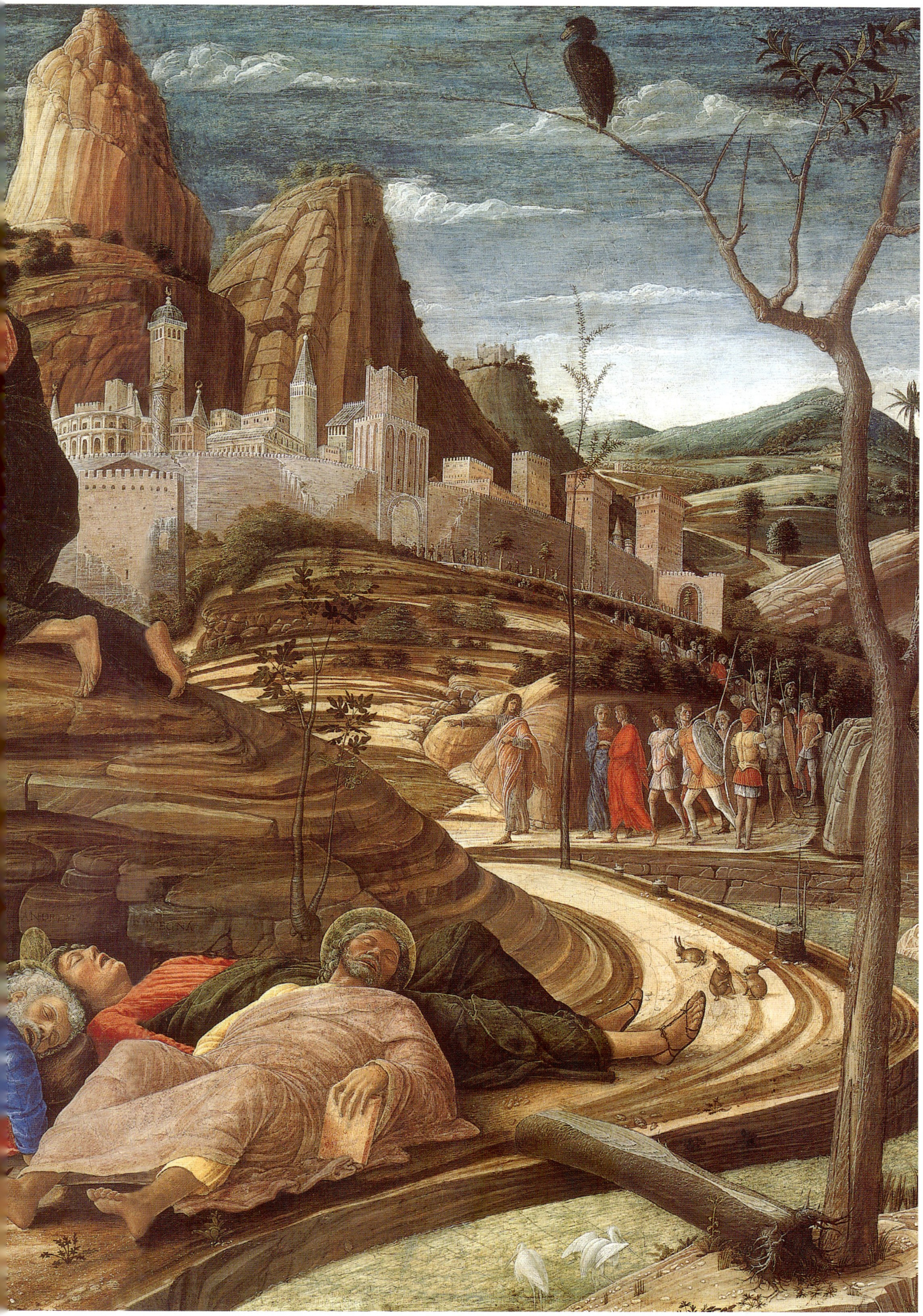

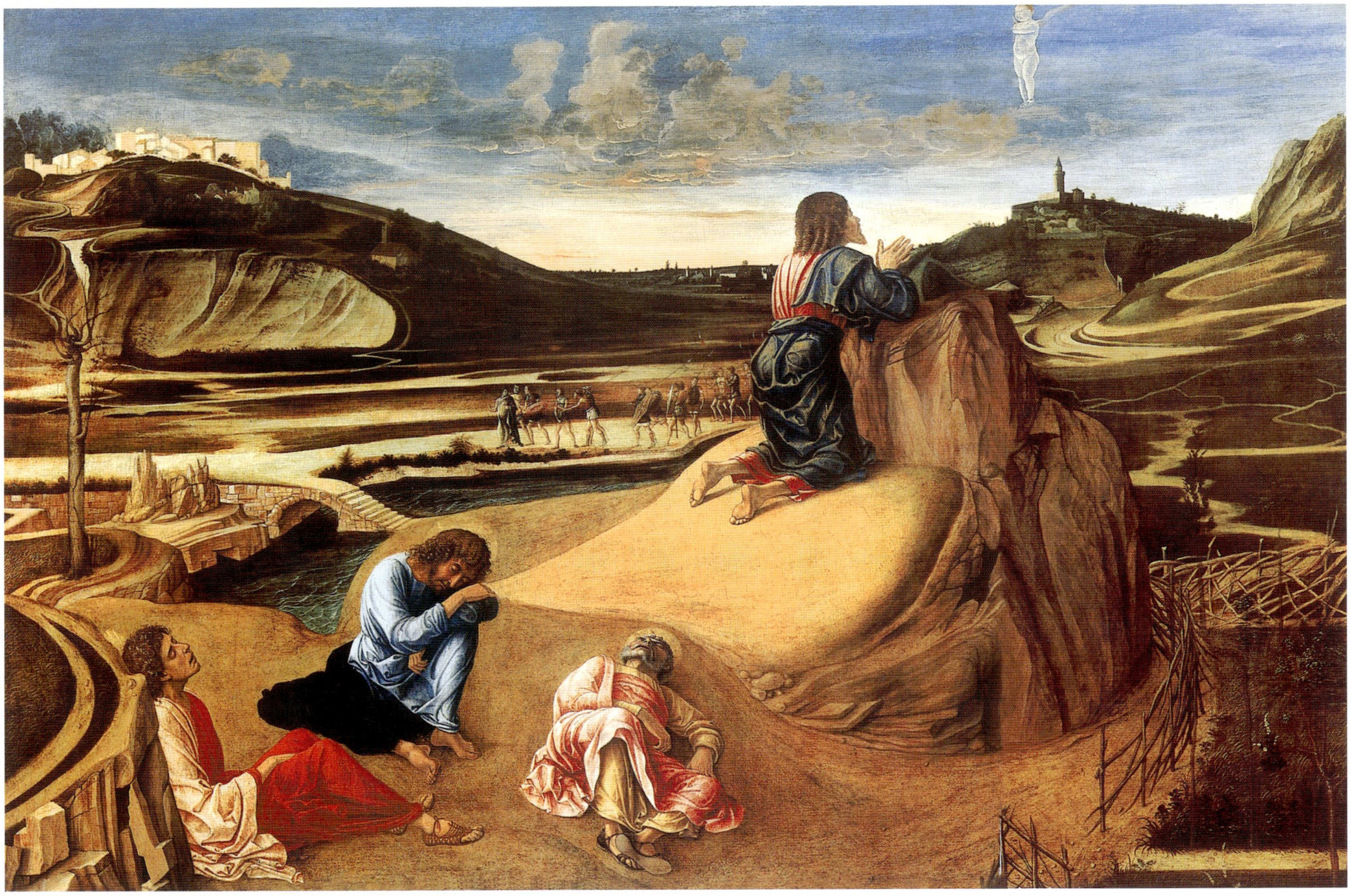

artists were often paid by the figure, and she argued the artist should receive less money than originally agreed because of the omission. Mantegna, given the restriction of space, thoughtfully limited the number of Apostles to eight, avoiding a consequent crowding and weakening of the composition.

One artist testified in court that Mantegna would have to have made the figures much smaller to fit them in, but he could have done so if he wished. Another master was more supportive of Mantegna. The sculptor Pietro da Milano argued Mantegna truly had room only for eight figures; adding the heads of the other Apostles would have spoiled the perspective of the picture. Pietro stated Mantegna's painting was made "*cum magna arte*," with great artfulness, and he should receive the payment the Ovetari family promised, which is how the matter was finally resolved. It is significant that Mantegna was willing to turn his back on tradition and represent not what was literally correct and usually done but what worked best artistically. Certainly this is a new dramatic type of *Assumption*, including vigorously gesturing Apostles who twist and turn in amazement as the Virgin ascends to Heaven. Mantegna increases the impact by making the action take place at night, set against a black backdrop. There is a flurry of active angels around Mary, and brilliant, eye-catching stars adorn the underside of the fictive arch.

22. Giovanni Bellini, *The Agony in the Garden*, c. 1460.
Tempera on panel, 81.3 x 127 cm.
The National Gallery, London.

Mantegna had other legal difficulties during these early years in the Ovetari Chapel. We have mentioned Niccolò Pizzolo as a contributor to the decoration of the Ovetari Chapel and, like

Mantegna, as an artist working in the new Renaissance style, however he also engaged in official challenges to Mantegna's work. Pizzolo fought to get as great a share as he could in the commission, and in September 1449 Pizzolo and Mantegna sought the arbitration of an outside expert. There was so much ill will between the painters it was necessary for the judge to decree neither should physically obstruct the work of the other, and Pizzolo must not block Mantegna's light by erecting a screen in the chapel. The arbitrator stated Pizzolo should be allowed to paint one of the histories on the Saint James wall, but the artist never took advantage of this opportunity. Mantegna had wanted to design the altarpiece, so the commission for the terracotta piece to Pizzolo was another favourable ruling for him from the arbitrator.

This altar and the ceiling vault paintings by Pizzolo (Figs. 11 and 20) show he was indeed a serious challenger, his bold foreshortenings and expressive figures at least equal to the work of Mantegna, who had also studied with the famous Squarcione. In 1448, one pupil wanted to study with Pizzolo with the intent of learning to "*pingere in recente*", to paint in the modern style, an indication it was well known that Pizzolo was practicing the very latest and most exciting style. It is easy to imagine the intensity of the emotional atmosphere as two brilliant artists, Pizzolo and Mantegna, worked in the same small chapel, fighting for space and for the accolades of the public.

This competition must have increased the inclination of both men to achieve the newest and most striking effects possible in their art. Indeed, the Renaissance writer Giorgio Vasari recorded working alongside Pizzolo gave to Mantegna "no little help and incentive by the competition."[2] This competition ended only when Pizzolo was killed in a fight in 1453; Niccolò had a history of trouble with the law, and apparently had an even more troublesome personality than Mantegna. These artists left further evidence of their great egos and intense personalities by painting their portraits in giant form just outside the chapel entrance. There has been some scholarly debate about which head is a portrait of which man; at any rate, both self-likenesses are characterised by tough realism and convey the combative natures of the artists (Figs. 14 and 15). Mantegna also left a searing self-portrait in the *Trial of Saint James*, showing himself as a scowling, terrible Roman soldier, offering us a glimpse of the strength of character of the artist who created these frescoes (Fig. 10). Indeed, all his later self-portraits indicate an intense, almost ferocious personality (see also Figs. 53 and 81).

The other artists working in the chapel were not as great as Pizzolo or Mantegna. Some other painters little known today, including Bono da Ferrara and Ansuino da Forli, helped Mantegna complete the wall on the right side of the chapel with scenes of the life of Saint Christopher. Their efforts are competent but without the novelty and incisive quality of Mantegna's work. Yet both their frescoes were in the new Renaissance style, and their art did not clash with that of the more progressive masters at work in the chapel. Christopher, a legendary saint whose story was again elaborately related in the *Golden Legend* of Voragine, was removed from the official list of Roman Catholic saints in 1969, but in the Renaissance and later he was revered as a protector of travellers and all who went about their daily rounds. Bono da Ferrara shows him in his most famous role, that of bearer of Christ across a river, the sins of the world contained in Christ's body straining Christopher's giant form. Mantegna's task was to show the execution of the saint, which takes place on the bottom register of the compartmentalised wall (Fig. 7). This part of the fresco cycle does survive, although it is much damaged, and to be able to make out large sections of the missing pigment it is necessary to turn to an important early copy.

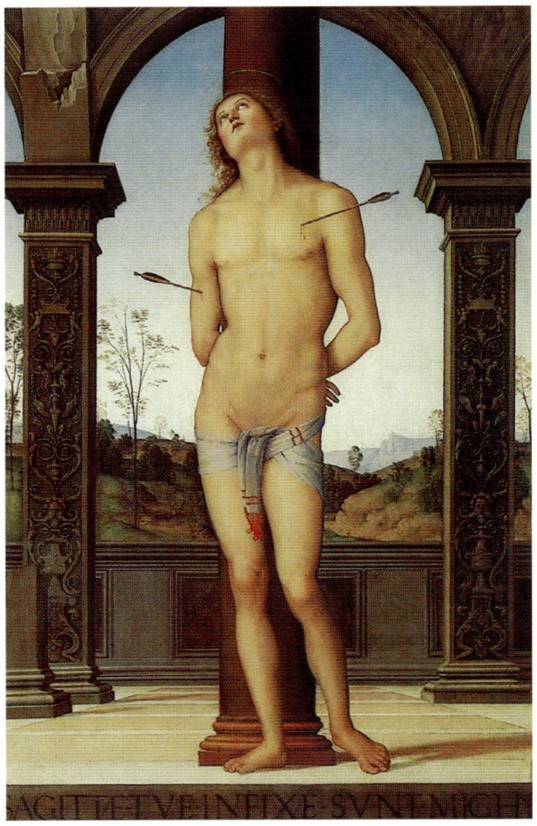

In medieval times, a new episode was added to early Christian legends of Christopher, relating how when his execution was ordered by the King of Lycia, forty archers were called on to kill the giant. Yet the arrows did not harm Christopher, and one of the arrows turned around in mid-air and landed instead in the eye of the king, who cries out as the arrow strikes and blinds him in Mantegna's rendering. In a characteristic spatial device, the painter sets Christopher outside the architectural moulding, putting him into the space of the viewer. The next part of the scene unfolds on the right side of this work; although spatially connected to the left side, it represents a later moment in time, when Christopher is finally beheaded (since the arrows failed), and his body is being dragged through the streets. The saint is depicted in bold foreshortening on the ground and his head, lying close by before the spectator, has a shock effect like that of the beheading of Saint James directly across the chapel. Early sources tell us many of the figures in the crowd on the right are portraits of Mantegna's contemporaries, most of them Paduan noblemen, doctors, and humanists, who formed an important component of the artist's appreciative public.

In his work for the Ovetari Chapel, Mantegna achieved an incredible feat, and one can argue the torch passed to him as the leading painter in Italy. In a perhaps unexpected turn of events, the young Paduan painter came closer than any other Italian painter to fulfilling the goals of the period as set out by a chief theoretician, Leon Battista Alberti who stressed, in his widely read and admired treatise *On Painting* of 1435, art should show figures who are alive down to their very fingernails, and painting should tell stories vividly and with an economy of means, representing in a memorable and accurate way human gestures, emotions, and attitudes. In accordance with the humanist's advice, Mantegna's art improves Nature, not just imitates it; the painter set out to better and ennoble the real world. Alberti, and many others, also recommended painters and sculptors borrow freely from Greek and Roman models. Because in the Renaissance no ancient paintings were yet known (this was before the excavation of such sites as Pompeii and Herculaneum in the eighteenth century), Mantegna had to borrow from the world of Roman sculpture and architecture, and he recreated his own inventive world of antiquity. In short, in these earliest works Mantegna changed the course of Italian art, and he fulfilled more completely than any other artist the aspirations the progressive Early Renaissance opinion about what it is that constitutes good, lively painting.

23. Pietro Perugino, *St Sebastian*, c. 1490-1500, Oil on wood, 176 x 116 cm. Musée du Louvre, Paris.

24. *St Sebastian*, c. 1455-1460. Tempera on panel, 68 x 30 cm. Kunsthistoriches Museum, Vienna.

25. *The Adoration of the Shepherds*, c. 1450-1455. Tempera on canvas (transferred from panel), 40 x 55.5 cm. The Metropolitan Museum of Art, New York.

This is not to say Mantegna faced no criticism in these early years. Certainly some of the late Gothic painters and their loyal public must have thought his work to be harsh, overly realistic, and lacking the suave gracefulness of the traditional style they practised. Even Mantegna's teacher, Francesco Squarcione, is recorded (by the biographer Giorgio Vasari) to have carped at Mantegna's murals in the Ovetari Chapel. He said Mantegna's figures looked as though they are sculptures rather than real people, saying of the frescoes in the chapel, "They were inferior work since when he did them Andrea had imitated marble statues. Stone", said Squarcione, "was essentially a hard substance and it could never convey the softness and tenderness of flesh and natural objects, with the various movements and folds."[3] This remark must have stung Mantegna (and puzzled him, since Squarcione had young Andrea learn by copying plaster casts), and it is possible the more supple figures and the slight softening of forms and colours occurring in the later Saint James scenes and in the *Execution of Saint Christopher* were a result of his adjustment to such criticism. And the young artist and his former master exchanged more than words at this time: in 1456, Mantegna sued Squarcione (and won) to break the legal partnership they had established in 1448 when he was still a minor.

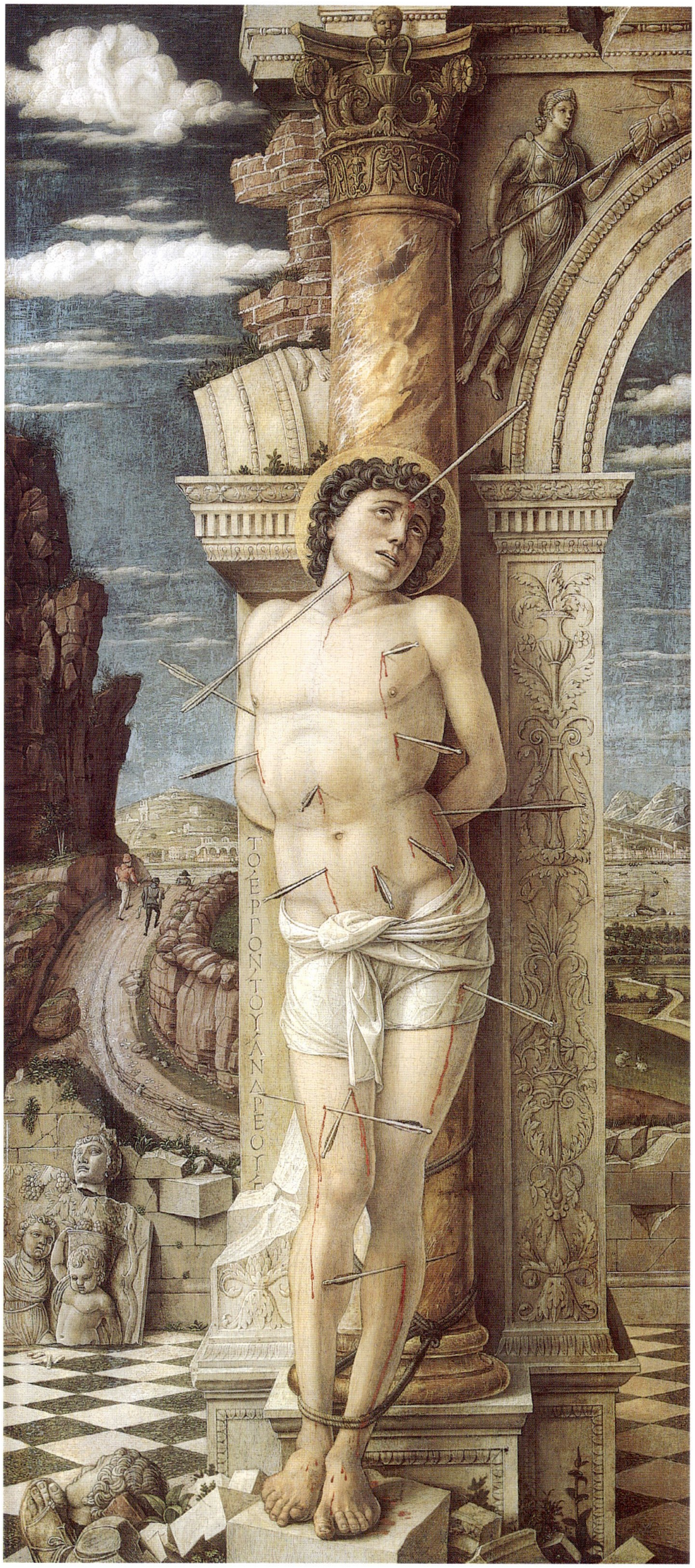
ΤΟ ΕΡΓΟΝ ΤΟΥ ΑΝΔΡΕΟΥ

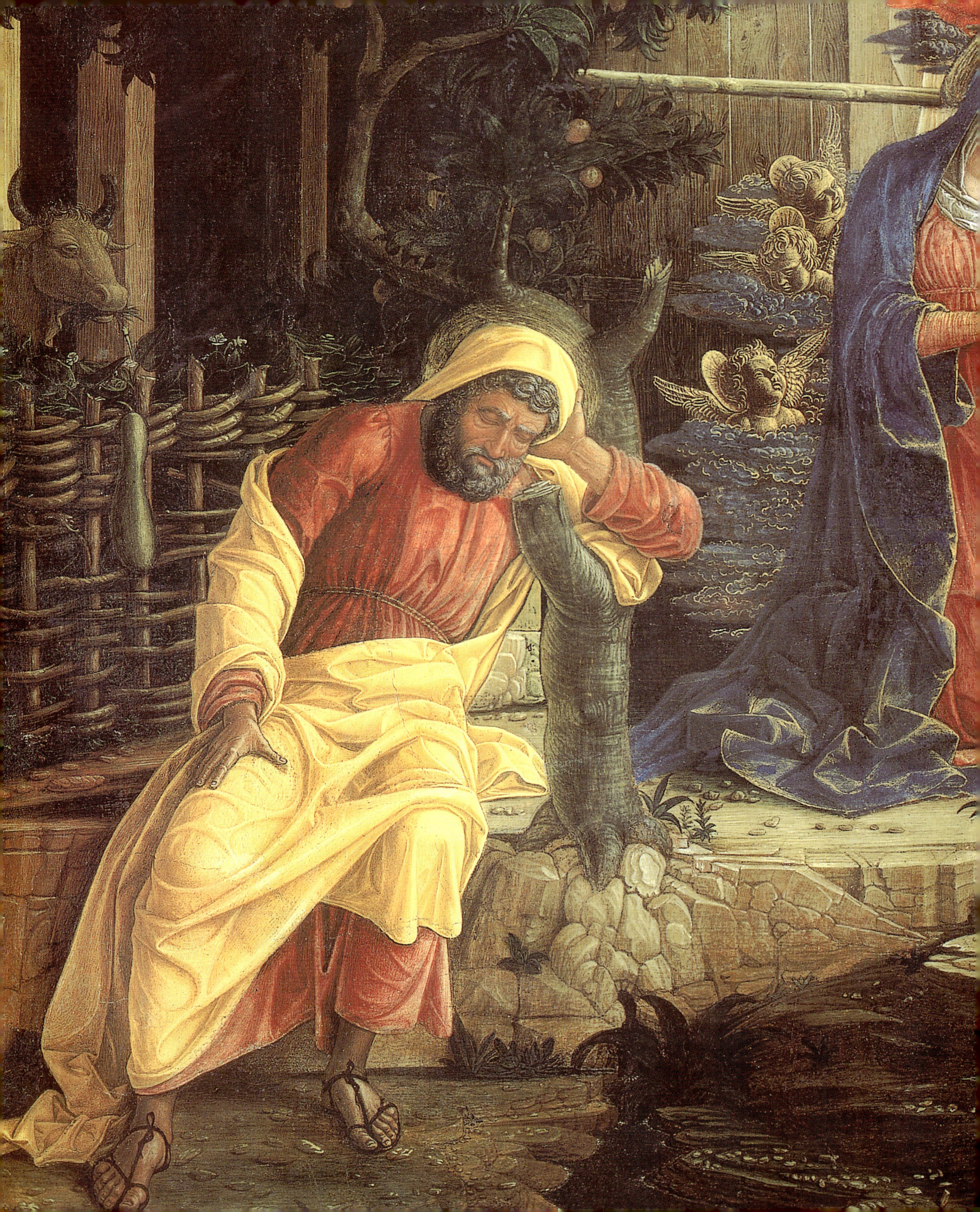

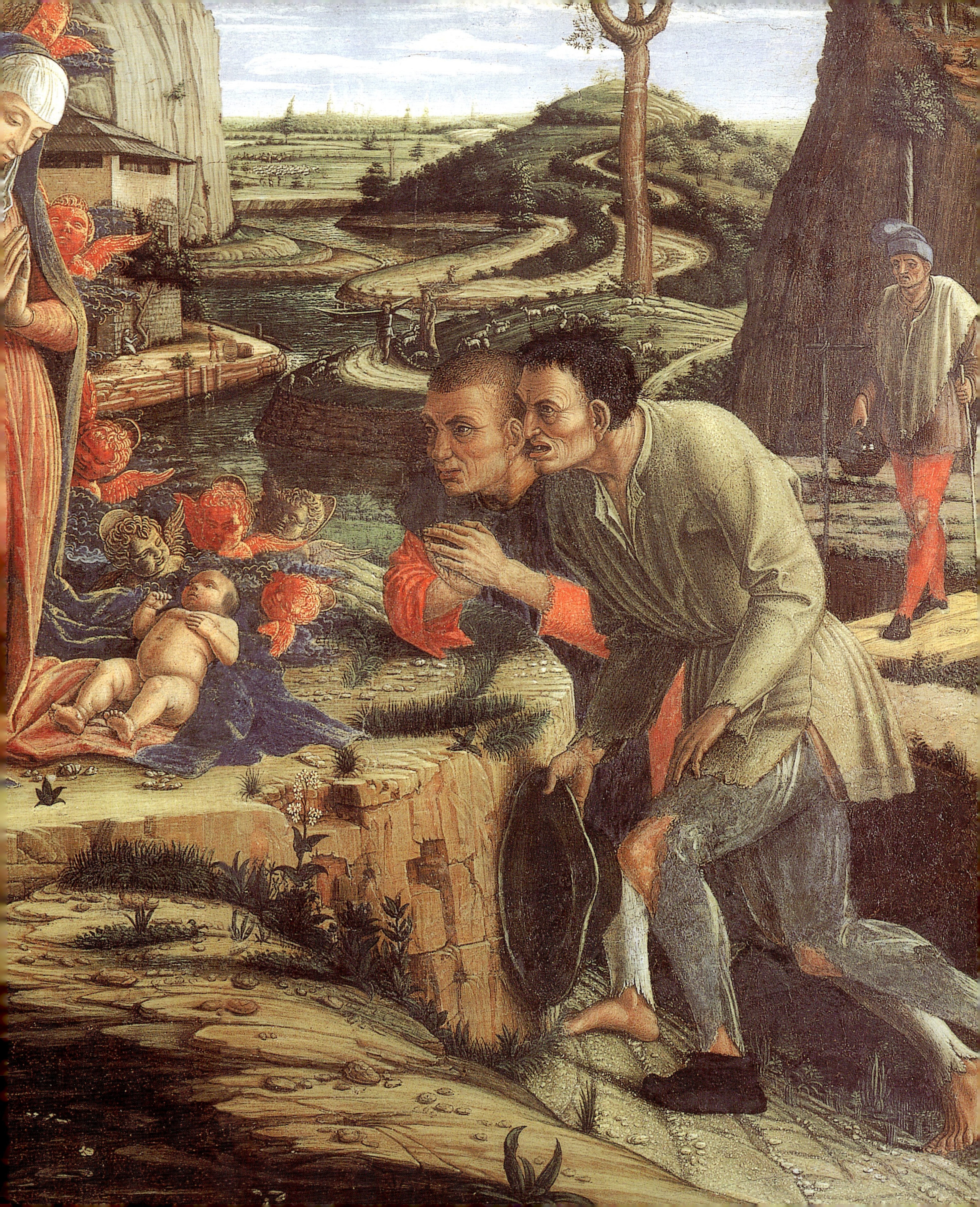

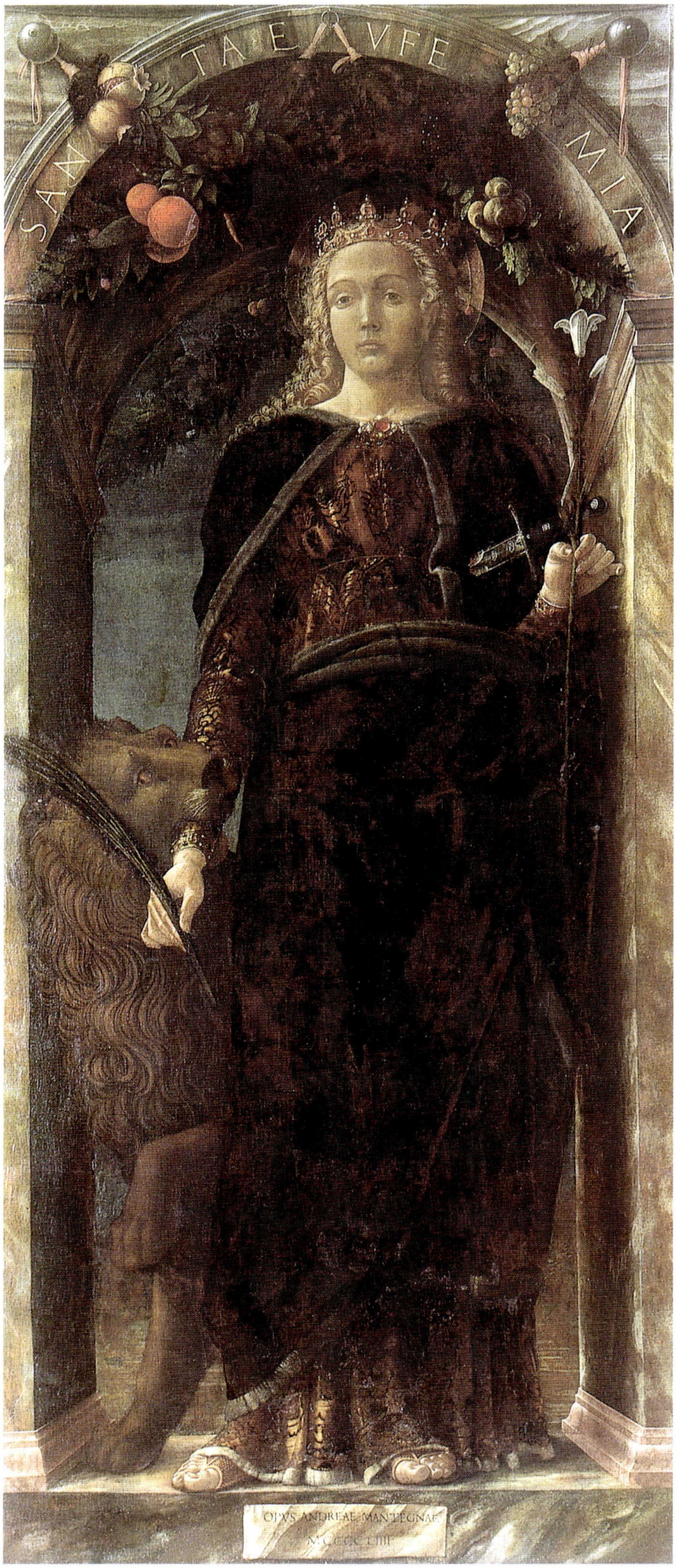
SAN TA E VFE MIA
OPVS ANDREAE MANTEGNAE
MCCCCLIIII

In addition to all his interactions with Squarcione and other artists during the years of the Ovetari Chapel, Mantegna also entered at this time into a long relationship with the great family of artists from Venice, the Bellini. It is even possible this new association helped to sour his relations with Squarcione, who might have resented his adopted son's new artistic relations. At any rate, Mantegna came into close contact with the work of the Venetian painter Jacopo Bellini, for in 1453 Mantegna married Bellini's daughter, Nicolosia. Jacopo Bellini's art contained much Mantegna must have admired. Bellini made many drawings of daring perspective views, and he was fascinated with fragments of antique sculpture and architecture, as we can see in one of his drawings.

Jacopo's painting style was subtle and showed great perception of the effects of light; perhaps his skill as a painter served as a model for Mantegna in his development. Jacopo's sons Gentile Bellini and Giovanni Bellini would become leading painters in Venice, and there would continue to be a mutual exchange of ideas between these brothers-in-law, all contemporaries and leaders in their field. One fruit of his association with the Bellini family is Mantegna's early *Agony in the Garden*, which recalls a similar work by Giovanni Bellini, both being based ultimately on a composition of the elder, Jacopo Bellini (Figs. 21 and 22). One of the last commissions Mantegna would undertake remained unfinished at his death, and the project was completed in part by his brother-in-law Giovanni more than fifty years after the time of the Ovetari Chapel (see Fig. 93). It is likely Giovanni Bellini learned a great deal from Mantegna in the early years of their contact, but later Giovanni's style moved in another, independent direction, becoming far softer than Andrea's and more harmonious in light and colouring. This can already be seen in the compositions on the same theme, hung nearby in the National Gallery in London. Giovanni's *Agony in the Garden* (Fig. 22), showing Christ and the sleeping Apostles approached by Judas and the Roman soldiers who will arrest Christ. Bellini's picture is luminous and soft in texture, with a pictorial unity created by the light and colour. In his version, Mantegna has created a stony sharp world, with bare branches against the sky, strongly foreshortened Apostles, and angels riding on a firm bank of clouds, the work dominated by pebbles, erupting masses of mountain, and striated rock in the middleground (Fig. 21). Not only do these paintings indicate the difference between the Venetian style of the Renaissance and Mantegna's stony approach; they are incipient examples of the divide between the linear and the painterly approaches to art-making, a contrast that would for centuries come to characterise two major schools of painting in Europe.

The fame that ensued from the work on the Ovetari Chapel frescoes would eventually bring Mantegna an opportunity to become a well-paid court painter in the city-state of Mantua. Before moving there in 1459, he completed several other notable works on religious themes. One of these is his *Adoration of the Shepherds* (Fig. 25), which he perhaps made for Borso d'Este, ruler of the city-state of Ferrara, located a hundred kilometres south-west of Padua (see Fig. 5). With this work we finally have a chance to assess a surviving easel painting by young Mantegna, painted in tempera, a mixture of egg and ground pigment that allows more minute and searching pictorial effects than the fresco technique he used in the Ovetari Chapel. Here Mantegna paints in incredible detail seemingly every stone, leaf, and sheep in the landscape. Mantegna's skill at representing Nature is apparent in the atmospheric clouds, which are beautifully struck by the light, reflecting his close observation of the natural world. This painting also reveals on a small scale Mantegna's emotional intensity, the picture including fervent shepherds and a loving, maternal Virgin. The *Adoration of the Shepherds* was widely admired and copied in Mantegna's lifetime, a remarkable homage to so young

26. *St Euphemia*, 1454.
Tempera on canvas, 171 x 78 cm.
Museo e Gallerie Nazionali di Capodimonte, Naples.

an artist, still in his early twenties. Surely one of the new and attractive elements of this painting for Italian contemporaries of Mantegna was the coarse realism of the two shepherds, who approach the foreshortened Child and begin to genuflect. In earlier traditions of Italian painting it was customary to make all the figures look ideal, whether heroic or merely pretty, but Mantegna gives these men – with their brutal faces, torn clothing, and bare feet – a rustic crudity that was new in Italian art. This is a good early example of the kind of biting realism that would continue to be a hallmark of Mantegna's artistry.

Humanistic themes never remained far off for Mantegna at any stage of his career. His *Saint Euphemia*, now in Naples (Fig. 26) seems to represent a classical Roman statue in a niche, with the swag of fruit, in ancient fashion, depicted overhead, and the inscription delineated in an accurate *all'antica* manner. The lion plays with the arm of the saint, his action helping to alleviate the severity of the spare Doric setting and the stoic reticence of Euphemia. This humanism can also be seen in his early, and justifiably famous, *Saint Sebastian* (Fig. 24). Sebastian was a Roman army officer of the third century who secretly became a Christian. When word of this conversion was known, his superiors ordered Sebastian's own troops to shoot him with arrows. Mantegna's saint makes for difficult viewing, as he is pierced with numerous arrows, including ones in his forehead and neck. We do not know for whom Mantegna painted the *Saint Sebastian*, but it is a perfect picture for someone with antiquarian or scholarly interests, and we must assume a learned patron enjoyed the classical references in this painting. At Sebastian's feet and behind him are fragments of Roman sculpture, the kind of marble pieces being eagerly collected at that time by growing ranks of connoisseurs of antique art. More than one ancient Greek and Roman writer noted Nature, like an artist, forms recognisable shapes in clouds, and Mantegna here shows a marvellous horse and rider in the cloud on the upper left, the kind of pictorial detail that would have delighted his erudite viewers. The saint is bound to the column of a classical triumphal arch, which includes a beautiful Victory in the spandrel. This triumphal arch serves a double purpose, to allow one to admire antiquity, but also to stress Christianity's triumph over Roman paganism, as attested by the crumbling condition of the arch. Thus, Mantegna manages to honour the Christian religion of his patrons as well as satisfy their interest in the classical past. Mantegna was surely pleased with this work, and proud of his liaison with the world of learning in Padua, for he prominently signed his name in Greek just to the saint's right; the inscription states this is "the work of Andrea M." Mantegna could not have known much Greek, and there is nothing Greek about the subject or the setting; but the young painter took the opportunity anyway to show off a bit of his own fascination with the classical past. This is Mantegna's form of classicism, however, not a timeless calm, but an aggressive, ruptured scene echoing the saint's suffering. The painter turns the paving squares in jarring points towards the picture plane, and the saint stands on a stone fragment with its pointed corner turned outward at an even more destabilising off-angle. The fragments consist of shattered bits of masonry, heads, and feet, and the triumphal arch has its brick core laid bare. The saint prevails over a moral world in collapse.

27. *San Zeno Altarpiece*, c. 1457-1459. Basilica di San Zeno Maggiore, Verona.

Despite his attempt at sharp realism, Mantegna's *Sebastian* is not rendered with complete anatomical accuracy. Although in the fifteenth century there was a growing interest in such subjects as the human body and medicine, it was not until later in the fifteenth century when artists such as Leonardo da Vinci would carry out dissections of the human figure in order to arrive at more scientific and convincing representations. Many of Mantegna's supporters in learned circles might

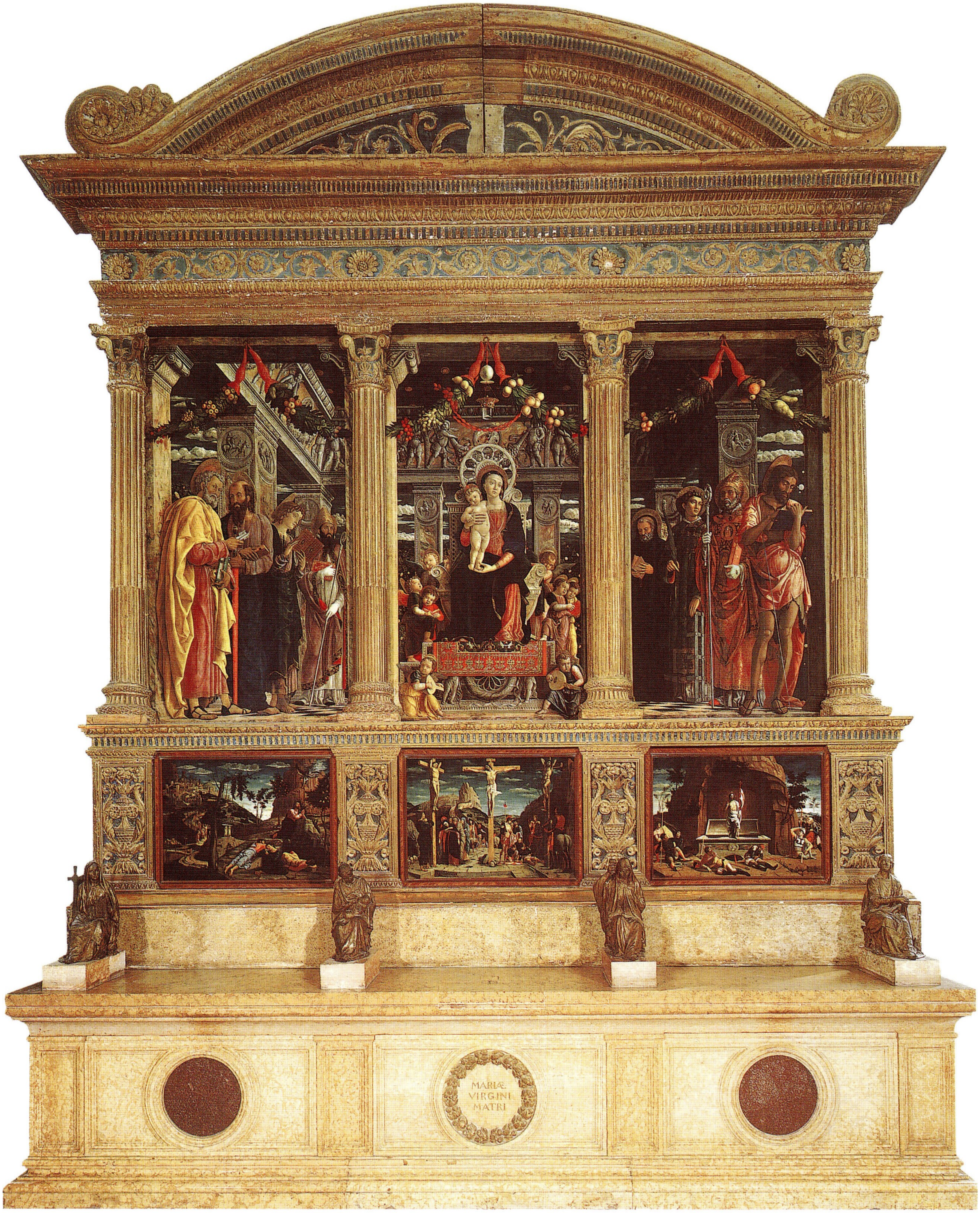
MARIAE
VIRGINI
MATRI

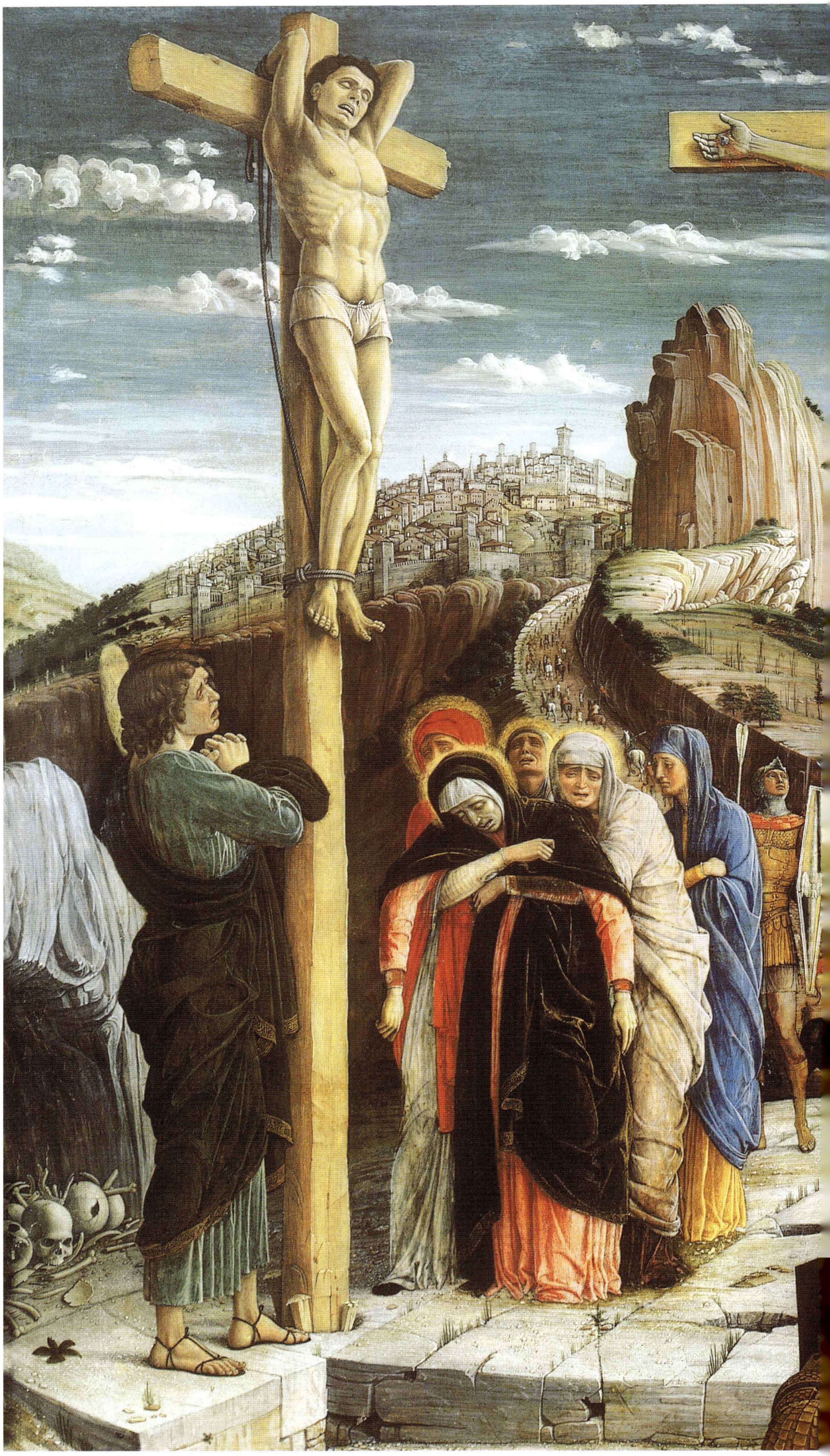

28. *The Crucifixion* (from the San Zeno Altarpiece),
c. 1457-1459.
Tempera on panel, 66 x 90 cm.
Musée du Louvre, Paris.

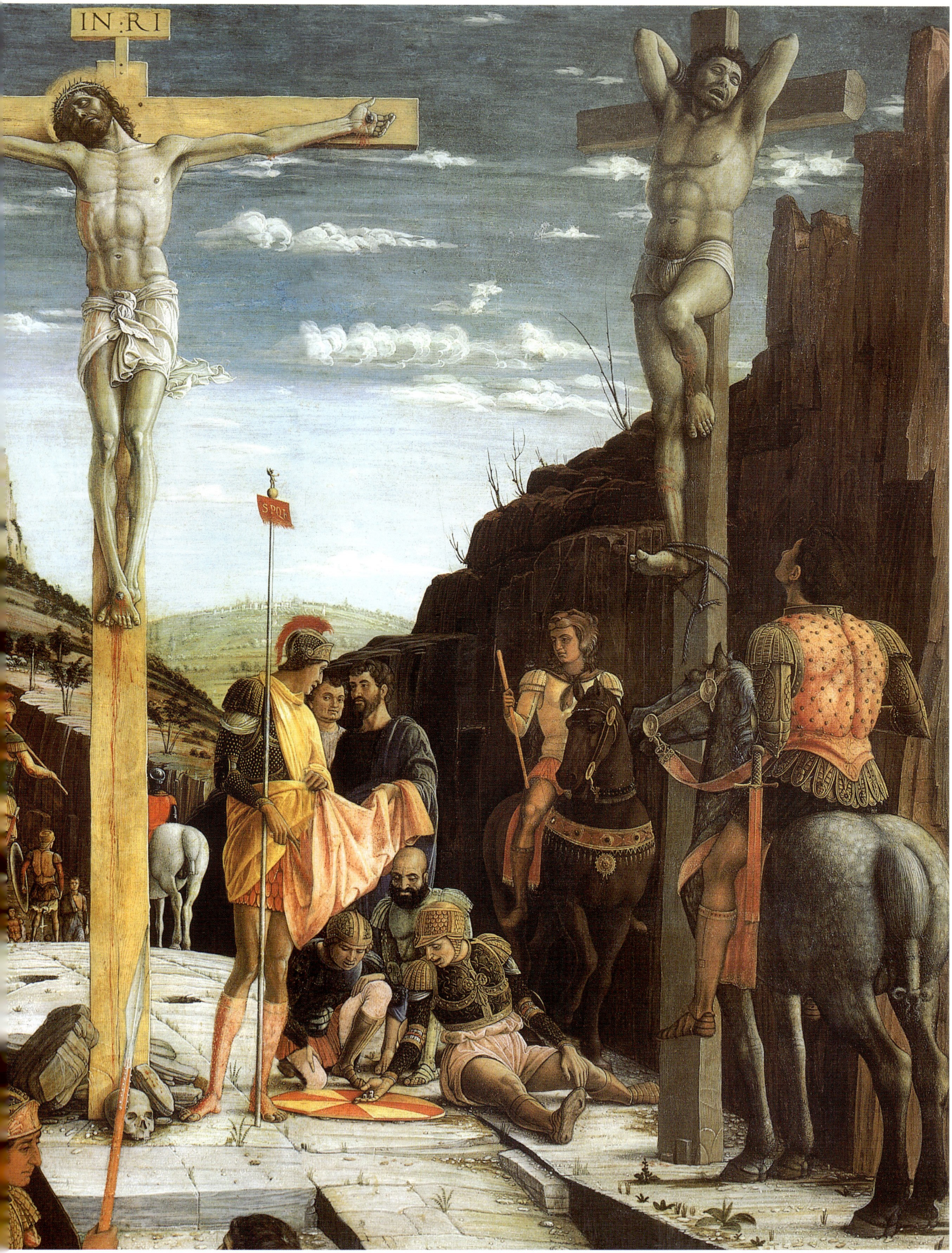
IN:RI

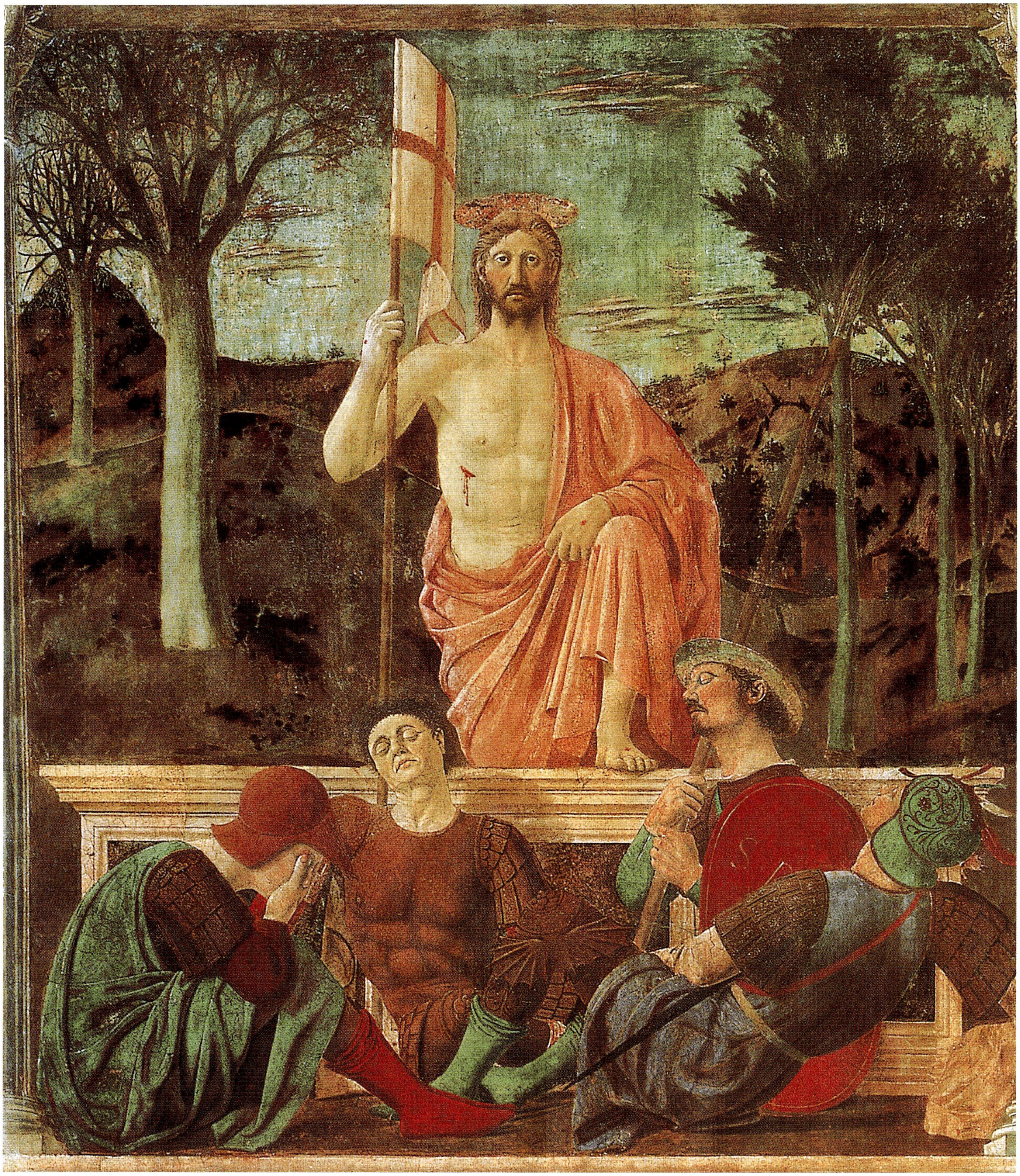

have praised his naturalism, just as so many ancient writers lauded the realism of their contemporary artists, but Renaissance humanists, being literary men, did not frequently spur on artists to dissect and scrutinise the human body. Instead, they emphasised the study of antique sculpture, and indeed the rib cage and abdominal musculature of Mantegna's tormented saint recall the anatomical definition of the male body as often found in classical sculpture. But whatever its deviations from natural appearance, Mantegna's saint probably seemed convincingly real to contemporary viewers who were accustomed to seeing rubbery, elegant Gothic figures. Here, as frequently happened in Mantegna's work and in other Renaissance painting, the investigation of the real world was filtered through the vision and artistic conventions of classical antiquity.

When Mantegna received the offer to move to Mantua in 1457 he delayed the move more than two years because he had other commissions to fulfil, especially his impressive San Zeno altarpiece (Fig. 27). In the larger panel stand the Madonna and Saints, and in the *predella* below are representations of *Christ in the Garden of Gethsemane* (left), the *Crucifixion* (centre), and the *Resurrection of Christ* (right). Mantegna painted the altarpiece in 1457-1459 for the church of San Zeno in Verona, where it is still kept, although all the smaller panels have been taken away to museums and have been replaced in the original altarpiece by copies. The work was commissioned by Gregorio Correr, a wealthy Venetian who had held a position of authority over the church in Verona, which is not so far from Padua and which, like Padua, was part of the Venetian Republic. Correr had received a solid humanist education in Mantua, studying with the famous humanist teacher Vittorino da Feltre. Later he wrote a tragedy which, for centuries, was mistaken for an original Roman work of drama. Because of his own interests in antiquity, Correr was undoubtedly attracted to the classical revival aspects of Mantegna's artistry.

This altarpiece is an exuberant exposition of Mantegna's style and must have created a shock when it was unveiled to the public in Verona, where the demure, polite traditions of International Gothic painting were still alive and widely practised. Here Mantegna unleashed a profusion of colour, three-dimensional form, and archaeological detail, all rendered in a crisp linear fashion. Even the frame is not in the usual Gothic form, which would have called for intricate foliage, slender colonnettes, and pointed arches. Well into the fifteenth century, works by Renaissance artists were frequently paired with frames made by artists working in the late, decorative Gothic style. But here Mantegna designed his own frame, which was carried out by a sculptor working under his instructions. The four great Corinthian columns and the other classical details make this monumental frame different from anything the public in Verona would have known. Moreover, in a clever stroke, Mantegna painted the swags of fruit between the real columns of the frame and the painted pilasters behind, setting up an effective and witty spatial continuity between the frame and the depicted world.

The form of the main panel is called a "holy conversation" (*sacra conversazione* in Italian) in which saints, who lived in various historical times, are shown gathered in one place to honour the Virgin and Child. The saints include most prominently Saint Peter on the far left and Saint John the Baptist on the far right, as well as several other bishop saints and female martyrs. Most of his earlier paintings depicted saints in separate isolated panels, not grouped together in this way (see Fig. 6). Indeed, a few years earlier, Mantegna – perhaps at the urging of the patron – made an old-fashioned polyptych for the church of Santa Giustina in Padua in 1453-1454 (Fig. 31), with figures

29. Piero della Francesca, *The Resurrection of Christ*, c. 1463. Fresco. Palazzo Comunale, San Sepolcro.

30. *The Resurrection of Christ (from the San Zeno Altarpiece)*, v. 1457-1459. Tempera on panel, 71 x 94 cm. Musée des Beaux-Arts, Tours.

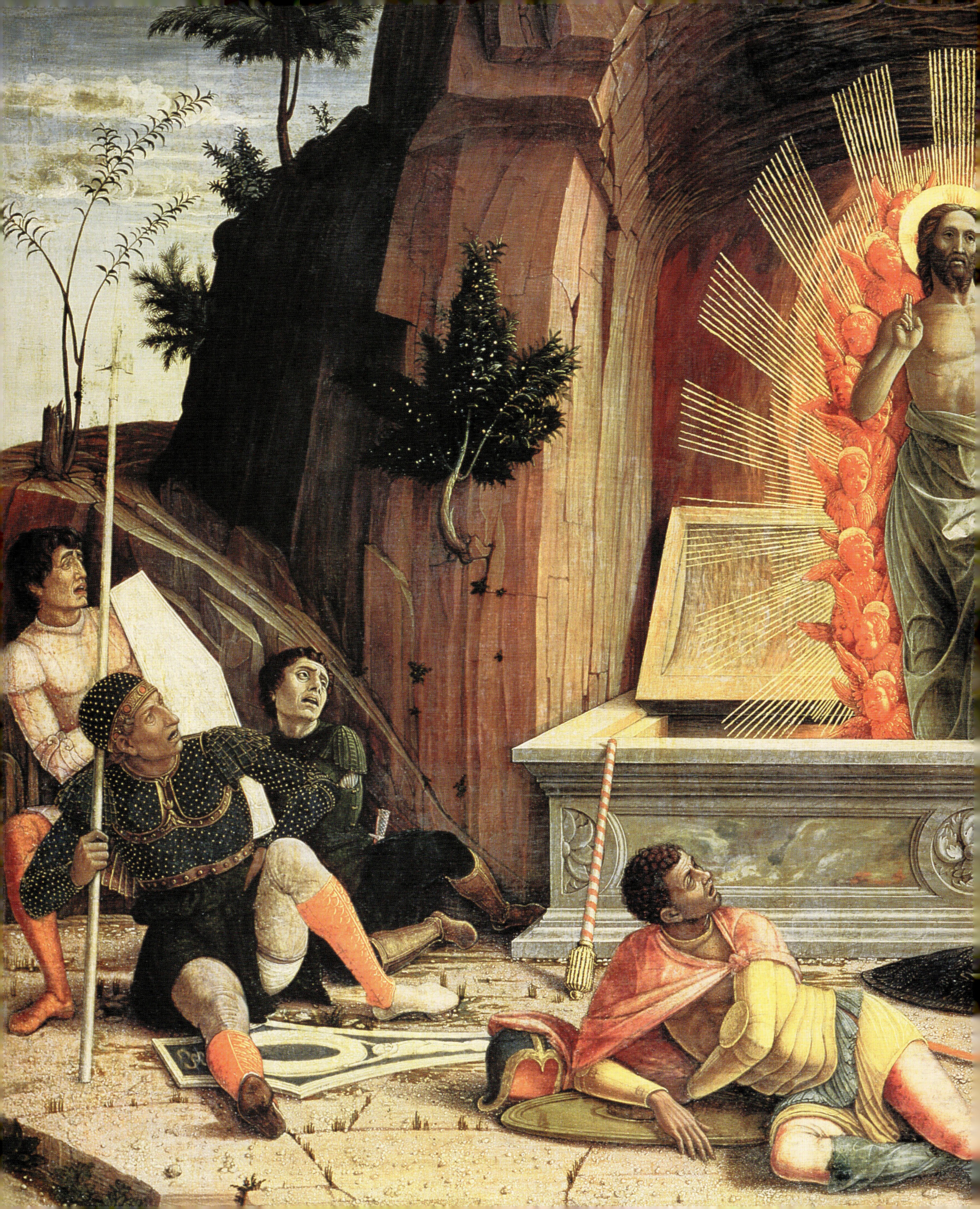

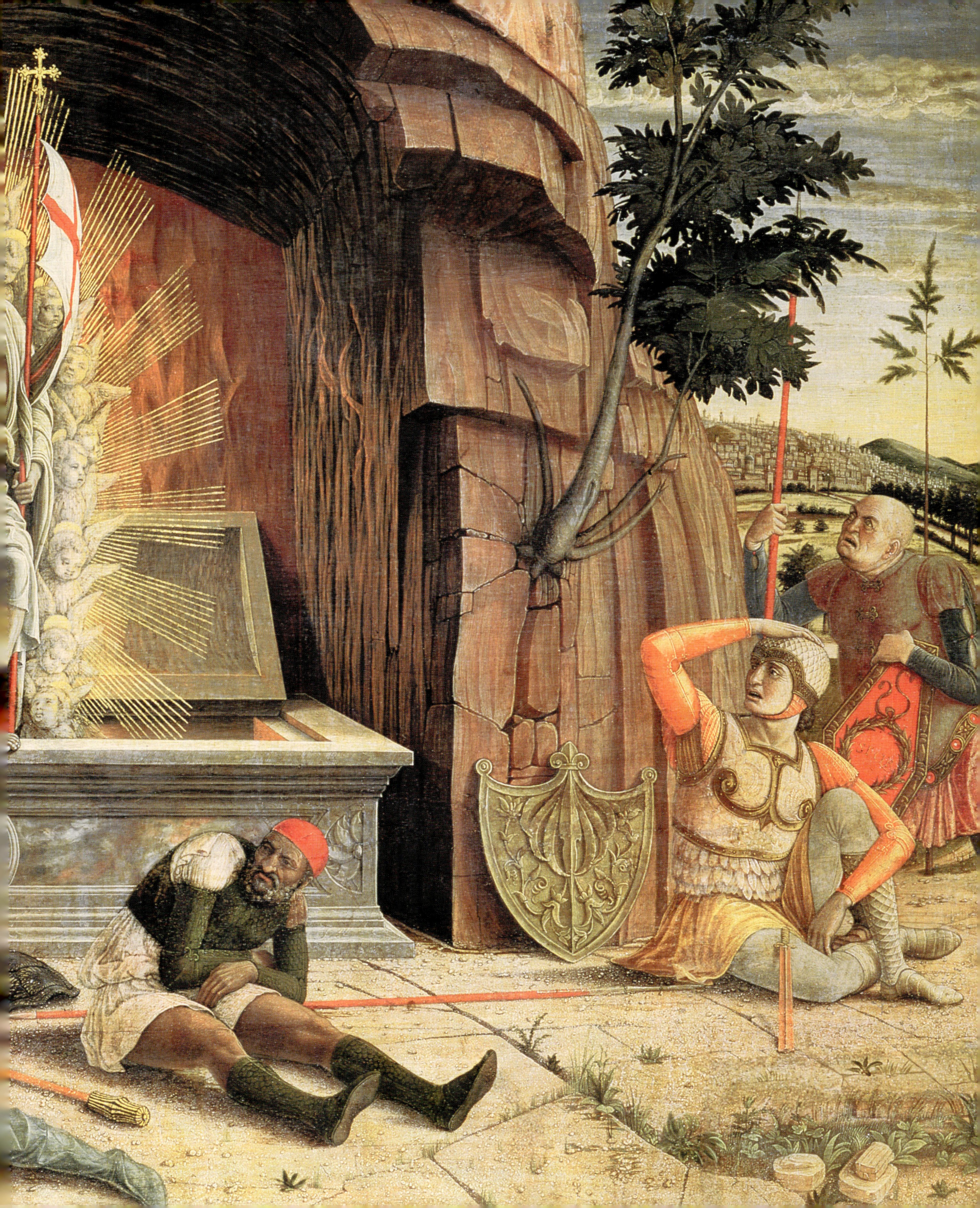

set isolated in niches and placed against gold backgrounds. But the San Zeno altarpiece is different in its spatial and figural unity. A few instances of the unified *sacra conversazione* had preceded Mantegna, but no other artist had included so many saints and so many other architectural and decorative elements in what had been a very conservative, staid tradition of altarpieces with compartmentalised panels. Mantegna took on the challenge of making a different kind of altarpiece, and he created one of his most striking works.

To help illustrate Mantegna's own particular contribution to Italian Renaissance art, we can turn to one scene from the *predella*, the *Resurrection of Christ* (Fig. 30). Mantegna's style would become a bit more restrained and controlled in colour and action later in his life, but here his youthful exuberance and ambition are full-blown. In order to gauge the extent of Mantegna's exciting earliest manner, it is illuminating to examine it with a comparable contemporary version by the central Italian painter Piero della Francesca (Fig. 29). Piero created a *Resurrection of Christ* in which the forms are heavy, geometric, and weighed down by gravity and by the pyramidal composition. As in the works of the Florentine painter Masaccio, one of his chief sources of inspiration, Piero creates a static, monumental scene that conveys a sense of grandiosity and calm. Mantegna, on the other hand, dazzles with an explosion of energy and excitement. Christ bursts out of his sarcophagus, surrounded by a bright aura of light rays and angels. The soldiers who were supposed to be guarding him react in surprise and horror, and seem to be physically thrown back by Christ's sudden return from the dead. Trees burst impossibly out of rocks, their roots having broken the substance of the stone in surface patterns, and isolated grasses cling tenaciously to the rocky ground. Christ strikes a confident, virile stance, in form an ancient Roman athlete posing as the Lamb of God.

The *Crucifixion* (Fig. 28) from the *predella* of the San Zeno Altarpiece is Mantegna's striking contribution to the history of the representation of this subject. The space – beginning with the *repoussoir* device of the soldiers at the bottom of the design area – shoots into the background, as the rocky surface forms a kind of lined piazza. The plateau composition, a device derived from earlier Netherlandish art, comprises an elevated foreground plane, a spatial descent, and a rising background, complete with a distant, winding road and hilltop city. As usual, Mantegna considers every detail. Christ's body is suspended against the sky, his feet just touching the level of the earth, a prefiguration of his coming Ascension into Heaven. The bad thief, on Christ's left, is in a contorted pose and is set against the sharp rock formations and brittle branches. The good thief is depicted more fully in the light, is set against the rounded hill, and stands above Mary and other holy mourners. Every anatomical detail of Christ's and the thieves' torsos is fully delineated, contributing to the tension of the narrative. The whole work has the feeling of a large scale mural, despite its modest size.

This dynamic narrative style, along with Mantegna's incisive realism and his abundant use of classical motifs, had won the artist a place in the highest echelons of critical acclaim. He was sought after, but rather than continuing to compete in the open market by seeking various public or private commissions in Padua or elsewhere, he took up the post of court painter in Mantua, a job that would provide a steady, guaranteed income and a chance for him to apply his artistic genius to a wide variety of projects. The twenty-eight-year-old Mantegna set out with his family for Mantua in 1459, probably not suspecting he would stay there until the end of his life nearly half a century later.

31. *St Luke Altarpiece*, 1453-1454. Tempera on panel, 230 x 177 cm. Pinacoteca di Brera, Milan.

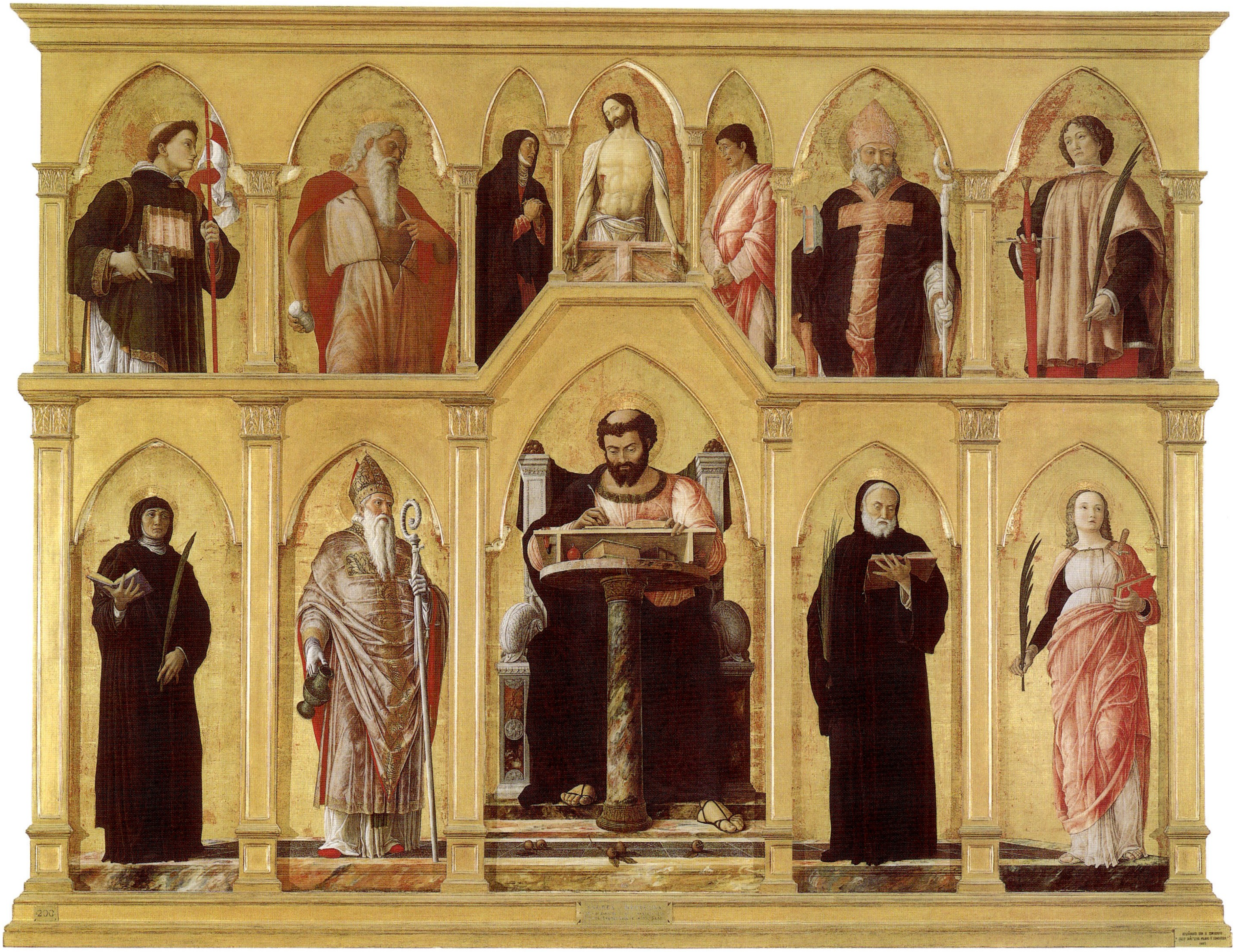

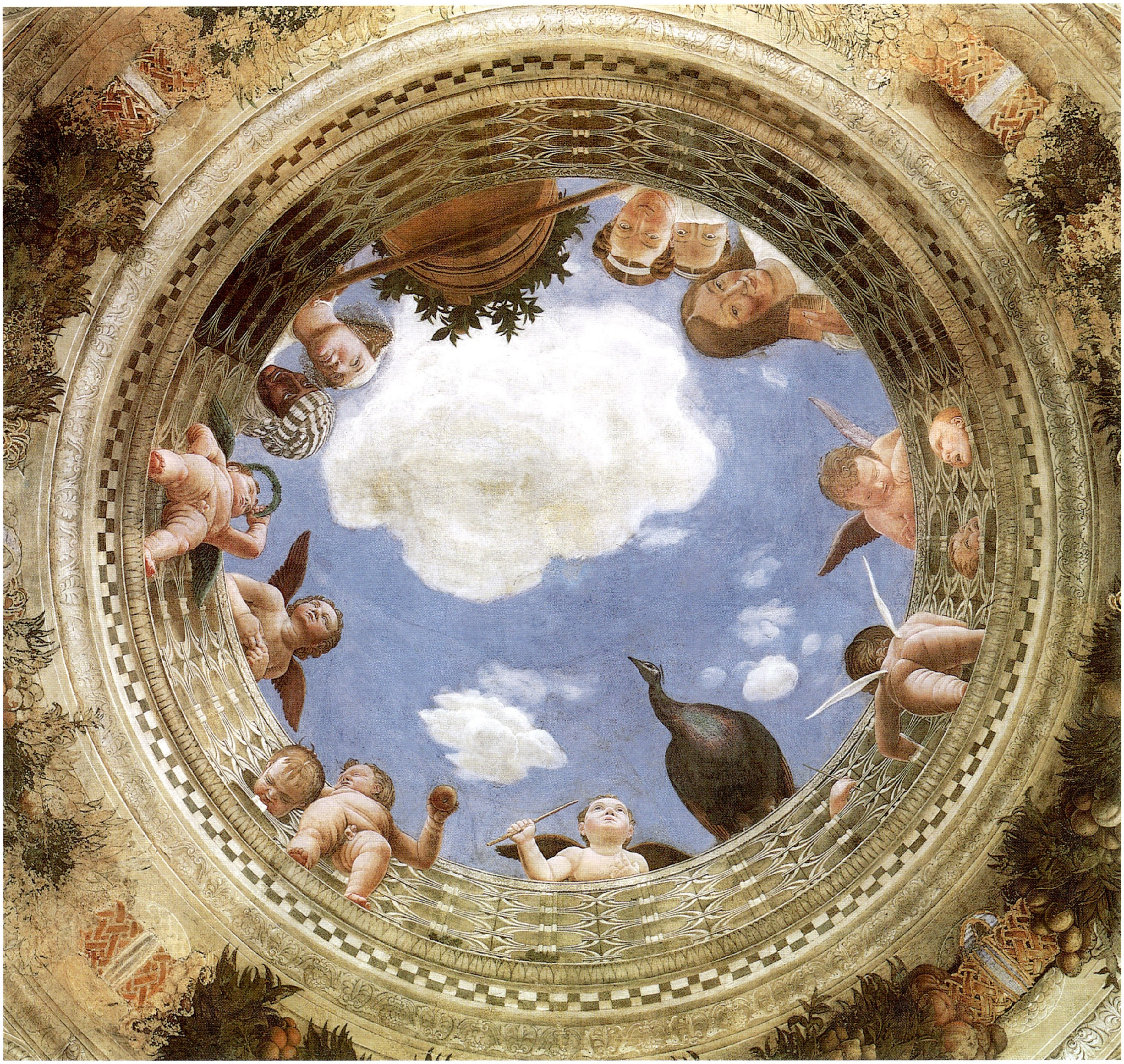

Mantegna as Court Painter in Mantua

The city-state of Mantua constituted the seventh largest nation in Italy, its lands gained from years of conquest and consolidation. Although many of the Italian city-states had relatively democratic governments when they were first established in the medieval period, only a few places, most notably Florence and Venice, retained anything close to a broadly participatory form of government by the fifteenth century.

Mantua, like the neighbouring duchies of Milan and Ferrara, was ruled by one family, the government held by physical might, moral suasion, and the hope for stability and rulership passed down by hereditary title.

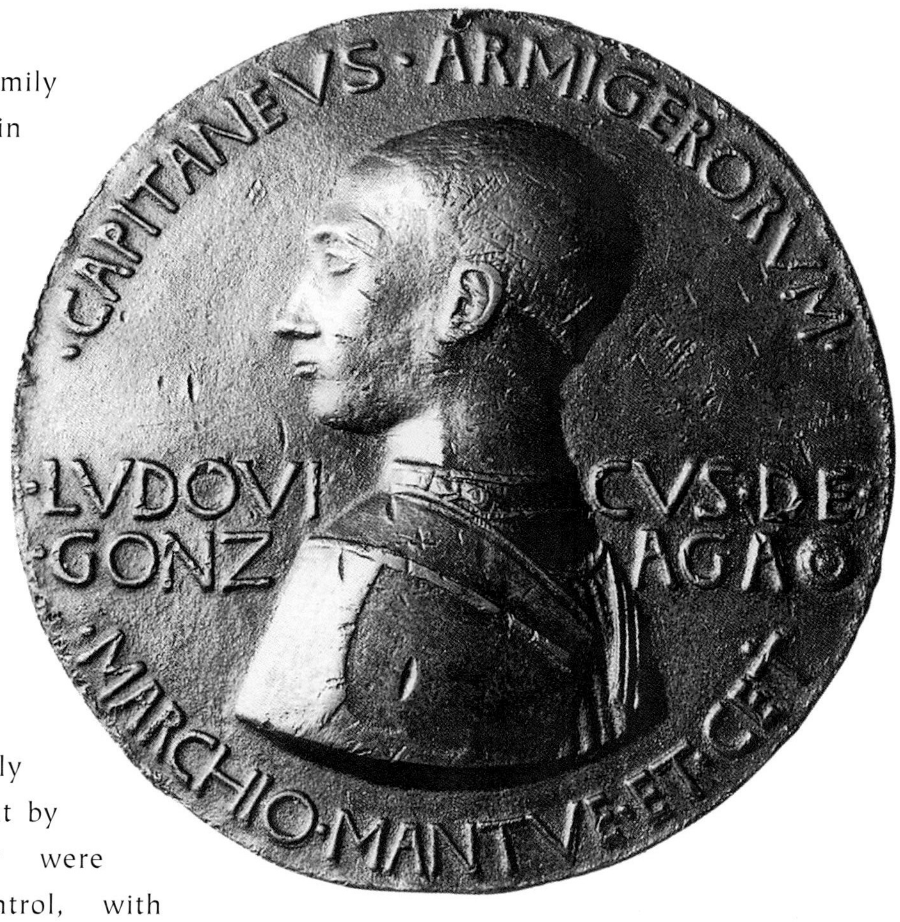

The Bonacolsi family maintained power in Mantua until 1328, when the Gonzaga took over. The overthrow of the Bonacolsi regime by the Gonzaga family was represented later in a dramatic battle painting from 1494.

The Gonzaga consolidated their power during the fourteenth and early fifteenth centuries, so that by Mantegna's time they were unquestionably in control, with landholdings and fortified castles spread across the territory (Fig. 5).

They held the title of *signore*, "lord", until they were proclaimed by the Holy Roman Emperor in 1433 to hold the higher designation of *marchese*, or marquis in English. The political arrangement in Mantua meant there was a heliocentric regime, consisting of a court and its dependents.

In Padua, Mantegna worked for members of a merchant oligarchy, and he had to answer to the dictates of the painters' guild; in Mantua, he served the needs of a single, powerful regime.

32. *The Oculus*, ceiling, Camera Picta, 1474. Fresco. Ducal Palace, Mantua.

33. Antonio Pisanello, *Portrait Medal of Ludovico Gonzaga*, c. 1447. Bronze, diam. 10.2 cm. Victoria and Albert Museum, London.

34. *The Oculus* (detail), ceiling, Camera Picta, 1474. Fresco. Ducal Palace, Mantua.

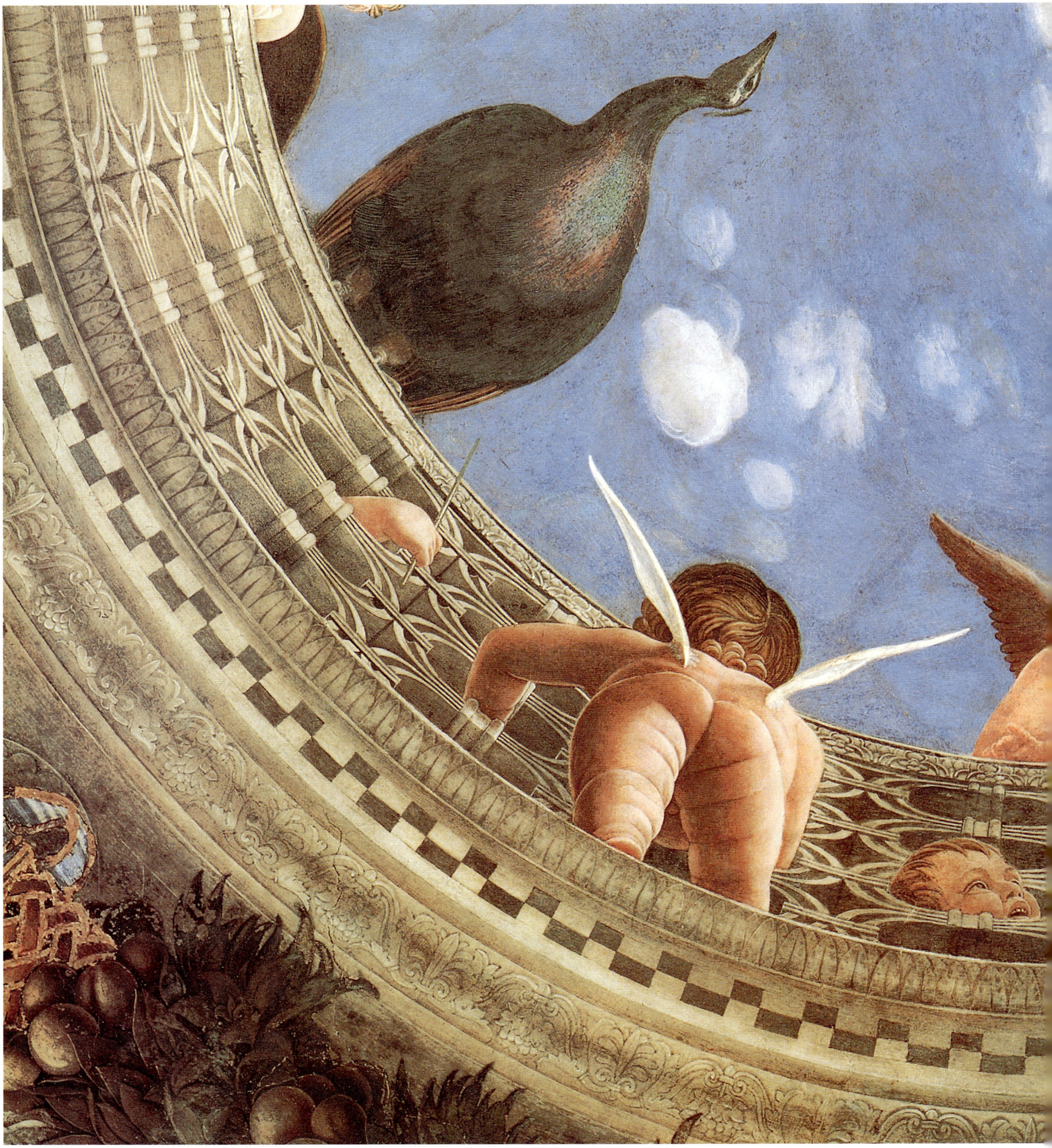

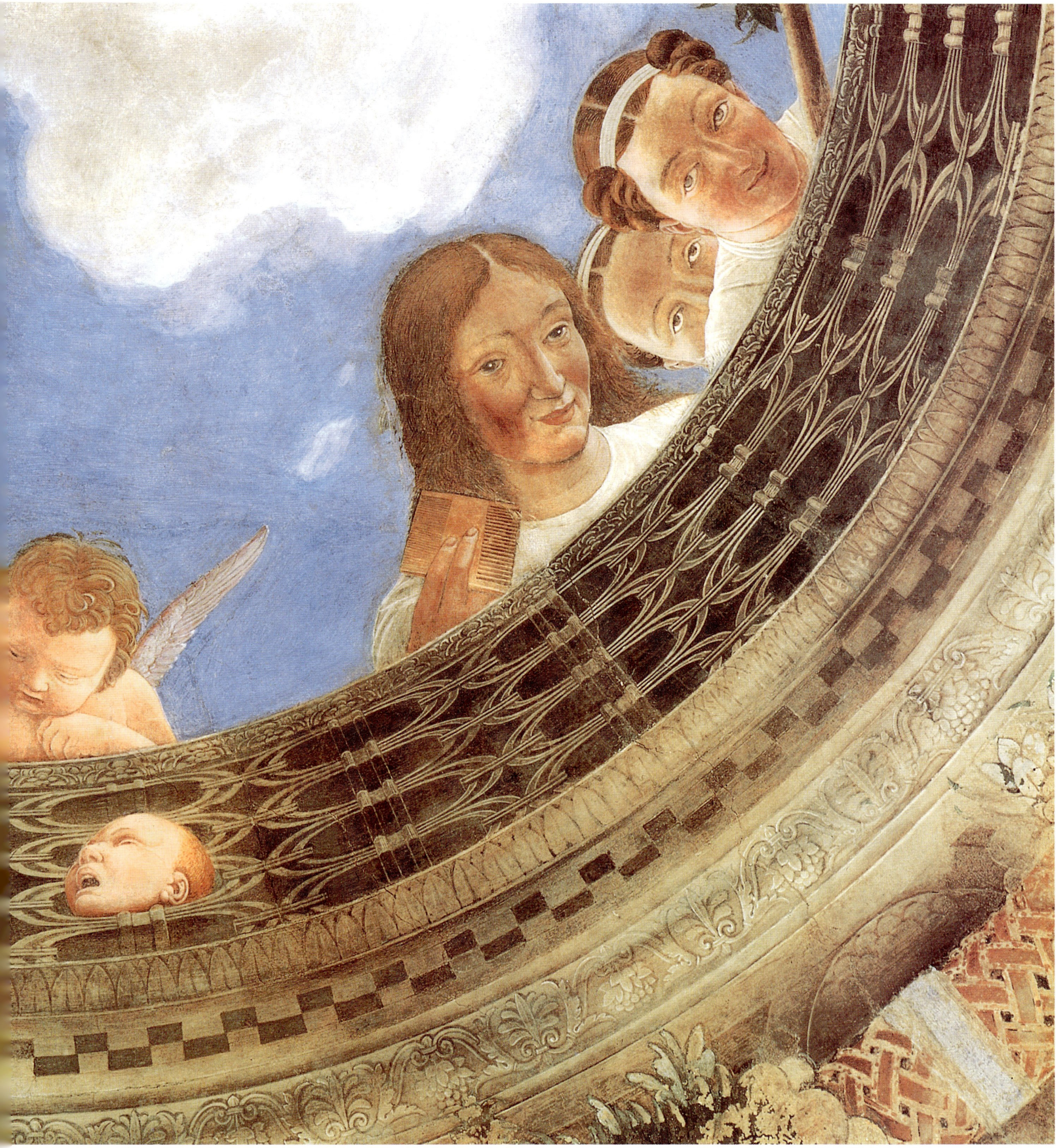

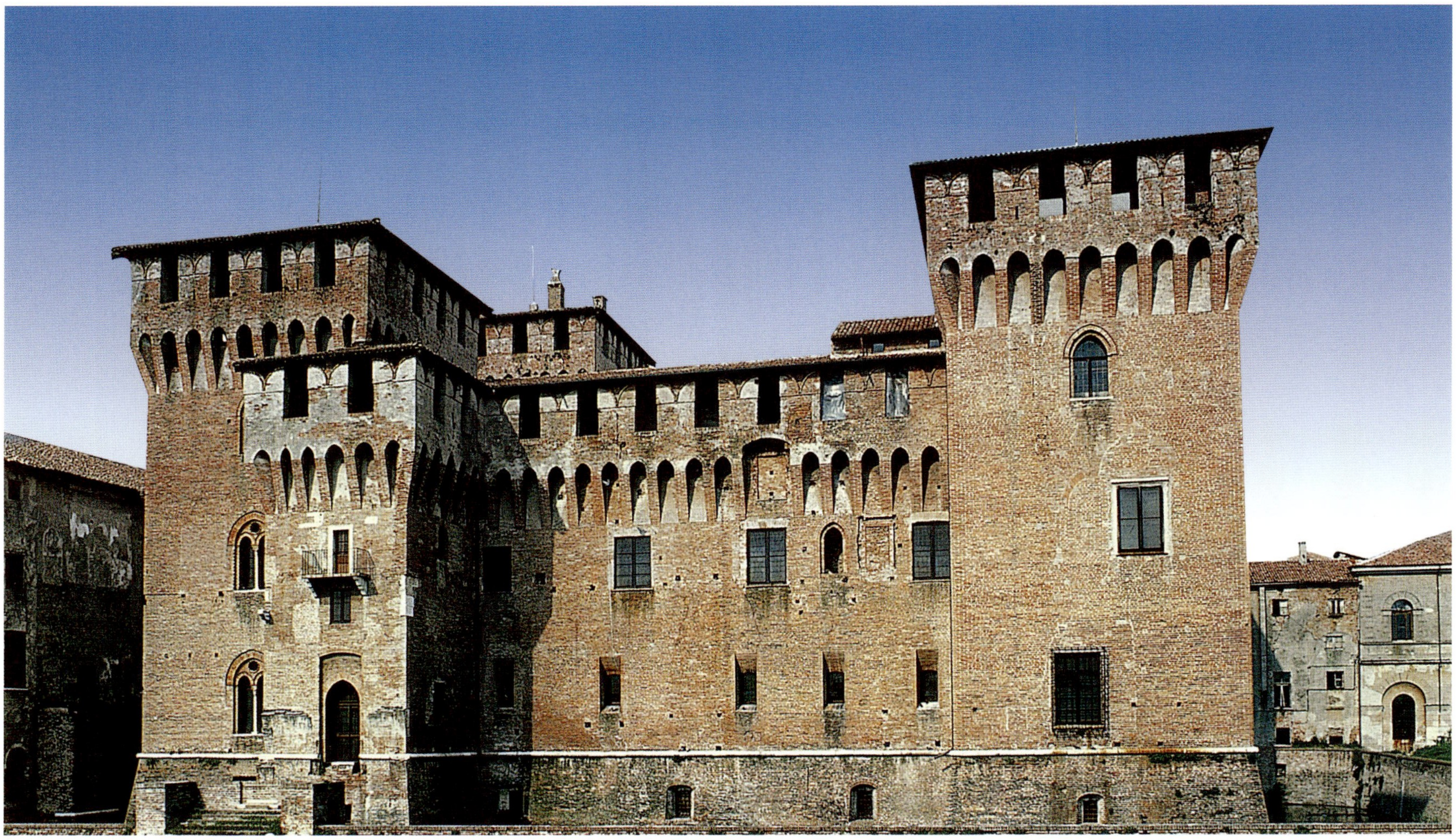

Mantegna entered the post because of the desirable security and prestige it offered. When he went to Mantua in 1459 he was promised transportation for his family (one of his sons, Francesco, would later become a painter and his assistant), a generous salary, and an allowance for food and firewood. He was also honoured by being granted a coat-of-arms of his own. Mantegna's tasks as court painter were not always lofty ones; he painted major works but also occupied himself with designing drinking cups and carpets. Even the great Leonardo da Vinci, when he became court painter in Milan in the 1480s, was asked to engage in such trivial duties along with his grander projects. The advantage of such a position was great, however, as the regular salary meant court artists did not have to wait for commissions, and they were still free to serve other patrons in different cities, as long as the ruler agreed to let them go, which he often did as a favour to the person requesting the artist's services. Since Mantegna was a master of the first rank, he was treated and paid far better than the average craftsman. Documents indicate he had a friendly rapport with his noble patrons, although he always maintained a deferential attitude to the Mantua rulers. As a court painter in Mantua, Mantegna had secured an enviable and honourable post of employment.

35. View of Castle of St. George showing area where Camera Picta and Studiolo were located.

36. *West Wall*, called *The Meeting, Castle* (left detail), Camera Picta, 1465-1474. Fresco. Ducal Palace, Mantua.

When Mantegna first arrived in Mantua, he was lodged at a residence provided for him but he eventually built his own house in the city, which still exists (Figs. 55 and 56). Over the years Mantegna acquired several pieces of property in the area which provided income, including farm lands in the outlying areas, and commercial and residential structures in the city. He was able to provide his daughters with substantial dowries, and his estate at the time of his death included property, money, and enough funds to establish a chapel for his family. Mantua was a city of moderate size, about the same as Padua but not nearly as large as nearby Venice. The city was nearly

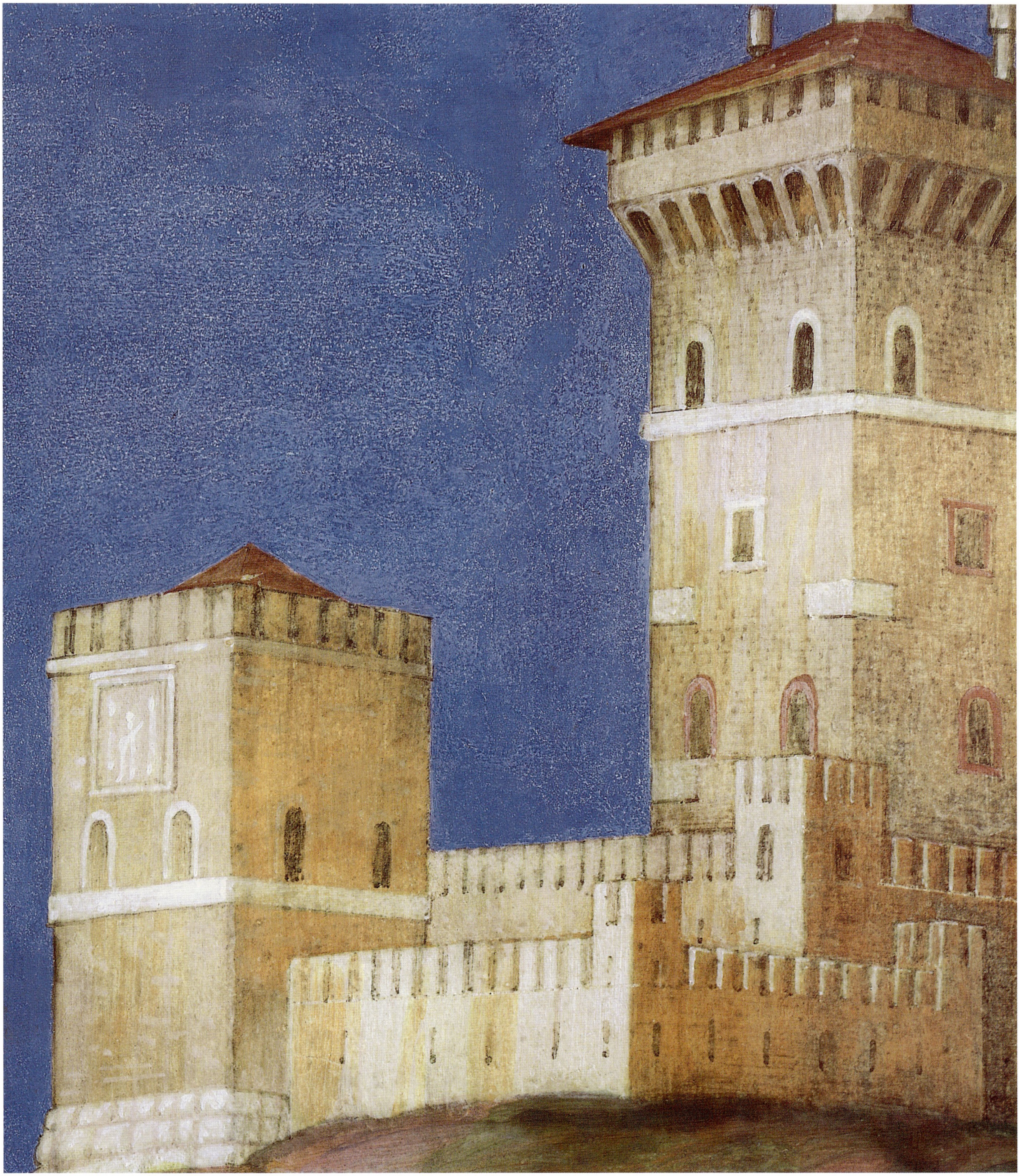

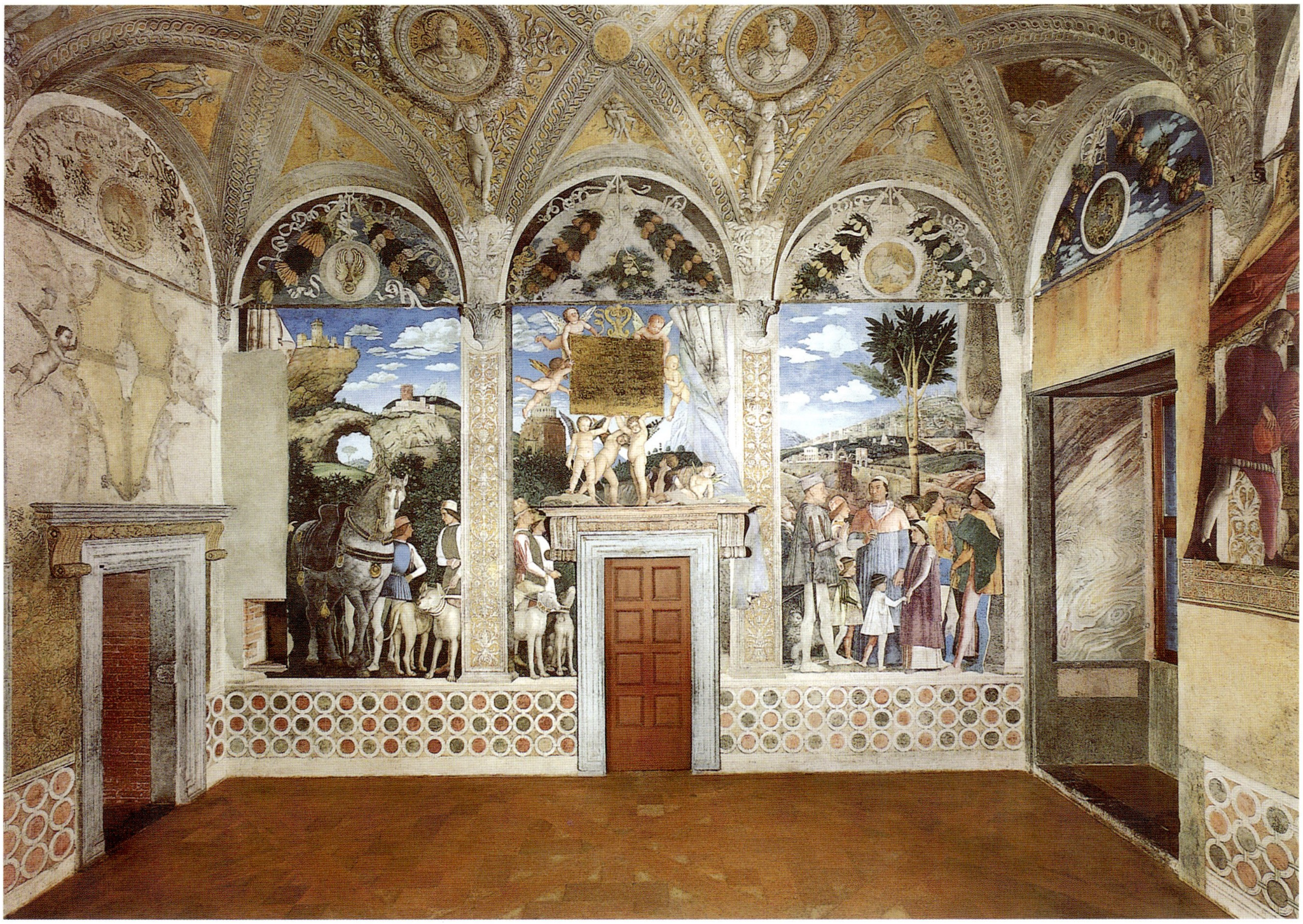

completely surrounded by a lake, making the place a haven for mosquitoes and frogs, although the watery setting embellished Mantua, making it among the most beautiful towns in Italy. Mantegna captured the attractive quality of the city early on in his *Dormition of the Virgin* (Fig. 57), which includes a view of the bridge of Saint George and several Mantuan buildings in the background. In Mantua, the imposing residences of the rulers stand near the city centre and the cathedral. Mantegna would spend much of his time labouring in the Castle of Saint George, which still exists with its impressive crenelations and thick walls (Fig. 35). That castle is connected to other palaces, altogether comprising a huge complex of rooms that is largely empty now but at the time bustled with activity and held splendid furnishings and other decorative arts. One of Mantegna's tasks as court painter was to add to this visual splendour, the amount and quality of the pictorial decorations reflecting the magnificence and prestige of the rulers. Mantegna's first employer in Mantua was Ludovico Gonzaga (b. 1412), who ruled from 1444 until his death in 1478. He occupied himself with many of the typical activities popular at that time among the ruling classes, including hunting, hawking, horse racing, and warfare. Ludovico, like his father and grandfather before him, helped to earn money for his state by serving as a *condottiere*, a hired general who served other cities needing professional military leadership. A bronze medal he commissioned in 1447 from Pisanello declares him to be a military leader as well as a *marchese* (Fig. 33).

37. *West Wall*, called *The Meeting*, Camera Picta, 1465-1474. Fresco. Ducal Palace, Mantua.

38. *West Wall*, called *The Meeting*, *Putti carrying the inscription* (central detail), Camera Picta, 1465-1474. Fresco. Ducal Palace, Mantua.

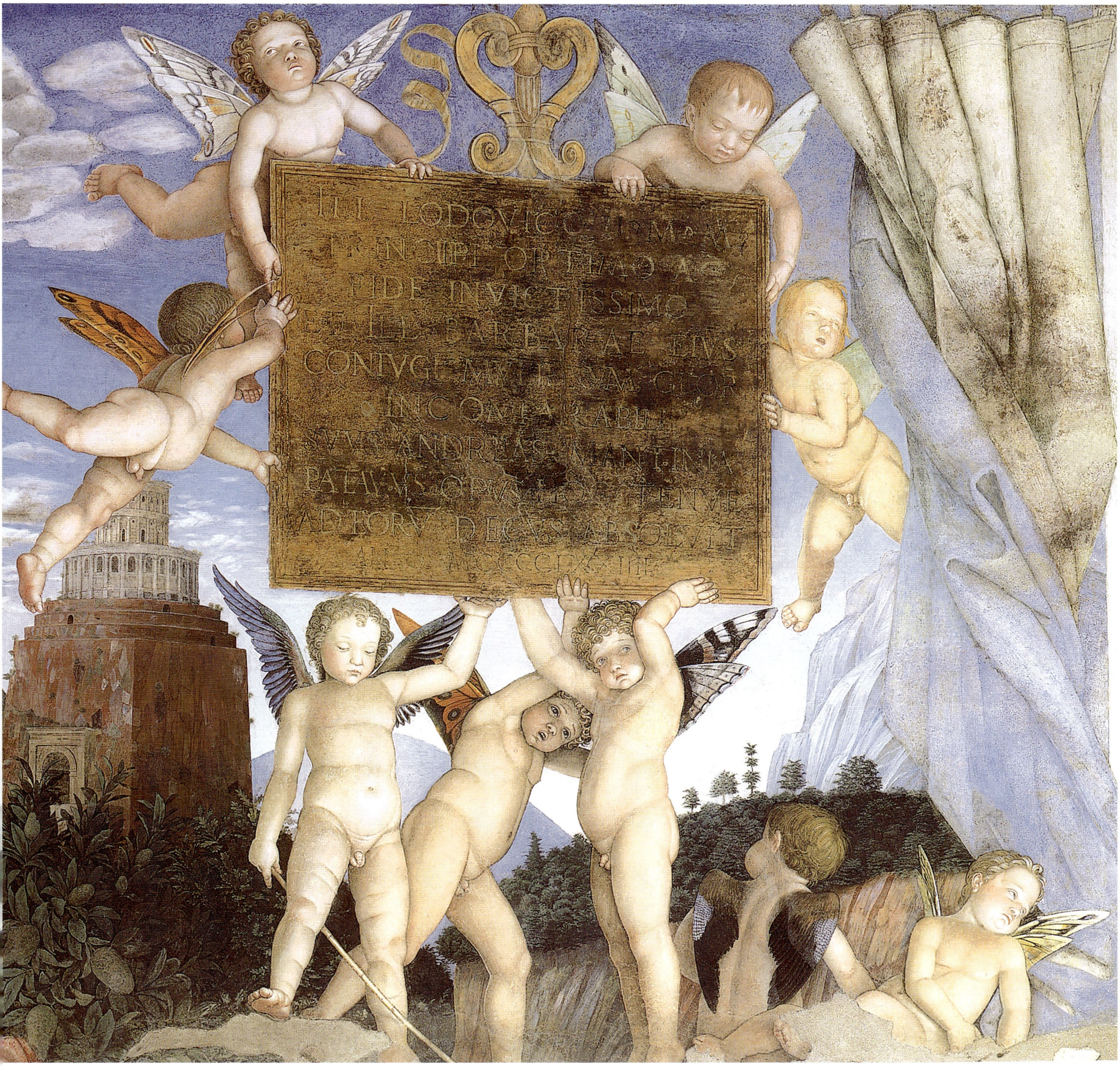
LODOVICO
PRINCIPI
FIDE INVICTISSIMO
BARBARAE EIVS
CONIVGE
INCOMPARABI
SVVS ANDREAS MANTINIA
PATAVVS OPVS TENVE
AD EORV DECVS ABSOLVIT

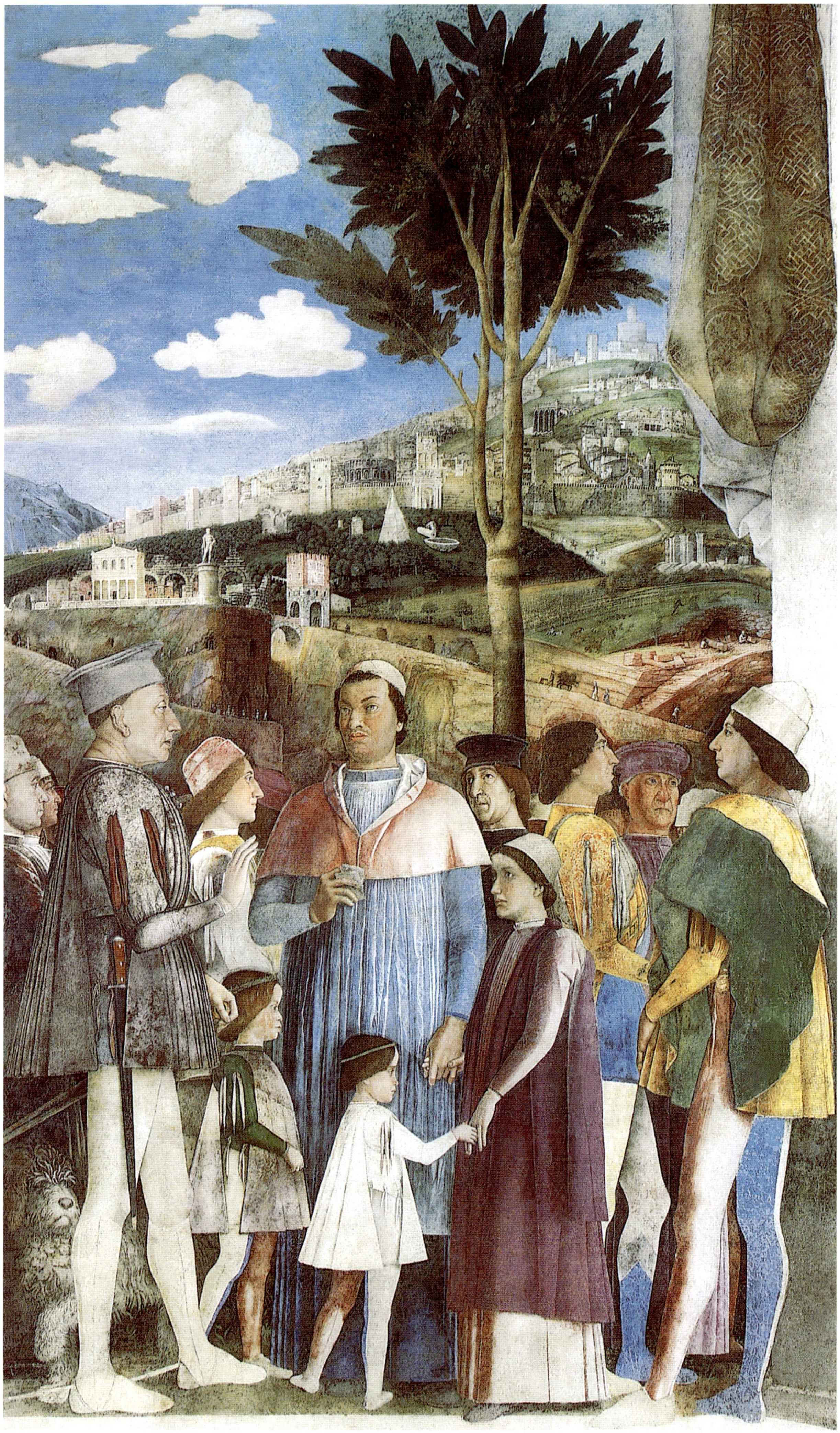

Most relevant for our study of Mantegna, Ludovico held a deep and genuine interest in reviving the culture of antiquity, commissioning for the city classical architectural structures and hiring numerous scholars and scribes to fill his library with copies of books by ancient writers. One contemporary said of Ludovico, "For his leadership in arms, above all else, he was commended as if he had invented this profession," but his more intellectual qualities were also widely recognised, for "some praised his learning, some his talent for different things, such as agriculture, architecture, and art." Ludovico, who was attuned to the advancing field of humanistic study and took a personal interest in art and architecture, was a responsive and interested patron and appreciative of Mantegna's talents. Like other Gonzaga rulers, he ruled by power and without prior approval of the popular will, but he was hardly cruel or uneducated. On the contrary, the Gonzaga court in Mantegna's time was a highly civilised place, where the arts, literature, music, and dance were fostered by the ruling family. Although they clung to medieval ideals of art and literature a generation or more later than the upper classes in mercantile cities such as Florence and Venice, the rulers of Italian city-states finally took up with enthusiasm the classical revival. Mantegna was part of this great cultural shift, and he brought the stylistic revolution in painting to the Gonzaga court.

Along with the revolution in painting style, a clear and tangible example of this shift toward classicism in Mantua was in the flowering of Renaissance architectural forms. The building of grand, magnificent palaces and churches in the new Renaissance manner gave lords such as Ludovico Gonzaga an air of refinement to their rule, linking them to the enduring classical past and demonstrating their good education. While Mantegna was serving as court painter in Mantua, Ludovico Gonzaga commissioned some important architecture done in the new style, favouring several architects working in the classical manner. The most famous of these was Leon Battista Alberti, the author of a treatise on architecture, a work Ludovico kept in his own library. He also wrote treatises on sculpture and painting, and studied Greek and Roman literature. He was a salient example of a humanist-artist, and his buildings in Mantua constituted important elements of his work as an architect.

Alberti was asked by the marquis to construct a new church of San Andrea, which now dominates the city centre of Mantua. With its huge barrel vaults, colossal classical façade, and giant pilasters it is an imposing and harmonious example of the Renaissance manner in building. Alberti's church of San Sebastiano, built on a Greek cross plan, also helped to adorn the city of the Gonzaga with simple classical building forms. Alberti, as an apostle of the Renaissance style, was Mantegna's counterpart in Mantua, each championing the great change in style. Although we have no sure record of their meeting, Alberti and the younger Mantegna certainly did know each other and exchanged ideas, as Alberti spent extended periods in Mantua in 1459-1460, 1463, and 1470-1471. The presence of both Alberti and Mantegna in Mantua was the fruit of Ludovico Gonzaga's conversion to classicism, a change recorded by a contemporary, Antonio Filarete, an architect and sculptor who wrote some lines of imaginary dialogue in a treatise on architecture and urban planning in which he expressed Ludovico's initial turning towards the Renaissance style of architecture. In a dialogue, Filarete has Ludovico say:

> "I too was once pleased by modern [i.e., Gothic] buildings, but as soon as I began to enjoy the antique ones, I grew to despise the modern [Gothic style in buildings]. In the beginning, if I had anything built, I usually chose the modern manner, because my lord father had used this fashion.... [But] when I heard they were building in the antique

39. *West Wall*, called *The Meeting*, *The Meeting* (right detail), Camera Picta, 1465-1474. Fresco. Ducal Palace, Mantua.

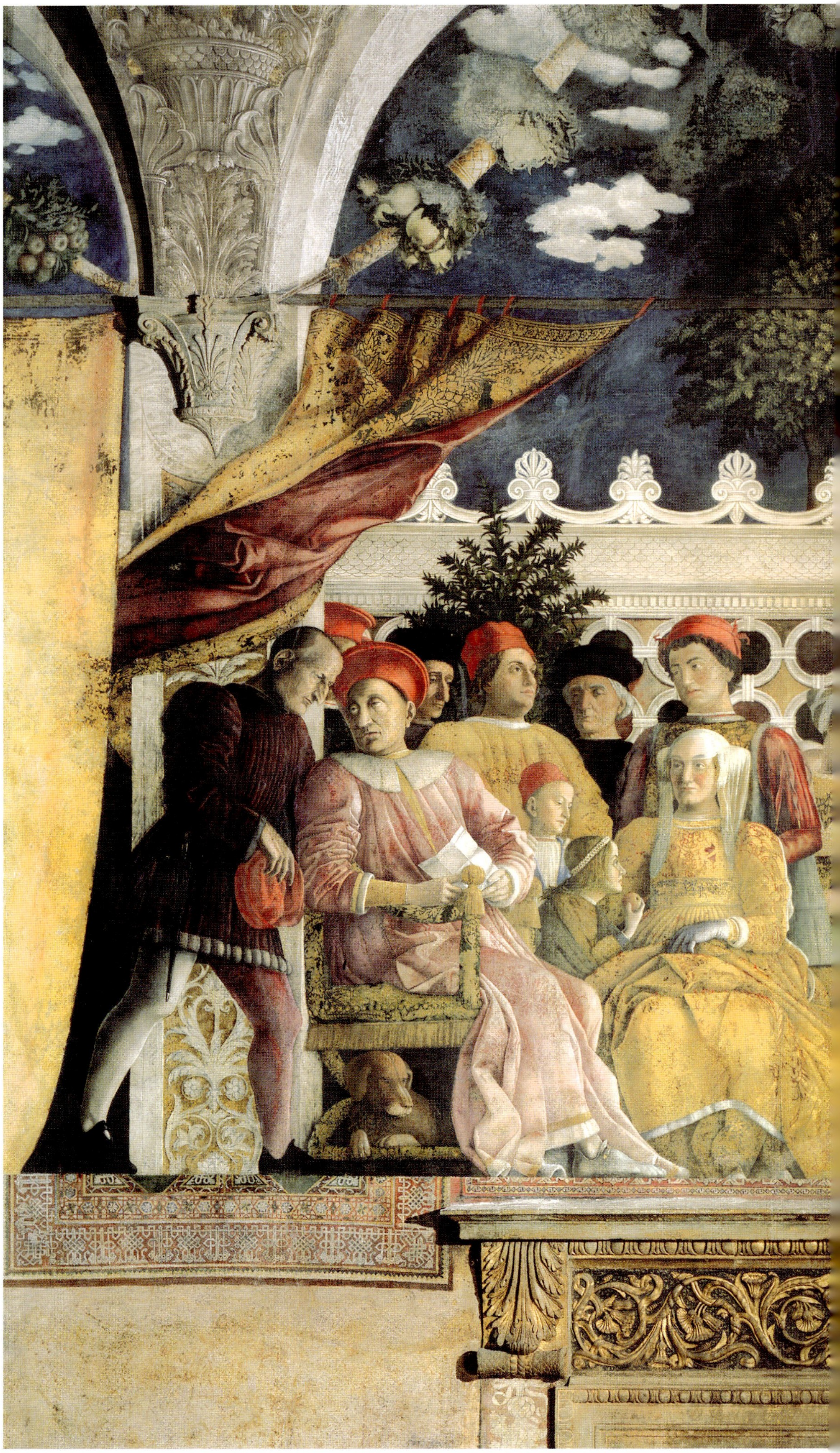

40. *North Wall*, called the *Fireplace Wall*, Camera Picta, 1465-1474. Oil on plaster. Ducal Palace, Mantua.

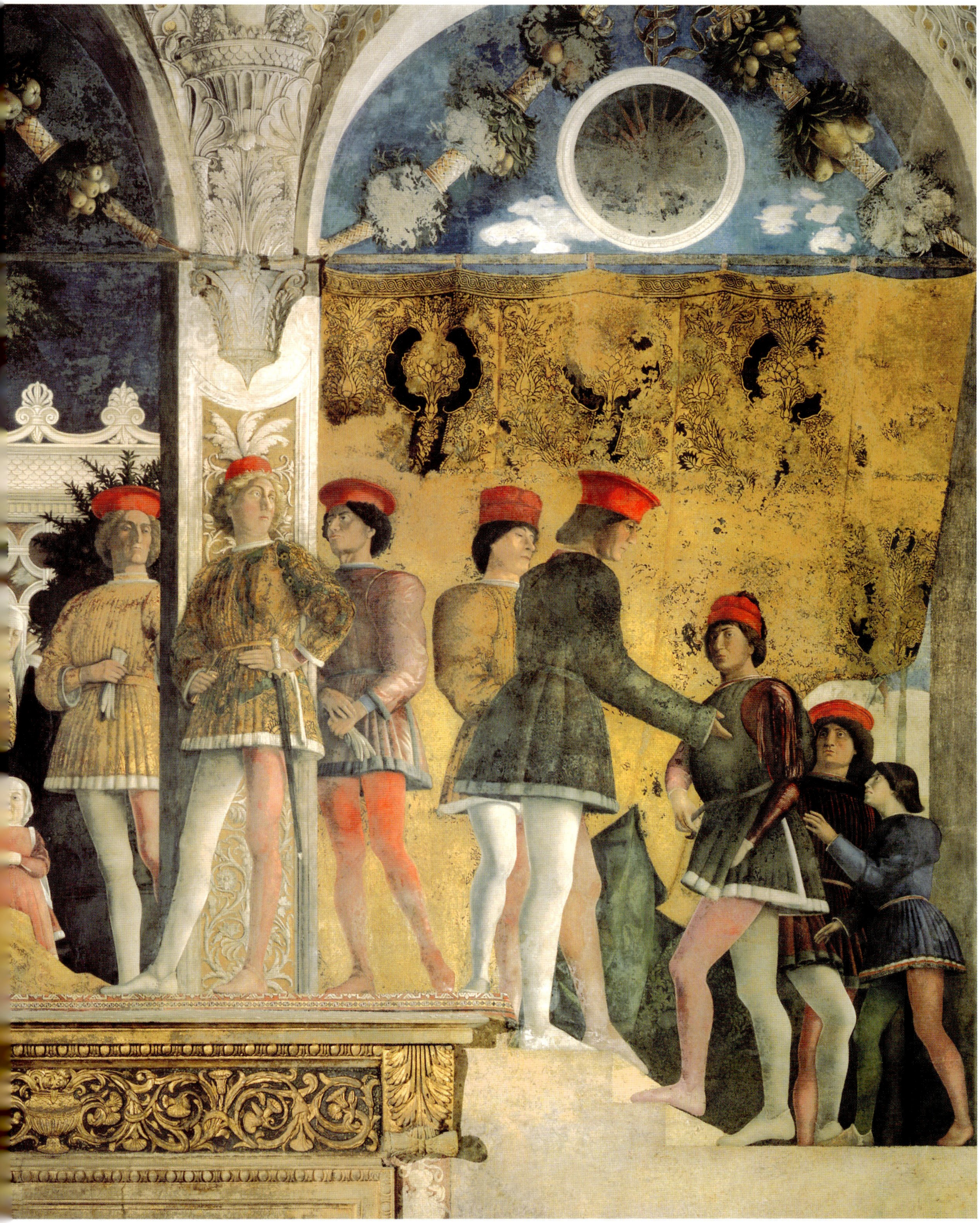

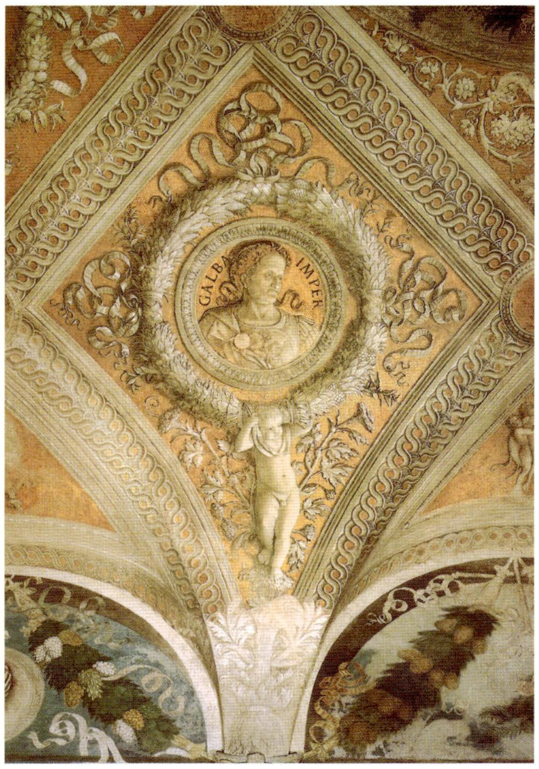

> [classical] style in Florence I determined to have one of the men I had heard named. While bargaining with them, I was so aroused that I would not build the slightest thing if it were not done in the antique manner."[4]

This quote refers to Ludovico's architectural commissions, but soon became true for painting and sculpture, as Ludovico sought a version of the Renaissance style that had commenced in Florence and would flourish under his aegis at his own court in Mantua.

When Mantegna came to Mantua, the Gothic style in art and architecture was still in vogue, a situation he soon did much to alter. The previous most prominent painter in Mantua was Antonio Pisanello, who worked for Ludovico soon after he became marquis (cf. Fig. 33). We saw in the quote from Filarete that Ludovico acknowledged it was because of the inertia of tradition at the beginning of his reign he commissioned Gothic architecture. Similarly, at the beginning of his reign, Ludovico asked Pisanello to paint murals on medieval romances of Arthurian legend. These works represent the famous knights of the Round Table, and the style and subject matter are decidedly late medieval, with flat space, cursive script in French identifying the various warriors, and lovely, fair-haired women elegantly watching a tournament from a balcony. The Gothic manner still prevailed in Mantua through the 1450s. Northern Italian humanist writers appreciated the realistic details and overall naturalism of Pisanello's art, but one should not overlook the dominant late Gothic character of his style.

41. *Galba,* Camera Picta, 1465-1474. Fresco. Ducal Palace, Mantua.

42. *Hercules fighting the Nemean Lion,* Camera Picta, 1465-1474. Fresco. Ducal Palace, Mantua.

43. *Hercules killing Antaeus,* Camera Picta, 1465-1474. Fresco. Ducal Palace, Mantua.

44. *Hercules and Hydra,* Camera Picta, 1465-1474. Fresco. Ducal Palace, Mantua.

45. *Hercules capturing Cerberus,* Camera Picta, 1465-1474. Fresco. Ducal Palace, Mantua.

46. *Orpheus Playing the Lyre,* Camera Picta, 1465-1474. Fresco. Ducal Palace, Mantua.

47. *Arion rescued by a Dolphin,* Camera Picta, 1465-1474. Fresco. Ducal Palace, Mantua.

Pisanello's death in 1455 meant the marquis was in need of a new chief painter, and this was an opportunity to hire someone with a progressive and different style. After Mantegna's failure to come immediately to Mantua when asked in 1457, Ludovico almost lost patience and hired a painter named Michele Pannonio to be his court painter. Pannonio, who was active in the nearby court in Ferrara, was a late Gothic artist (see also Fig. 118), and his hiring would have delayed the coming to Mantua of the forcible Renaissance manner of Mantegna. But Ludovico did wait for Mantegna, and his eventual arrival transformed that city into a leading centre for painting done in the new Renaissance style, the advent of which would have been slowed had the marquis indeed settled for the conservative artistry of Pannonio.

Mantegna began his work for Ludovico in a project that, although minor, reflected the humanistic interests of the Gonzaga court: Mantegna designed a shield on which some verses of the ancient Roman writer Plautus were to be inscribed. Apart from such lesser assignments, the first major task undertaken by Mantegna in Mantua was decoration of an elaborate chapel in the castle. Despite the importance of the commission, the length of time spent on it, and the critical success, we know nothing for sure about its appearance. However, a major mural project Mantegna painted after this chapel does indeed survive, and it constitutes his most famous work: the Painted Room, or *Camera Picta* (or *Dipinta* as it was sometimes called in early documents), a chamber in the Castle of Saint George that he began in 1465 and finished nearly a decade later (Fig. 37). An inscription in the room (Fig. 38) marks the year of completion as 1474. This project offers a vivid picture of court life in Renaissance Mantua, and the work was particularly striking for Mantegna's contemporaries. The year after the room was finished Ludovico Gonzaga received a letter noting the Milanese Duke Galeazzo Maria Sforza considered this to be the "most beautiful room in the world," and the Duke of Milan lamented his own portrait was not included in the paintings there.

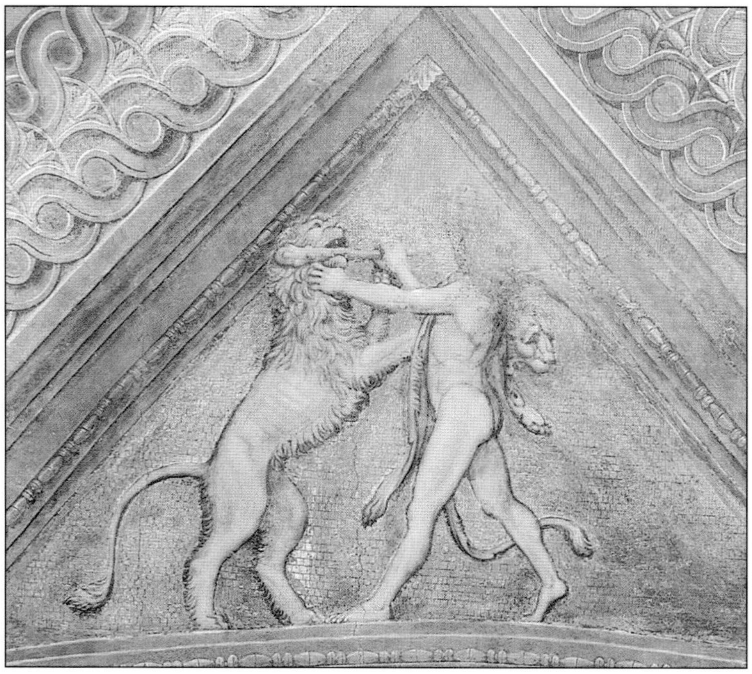
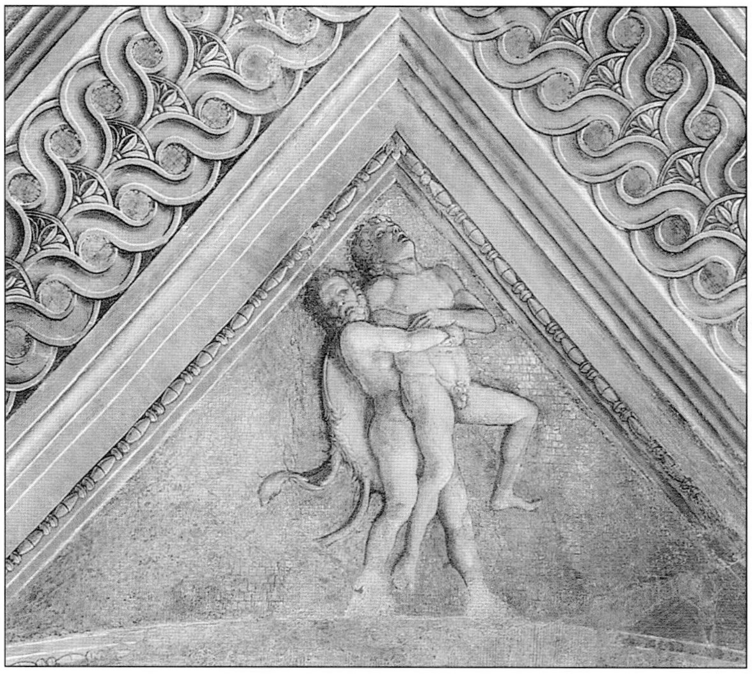
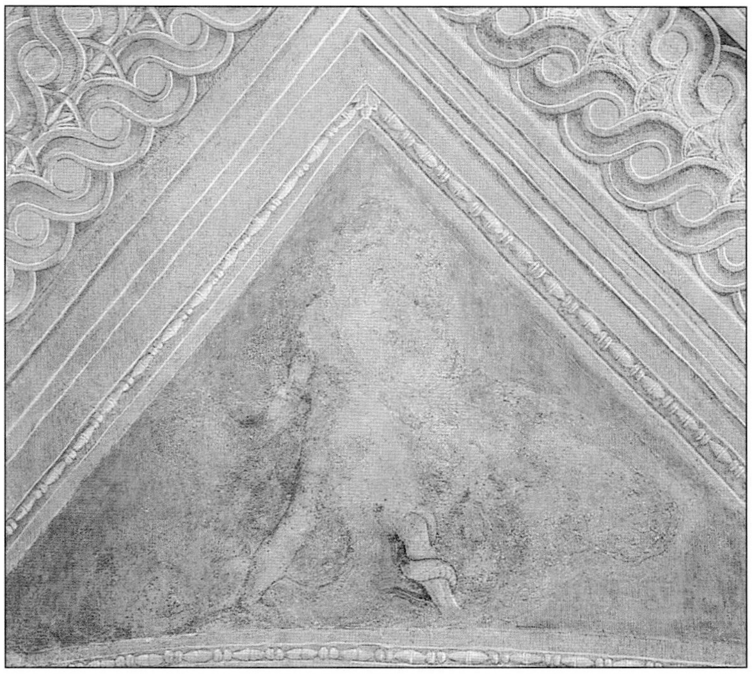
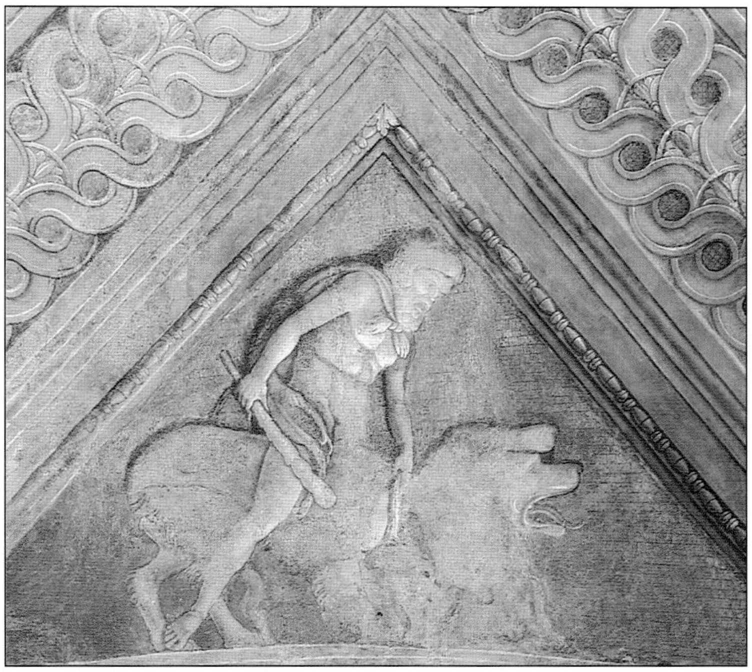
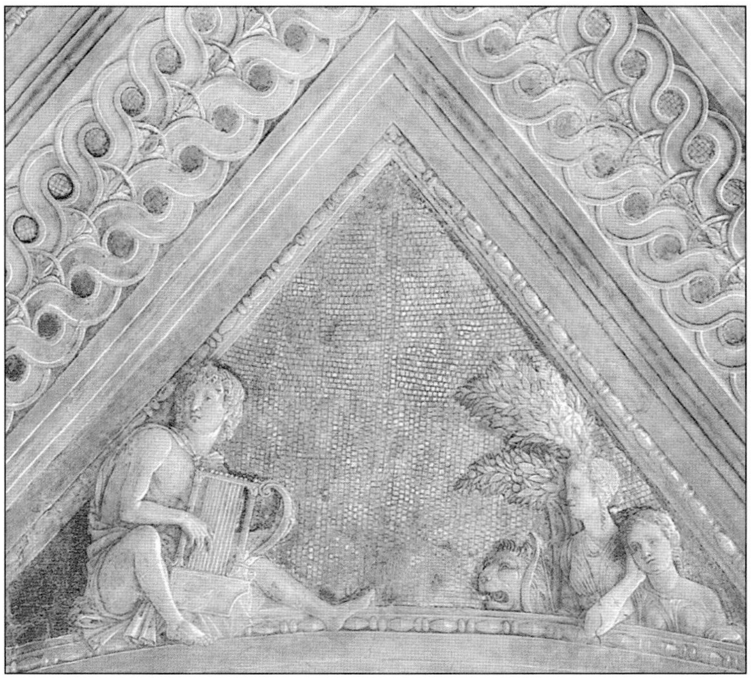
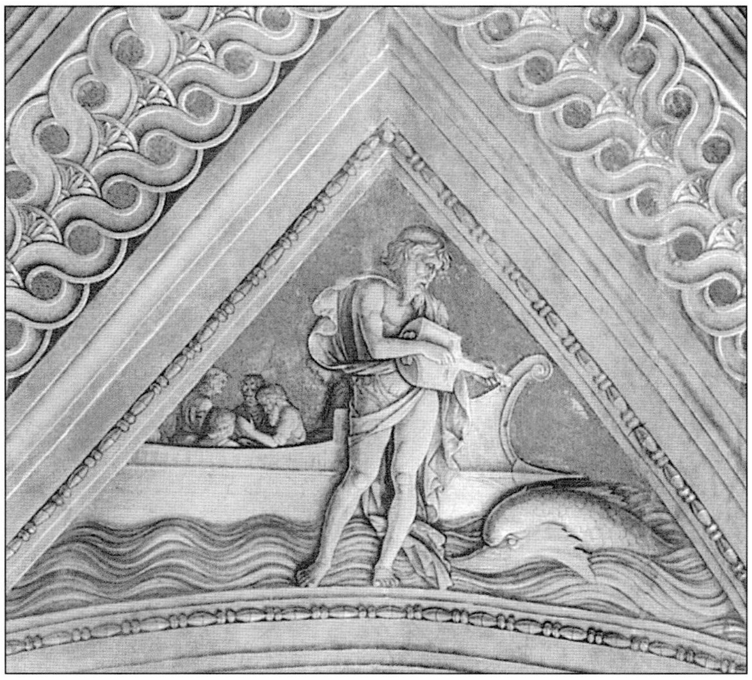

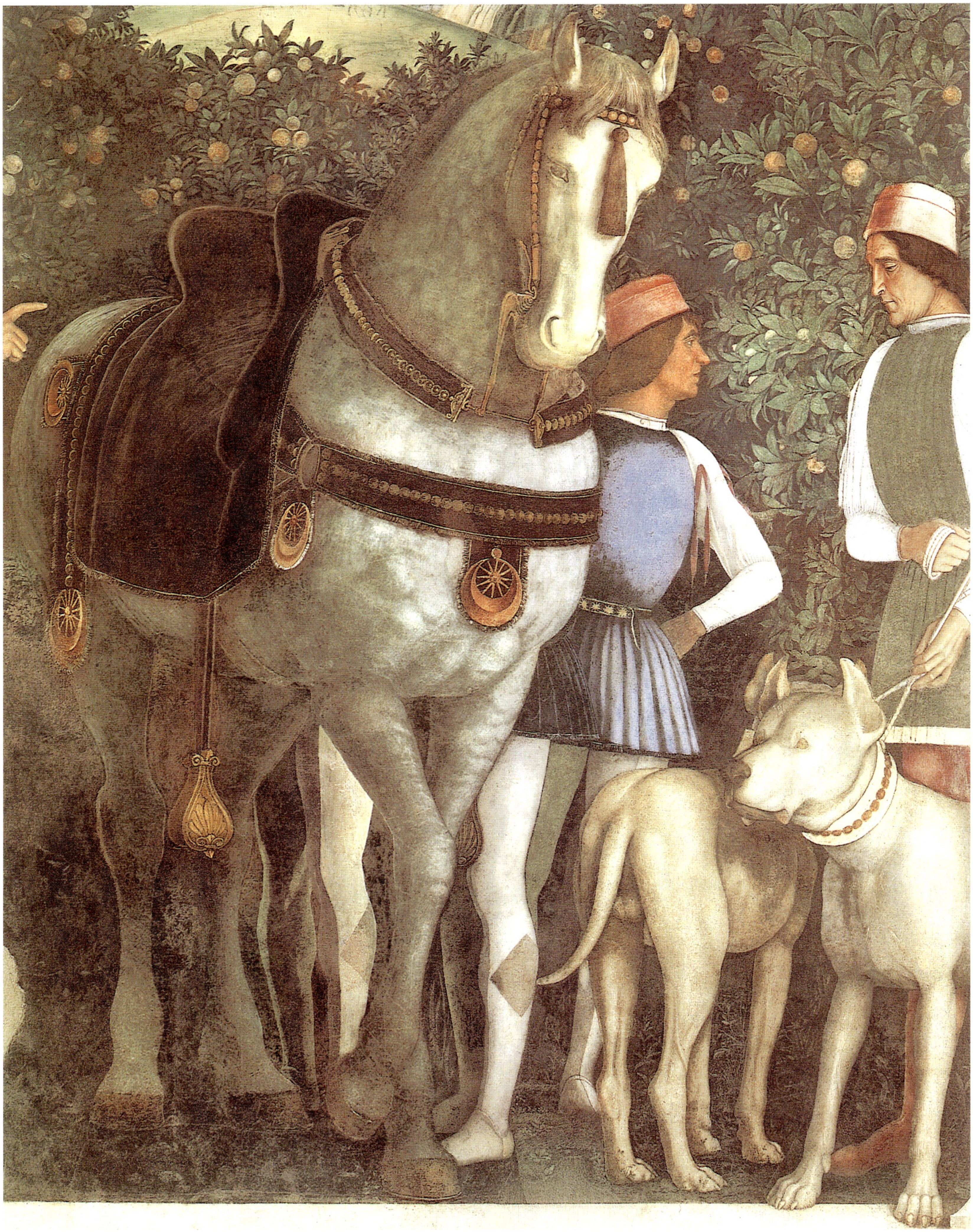

The architecture of the room is rather plain, but Mantegna elaborated the structure and created his own; the room became a chamber in the new classical style, with pilasters and Corinthian capitals providing an *all'antica* framework for the room, which appears to be an open, colonnaded hall. The chamber is not meant to recreate any specific kind of contemporary structure, although to some extent the room resembles the temporary, open pavilions erected at the Gonzaga court for festive occasions. Here, perhaps more palpably than any other interior space of the Italian Renaissance, one comprehends the pleasures and duties of an Italian ruler, from the delights of hunting, to the sociable gathering of dignitaries, to the ease of the pleasure garden, to the engagement with the demands of rulership, carried out in the context of familial bonds. The architecture, at once both timelessly classical and with the immediacy and festive quality of an ephemeral decoration, is cleverly compatible with the broad array of actions taking place, which range from the epicurean to the soberly functionary. The unity of painting, sculpture, and architecture – both real and apparent – is manifest, and the room would have allowed analysis and discourse by viewers who were intensely interested in questions of representation and imitation.

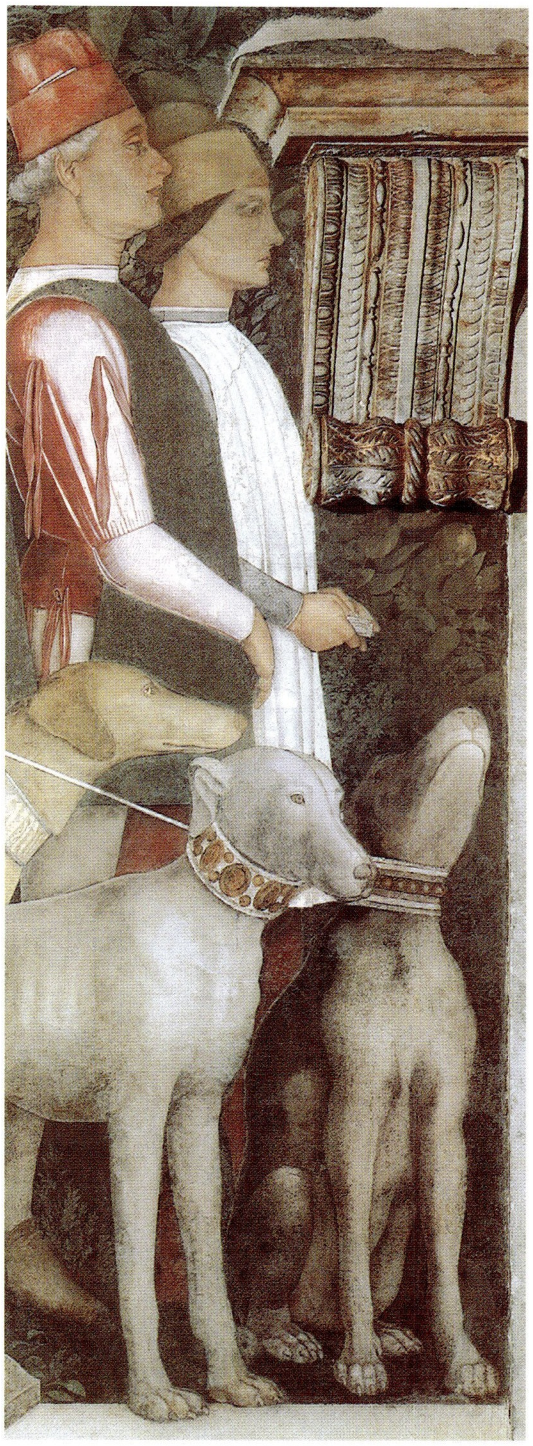

The *Camera Picta* is a masterpiece of illusionism, painted on all four walls as well as on the ceiling. Even all the apparent stone – meant to imitate red, green, and white marble – found around the lower part of the walls is fictive; this was ideal for the patrons, who could admire the ingenuity of the artist and also save money by not having to pay for real marble! The room is conceived so it appears curtains have been pulled aside on two of the walls, revealing brilliant scenes of court life. Two of the walls are painted with the "curtains down" and one can admire the fine materials and embroidery work represented but no view is offered beyond the fabrics. In one place the blue curtain cleverly wraps around one of the few real pieces of architecture in the room, the stone lintel of a door (Fig. 38). The effect of the whole room is, typically for Mantegna, both clever and intensely real, and – as in a theatre – it seems a glimpse of life has been dramatically revealed.

The most elaborate of the scenes takes place in a fictive space over the mantelpiece (Fig. 40). The marquis, Ludovico Gonzaga, is seated in a great chair receiving a letter from a messenger. The importance of the Gonzaga lord is immediately apparent in Mantegna's arrangement, as the messenger bows slightly to the ruler and Ludovico's own family members stand farther back. One of the curtains overhead sweeps dramatically back over the *marchese*, a forerunner of the use of dramatic curtains in bombastic aristocratic and state portraiture that would be in vogue over the coming centuries. Although we do not know the exact message being sent, it shows Ludovico in action, the head of his state and of his family. The room came in later history to be called the *Camera degli Sposi*, or the "Room of the Newlyweds", but this was a misnomer (it was not built for any recent spouses) and does not reflect its original function. In the Renaissance, the Painted Room (*Camera Picta*) served only sometimes and in part as a bedroom (the beds would have been placed against the walls without any painted figures). And while it probably had furnishings fitting for a sleeping chamber, such as chests, tables, and mirrors, it was often used as a reception chamber for ambassadors, one of Ludovico's official receiving rooms. This scene, therefore, reflects the function of the chamber. Ludovico must have frequently looked at Mantegna's painting and seen an echo of the duties he regularly carried out in that very place. Foreign ambassadors, dignitaries, and local courtiers could admire the painting of the marquis in action, surrounded by his family; even his favourite dog, Rubino, is faithfully sitting beneath his seat.

48. *West Wall*, called *The Meeting, Servants with Horse and Dogs* (left detail), Camera Picta, 1465-1474. Fresco. Ducal Palace, Mantua.

49. *West Wall*, called *The Meeting, Servants with Dogs* (central detail), Camera Picta, 1465-1474. Fresco. Ducal Palace, Mantua.

Just to the left of Ludovico is his wife, Barbara of Brandenberg. She is one of the several German wives the Gonzaga rulers married in order to strengthen their ties to the north and to the Imperial crown. It was a German, the Holy Roman Emperor Sigismund, who in 1433 first made a Gonzaga ruler *marchese*, and the family was always eager to build on this important northern European connection by intermarrying with noble German women. It even happened the Gonzaga were willing to forgo the usual dowry from the fathers of the German brides and indeed paid for the privilege of marrying them. Barbara's family received a huge nuptial gift of 50,000 florins from the Gonzaga court for her marriage to Ludovico. The union of Ludovico and Barbara was a dynastic triumph for the Gonzaga, and her place in the family and court life was an honoured one. This tradition would continue in 1463, just before the time of the *Camera Picta*, when Ludovico's son Federico would marry the noble lady Margaret von Wittelsbach, daughter of the Duke of Bavaria.

Barbara is shown near to her husband, ready to take part in political life, but for the time being she is relatively passive and surrounded by her children and servants. Directly behind her is one son Rodolfo, and standing between her and her husband is another son, Gianfrancesco. Leaning across her lap is Paola, her last child, who was born just two years before the room was started. The adolescent girl looking off to her left is Barbara (between the marquise and the court dwarf), who would later, in mirror image of her mother, marry a German nobleman, the Duke of Wurttemberg. Just to the left and behind Barbara is a favourite female dwarf. Although the practice seems cruel to us today, dwarves served the purpose of entertainment in Renaissance courts, being targets of verbal abuse and teasing, while they also frequently dished out witty taunts to courtiers. The most famous "court jester" in history, a hunchback named Rigoletto, was the subject of an opera in the nineteenth century by Giuseppe Verdi, set in Mantua of the early seventeenth century. Court dwarves were sometimes forced to wrestle with each other or to perform other strange feats. One female dwarf at court could urinate on demand, raising her skirt and peeing on the floor whenever asked, to the merriment of the gathered crowds of lords and ladies. In the *Camera Picta*, this dwarf looks out at the viewer, reflecting her special rapport with the audience. Mantegna depicts her with a certain decorum and dignity, recalling the work of another great court painter of two centuries later, the Spaniard Diego Velazquez, noted for his sympathetic and insightful portraits of the dwarves of the court in Madrid. More than once in his art, Mantegna demonstrated a certain sympathetic feeling for underdogs, as revealed in his dignified representation of lower classes in religious paintings, and his noble depiction of captives in the *Triumphs of Caesar*. In the *Camera Picta* he painted the court dwarf with a great deal of sensitivity and humanity.

On the right there are young male courtiers; some on the farther right belong to foreign courts, although others in the scene wear the colours of the Gonzaga court and stand in support of their ruler. These young men keep a respectful distance from Ludovico Gonzaga, and they await a closer audience with him. On the far right, the action is quite animated, contrasting to the stately images of Ludovico and his nearby family and courtiers. In the centre, Mantegna has one young man stand in front of a (painted) pilaster, and he seems to be atop the room's mantelpiece, appearing to be in the viewer's space. Since he and the other figures in the murals are painted more or less life-size, the illusionism is powerful and effective. Mantegna surely cleared the overall program with his employer, and perhaps even received advice, but only he could invent the details of gesture and placement of the figures that makes the *Camera Picta* a success. His inventive design is apparent on the other wall of the chamber in an outdoor group gathering (Figs. 39), the wall including

50. *West Wall, called The Meeting, Putti carrying the Inscription* (central detail), Camera Picta, 1465-1474. Fresco. Ducal Palace, Mantua.

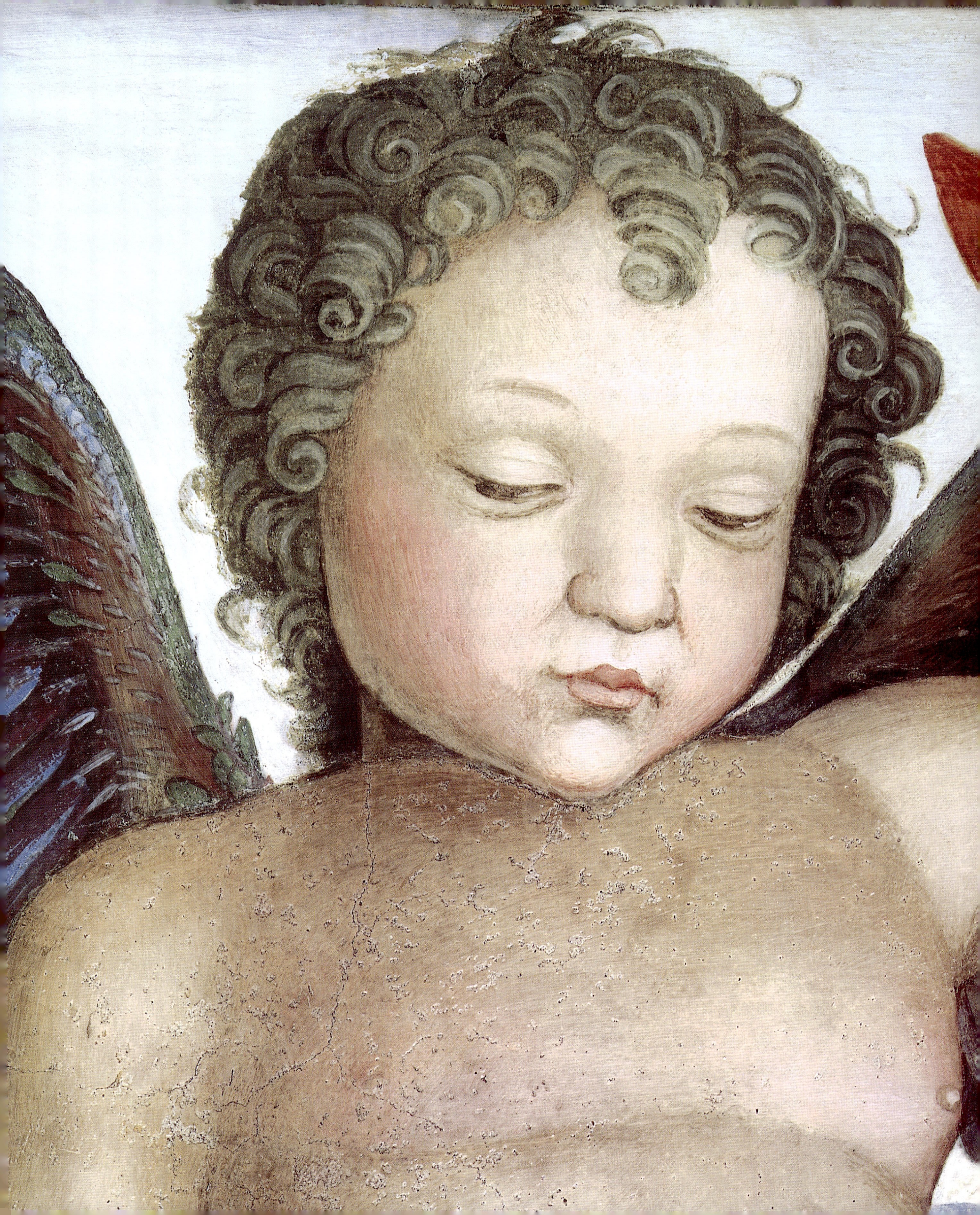

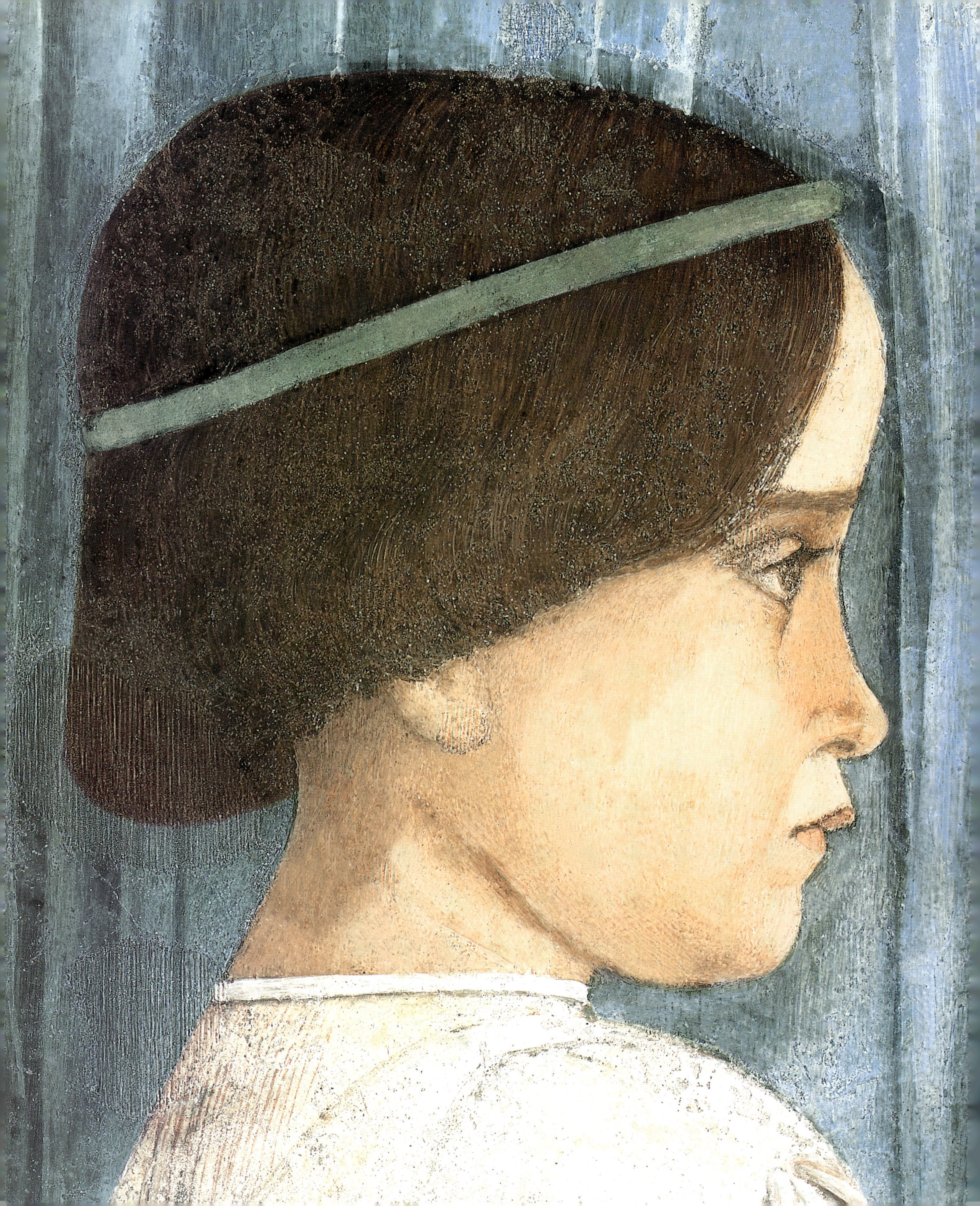

imaginative landscape and cityscape background. The scene on the right, usually referred to as *The Meeting*, takes place outdoors in the realm of males, so no women appear here. Ludovico, who is armed and ready to defend his realm, stands in the right-hand section and makes a formal gesture with his right hand toward his son, Cardinal Francesco. Between his uncle and grandfather is young Gianfrancesco Gonzaga, usually called Francesco, who would become the Marquis of Mantua in 1484; Francesco's distinct profile, with large, arching forehead will be captured in later works by Mantegna (cf. Fig. 67). The smaller boy next to Francesco, holding the hand of his young uncle Ludovico (future bishop of Mantua), is Francesco's brother Sigismondo, who would become a Cardinal in 1506. On the far right is Federico Gonzaga, who would become *marchese* at the death of his father Ludovico, only holding the position for five years, from 1479 until 1484.

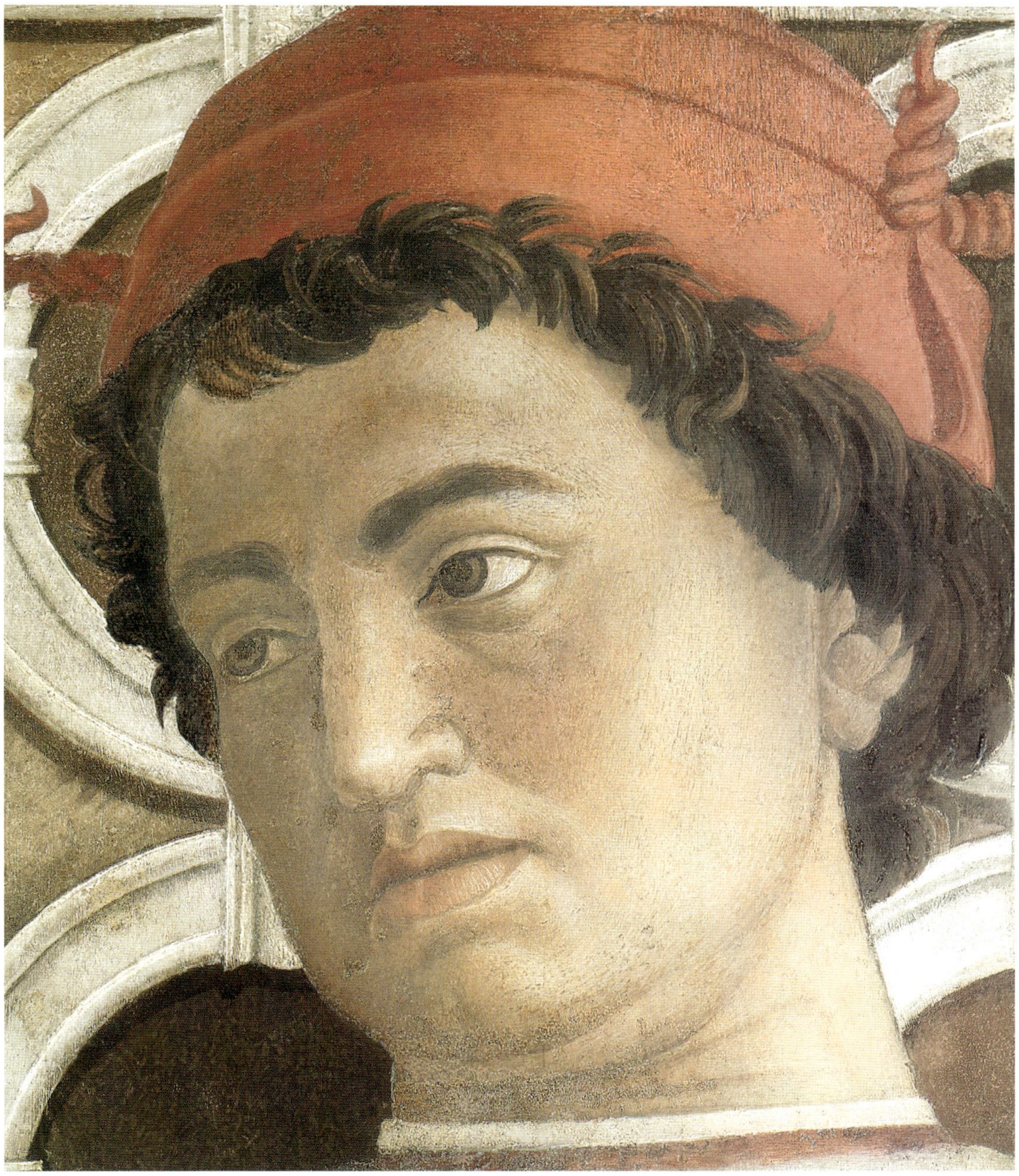

In 1475, the Duke of Milan, Galeazzo Maria Sforza, complained to Ludovico Mantegna depicted in the *Camera Picta* portraits of "two of the worst men in the world," namely, the Holy Roman Emperor Frederick III and Christian I, the King of Denmark. These rulers had become political enemies of Sforza, but Ludovico was officially at the service of Frederick, and Christian was the brother-in-law of his wife, so the marquis was glad to have had Mantegna paint their portraits. Some observers have plausibly identified these men as the first two to the left of Federico on the right side of *The Meeting*, the king seen frontally and the emperor shown in profile and facing to the right of the viewer (Fig. 39). These important figures, like Ludovico in the same scene, stand in stoic calm, befitting their political status, and representing the kind of moral character they would wish to have a painter capture.

Characteristic of Mantegna's inventive contribution to art of this period is the cityscape behind, which is of no particular place, but is an inventive mixture of classical architecture and contemporary structures (Fig. 54). The antique buildings are somewhat in disrepair, as they were in the fifteenth century, with gaps in the stone filled in with bricks. Mantegna knew classical buildings from his field-trips, and he reflects the contemporary appearance of them in his own time in his paintings. One tower even has laundry hanging out to dry on a cord! This city-view includes a pyramid, temples, ruins of an aqueduct, and a theatre or small amphitheatre, constituting an imaginative evocation of a ruined Roman city that

51. *West Wall*, called *The Meeting, Head of a Child* (right detail), Camera Picta, 1465-1474. Fresco. Ducal Palace, Mantua.

52. *North Wall*, called the *Fireplace Wall, Head of a Man* (detail). Camera Picta, 1465-1474. Fresco. Ducal Palace, Mantua.

has been fortified and inhabited by his contemporaries. There are no Christian buildings in this city; Mantegna wanted to evoke a classical city, which would have delighted his educated viewers, whether professional humanists or the enlightened rulers of Mantua interested in classical art and architecture. At the base of the hill a criminal hangs by the neck from the gallows, a reference to good government and a reminder of the effective justice to be found in the city-state of the Gonzaga.

The left side of the wall echoes life at the Gonzaga court, illustrating Ludovico's interest in hunting, with the inclusion of valets, dogs, and horses (Fig. 48). One of the dogs stands on a ledge and, once again, protrudes into our space. The land behind is remarkably hilly, with a wonderful natural bridge. This must have been an enjoyable sight for any Mantuan courtier, who when looking around the city would see much flatter terrain. In this setting of deep greenery and fantastic rock formations, Mantegna offers a rich and abundant scene of the pleasurable, healthy aspects of masculine society at the Gonzagan court. The landscape, once more in the room, shows the effect of good government; there men go about safely, and there is a watchful Gonzaga castle. Again, Mantegna is not making specific record of a real place or event. That is further demonstrated by the presence of the fluttering, humorous *putti*, who struggle to hold up a heavy plaque recording the finishing date (1474) and other information about the commission. In this inscription, Mantegna pays honour to the marquis and marquise, and calls his chamber "this meagre work" ("*hoc opus tenue*"), a conventionally modest designation unlikely to express his true feelings about his monumental accomplishment.

Much of the *Camera Picta* concerns portraiture, and forms a showpiece for Mantegna's skills in this regard. Despite his reputation as realist, Mantegna does far more than mirror nature in his portraiture. His patrons expected some idealisation to occur, and he did refine his subjects to some degree. For example, Ludovico Gonzaga was something of a hunchback, but this is barely detectable in either of his portraits in the *Camera Picta*. Moreover, Ludovico's teacher, Vittorino da Feltre, complained his lordly pupil was clumsy and fat, too desirous of fine foods, and he remained slightly overweight his whole life. In the *Camera Picta*, Mantegna de-emphasises this aspect of Ludovico, especially in the standing portrait (Fig. 39). We do not always have corroborating portraits for the other figures, but we can suppose Mantegna prudently improved his sitters whenever he needed to give them finer skin, a better physique, a more intelligent face, or a more serious, grave appearance.

The ceiling of the *Camera Picta* contains a number of classical and learned elements that advance the interests of Ludovico Gonzaga. The ceiling is painted in fictive sculpture to look like raised stucco relief, with various roundels containing portraits or other scenes. The ceiling includes the representations of reliefs of Roman Caesars held up by *putti*, chubby boys who appear frequently in ancient Roman art (Fig. 41). The Gonzaga clan received the designation of marquis from the Holy Roman Emperor, who was a distant political descendant of the emperors of ancient Rome. The inclusion of these portraits in the *Camera Picta* therefore helps suggest the rule of the Gonzaga was not an evanescent aspect of history, but was rooted in distant antiquity. Here is a powerful political use of classicism, as Mantegna presents the Gonzaga as heirs of ancient Roman power. These portraits of the Roman rulers are not direct copies of any specific known portraits, but are the artist's own inventive variants. The style is particularly intense in facial expression, conveying the message of permanence and power. Six of Mantegna's other fictive reliefs, placed in the spandrels of the room represent the legend of the god Hercules, who was a model of virtue, strength, and action; the depiction of these reliefs in the *Camera Picta* reflects well on Gonzaga rule. One of the

53. *Portrait of Ludovico Trevisan*, c. 1459-1460.
Tempera on panel, 44 x 33 cm.
Gemäldegalerie, Berlin.

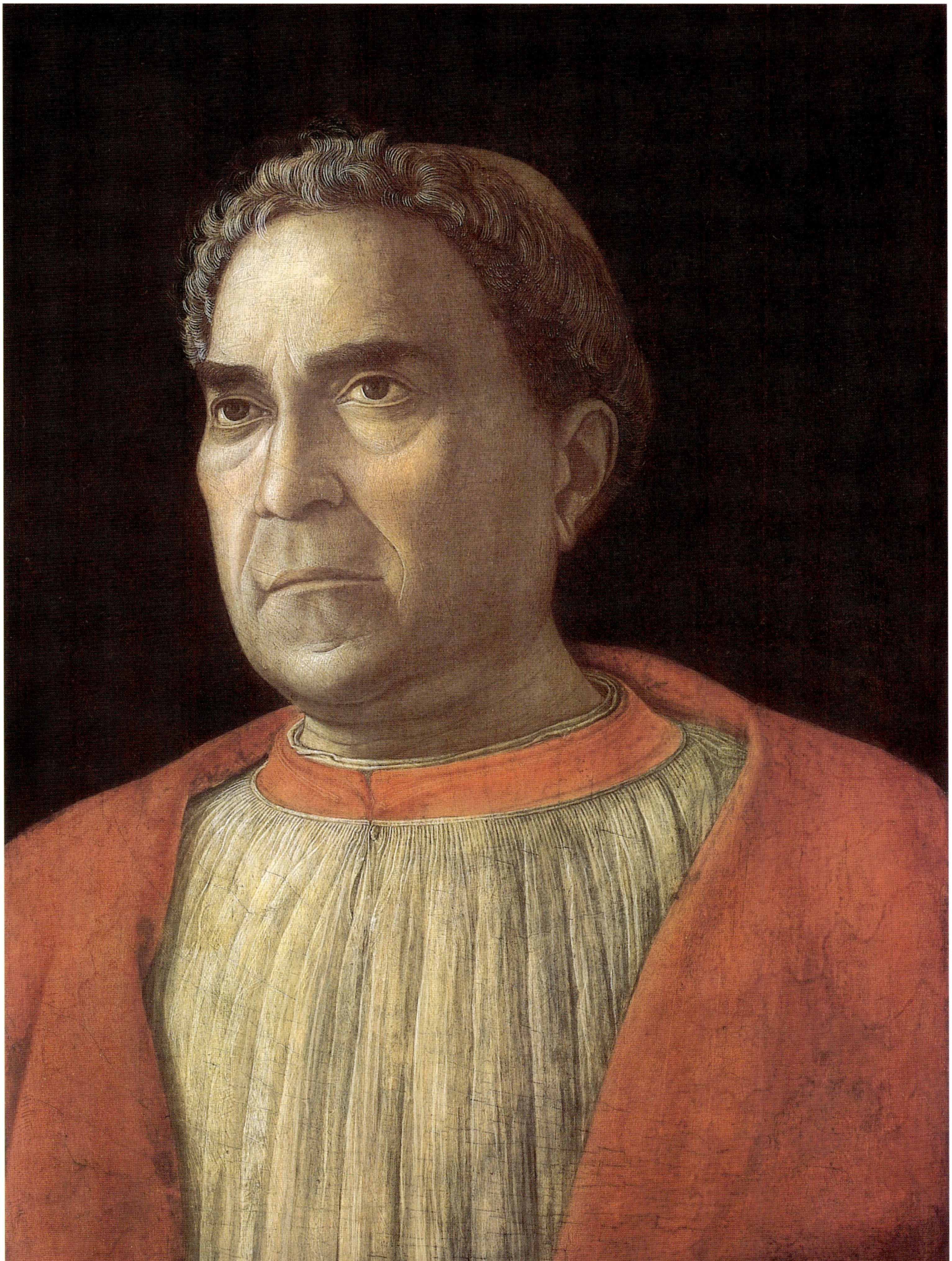

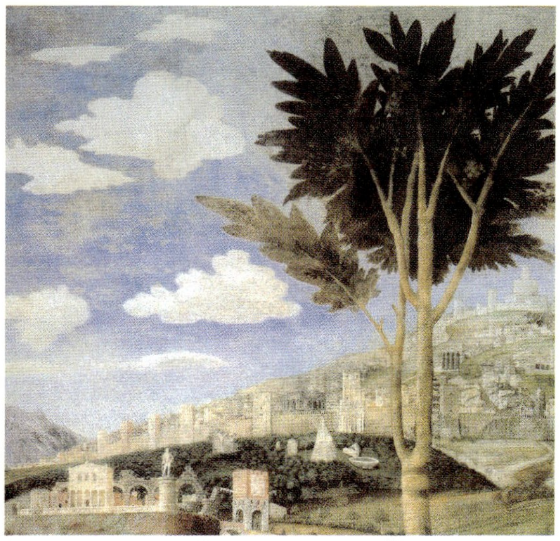

aspect of Ludovico, especially in the standing portrait (Fig. 39). We do not always have corroborating portraits for the other figures, but we can suppose Mantegna prudently improved his sitters whenever he needed to give them finer skin, a better physique, a more intelligent face, or a more serious, grave appearance.

The ceiling of the *Camera Picta* contains a number of classical and learned elements that advance the interests of Ludovico Gonzaga. The ceiling is painted in fictive sculpture to look like raised stucco relief, with various roundels containing portraits or other scenes. The ceiling includes the representations of reliefs of Roman Caesars held up by *putti*, chubby boys who appear frequently in ancient Roman art (Fig. 41). The Gonzaga clan received the designation of marquis from the Holy Roman Emperor, who was a distant political descendant of the emperors of ancient Rome. The inclusion of these portraits in the *Camera Picta* therefore helps suggest the rule of the Gonzaga was not an evanescent aspect of history, but was rooted in distant antiquity. Here is a powerful political use of classicism, as Mantegna presents the Gonzaga as heirs of ancient Roman power. These portraits of the Roman rulers are not direct copies of any specific known portraits, but are the artist's own inventive variants. The style is particularly intense in facial expression, conveying the message of permanence and power. Six of Mantegna's other fictive reliefs, placed in the spandrels of the room represent the legend of the god Hercules, who was a model of virtue, strength, and action; the depiction of these reliefs in the *Camera Picta* reflects well on Gonzaga rule. One of the apparent reliefs illustrates Hercules killing Antaeus, the king of Libya, who thought himself invincible; this labour of Hercules, like the others shows heroic physical action, as good triumphs over evil (Fig. 43). Apart from the general ethical importance of Hercules, the scenes carried a personal meaning for the marquis, for in his school days Ludovico was nicknamed Hercules (Ercole) by the tutor Vittorino da Feltre. In addition to inclusion of Hercules in the spandrels, Mantegna placed a statue of Hercules behind Ludovico in the mural of *The Meeting* (Fig. 54). In this *grisaille* (from the French for "grey") of Hercules and Antaeus, as with the other spandrel scenes (see Figs. 46 and 47), there is a witty blurring of the distinction between painting and sculpture, and sculptural reality, as the figures resemble ancient sculpture, but possess a new level of verisimilitude because of the internal lighting and the suppleness of representation.

Mantegna's originality comes to the fore most obviously in the central part of the ceiling, which breaks from the seriousness and formality of the rest of the room (Figs. 32 and 34). It is perhaps Mantegna's most delightful and creative invention: the centre of the vault seems to open up, the first painting of the Renaissance to apply the notion of illusionism not just to an easel picture or wall but to a ceiling as well. This view upwards completes the *trompe l'oeil* vision Mantegna created in the *Camera Picta*, which is the first illusionistic room of the Renaissance; the ideal of the flat picture space as an extension of the real world is here given a spectacular expression, as a viewer in the middle of the room can see clouds overhead, fictive curtained walls, a classical architectural framework, and an idealised vision of the Gonzaga court. Overhead in the *Camera Picta*, Mantegna shows us a court matron (next to the Moorish servant) and smiling ladies-in-waiting looking down on the viewer, one of them combing her hair. A potted plant seems ready to fall off, and through a balustrade little winged boys are poking their heads out, and some are clinging to it, also ready to fall. One winged child threatens to drop an apple on our heads, and two other little boys are attempting to get their

54. *West Wall*, called *The Meeting*, *Cityscape* (right detail), Camera Picta, 1465-1474. Fresco. Ducal Palace, Mantua.

partly explained by the other commissions and travels he undertook during this time. In fact, in 1470 the marquis complained of these delays, writing to Alessandro Sforza in Milan, "Andrea is the kind of man that, even though he started to paint our chamber many years ago, still has not provided the half of it. And if he is given the slightest disturbance, he drags out the work for months and years."[5] For lesser artists or craftsmen a delay may have meant a fine or other punishment by the court, but Mantegna was allowed to proceed at his own pace. The indulgence of the court and the artist's slow progress paid off, for the *Camera Picta*, painted with great care and delicacy, includes many convincing and realistic portraits, landscapes, and illusionistic architecture.

Although we might think his artistic skill and good reputation at the Gonzaga court would have made him greatly appreciated there as a portraitist, this was not always the case. We have seen Mantegna did, to some extent, idealise his portraits but he apparently did not always do so to a great enough extent. Ludovico Gonzaga noted in 1475 in a letter to Galeazzo Maria Sforza of Milan, "It is true that Andrea is a good master in other things, but in portrait painting he could have more grace, and doesn't do so well."[6] Ludovico apparently found a lack of the suave grace and reserved demeanour that had been become traditional in court portraiture. Indeed, the Duke of Milan had earlier destroyed several portrait drawings by Mantegna because he did not like them. Later on, the marquise Isabella d'Este would lament Mantegna did not portray her to her satisfaction. She was stout and ever concerned about her age, and she preferred portraits which made her as thin, young, and blonde as possible. Mantegna's strong point as an artist was his realism, but there had been a tradition in courtly portraits for artists to gloss over cruel details and imperfections. The portraits in the *Camera Picta* are by *Quattrocento* standards rather direct and unembellished, their accuracy and the noble air of the sitters partly compensated for this bluntness, yet documentary evidence suggests the Gonzaga always had some reservations about being portrayed without the falsifying idealisations traditional in portraits of rulers. Mantegna improved reality, and ameliorated some of the flaws of the sitters, conveying on them a sense of *gravitas*, but he did not set out to achieve the suavity, charm, and generalised surfaces his patrons often preferred. A few at court might have wistfully remembered late Gothic portraiture, preferring its flattering falsehood to Mantegna's intense and dry manner.

A fascinating letter survives from 1477 indicating Mantegna objected to the patron's demand that he paint from memory. Ludovico preferred to have a more generalised image, while Mantegna wanted to have all the physiognomic details before his eyes. Mantegna responded to the marquis in a letter in which he makes it clear he could work only from a live sitting:

> "Most illustrious and excellent lord, after the compliments due, I inform your excellency that, as you wish these portraits done, I do not understand, since your excellency wants them so quickly, in what manner they are to be done, in a drawing only, or in colour, on panel or on canvas, and what size. If your lordship wants to ship them far away, they should be done on thin canvas so that they can be wrapped around a little pole. Further, as your excellency knows, one cannot do something well from life if one has no arrangements for seeing it. Your Excellencies [the marquis and marquise] are out of the territory. I will await the instruction that you wish to give... [Signed] Your excellency's follower, Andrea Mantegna."

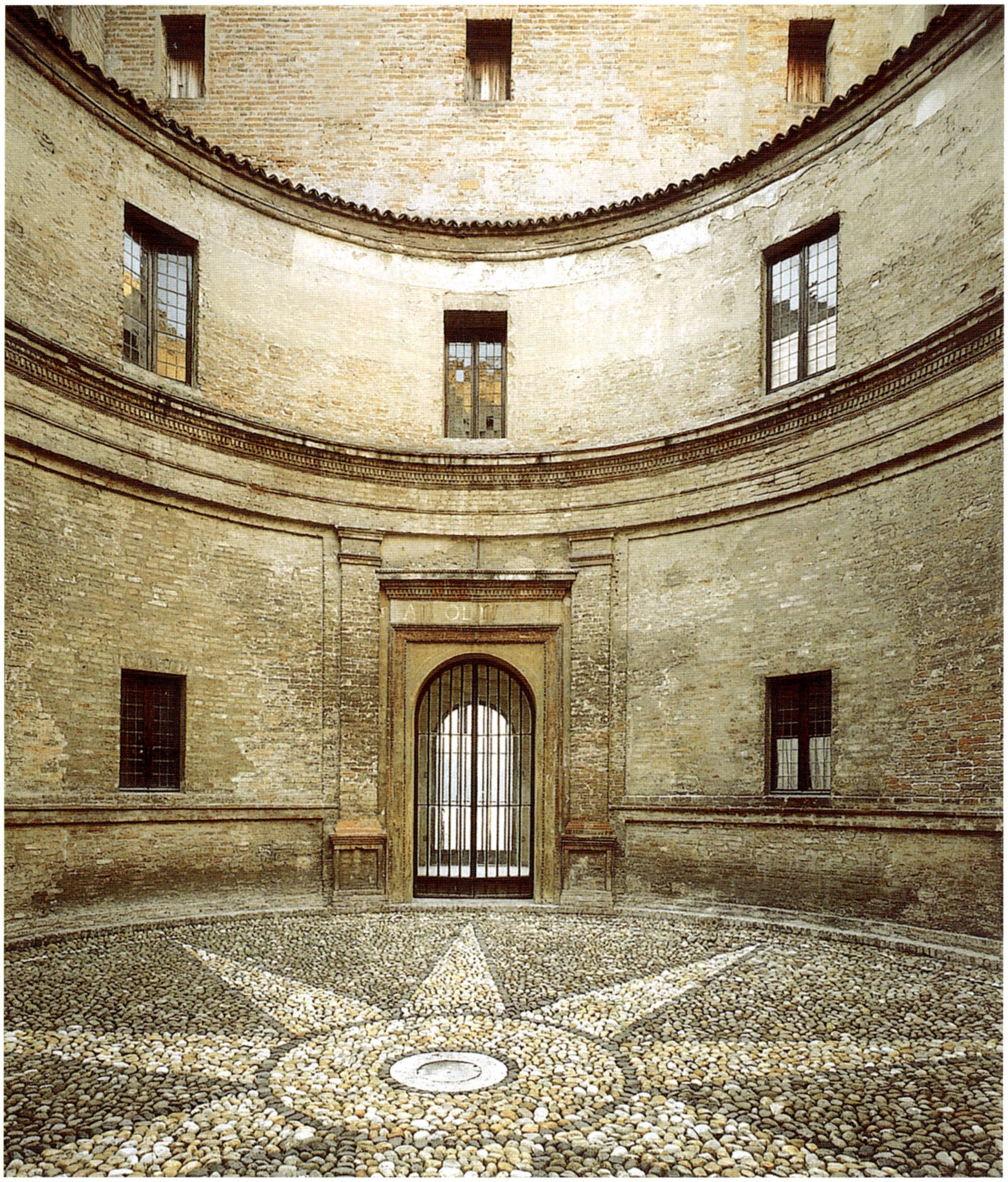

Despite the ironic signature in which the painter claims to be the ruler's "follower," Mantegna let the *marchese* know he must make portraits in his own way.

Mantegna was conscious of his social position at the Gonzaga court, which was less lofty than his ranking as the premier painter in town. His awareness of social relationships is obvious in the group portraits in the *Camera Picta*, and it is telling how the artist included himself in the room in a self-portrait: with his usual wit, he painted his features on a head hidden among an acanthus leaf, a most self-effacing and ironic inclusion of himself in this courtly gathering. As a painter, Mantegna held only limited status, and he tried over the years to elevate himself. He was made a knight by the *marchese* by 1484, and he later received the title of count, noble titles he proudly used in signing his name. Mantegna was one of the first painters of the Renaissance to raise himself up, not just by impressing others with his skill as a painter, but through receiving aristocratic titles. Later, throughout the

55. *Mantegna's House*, view of courtyard, c. 1466-1474. Mantua.

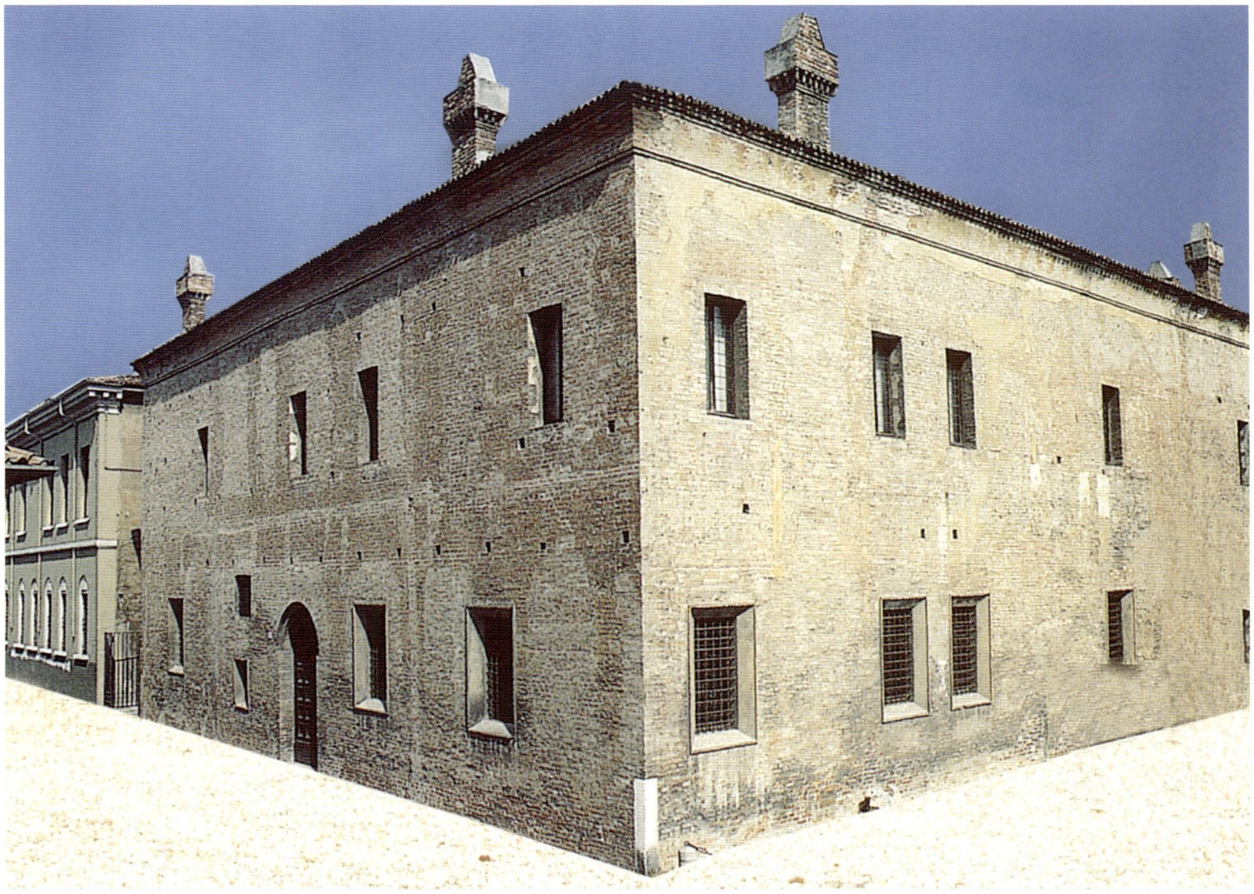

Renaissance and Baroque periods artists would seek to ennoble themselves by such appointments, either buying them or receiving them for services rendered. For his part, Mantegna was keenly aware of social hierarchies, and is probably what makes his *Camera Picta* portraits so insightful, his awareness of the nuances of courtly position especially obvious on the fireplace wall (Fig. 40).

As a group portrait of rulers and their court dependents, the *Camera Picta* was not a new subject in the artistic culture of Europe at this time. However, Mantegna also painted several independent portraits during his lifetime, including those of non-rulers. The practice of portraying individuals in easel paintings was a practice that had almost completely fallen into disuse during the Middle Ages. Before the second quarter of the fifteenth century, likenesses of non-rulers were generally restricted to tombs (which are, after all, religious monuments), or to representation as donors in altarpieces; rulers were also sometimes portrayed on coins or in group portraits. But in the fifteenth century independent portraiture came to extend to a wider range of social classes and to more secular contexts. Renaissance portraits were just one manifestation of a new interest in the individual personality. This individualism and secular spirit of the time meant people commissioned portraits of themselves, their wives, and their children to set up in their homes, to take with them on travels or during other separations, or to send as gifts. Mantegna would have a busy practice in his life catering to this desire of patrons to have their features recorded.

Many more portraits by Mantegna for the Gonzaga and for others are recorded than survive, although the extant ones demonstrate his skills at easel portraiture. One of these, of Francesco Gonzaga, was commissioned from him almost immediately after he became court painter in 1459 (Fig. 58). This boy became a cardinal at the age of sixteen, about the time of this portrait. Mantegna gives him a noble, confident air appropriate for a member of the ruling house, yet also shows the

56. *Mantegna's House*, c. 1466-1474. Mantua.

delicate skin and the shyness of youth. In the sixteenth century more dynamic forms of portraiture would prevail, but in the *Quattrocento* the more static profile portrait was quite widespread. The profile is also a good shorthand way to express accurately the main features of the sitter. Yet the profile was more than just for ease or as a staid conservatism; it was also reminiscent of classical Roman portraiture because so many profile likenesses survived from antiquity in the form of coins and medals. The likeness of Francesco Gonzaga would have recalled for fifteenth-century viewers standard Roman portrait types. Mantegna also utilised the three-quarter type of portrait which was growing in popularity in the later *Quattrocento*, a method allowing the artist to show more modelling and more of the sitter's character. This was a form very widespread in Netherlandish painting, and was increasingly favoured in Venice. In a portrait from about 1460, a likeness of Cardinal Ludovico Trevisan, Mantegna conveys the strong moral character and firmness of conviction of the sitter, who served as a Papal legate and an admiral at the time in a war against the Turks (Fig. 53). He was in Mantua for a Church Council in 1459 and 1460, when Mantegna had an opportunity to capture the moral strength and forcible character of the cardinal. In addition to his ecclesiastical offices, Trevisan was also a humanist who collected ancient medals, and he once purchased a Roman cameo from the famous humanist Niccolò Niccoli. Despite its relatively small size, the portrait of the cardinal somehow appears larger than it is, and the sitter seems to tower high, an impressive portrait specimen by Mantegna.

We can conclude this discussion of Mantegna's place in the Gonzaga court with a mention of his building of a fine house in Mantua. Mantegna raised his social status through his work as a painter, in becoming a member of the lower nobility by achieving knighthood and gaining the title of count. In addition to the quest for aristocratic titles, soon after he finished painting the *Camera Picta*, Mantegna set about in another fashion to establish his position in society more visibly and impressively by starting to build a grand house in Mantua. The land was provided by the *marchese*, and the artist spent much of the rest of his life financing its construction costs. This house, containing fifteen rooms, was unusually large for an artist's house of the time. It still stands, although it now lacks much of the exterior frescoed decoration Mantegna had designed (Figs. 55 and 56). It is impressive in size, and stands as a monument to his social status and professional success.

Two elements of the building specifically link it to humanistic thought and culture. First, the house has a round, central courtyard, a highly unusual feature for a private dwelling of the fifteenth century. It was known that ancient Romans often built rounded or domed structures, and the round floor plan was frequently favoured by Renaissance architects for all kinds of structures, both secular and sacred. Indeed, the house is a cube, and the circle-in-a-square plan was characteristic of architecture of the *Quattrocento*. The simple form of the circle appealed to the Renaissance sense of geometry and unity, while the circular form reverberated with associations with circular courtyards, temples, and monuments from the Greco-Roman past. Also, the open courtyard is reminiscent of the ancient Roman atrium, another classical allusion. The resemblances to the *Camera Picta* are obvious, both being attempts in the classical tradition to offer a view upwards as if through a rounded oculus or opening above an atrium. The *all'antica* inscriptions on the house are also worthy of note. The building has an inscription carved in on the foundation stone (dated 1476) in beautiful, Roman lettering telling the width and breadth of the home, using Latin abbreviations and language of the type that frequently appear in original Roman inscriptions. For example, this inscription refers to "*Ludovicus Divus*," the Divine Ludovico, a borrowing from Roman antiquity when emperors were

57. *Dormition of the Virgin*, c. 1460. Tempera on panel, 54 x 42 cm. Museo del Prado, Madrid.

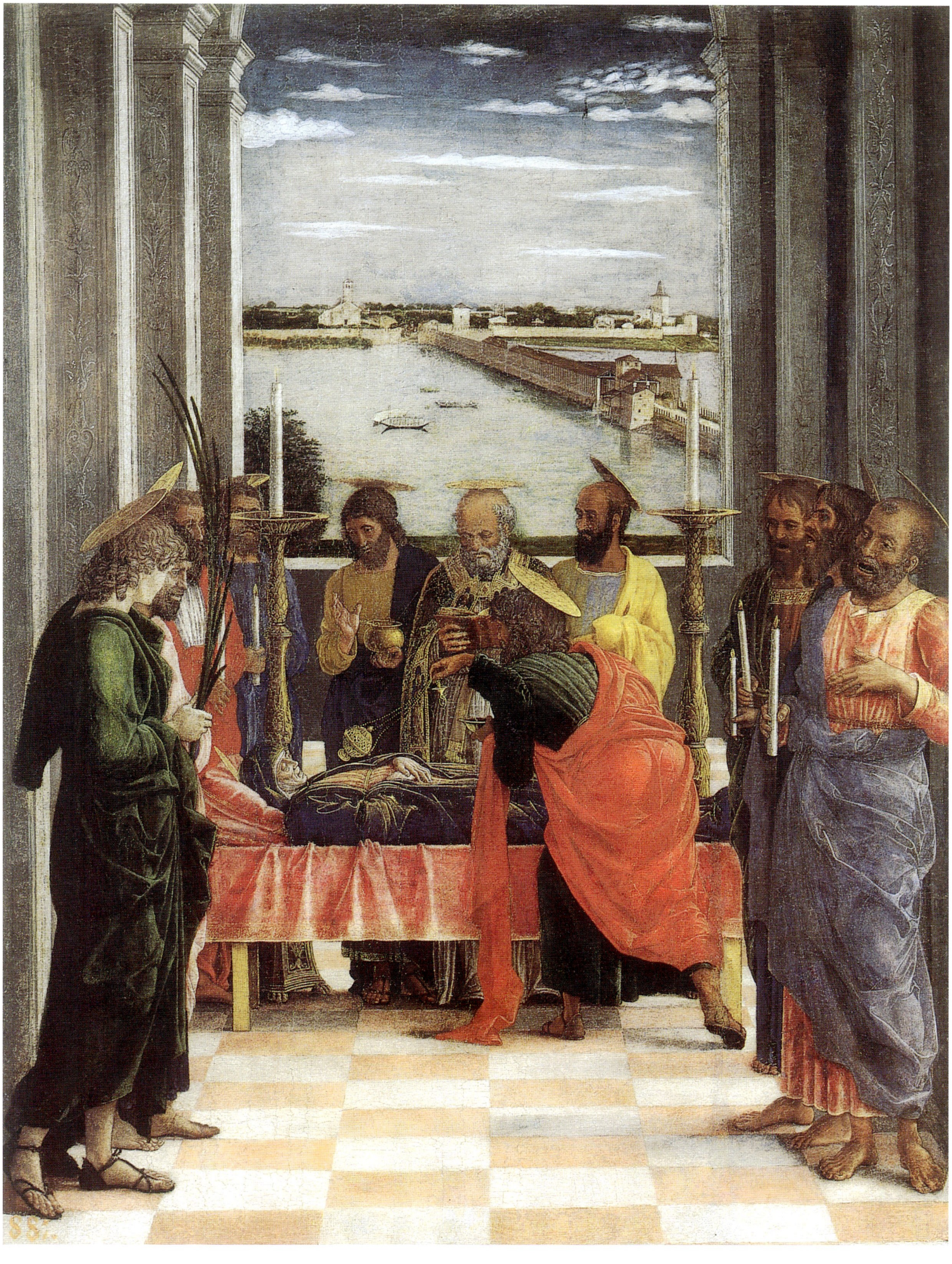

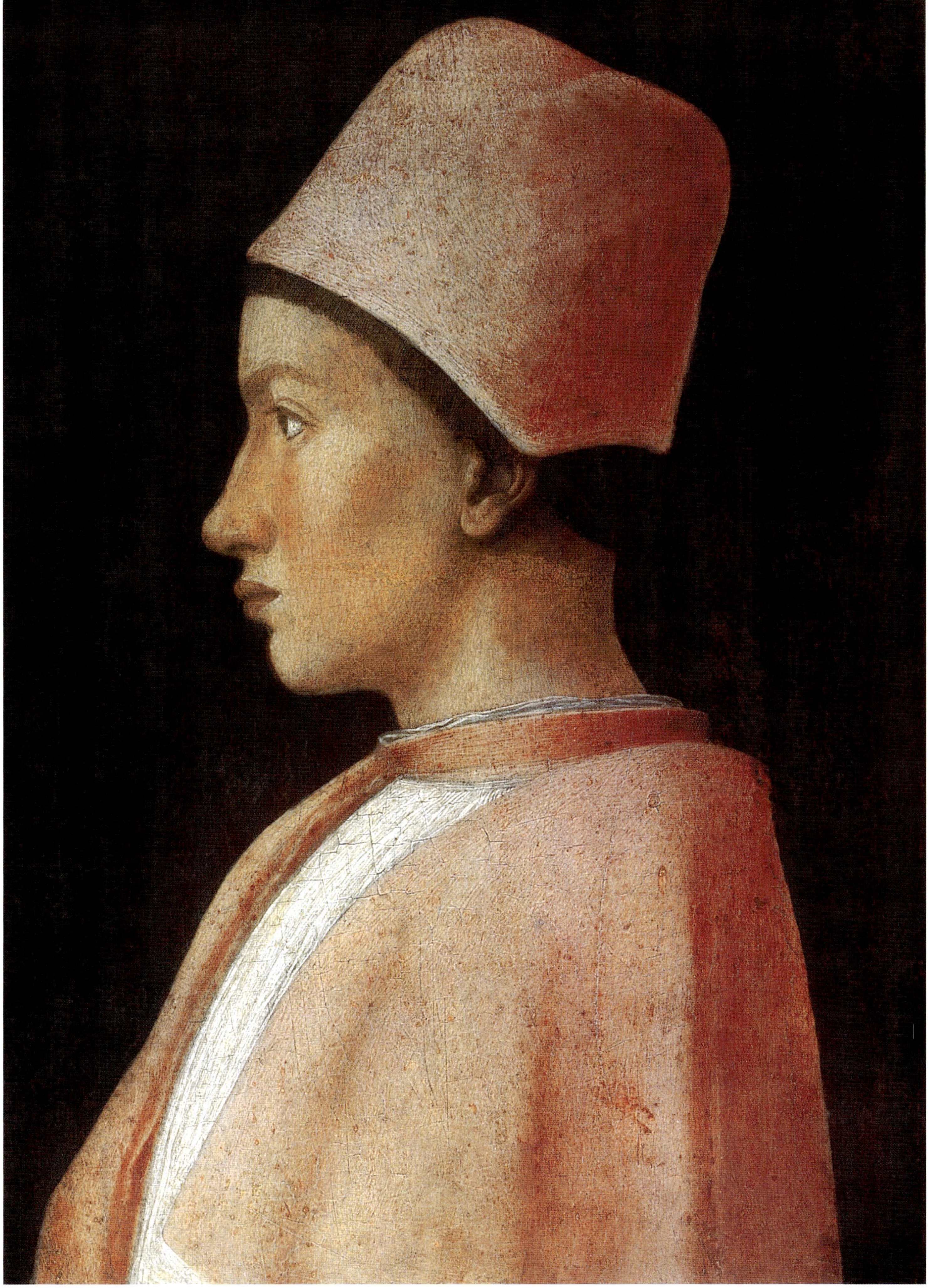

considered god-like. There are other inscriptions over each door in the courtyard stating "*Ab Olympo,*" "from [Mount] Olympus," one of the mottoes of the Gonzaga family, referring immodestly to the abode of the gods. The inclusion of this inscription was not an appropriation by Mantegna of an aristocratic motto, but was rather an act of loyalty by Mantegna to his lord and employer. Rulers like the Gonzaga ruled by power and needed the loyalty of courtiers and other Mantuan citizens. Mantegna was happy to link himself with the court, being grateful to the Gonzaga for their support of his work and for allowing him from the beginning to use their coat-of-arms when he wanted. The son of a country carpenter had become an esteemed and learned artist, a member of the lower nobility, and he had achieved a degree of financial success and security at the Gonzaga court, all this symbolised to the world by his impressive *palazzo*. There was another method of social and economic advancement open to Mantegna, and that was through land ownership. In 1472 he obtained 110 acres of land in the Mantuan countryside, and later in the 1470s and 1480s he acquired other small pieces of property, all of which yielded some rent. One acquisition brought Mantegna headaches, because he was in dispute with some neighbours, who belonged to a noble and long-established family in the area. Mantegna, whom they regarded as a newcomer and a social upstart, accused them of encroaching on his land, and they settled the argument only after litigation. More than one neighbour accused the artist of stirring up trouble, and the picture of Mantegna we get from the legal records is of a quarrelsome, difficult absentee landlord. A neighbour, whom the painter accused of stealing fruit from his trees, said Mantegna "is a disagreeable and objectionable person," noting further "he has had a quarrel with every neighbour in the area." This sort of conflict did not help his social status, but the income from these lands did boost his fixed salary, which during times of financial crisis at the Gonzaga court he did not always receive in full.

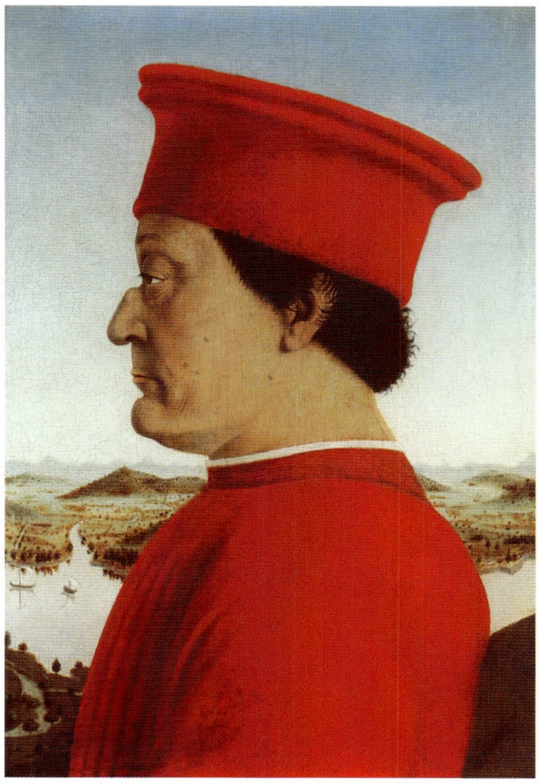

Rather than indicate some entrance into a genteel, traditional class of land owners, these feuds with neighbours place Mantegna squarely in the aggressive, competitive world of the Renaissance, a time of strong individual personalities and egotism. His problems as a landowner also allow us insight into his personality, which in turn sheds light on his art, characterised by a certain tough and hard-edged quality. Ludovico Gonzaga recognised Mantegna's difficult personality when he told another ruler whom Mantegna had refused to serve, "You know how temperamental these artists can be." Mantegna eventually acquired more learning than painters who were mere craftsman, more land than most court servants, and more titles of nobility than others of his profession, but he never acquired the suave, easy behaviour possessed by aristocrats of the fifteenth century. Like the man himself, his pictures are tough and pragmatic, characterised by hard edges and a flinty quality. Despite these petty squabbles, the picture we have of Mantegna's overall social position is an unusually lofty one for a painter of his time. The circumstances of his coming to Mantua meant he arrived with privileged status, since he honoured the marquis by leaving his own country and moved to the city-state of Mantua, which was artistically more provincial than the area of Venice and Padua. In Mantua, Mantegna was free from the necessity of maintaining a commercial workshop and waiting for commissions from various patrons, and he was therefore in a secure financial situation. It was also true he could not leave Mantua without permission nor serve any other patron than the Gonzaga. Yet, the rulers of Mantua did on occasion allow him to travel to other places, something which honoured other rulers and patrons, and helped to link them politically with the Gonzaga because they were being granted a favour by benefiting from Mantegna's release. A highly sought talent, Mantegna was glad to demonstrate his skills by serving a variety of patrons, making artworks outside of Mantua, and as we will see in the next chapter he had a chance to work in Rome for the Pope.

58. *Portrait of Francesco Gonzaga*, c. 1460. Tempera on panel, 25 x 18 cm.
Museo e Gallerie Nazionali di Capodimonte, Naples.

59. Piero della Francesca, *Diptych: Portrait of Duke Federico da Montefeltro and Battista Sforza (right panel)*, 1472.
Oil and tempera on panel, 47 x 33 cm.
Galleria degli Uffizi, Florence.

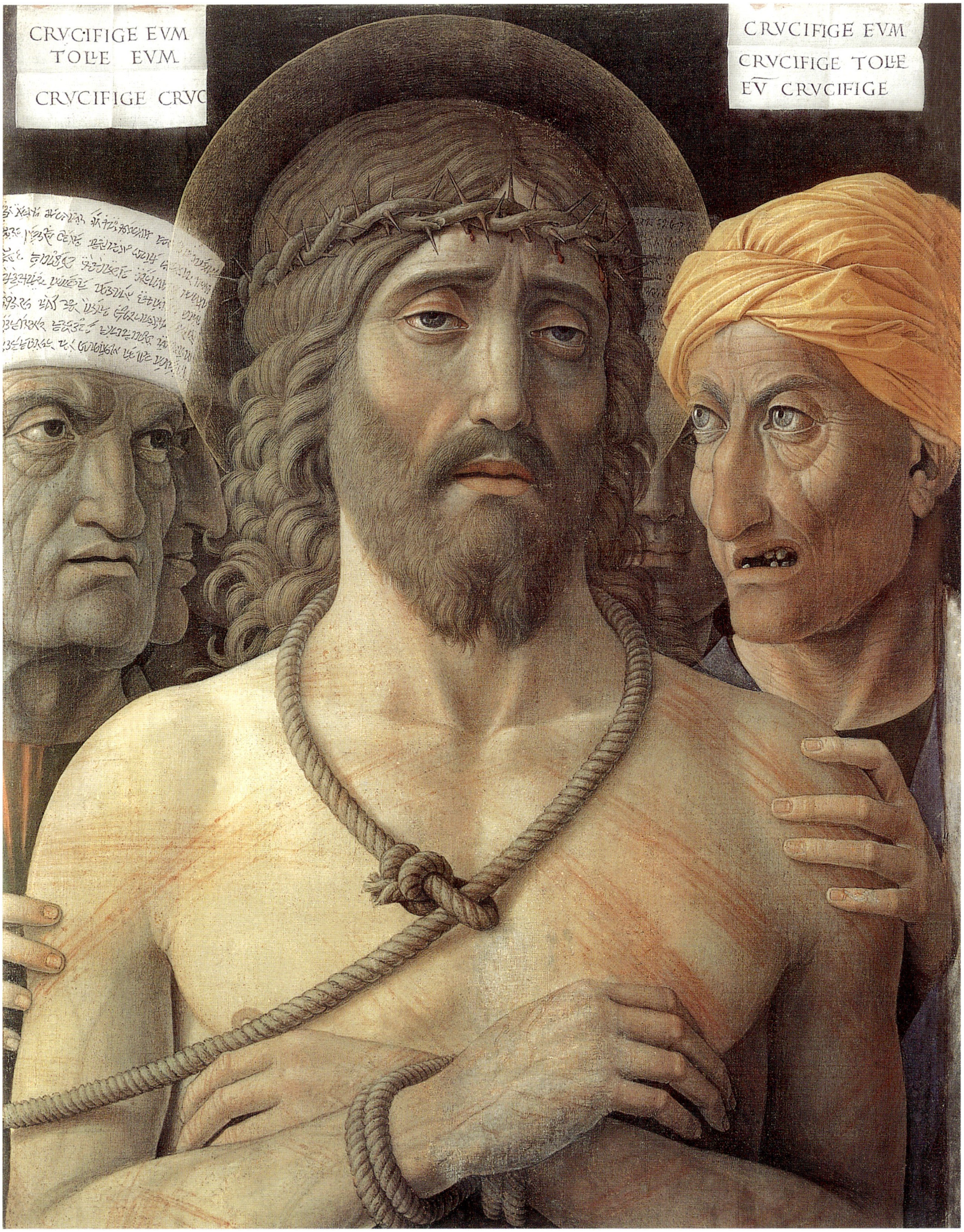
CRVCIFIGE EVM
TOLLE EVM
CRVCIFIGE CRVC
CRVCIFIGE EVM
CRVCIFIGE TOLLE
EV CRVCIFIGE

Piety and Passion in Mantegna's Later Religious Works

Unlike some other Renaissance artists, Mantegna was not known to have had strong, lifelong affiliations with any religious cause. Alessandro Botticelli's devotion to the fire-and-brimstone preacher Girolamo Savonarola, or Michelangelo Buonarroti's passion for theological discussions and philosophical poetry, were not shared by Mantegna. Still, Mantegna's religious works are among the most memorable of the fifteenth century, and he created some of the most poignant sacred scenes of the Renaissance. This is partly owing to the strength of his own religious feeling, which can be gauged by the stipulations in his will that called for the creation of a family chapel where Mass would be said for him and his relations. Moreover, his natural power as a narrator lent itself to illustrating both sacred and secular stories, his biting realism especially successful when representing the Passion of the Christ. The emotionalism and drama of his Christian imagery, seen best in his smaller works, appealed to the people's mystical desire to feel a mystical, personal communion with the divine.

As we saw in our exploration of his early career, it was as a painter of religious works that Mantegna established his professional reputation, beginning in the Ovetari Chapel in Padua and then in the San Zeno Altarpiece in Verona. Beyond this initial period, he carried out a number of sacred paintings over the decades after coming into the service of the Gonzaga. Mantegna's religious artistry from this beginning of this period as court painter can be seen in small but striking pictures intended to adorn the walls of the Castle of Saint George in Mantua: his *Adoration of the Magi*, *Circumcision* (Fig. 62), and *Ascension of Christ* (Fig. 61), dating to the earlier 1460s. (The *Dormition of the Virgin* (Fig. 57) has also been associated with this project). These three paintings reveal the incisive and detailed realism of the artist, and his fascination with antiquity is reflected most powerfully in the architecture and sculpture of the *Circumcision*, which includes an elaborate reconstruction of ancient temple-like rchitecture revealing his own florid classicism and stands as an attempt to reconstruct the ornate decoration of a Jewish temple. The *Circumcision* shows us Mantegna's narrative insight, as the Christ Child attempts to flee the knife and looks up to his mother for help; she is sympathetic, but stands firm. The priest, utterly determined and intent on his task, is prepared to use the knife with precision, and is equipped with scissors and bandages to soak up this first shedding of Christ's blood. The sacrificial aspect of the *Circumcision* is underscored by the relief on the upper left of the Sacrifice of Isaac, itself a prefiguration of a father's willingness to sacrifice his own son.

The *Adoration of the Magi* is painted on a curved panel, which increases the spatial illusion and is a subtle forerunner of the panoramic paintings so popular in the nineteenth century. An almost cinematic progression of Magi approaches the Mother and Child, including the first representation in Italian art of a black Magus. The unexpected visitors approach via the pinched perspective of the winding road. The sharp expressionism of Mantegna's art is evident, as plant and tree forms fight for their lives, rising tenaciously out of the stony soil or springing improbably out of sheer rocky walls. Impossible outcroppings of rocks and thin, petrified clouds add to the visual intensity of the

60. *Ecce Homo*, c. 1500.
Tempera on canvas, 54 x 42 cm.
Musée Jacquemart-André, Paris.

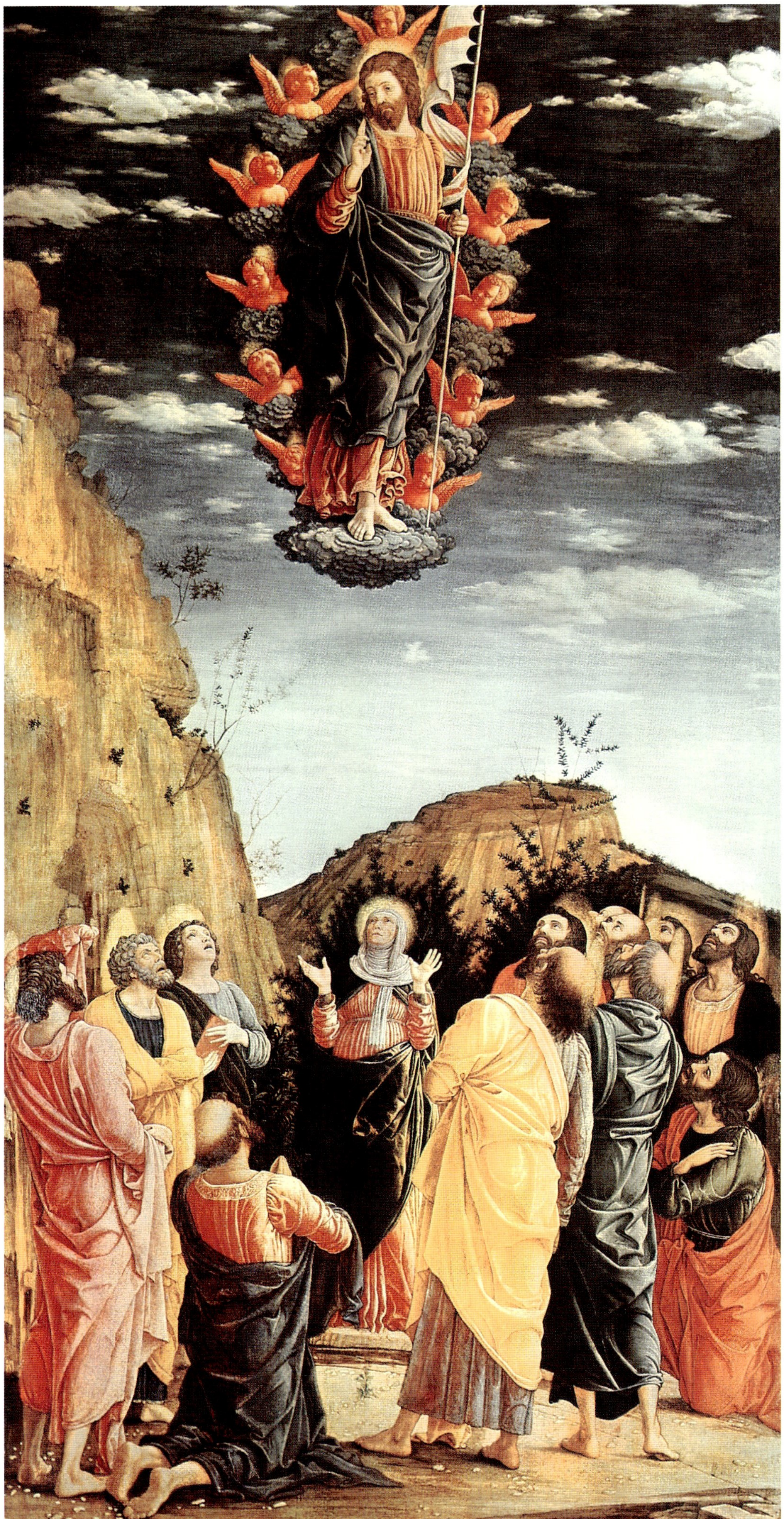

scene. Every pebble, drapery fold, and face is painted in graphic detail, the product of Mantegna's keen observation, and the whole work is a cornucopia of exotic human presence and peculiar natural forms. If early contemporary opinion is right, Ludovico Gonzaga wanted to get away from the soft, elegant, and suave painting style of the Gothic style, and he succeeded beyond measure in commissioning the intense and flinty paintings by Mantegna. The *Ascension of Christ* (Fig. 61) offers a bit of visual relief, as Mary and the Apostles stand in classical balance below, but the group above comprises the ascending Christ is like a coiled spring, and our eyes are drawn to his complex draperies, furling flag, and the overpopulated, brightly coloured crowd of seraphim.

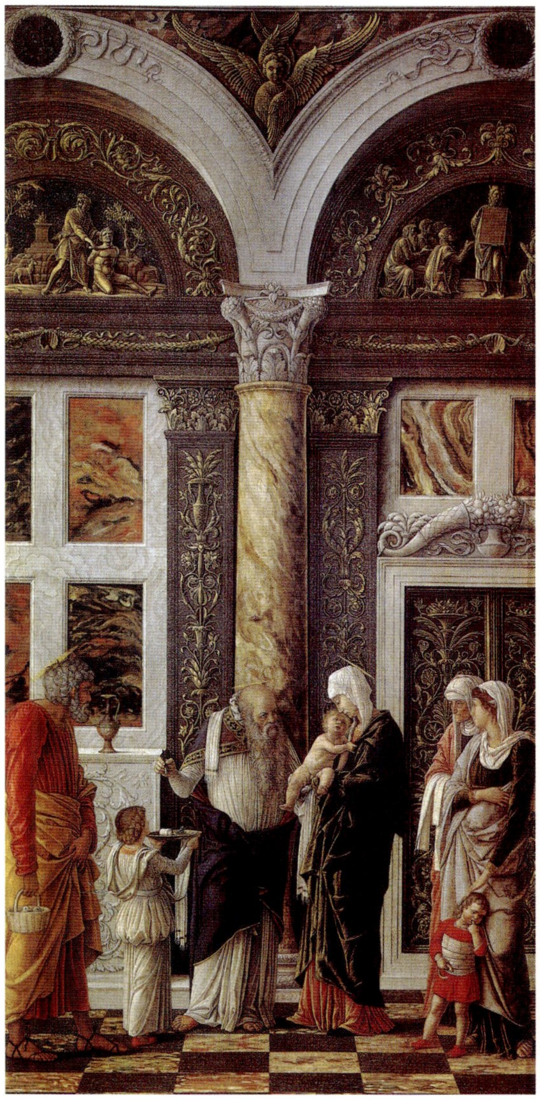

Many of Mantegna's surviving religious works, including his very earliest efforts, have an historical, classical air to them. This became further accentuated after a trip to Rome in 1489-1490. He went there to work on religious paintings for the Pope, but while he was there he availed himself of the opportunity to study antique ruins and sculptural remains of pagan antiquity, as there were ancient works he admired or copied. Like his early paintings, Mantegna's mature religious works are a combination of Christian subject matter and classical accoutrements of costume, architecture, armour, and so forth. In this spirit, Mantegna invented a new type of Holy Family image, several versions of which exist from the later years of his life (Fig. 63). Also in this vein is Mantegna's late, relief-like *Adoration of the Magi* (Fig. 66); it lacks the stone framing seen in some of his works in this format, but there is an intense physical presence of the figures, and a lively composition with a variety of glances and a subtle counterpoint of heads and hands. All these works are roughly based on Roman funeral portraits of individuals or families, which represent the couple carved in relief, shown in bust or half-length and facing out. Such ancient reliefs were quite numerous, and there are several Mantegna could have seen in Rome and elsewhere. Mantegna borrows not just the form of the antique compositions but also the stoic quality and the incisive realism that are characteristic of much classical art. In general, his Christian saints have the firm stance, strong character, and the convincing, natural features found in Roman portraiture. He expresses the physical and moral perfection of his saint, using the art of antiquity as his essential model. These paintings probably postdate his trip to Rome, so here we have some visual evidence that he was undertaking sketching expeditions and was collecting ideas during his stay in the Eternal City. These pictures all demonstrate the warm texture resulting from Mantegna's innovative use of canvas, a support he had used already in his earliest signed work (cf. Fig. 4) and which he often coupled with the animal glue (distemper) medium to bring about a matt, unified surface and naturalistic appearance.

While at work on the large project for the Pope, Mantegna painted at least one small painting, *Madonna of the Stonecutters,* during his stay in Rome, if it as Giorgio Vasari argued in 1550 (Fig. 131). Still, little about this little picture bespeaks his time in the seat of ancient Roman civilisation, except perhaps the boldness of the invention. Even in this tiny panel an expressive and imposing mountain rises up behind in an explosion of energy. On the right some carvers are cutting a column and a stone slab from the quarry, symbols of the forthcoming sacrifice and suffering of Christ, who will be tied to a column and whipped, and later buried in a sarcophagus. This is one of the painter's more memorable works, and the motif of the great mountain is without precedent in the history of the subject of Madonna and Child. This kind of invention and originality must have impressed the humanists at the Papal court, justifying the growing number of assertions that Mantegna was the leading painter in the world at the time.

61. *The Ascension of Christ,* c. 1460-1465.
Tempera on panel, 86 x 42 cm.
Galleria degli Uffizi, Florence.

62. *Circumcision,* c. 1460-1465.
Tempera on panel, 86 x 43 cm.
Galleria degli Uffizi, Florence.

After he returned from Rome in 1490, Mantegna spent much of his time on his *Triumph of Caesar*, which we will consider in a later chapter (see Figs. 82 and 87, 88, 90, 91, 92); these canvases would occupy him through the end of the 1490s. By the middle of the decade, the marquis of Mantua, Francesco Gonzaga, would have Mantegna paint an altarpiece with deep personal meaning for him, the *Madonna of Victory*, now in the Louvre Museum in Paris (Fig. 67). The Virgin and Child dominate a painting rich in fruit and foliage and populated by heroic saints and the kneeling, victorious Francesco Gonzaga. The story of how this altarpiece originated is one of the richest tales known regarding the creation of any Renaissance painting, and it throws a considerable amount of light on political and social relations in Italy at the time.

In 1494 the French, under King Charles VIII, invaded Italy, hoping to conquer the Kingdom of Naples in the south; they counted on finding little resistance from the squabbling city-states of Italy, all of them much smaller than the ever-growing and united French kingdom. The French entered the Italian peninsula with a formidable military force. On the way to Naples they wreaked havoc with Italian politics; the invasion helped lead to the overthrow of the Medici family in Florence, and later in the Italian Wars caused the downfall of the Sforza, rulers of Milan. The French faced a united force of several Italian states, including those of Mantua and Venice. The chief military general for the Italian army was Francesco Gonzaga, whose portrait as a child we saw in the *Camera Picta*. Like his grandfather Ludovico, he was a military specialist and a *condottiere* for the Venetian Republic, which paid him a large annual salary to serve as a captain general. He received this salary even during peace time, but in 1495 it was his duty to serve in the field; the Venetians had him lead a force totalling about five thousand foreign mercenary and native Italian troops.

On 6 July 1495 he met the French near the northern Italian town of Fornovo. The battle was brutal, and Francesco almost lost his life during a darker moment in the struggle. Francesco's troops fell into disarray, but they inflicted heavy damage on the French, who only wanted to leave Italy and return to France anyway, which most of them were able to do. Because of the numerous French casualties, their departure from the field of battle, and the seizure of the king's personal supplies and luxury items he was carrying, Francesco and the Italians declared a victory. The *Marchese* of Mantua proclaimed himself the redeemer of Italy. Certainly, Francesco fought well, and he rallied his troops in the battle; he felt fortunate to be alive and to be able to claim the title of victor. A contemporary portrait conveys some of Francesco's fortitude and military valour.

During the Renaissance, as in earlier times, it was customary to erect churches, chapels, altarpieces, or smaller votive offerings to the Virgin whenever a great difficulty was overcome or a danger avoided. When one survived a shipwreck or storm, lived through an illness or a time of plague, or when one's child did, it was usual to offer tribute to Mary, the protector and intercessor for mankind. It is hardly surprising Francesco asked his best painter, Mantegna, to make an altarpiece dedicated to the Virgin. However, the nature of the painting and the site for it had its own extraordinary circumstance. The story involves a certain Jewish banker in Mantua named Daniele di Leone da Norsa. The Jewish population faced many legal restrictions and other prejudices in Europe during this time, and they were even expelled *en masse* from Spain in 1492. Still, Jews often received protection from the rulers of Italian city-states, including Mantua and nearby Ferrara, because the rulers welcomed the additions of population to their realms and because Jews could deal more easily in trades such as banking which were supposedly off limits to Christians because of Church admonitions against money lending.

63. *The Holy Family with the Infant Baptist*, c. 1490-1500.
Tempera on canvas, 71 x 50.5 cm.
The National Gallery, London.

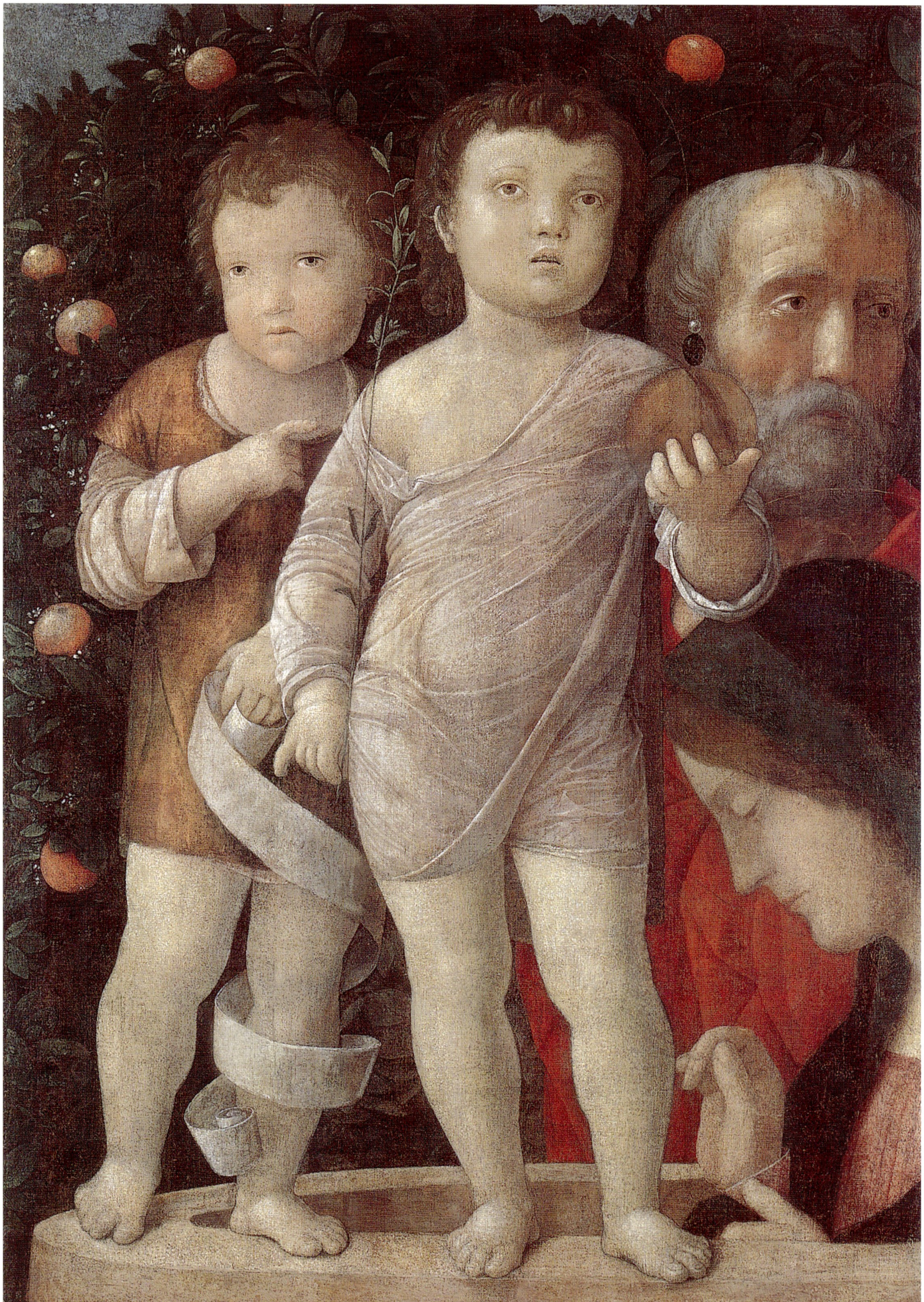

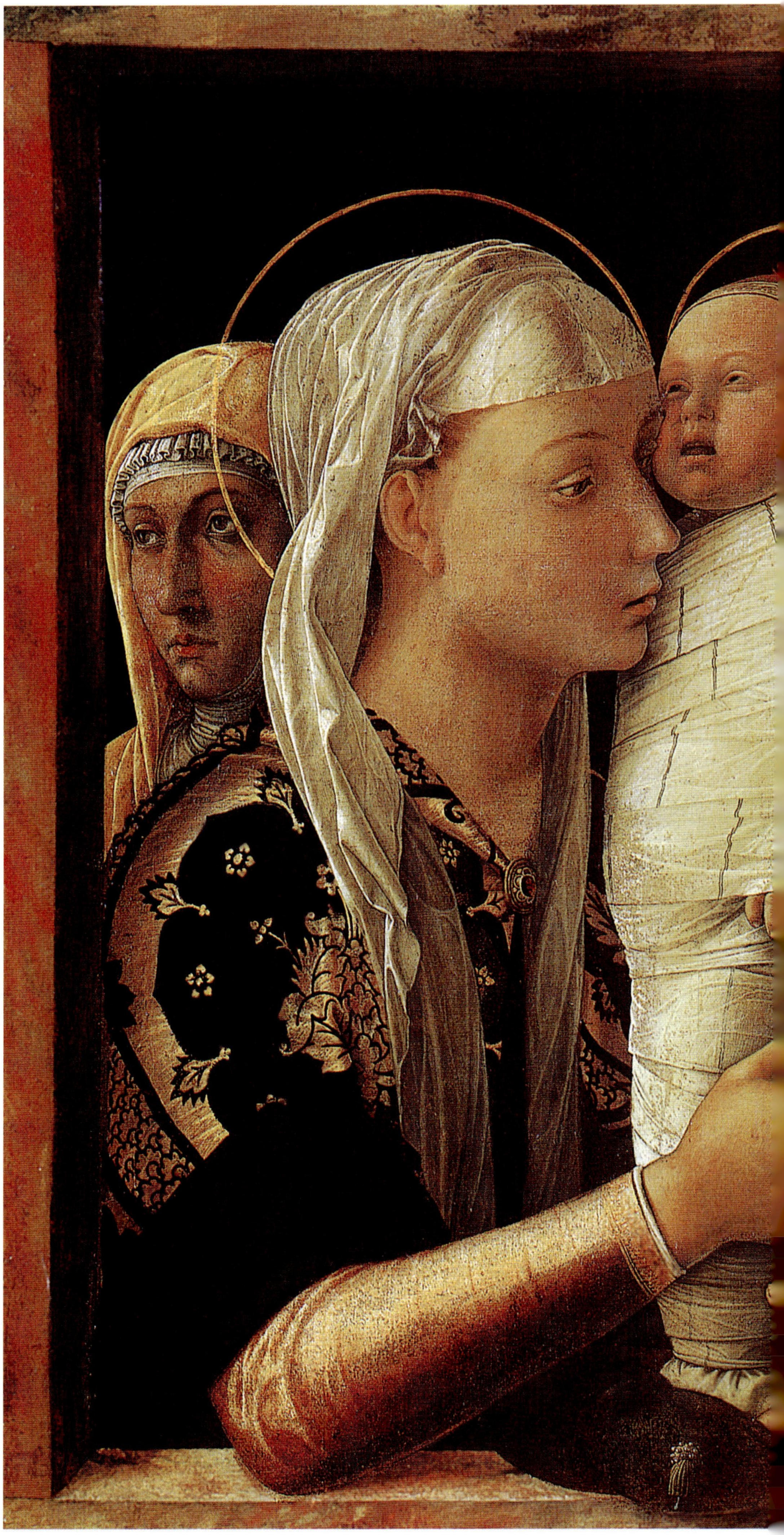

64. *The Presentation at the Temple,*
Tempera on canvas,
68.9 x 86.3 cm.
Gemäldegalerie, Berlin.

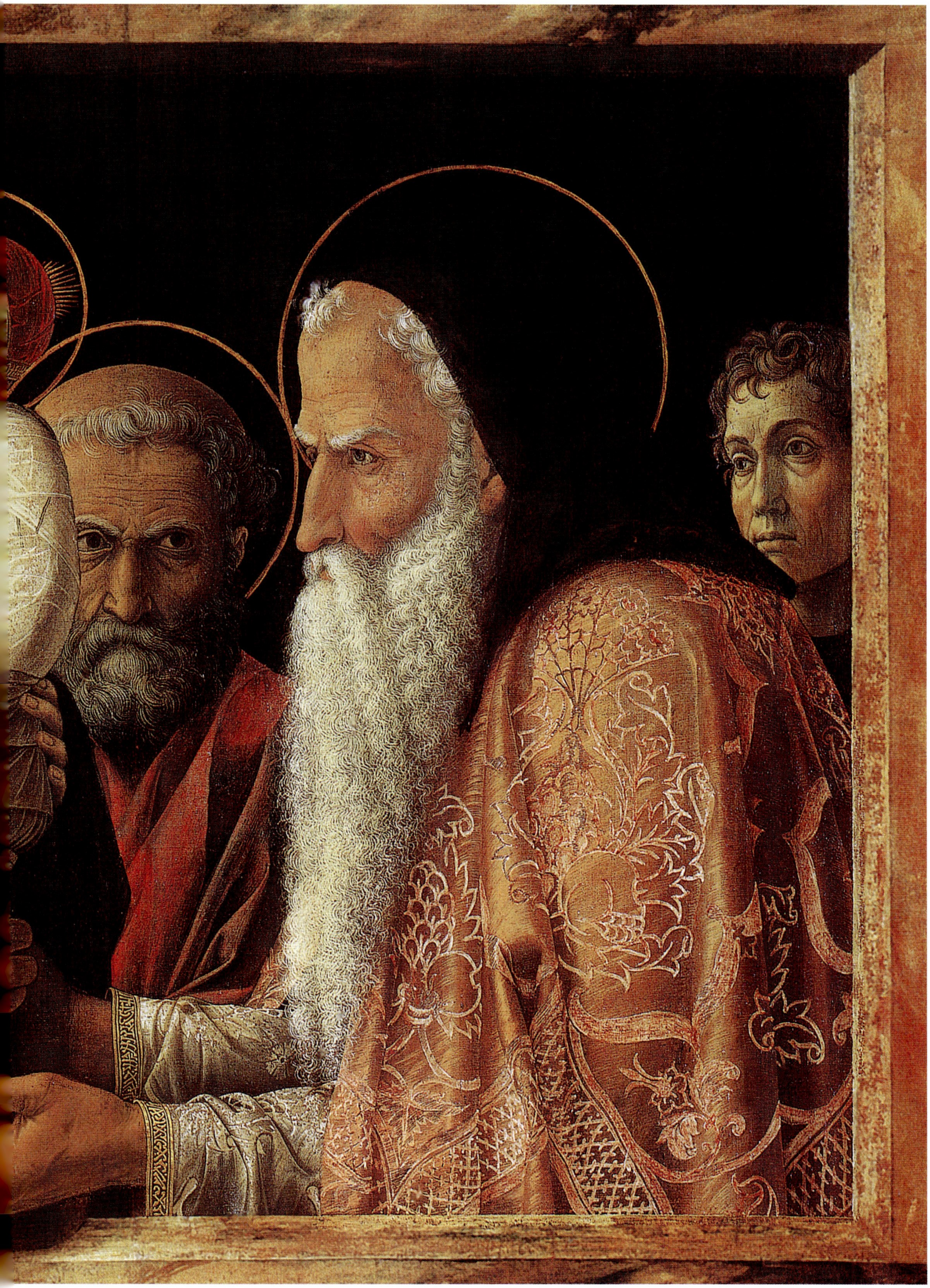

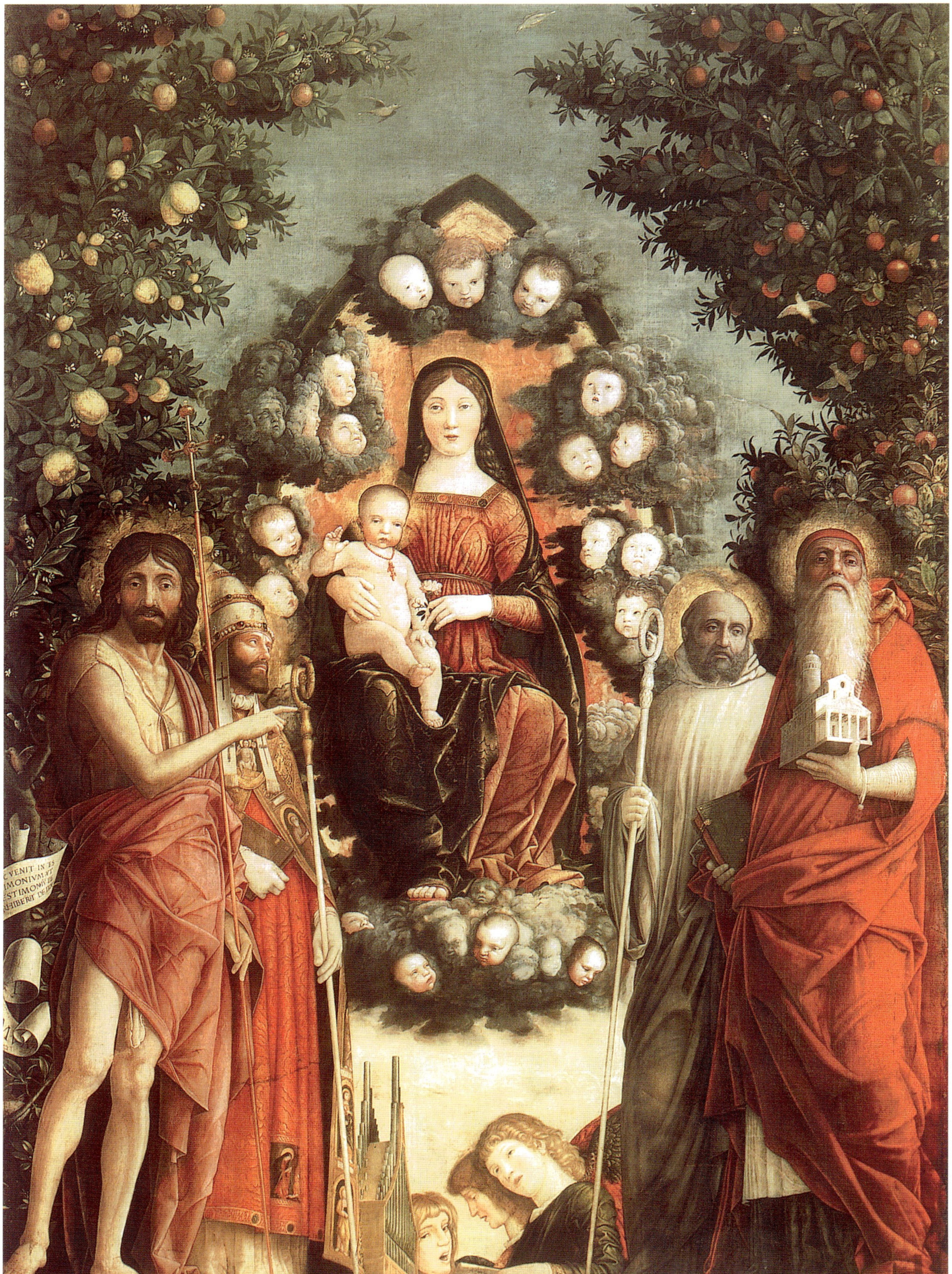

It happened more than once that Italian rulers protected Jews from mob violence, which occurred frequently after Lenten sermons. Isabella d'Este, Francesco's wife by 1490, once told a preacher in Mantua to keep his sermons in check and not stir up rioting against the Jews. A governor in a smaller town of Reggio, which was under Estense rule, acted similarly; the courtier and poet Matteo Maria Boiardo, once commuted a death sentence to a Jew (who had had sexual relations with a Christian woman) to a mere fine, and then he forgave him the fine as well. Yet there remained in Italy deep anti-Semitism, especially from the lower classes and the clergy. The site and financing of Mantegna's *Madonna of Victory* came about after the marquis was convinced by local clergy to seize the assets of the banker Daniele when he destroyed an outdoor fresco on his house representing the Virgin with saints. Daniele wanted the work to be removed legally and systematically, since he did not want to be blamed if others harmed the work, and he obtained legal permission to destroy the fresco, but some Mantuan Christians soon painted crude figures of saints on his wall accompanied by mocking verses. A mob attacked the house with stones, and even Francesco, who was far away fighting the French, heard news of the controversy and ordered the banker to pay immediately for a new fresco.

The whole affair then grew worse for Daniele. A theologian and mystic in Mantua entered the scene, writing to the marquis he had had a vision that His Lordship would destroy the Jew's house and build a church on the spot, calling it Santa Maria della Vittoria, Saint Mary of Victory. This visionary, Fra Girolamo Redini, included Mantegna in his "dream," envisioning Mantegna would create a picture with the Virgin in this church. Redini wrote to Francesco, who was still serving as captain general outside Mantua, that in this picture "under the mantle on one side shall be you, fully armed as a victorious captain with your brothers, and on your other your most illustrious consort [the marquise, Isabella d'Este], which will be a most noble work." This splendid vision was not yet enough to tempt Francesco to destroy the home of the banker Daniele, who, after all, had obtained permission to remove the first fresco. But Francesco did eventually go beyond simply fining him and asking him to replace the old fresco with a new one. The marquis soon succumbed to the advice of his clerics and advisers in Mantua: the house of Daniele da Norsa was razed, and he was forced to fund the construction of a small church and pay for Mantegna's painting of the Madonna of Victory.

Redini, in consultation with others in Mantua, decided on a new scheme for the altarpiece, including the warrior saints George and Michael, and now omitting Isabella; he wrote in a letter to the *marchese*:

> "I have learned the answer your lordship gave to the Jew, that he had to have the blessed image of the glorious Virgin Mary painted, which he had erased... Master Andrea Mantegna [will] make two saints, one on each side of the Madonna, holding her mantle, under which there will be your lordship, armed; these saints will be Saint George and Michael, and everyone, I most of all, liked the words he added, inspired I believe by God, that these two saints were victorious, one in body and one in soul, and that they, together with the most holy and devout mother of God, your intercessor and sole hope, will give victory to your most illustrious lordship, and finally he said he hoped to see a fine cult grow up in that place."[9]

In 1496 a small church was erected on the spot where the Jew's house stood, and Mantegna painted his picture much as stated in this letter. Francesco was still in the field against the enemy, but he soon returned to see the altarpiece commemorating his victory of 1495 at Fornovo.

65. *Madonna and Child in Glory*, called *Trivulzio Madonna*, 1494-1497.
Tempera on canvas,
287 x 214 cm.
Castello Sforzesco, Milan.

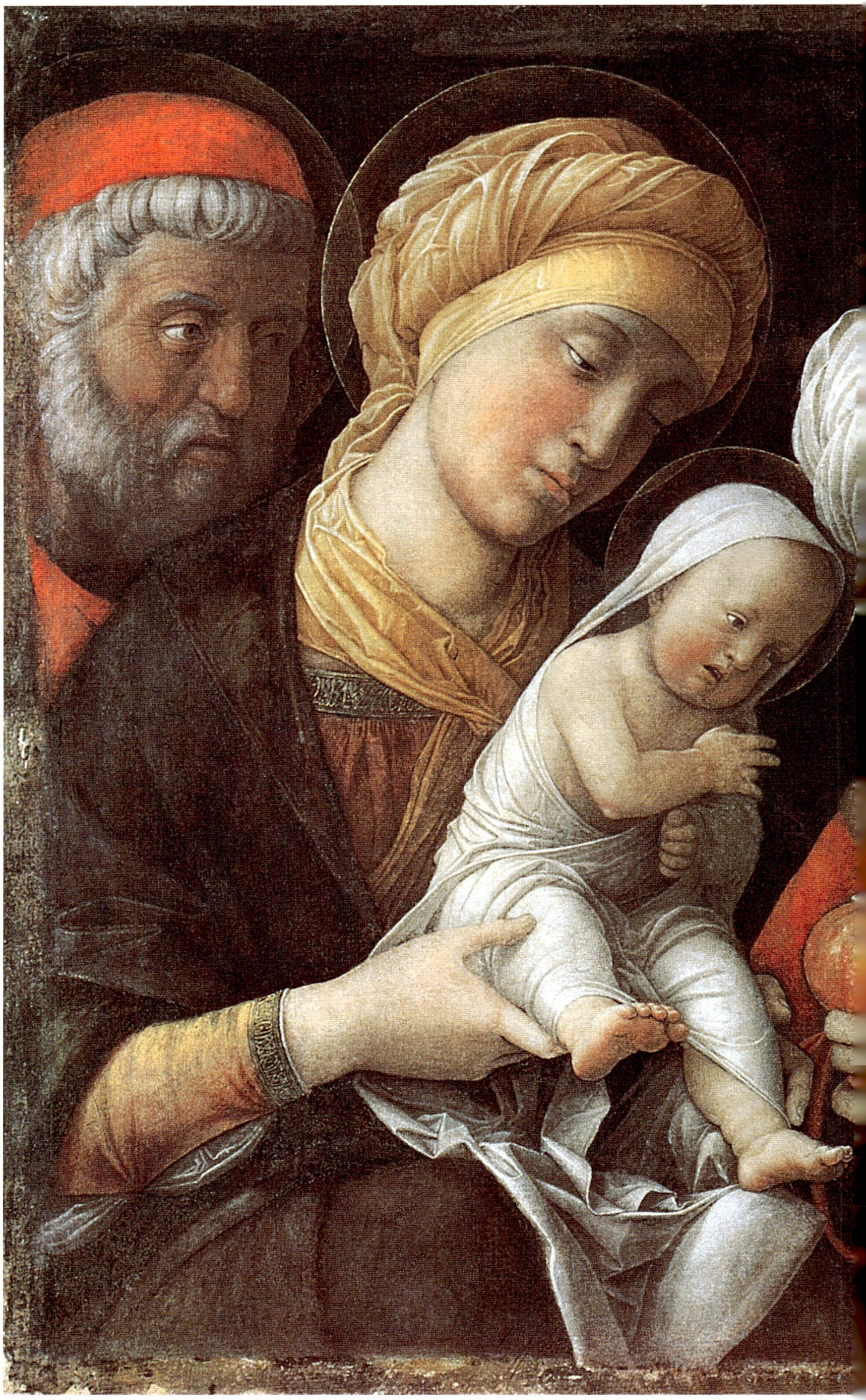

66. *Adoration of the Magi*,
c. 1497-1500.
Tempera and gold on linen canvas,
54.6 x 70 cm.
The J. Paul Getty Museum,
Los Angeles.

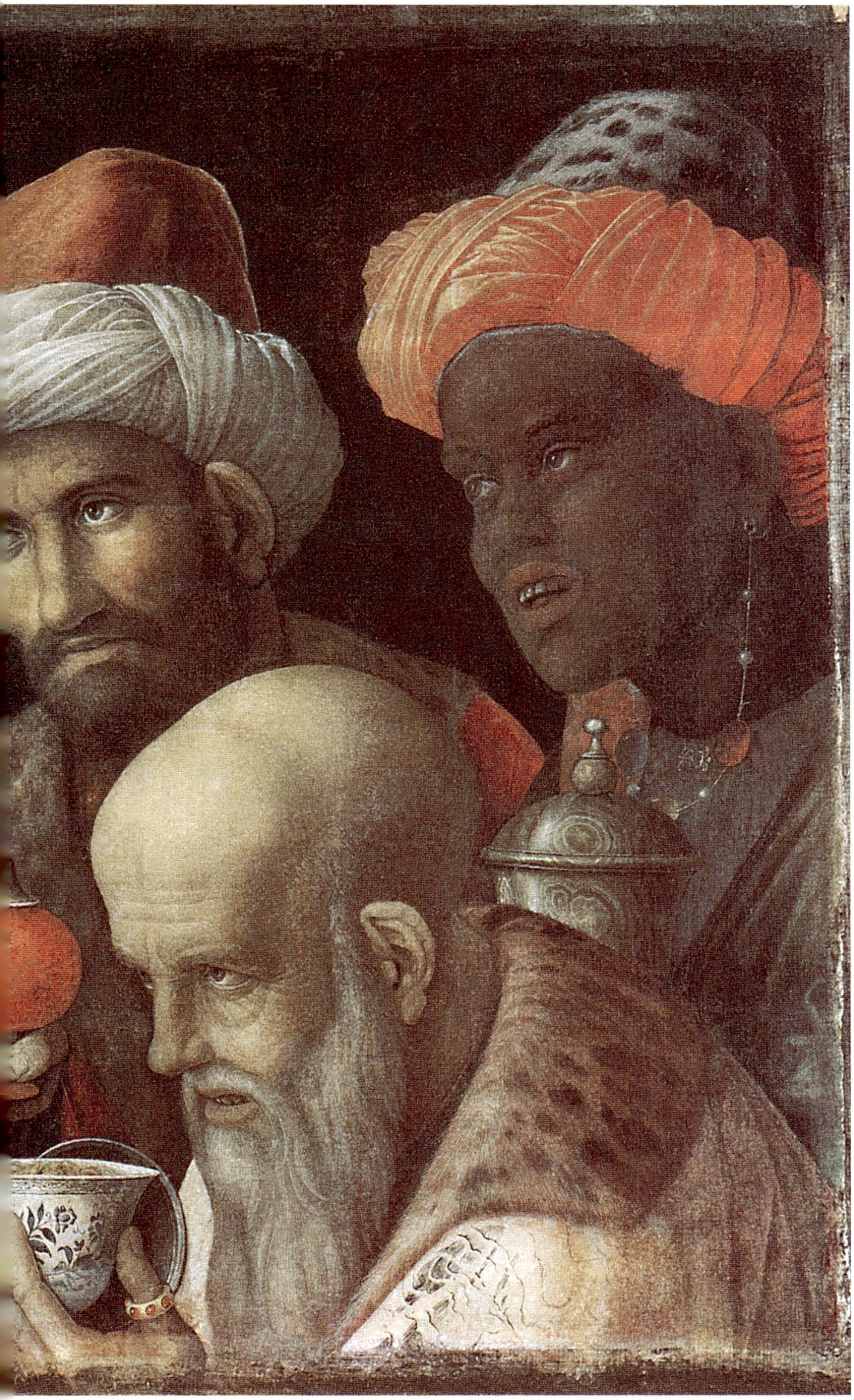

The painting is one of Mantegna's finest creations. Characteristically, Mantegna's *Madonna of Victory* contains some classical elements, including the inscription (in Roman lettering), the style of the footstool, and the spectacular frame and architecture within the painting. As described in Redini's letters, the altarpiece does include the warrior saints George and Michael, as well as saints Andrew and Longinus, who are farther back in space. These latter two are patriotic saints. Mantua held in the church of San Andrea (i.e., Saint Andrew) a relic of the Holy Blood of the Redeemer. The blood had flowed from the side of Christ after the wound delivered by the Roman soldier Longinus, who then converted and became a follower of Christ, later to be canonised as a saint. On the right of the *Madonna of Victory* kneels Saint Elizabeth, supporting the nude, infant Saint John the Baptist; this reference to baptism is perhaps an anti-Semitic aspect of the painting, since it is the initial sacrament separating Christians from Jews. The Virgin is seated on an elaborate throne, holding her hand in a soft, maternal fashion over the armed and relaxed figure of Francesco, who piously looks up at his holy protectress.

The setting is beautifully conceived as a bower, with luscious fruit growing on it, like the court gardens in Mantua of the Gonzaga. Over the head of Christ is a brilliant red coral. He is sometimes shown in pictures with coral around his neck, but here it hangs in the air, echoed colouristically by red beads. Coral was a symbol of protection, as it was thought to ward off evil and heal wounds. Coral is a symbol for Christ, and also reinforces the idea of the protection Mary provided for Francesco on the battlefield. Mary is shown as the *Regina Caeli*, the Queen of Heaven, according to an inscription under her foot, and her high position reinforces this title, as she is raised up above the earthly level. Traditional Christian iconography in Mantegna's painting includes Adam and Eve, shown in fictive sculpture on the base of the throne: mankind has sinned, and Christ must come as Redeemer. They are conceived with a smooth, classical beauty.

Mantegna's painting was celebrated by the general Mantuan populace as well as by its rulers and clergymen. In a letter of July 1496 to his brother the marquis, Sigismondo Gonzaga described the public adulation of the picture and the celebration of the anniversary of Francesco's victory. First, the altarpiece was set up in the church of San Sebastiano (near the painter's house), where it was celebrated with songs performed by figures dressed as angels, saints, prophets, and God the Father. After being carried from there to Santa Maria della Vittoria, Mantegna's masterpiece was illuminated with votive candles and common people placed before it popular wax images of saints.

> "My most Illustrious Lord. Since I continuously remember the harsh and cruel day of the battle, one year ago in Parmigian territory, in which the supreme deity and his glorious mother saved your excellency, after many brave and forceful actions for the death and destruction of the enemy done for her, I thought that today, along with my most illustrious lady, I would make some praiseworthy memorial, in praise of God and his glorious mother. And so we arranged a fine procession, which took place this morning solemnly, with all the orders of monks and priests, in the following manner: all the religious assembled at San Sebastian, with the greater part of the people, where the image of the glorious virgin which Master Andrea Mantegna has finished was raised up on a great platform, very admirably framed, and above this image was a youth dressed as God the Father, and two prophets were on either side, and at the sides three little angels singing certain lauds, and opposite were the twelve apostles. When it was time... Fra Pietro da Caneto gave a fine speech in Italian to the people, in praise of the glorious virgin, exhorting them to devotion to her,

67. *Madonna of Victory*, c. 1495-1496. Tempera on canvas, 280 x 166 cm. Musée du Louvre, Paris.

68. *Madonna with Sleeping Child.* Tempera on panel. Museo Poldi Pezzoli, Milan.

69. Sandro Botticelli, *Madonna of the Book*, c. 1483. Tempera on panel, 58 x 39.5 cm. Museo Poldi Pezzoli, Milan.

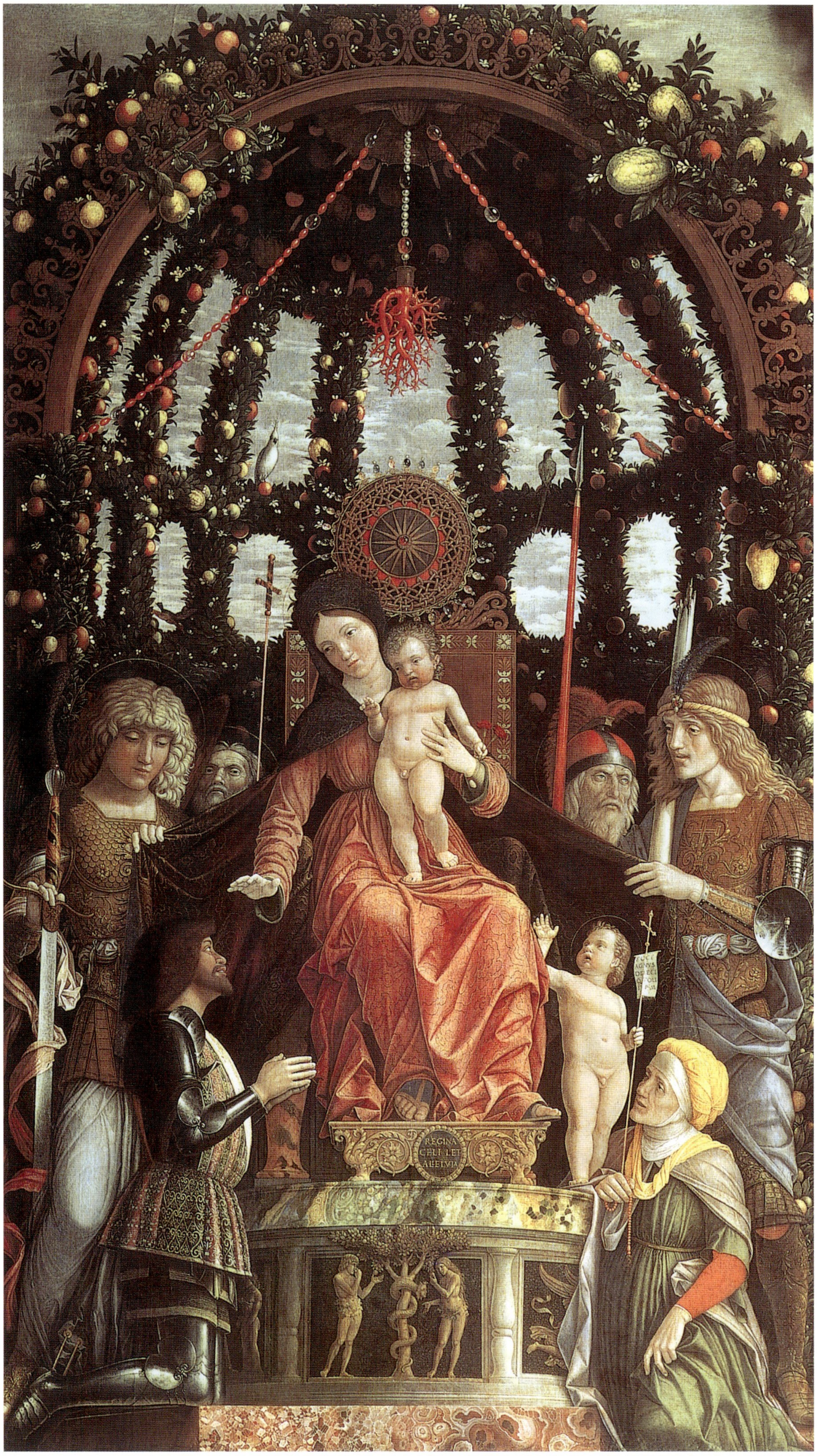

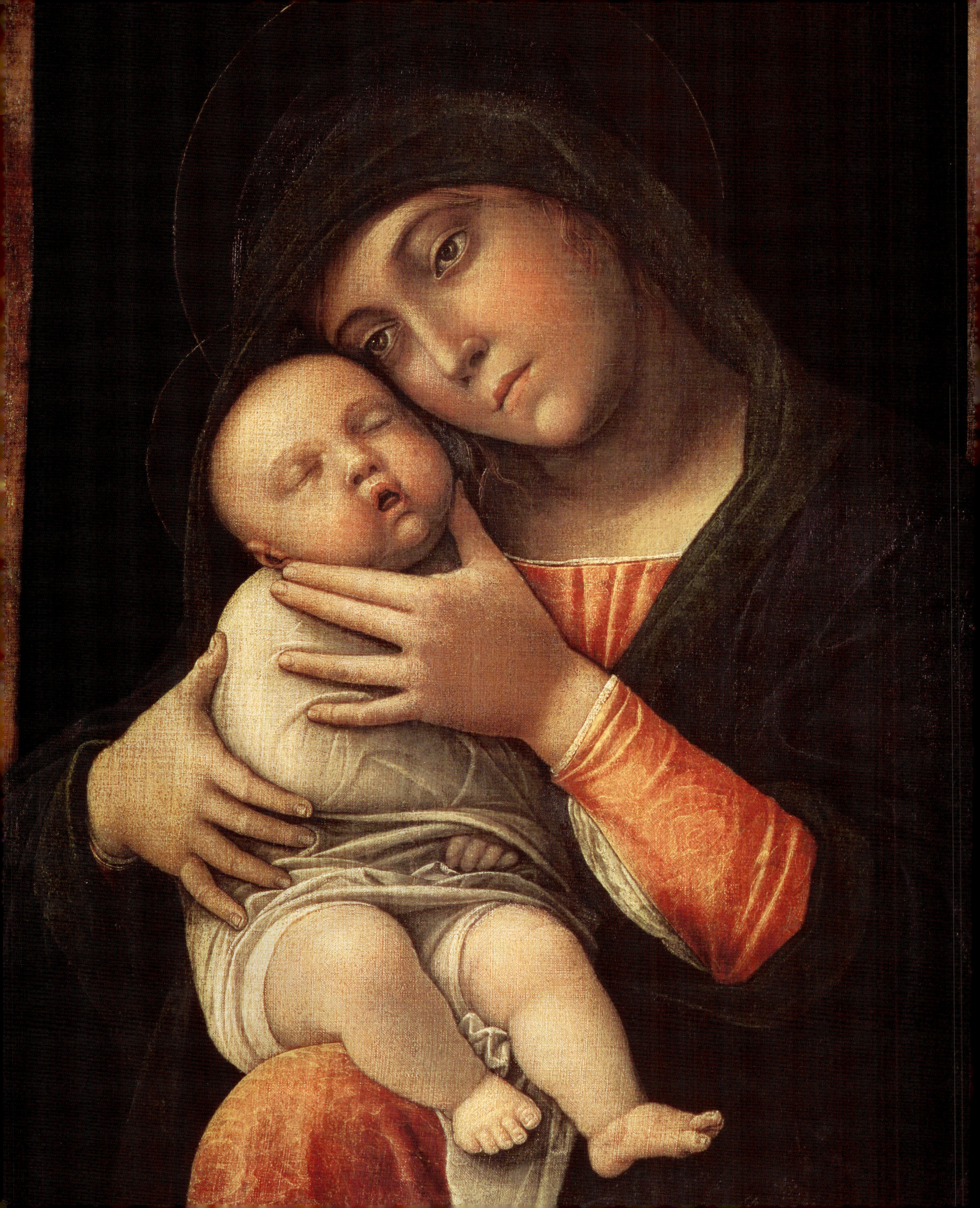

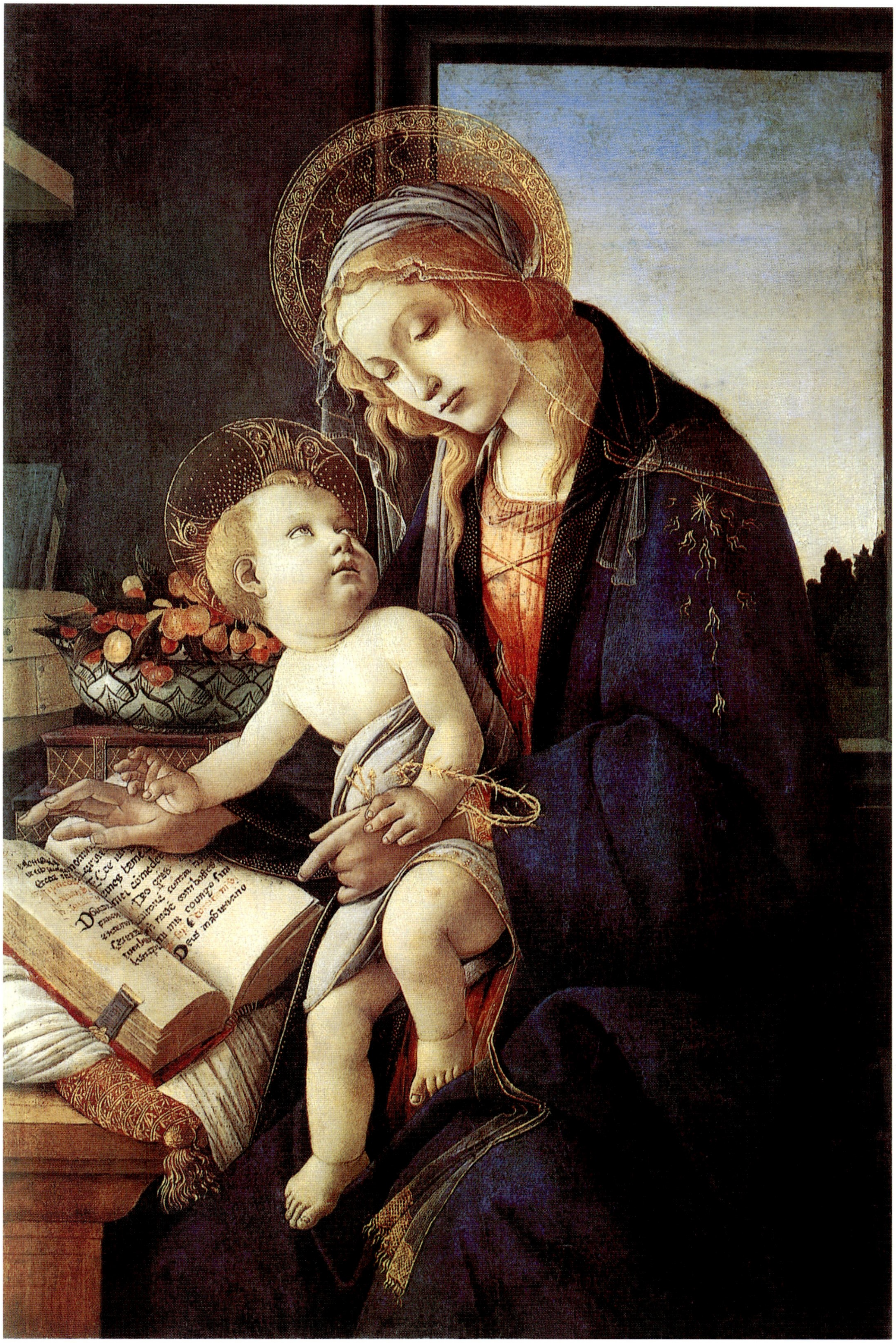

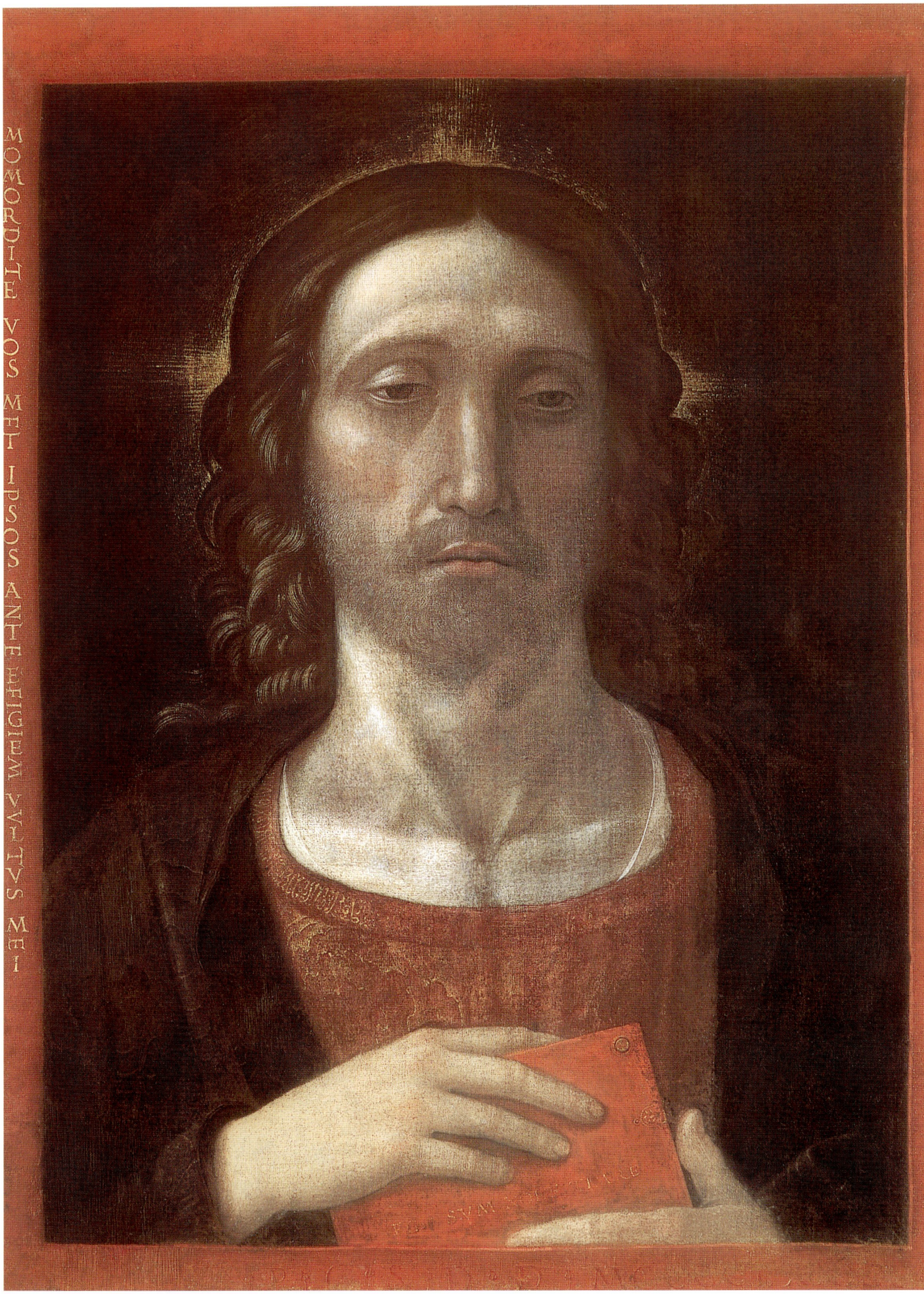
MOMORDITE VOS MET IPSOS ANTE EFFIGIEM VVLTVS MEI

> reminding them it was she who had freed your excellency on that day from dangers, and they should all pray to her to preserve you in happiness for the future. And so in truth all did pray, with one voice... After lunch the image was set in the appointed place, where it was not three hours before some wax images were presented to it, and torches and other ex-votos, so I believe that in a short time a great devotion will attach to it, and of all this good your excellency will have been the cause."[10]

Francesco Gonzaga thus would return to Mantua to find the altarpiece made to celebrate his victory already had a devoted following among all classes of the Mantuan people.

Ironically, the *Madonna of Victory* was carried off to France in 1797 after Napoleon's successes in Italy. It now stands in the Louvre Museum, isolated from its original context. Like other great works that have found their way to museums, this one has an individual history, in this case one of military victory, devotion by a patron, the vision of a mystic priest, anti-Semitism, a public parade at its installation, and the cult devotion among the people after it arrived at its final location. We are fortunate the importance of Mantegna's position meant letters exchanged at the court of Mantua recorded the history of this still-famous work. The *Madonna of Victory* has a particularly rich history, but every work of art in a museum could tell a story if we only knew it.

Because of the military subject, the festive occasion, and the public setting (which called for a work of popular appeal), the *Madonna of Victory* is quite colourful and dynamic. Mantegna could change his modes of painting, and he was flexible when the circumstances of the commissions called for different kinds of painting. For example, another mature altarpiece made for a specific religious order shows Mantegna changing his style to suit the site and patrons. By 1497 Mantegna had painted an altarpiece for the church of Santa Maria in Organo in Verona (Fig. 65). The religious order, the Olivetans, followed the monastic rules of Saint Benedict, who is shown in a white robe on the right. He is worshipping the Madonna and Child, along with Saint John the Baptist (pointing), Saint Jerome (holding a model of the church), and Saint Gregory on the left behind John. The fruit trees and the singing angels on the bottom add festive notes to the picture, but otherwise the painting is consciously subdued and sober in design and colouring. The figures are more static than in the *Madonna of Victory*, more in keeping with the style expected for a monastic church. The conservatism of the composition extends to the use of perspective, as the Virgin and Child are not seen in foreshortening from below, but appear as if seen straight on; this lends them the formal, timeless look of an icon. Thus, Mantegna bends the rules of perspective and creates a relatively subdued work appropriate for the monastic setting of the altarpiece.

The documentary evidence shows Mantegna, who was temporarily released by the Gonzaga in order to work in nearby Verona, was treated very well by his hosts at the monastery. The master in charge of the new architecture and decoration of the church, Fra Giovanni da Verona, gave Mantegna some pheasant, partridge, and thrush in October 1496. In November, Verona provided him with some thrushes and hares, and soon thereafter gave him some olives. Clearly the painting was appreciated, and the Olivetans knew they had the work of a leading master adorning their church. This altarpiece presents the kind of mystical vision of saints that was well appreciated at the time. In some verses published in 1499, an admirer of his art, Panfilo Sassi, described a painting by Mantegna in which Mary seemed so real, he somewhat fancifully wrote, if the Holy Spirit descended to the image a

70. *Christ the Redeemer*, 1493.
Tempera on canvas, 55 x 43 cm.
Museo Civico, Correggio.

71. *Madonna and Child*,
c. 1470-1480.
Tempera on canvas, 43 x 32 cm.
Gemäldegalerie, Berlin.

72. *Madonna and Child*, c. 1490.
Tempera on canvas, 43 x 31 cm.
Accademia Carrara, Bergamo.

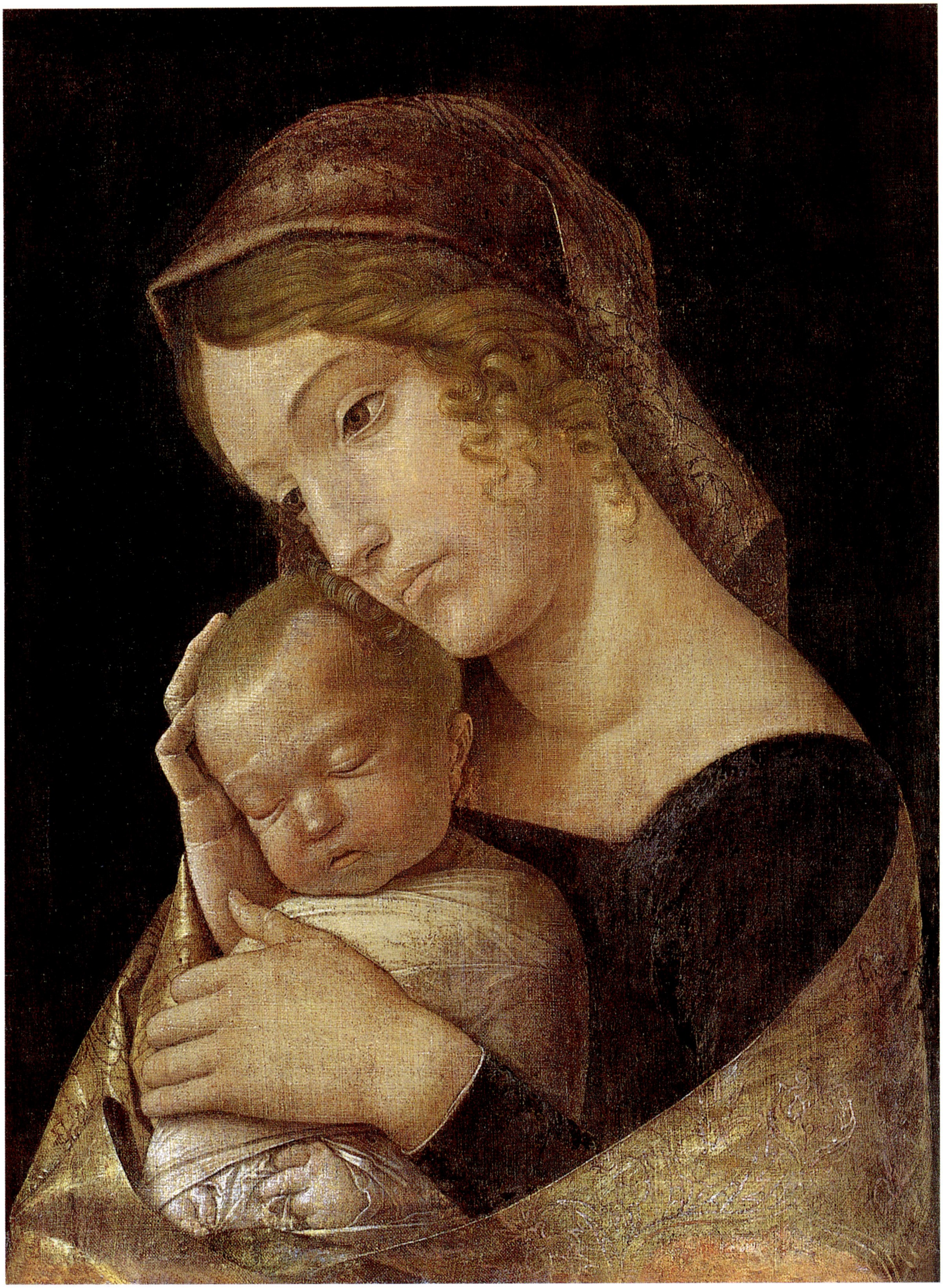

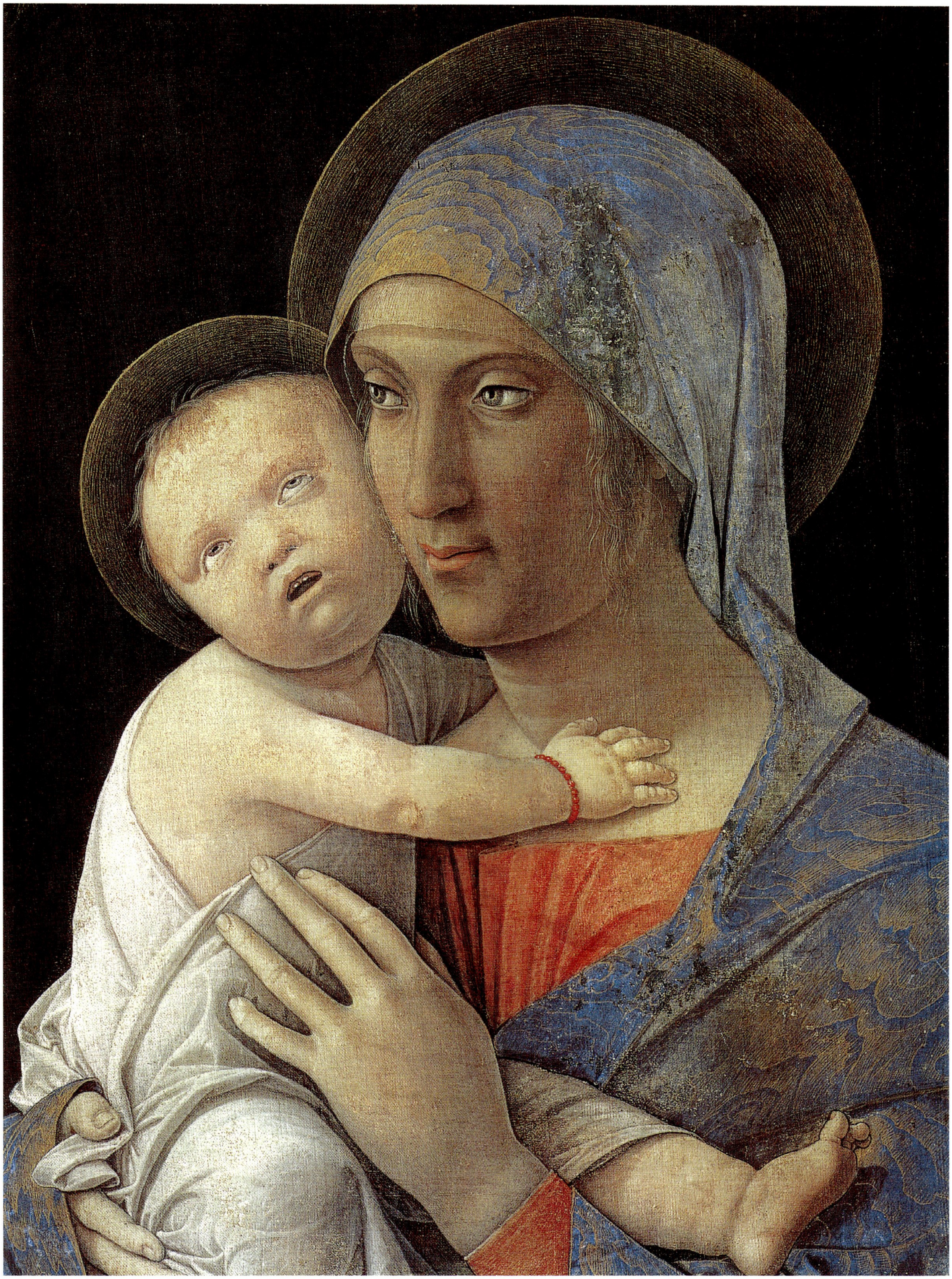

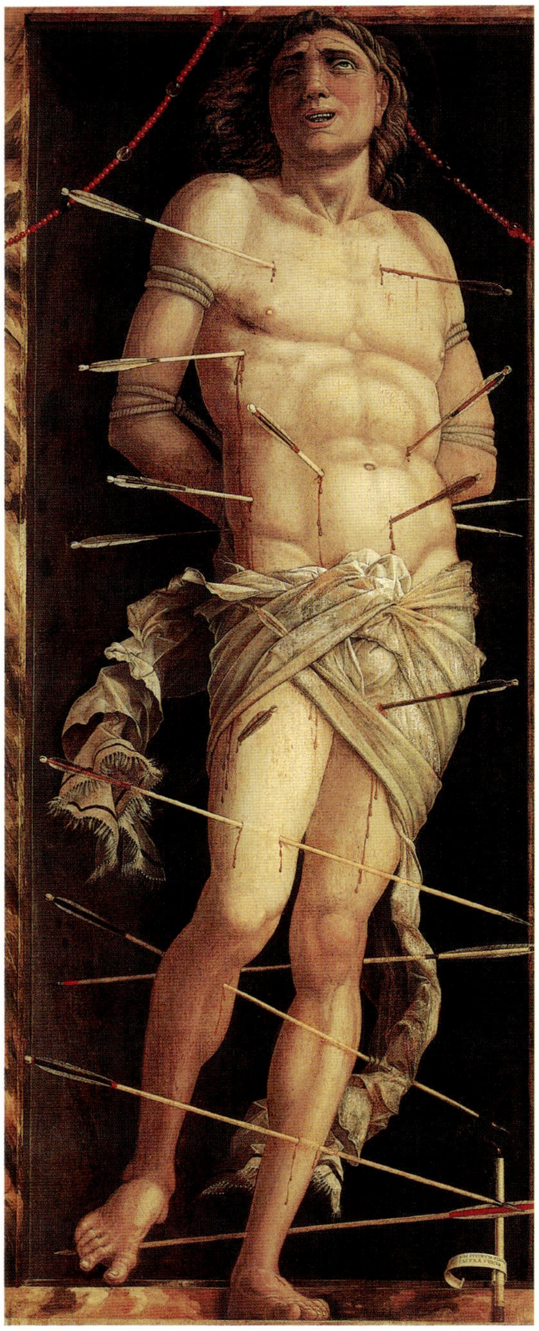

second birth of Christ might ensue! The altarpiece for the Olivetan church, embodying Mantegna's realistic manner, is the kind of work which aroused among contemporary viewers the intense, mystical feeling they were confronting the Virgin and saints as if in the flesh and blood.

The desire for immediacy and intensity was a mark of the times, and was a general feature of fifteenth-century European culture, continuing a trend that had it origins in the later Middle Ages. Many philosophers came to embrace nominalism, holding that material facts precede mere verbal constructions or conceptualisations, and other aspects of scientific investigation, such as the study of the human body, were all part of this same broad trend towards particularisation and a new realistic attitude. This trend had its secular side, but also fused with religious devotion. For his part, Mantegna embraced a relative realism of style, and in subject matter many of his religious works are deeply rooted in the late medieval trend in art toward devotion to the Passion of Christ. The particular emphasis on Christ was part of an even more widespread, popular devotionalism that comprised the spread of lay prayer groups and organised pilgrimages, the movement coming at a time when holy relics were increasingly venerated. The trend was ever more toward direct, emotional contact with the divine or saintly, taking the form of intense, direct piety.

There was a literary and an artistic side to the empathy with the suffering and death of Christ. There had been throughout the Middle Ages an attempt to share Christ's pain and try to understand the agony he experienced at the time of his Passion. In the fifteenth century in both Italy and the north of Europe there was an expansion and a popularisation of this practice. This movement was certainly abetted by the publication of books that encouraged intense devotionalism. The most famous of these was written by the German author Thomas à Kempis, who's *Imitation of Christ* became a best-seller all across Europe, its sentiments repeated in sermons and private conversations across national borders and social classes. Kempis advised the reader to leave aside the mundane world, and concentrate on feeling a union with Christ, attempting to understand his words and deeds. This close communion with the divine was intensely personal and subjective, rather different from formal worship in church and unlike the traditional practice of praying to an intercessory saint.

Today we can hardly imagine the intensity of religious life that still existed in the fifteenth century. Preachers moved great crowds to tears, and men, women, and children saw visions and believed in miracles. A fervent few engaged in self-flagellation, and others expected the momentary end of the world. Many saw statues move and could hear paintings speak to them. This widespread intensity of devotion and faith led not only to the experiencing of visions, but also to the strong need to see vivid images before one's eyes.

What better way to understand and sympathise with Jesus than to see the suffering during his arrest, torment, and death by crucifixion? Sometimes this close communion occurred at what we might call street theatre, or Passion plays that took place in the churches and piazzas of Italy. In this theatre, actors would play Christ and other New Testament figures, giving a vivid and palpable dramatisation of Christ's arrest, torture, and death, the Passion of Christ brought before the very eyes of fifteenth-century Christians. This thirst for visualisation of Christ's life frequently found expression in sculpture and painting, especially in smaller paintings owned by private citizens and utilised for personal, devotional worship. Mantegna's devotional images, represented in great naturalism and with the figures placed close to the viewer, catered to this need to have the holy

73. *St Sebastian*, c. 1495-1505.
Tempera on canvas, 210 x 91 cm.
Galleria Franchetti, Ca d'Oro, Venice.

74. *St Sebastian*, c. 1475-1485.
Tempera on canvas, 275 x 142 cm.
Musée du Louvre, Paris.

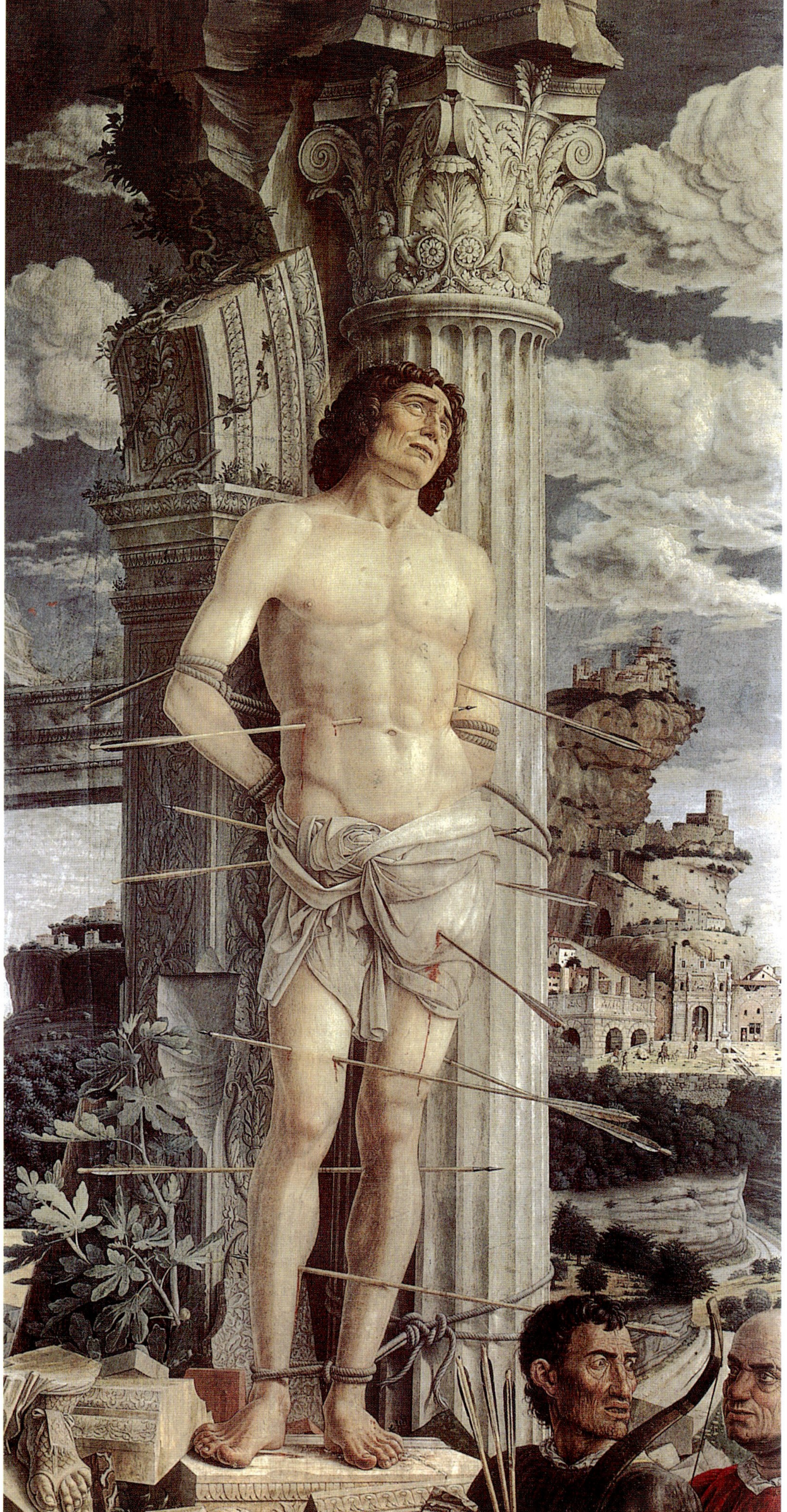

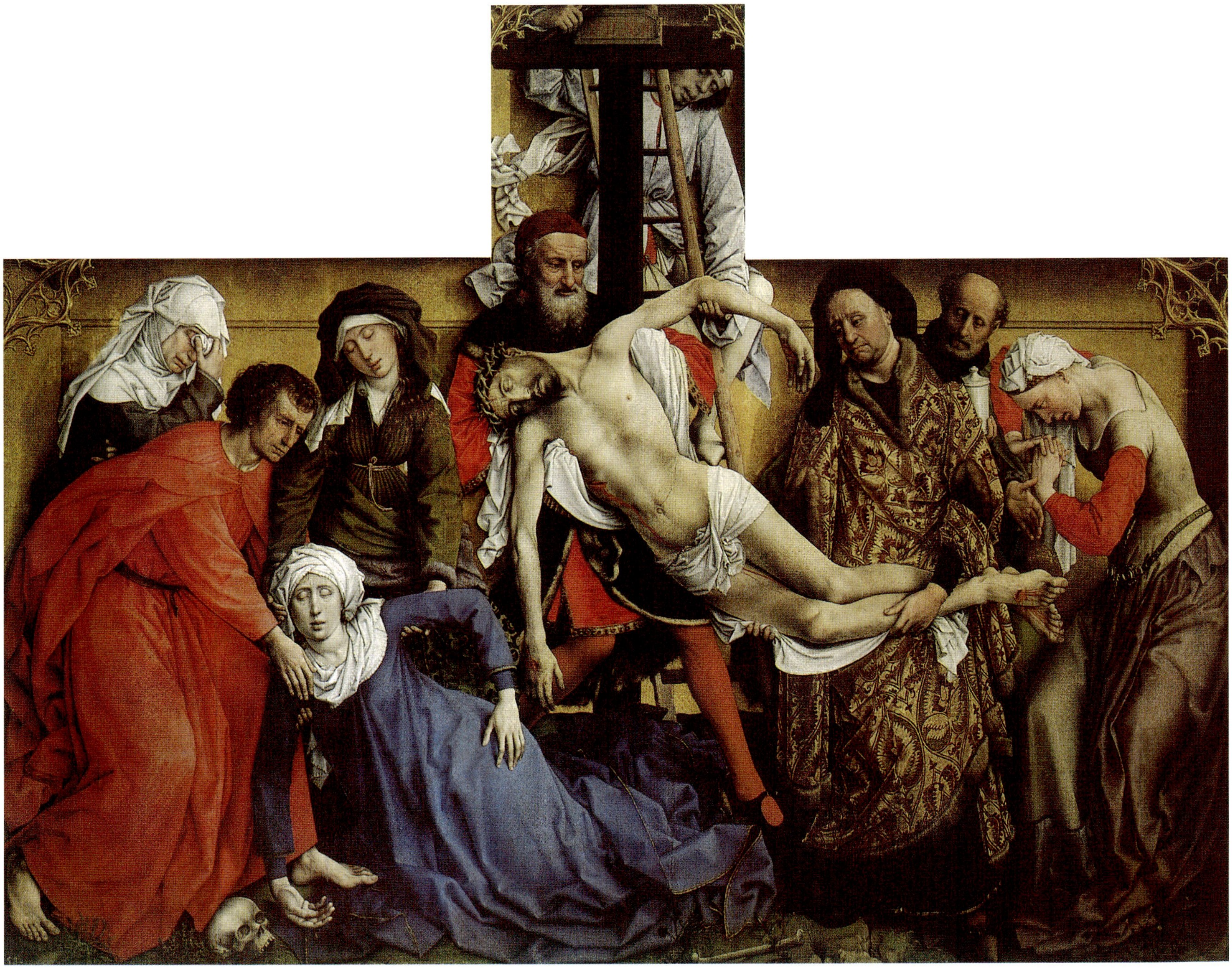

75. Rogier van der Weyden, *Deposition from the Cross*, c. 1435. Oil on panel, 220 x 262 cm. Museo del Prado, Madrid.

seem to appear before the devoted faithful. We have noted people of the fifteenth-century, because of their growing interest in the natural world, were tending to favour realism in art. This was reinforced by the religious considerations discussed here, also leading to the trend toward detailed verism in art. Mantegna's paintings, like those of many of his Early Renaissance contemporaries in painting, catered to both the sacred and the secular desires of his viewers. This tendency was also very strong in the north of Europe, where artists such as Hugo van der Goes and Petrus Christus painted minute and detailed images of the suffering Christ and mourners (Fig. 76). Works from the hand of the Netherlandish painter Rogier van der Weyden were in Italy by the middle of the century; his style can be seen in his highly polished and theatrical *Deposition from the Cross* (Fig. 75). To any worshipper interested in experiencing the feeling of the Holy, how effective these Netherlandish works must have been, with their depiction of individual features such as hair, veins, and brilliant translucent tears that stream down the faces of mourners. Mantegna knew such works, and their detailed quality and vivid realism are reflected in his works of all types, but especially in his Passion images. Mantegna was just one of the *Quattrocento* Italian artists to borrow heavily in his Passion

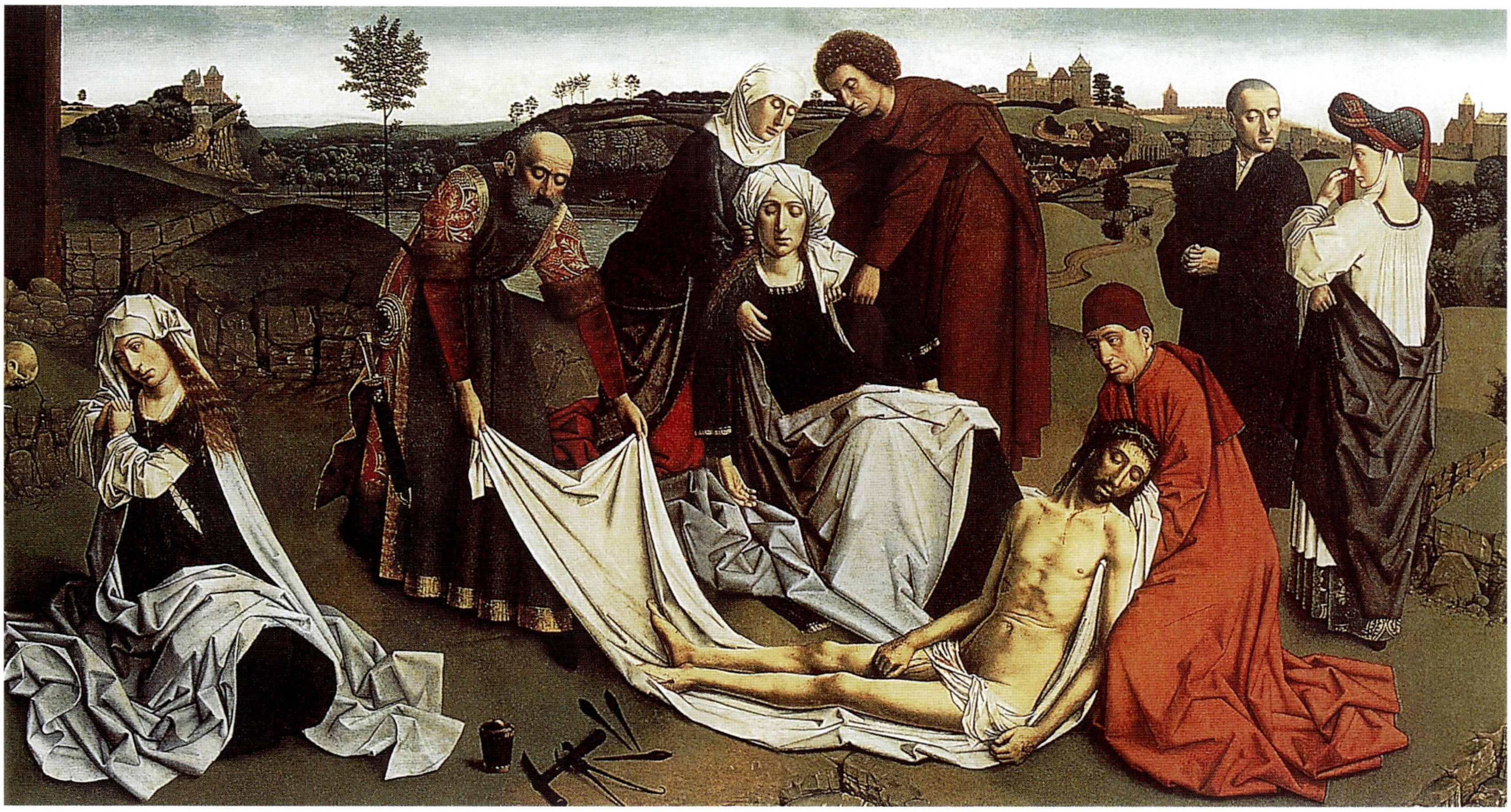

imagery from art of the northern Europeans. Painters like the Ferrarese Ercole de' Roberti and the Venetian Carlo Crivelli shared with him a common visual culture that combined a dry realism with a painful, detailed evocation of the death and suffering of Christ.

A good example in Mantegna's oeuvre of this manner of Passion imagery is his *Ecce Homo*, now in the Musée Jacquemart-André in Paris (Fig. 60). The title, meaning "Behold the Man," expresses the words Pontius Pilate used when he presented Jesus to the crowd to have them decide whether or not to crucify him. In the painting, Christ is held by two torturers, their ugliness symbolising their moral corruption; his beauty contrasts with the assailants. Mantegna convincingly depicts the painful red stripes from the whips and the puncturing of his skin by the thorns from the mocking crown. On one side is an inscription saying "Crucify him. Crucify, take him away, crucify him." The practice of contrasting the comely Christian hero with ugly torturers was especially widespread in the art of northern Europe, and Mantegna presents such a dramatic and meaningful contrast in this painting. The man on the left has an inscription in pseudo-Hebrew on his cap. This latter "inscription" is a

76. Petrus Christus, *Lamentation*, c. 1448.
Oil on panel, 101 x 192.1 cm.
Musées Royaux des Beaux-Arts, Brussels.

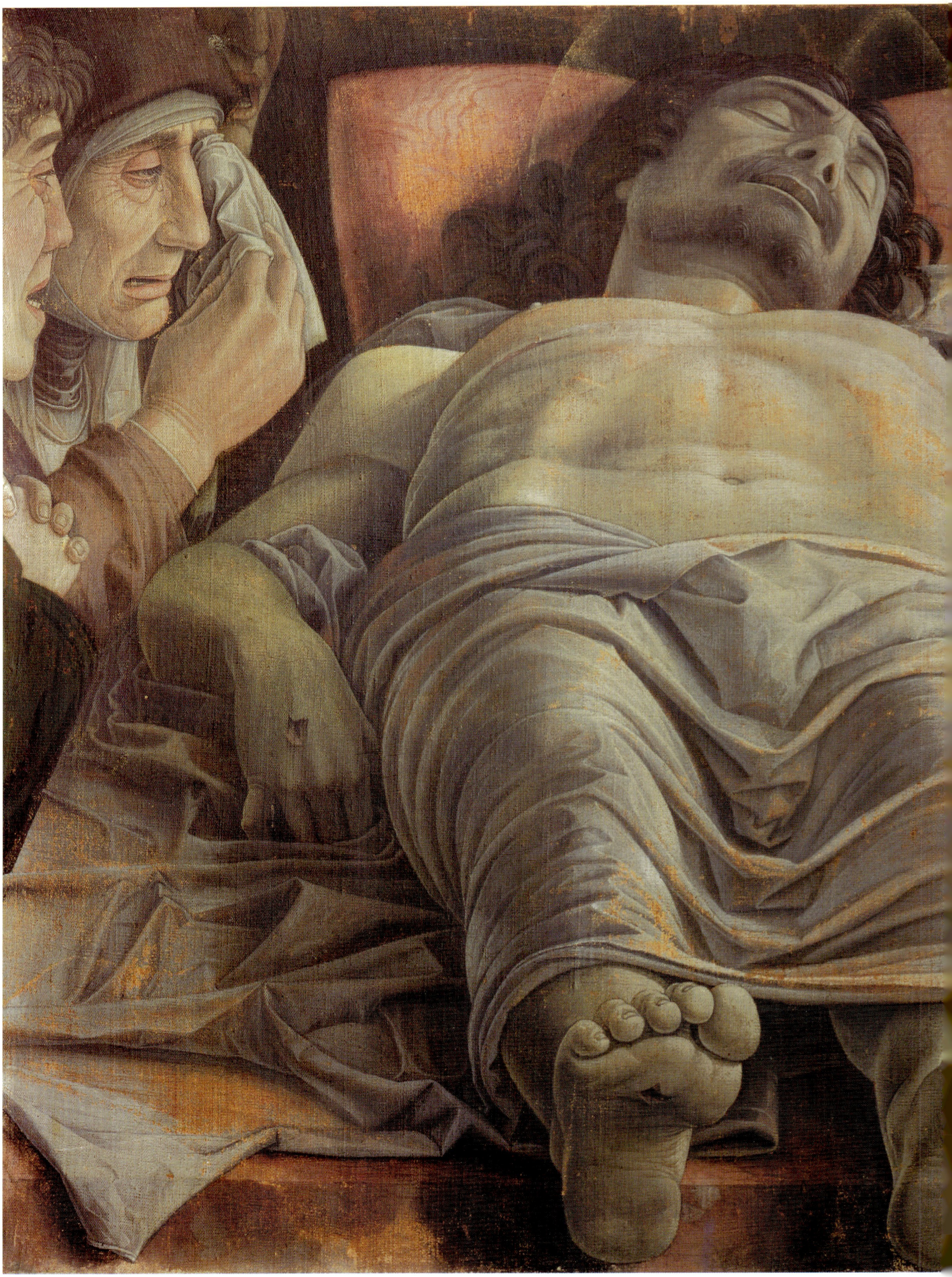

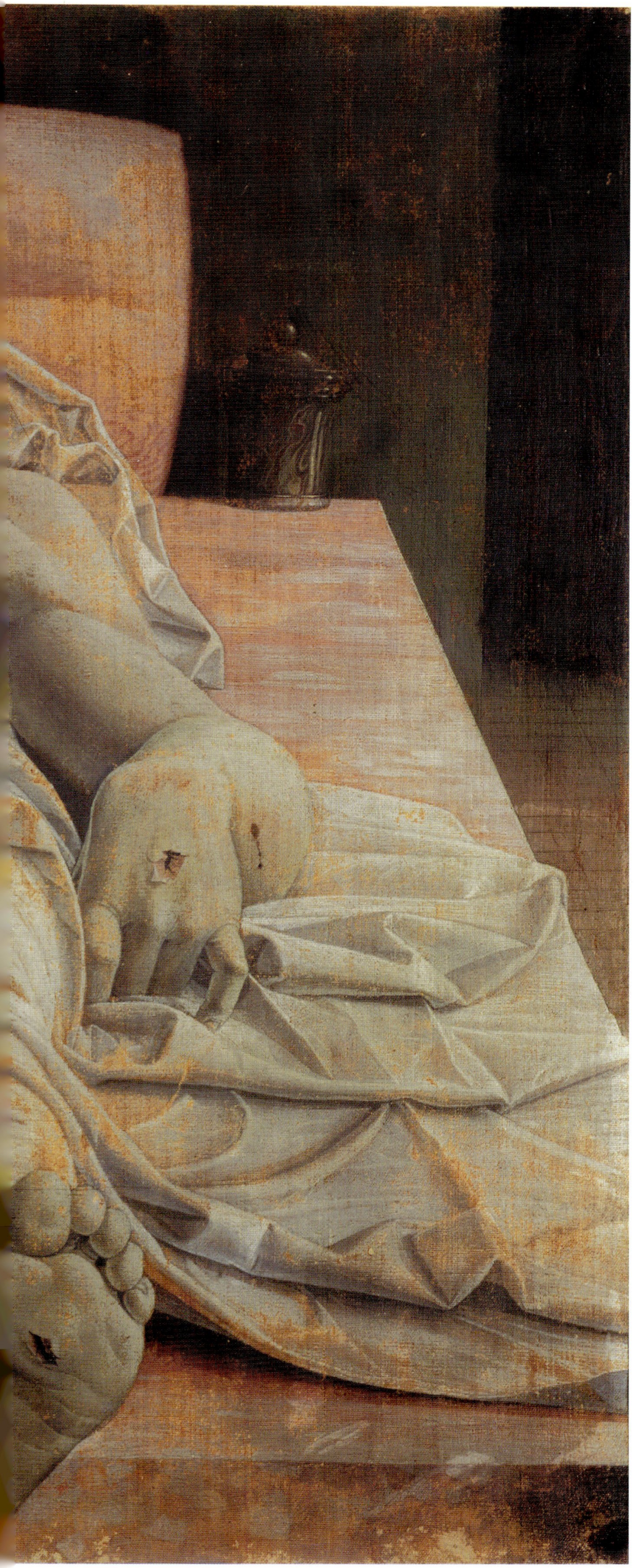

77. *The Lamentation over the Dead Christ*, c. 1490.
Tempera on canvas, 68 x 81 cm.
Pinacoteca di Brera, Milan.

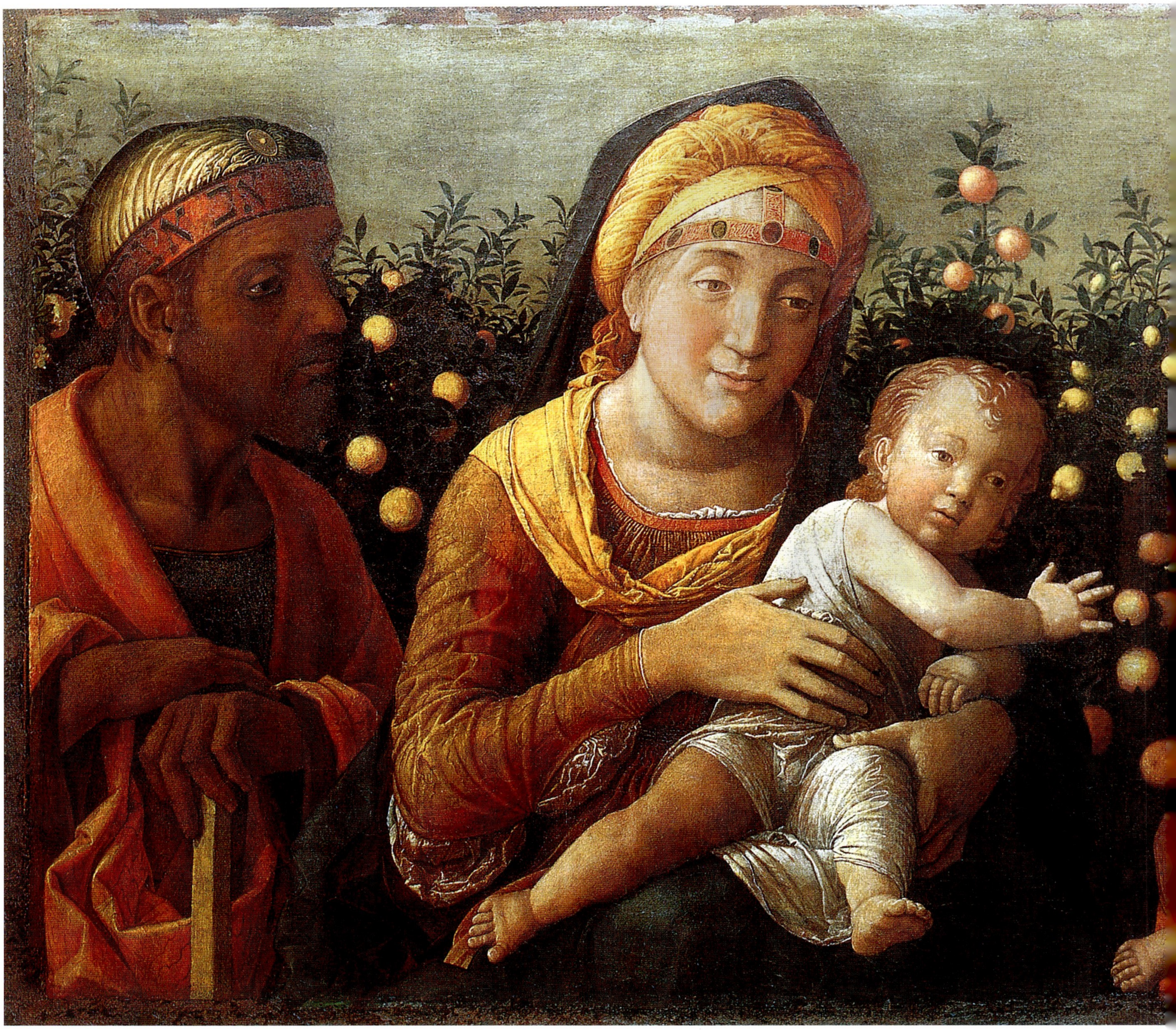

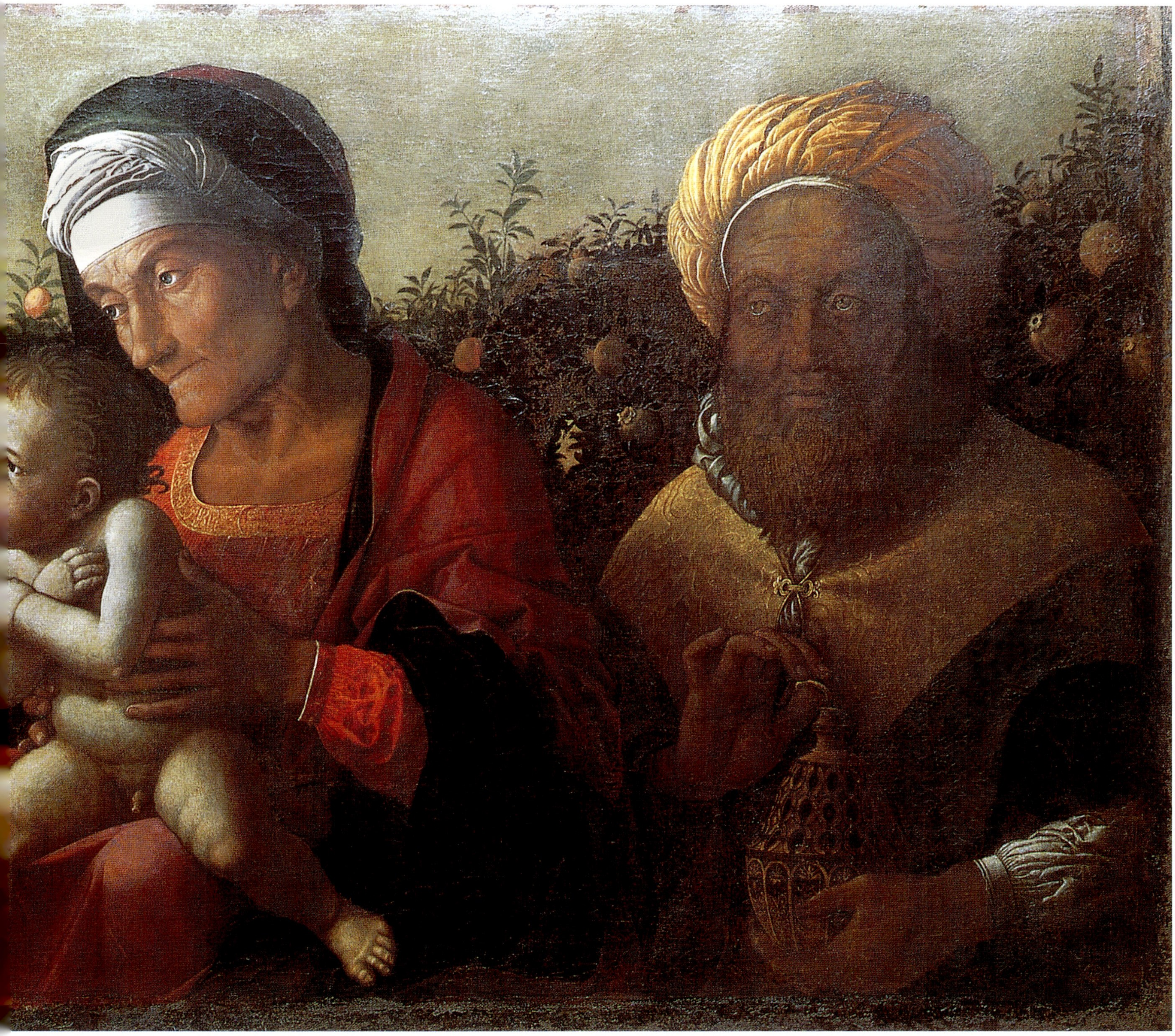

78. *The Families of Christ and St John the Baptist*, c. 1500-1505.
Tempera on canvas, 40 x 169 cm.
Church of Sant' Andrea, Mantua.

reminder of one of the unfortunate aspects of the experiencing of Passion imagery and literature of the time. It frequently happened after a sermon during Lent or after a Passion play that crowds went through the Jewish areas of the towns and cities of Europe (including Italy), damaging property and inflicting personal injuries as well. Mantegna's *Ecce Homo* conveys, in its caricatured brutality and in the inflammatory inscriptions above, some of the crudity and popular sensibility of Passion theatre or popular preaching of the time. The compelling desire of fifteenth -century people to imagine as vividly as possible the presence of Christ also finds expression in Mantegna's *Christ the Redeemer*, painted in the 1490s (Fig. 70). Jesus appears with no wounds, but has an intensely sad face and is close to the frame confronting the viewer. An inscription says in Latin "Do not fear, it is I," and another (on the left) states "Mortify yourselves before this effigy of my face". Yet another inscription states this was a gift from Mantegna; *Christ the Redeemer* is a heartfelt, personal image of Christ made by Mantegna to honour an unknown recipient, who was expected to feel mortification before the picture. Here, as in so many of his works, Mantegna's makes an innovative use of canvas support and distemper paint. Distemper technique, the binding of pigments in animal glues, produces more uniform and less glossy results than egg tempera or oil; the use of distemper helped him achieve a dry naturalism in his artistry, with an effect closer to fresco technique.

The best preserved of the Passion images by Mantegna is his *Man of Sorrows* in Copenhagen (Fig. 79). Many of Mantegna's works have been over-cleaned by restorers in recent centuries, removing the final magical glazing and varnishes the master put there. Even without over-cleaning, years of blistering, abrasion, and cracking have wrought great destruction to many fifteenth-century paintings, Mantegna's included. This well-preserved work has not undergone such damage. Here Mantegna presents the Body of Christ, which is celebrated in the mystery of the Eucharist at the Mass. He is shown with an agonised face as if still alive, although the story of the Crucifixion is indicated on the upper right by the presence of the three crosses atop Golgotha. This intensely pious image presents the wounds in Christ's hands and side, his death mourned by two angels. The image is especially dramatic, with a glorious sunset behind and active, complicated drapery folds echoing the emotional subject matter. The overall effect is realistic, almost illusionistic, in its immediacy.

Much of Mantegna's religious imagery is dramatic and even violent, yet there was also a gentler side to his sacred art. It was more and more the custom throughout the course of the Renaissance to keep religious images in one's private residence, especially in bedrooms. Mantegna's smaller religious paintings, such as his half-length narratives of the childhood of Christ, responded to this growing demand for such art (cf. Fig. 63). Especially popular for personal devotions were Madonna and Child paintings. Whereas earlier in the Middle Ages Christ was represented as a king, with crown and sceptre and long robes, in the Renaissance the Christ Child was humanised, and he appeared as a tender infant. Mantegna depicted a humanised, down-to-earth Christ in close emotional union with his mother, sometimes even cheek-to-cheek (Figs. 68 and 72). We might imagine these over the beds or private altars of Mantegna's patrons, an appealing and intimate representation of Christ and his mother, shown in a way Renaissance viewers appreciated: real and believable. Some critics have asserted Mantegna was a cold antiquarian, but works such as this show his warm, human side. Mantegna's mature style is epitomised in a large image of *Saint Sebastian*, now in the Louvre (Fig. 74), a working dating to the 1480s. Unlike his early version of this subject, which is tense and wiry, and replete with details (Fig. 24), this later work includes a much more broadly proportioned, heroic saint, whose physical beauty contrasts to the ugliness of the soldiers shown on the lower

79. *The Man of Sorrows*, c. 1490-1500. Tempera on panel, 78 x 48 cm. Statens Museum for Kunst, Copenhagen.

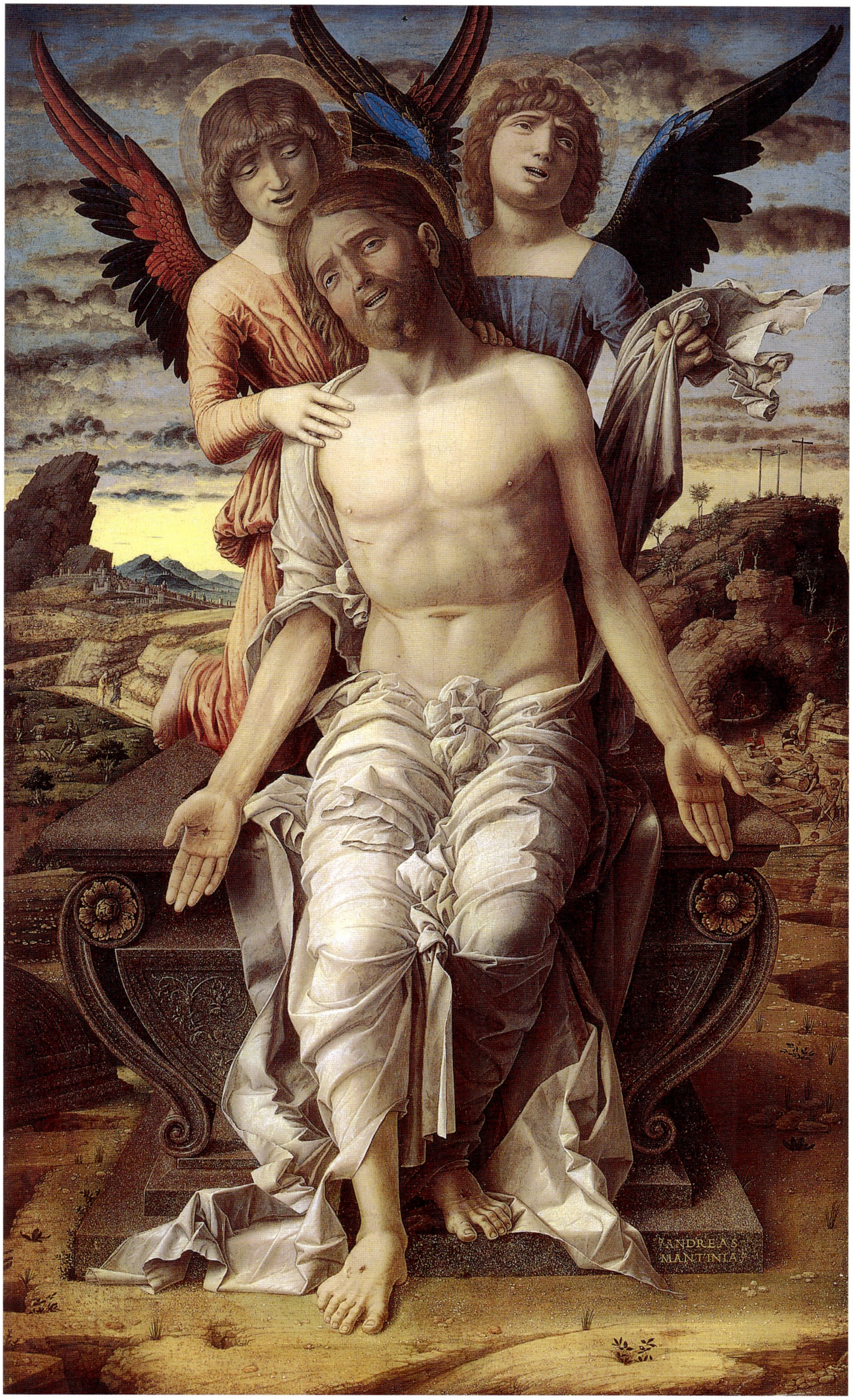
ANDREAS
MANTINIA

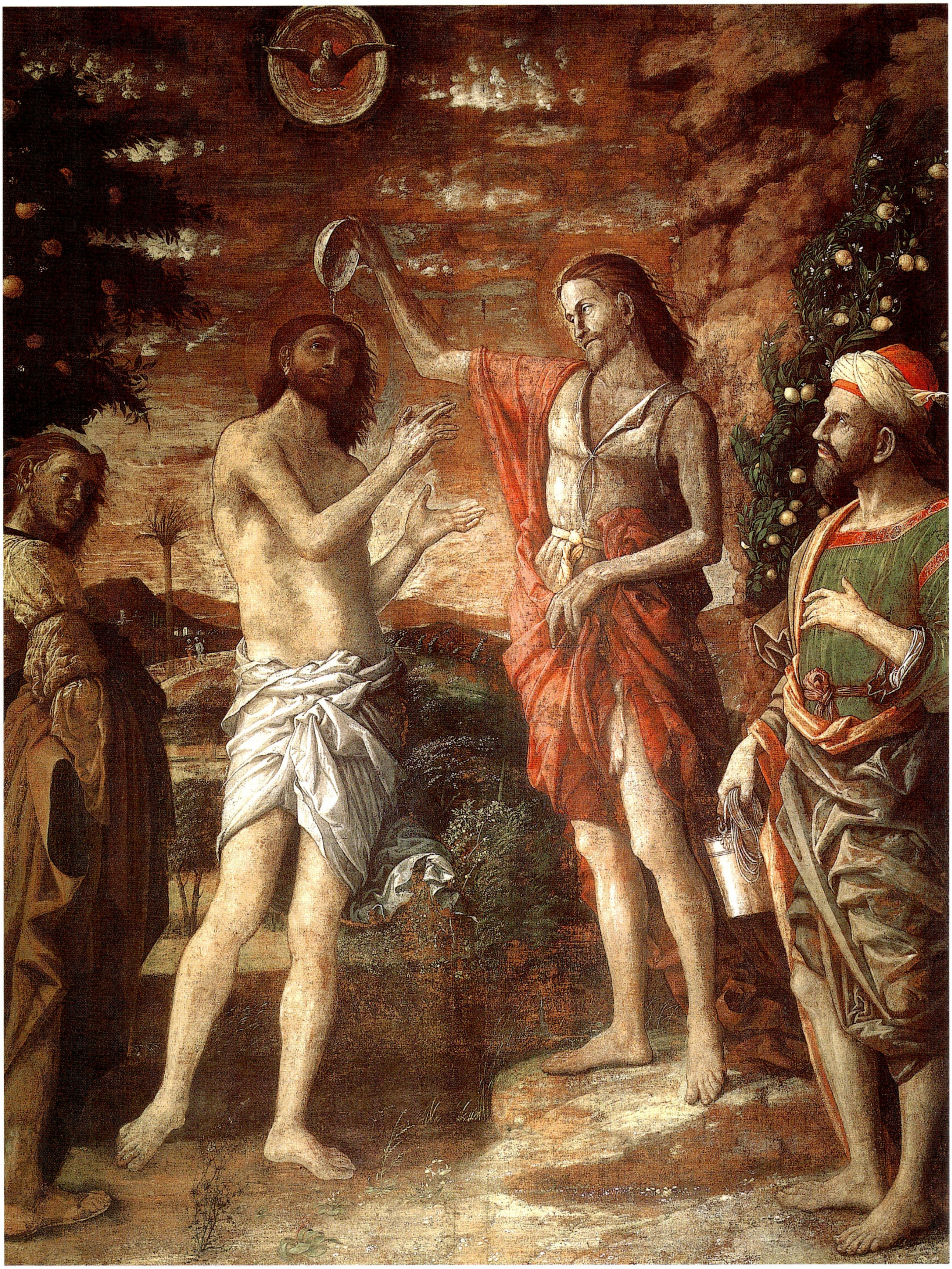

right. The handsome saint's body is hardly marred by arrows. Following the Renaissance ideal of beauty as a mirror of moral character, Sebastian's handsome face and athletic body stand in distinction from the vulgar soldiers who are cut off by the frame and look away from the suffering saint. This version of the subject comprises a broad mass of classical ruins, which echo the solidity of the saint, and a distant view of a ruined, ancient hill city is well calculated to appeal to humanistic viewers who would delight in recognising such particulars as the variant copy of the Arch of Constantine. Compared to the more emotional saint in the early version now in Vienna, this saint suffers his torture in a state of philosophical calm.

As he grew older, Mantegna's thoughts increasingly turned to death and future salvation. This is attested by two extraordinary works which remained in his collection at the time of his death, perhaps indicating they were painted by him in his later years to be used for his own private devotion and prayer. One of them is a *Saint Sebastian*, now in the Ca' d'Oro Museum in Venice (Fig. 73); the other is a *Dead Christ* (Fig. 77). The *Saint Sebastian* is the third extant work of this subject Mantegna painted. The first, and earliest, was replete with humanistic references such as sculpture fragments and a Greek inscription, and represented a tortured, gaunt saint (Fig. 24). The second version in the Louvre we have just seen (Fig. 74), and includes a broad view of figures and landscape. This latest final version, though, concentrates intensely on Sebastian, who looks up imploringly to Heaven, his body riddled with arrows (Fig. 73). Of all the exuberant decorative flourishes that Mantegna learned at the workshop of Squarcione in Padua, there remains here only the bright red beads at the top. Otherwise, the painting has little charm, and the artist concentrates instead on expressing Sebastian's passion and suffering. Mantegna's own growing consciousness of the afterlife and of salvation is expressed in a powerful motif, a recently extinguished candle on the lower right, accompanied by the inscription: "Nothing is lasting except the divine; all else is smoke." This saint is posed in an unstable and fervent manner. We have few written statements by Mantegna concerning his religious beliefs, but the visual evidence from a work such as this, especially if he made it for himself, indicates his own piety and intense Christianity. Since he asked in his will that Bishop Ludovico Gonzaga (son of the Ludovico of the *Camera Picta*) receive the work is evidence that a taste for such striking naturalism and intense piety was shared by his patrons. A nearly monochromatic vision of Jesus mourned by three figures was in Mantegna's collection at the time of his death; this *Dead Christ* includes Saint John, Mary, and Mary Magdalene (Fig. 77). His inventory of 1506 referred to a work fitting this description, presumably the very same picture, and it ended up in Gonzaga collections later in the century. This is a searing image of Christ laid out on his funeral slab, an intense vision of Christ's suffering and death. The wounds in his hands are like torn paper, as is the spear gash in his side. Mantegna has played with the rules of perspective here, making the head large; it should be much smaller than the feet because the figure is strongly foreshortened. To make the work in proper perspective would have made the face of Christ too small to elicit strong empathy from the viewer. This is a brutal and dramatic image, completely lacking in any particular beauty, and the murky, monochromatic, golden-brown colouring helps to move this painting to another realm of passion and religious fervour. The viewers would sympathise with the sorrowful Mary, John, and Mary Magdalene who appear in truncated form on the left, pouring out their grief in open mourning.

An important manifestation of Mantegna's personal piety in his later years was his plan for his family chapel and tomb. It was common during the Renaissance to plan one's own tomb well in advance even of serious illness, and artists were especially fortunate in that they could plan and design their

80. *The Baptism of Christ*,
c. 1500-1505.
Tempera on canvas,
228 x 175 cm.
Church of Sant' Andrea, Mantua.

own funerary decorations, although only highly successful artists could afford elaborate tombs. In the sixteenth century, the Florentine artist Michelangelo and the Venetian painter Titian made works of art for their own tombs. Mantegna planned an elaborate funerary chapel for himself and his family, which still exists and includes some work from his own hand. Andrea Mantegna died on 13 September 1506, but two years earlier he had already made provisions for the character of his final resting place. In 1504 Mantegna applied for the right to turn an empty chapel on the left side of the great Mantuan church of San Andrea into his family chapel. A local mason and a sculptor accompanied Mantegna as witnesses as he appeared before the church council and was granted permission to adorn the chapel. He even bought the plot of land just outside the window of the chapel, and legal documents state, like a good painter, he did so to make sure no one built any structure too close to the church and blocked the light. The land would also serve as the place of his family's burial ground. He also intended to build a small cell there so he might spend leisure time there in his remaining days as a place of contemplation and retreat. The vision of the aged and infirm artist seated and lost in thought near his place of burial is a touching one.

The bare and unadorned chapel was already dedicated to Saint John the Baptist before Mantegna got control of it, so the paintings he planned for the site included a *Families of Christ and Saint John the Baptist*, representing Saint John along with Mary, Christ, and John's mother, Elizabeth (Fig. 78). This picture was to be grouped in the chapel with a *Baptism of Christ* (Fig. 80) and another work of unknown subject. The two surviving paintings were in Mantegna's studio at the time of his death, but are now placed in the chapel. Although the master probably designed and commenced both paintings, the *Baptism of Christ* is somewhat more crudely painted than the *Families of Christ and Saint John the Baptist* and the former was perhaps finished by Francesco, Mantegna's son. It was also probably the son who set in place the bronze portrait of the father, a moving of image of the master that conveys his determination and intelligence (Fig. 81). The work shows the painter crowned with laurel leaves, the manner of bestowing honour widespread in Roman antiquity. The portrait is attributed by many scholars to Andrea, and it is even possible he was responsible for its casting. He most likely designed the fresco decoration in the chapel, although again Francesco probably executed the scheme in the domed chapel, which included fictive architecture, a great shell over the altar, Virtues (among them Justice), foliage, and the Four Evangelists. The overall appearance recalls the descriptions we have of the Papal chapel Andrea painted by 1490, and if the master did not design this chapel, someone managed to imitate in convincing form Andrea's decorative approach.

Mantegna set aside money to provide for the saying of Mass for his soul and those of other family members in the future. The chapel is a public display of his piety, as well as a monument to his own accomplishments as a man and an artist. As an elaborately decorated family chapel, it glorifies Mantegna, in the tradition of chapels commissioned by leading families. The location is a prestigious one, being in a conspicuous chapel of a major church in Mantua. The artistic qualities of the invention here are also extraordinary, and it is little wonder the priests of San Andrea readily accepted his application to adorn the chapel, for it brought honour to the church. Nor is Mantegna's connection to the Gonzaga court missing in the project. True, he was owed a considerable amount of money by the Gonzaga court at the time of his death. Still, comprised in the fresco decoration is Mantegna's coat-of-arms (Fig. 81) coupled with the Gonzaga's, and included is their motto "*Ab Olympo*," which he also used in his house to demonstrate his allegiance to his patrons. Even in death and in a religious context, Mantegna expressed his worldly loyalty to the Gonzaga court.

81. *Portrait of Andrea Mantegna*,
c. 1480-1485.
Bronze, h: 47 cm.
Church of Sant'Andrea, Mantua.

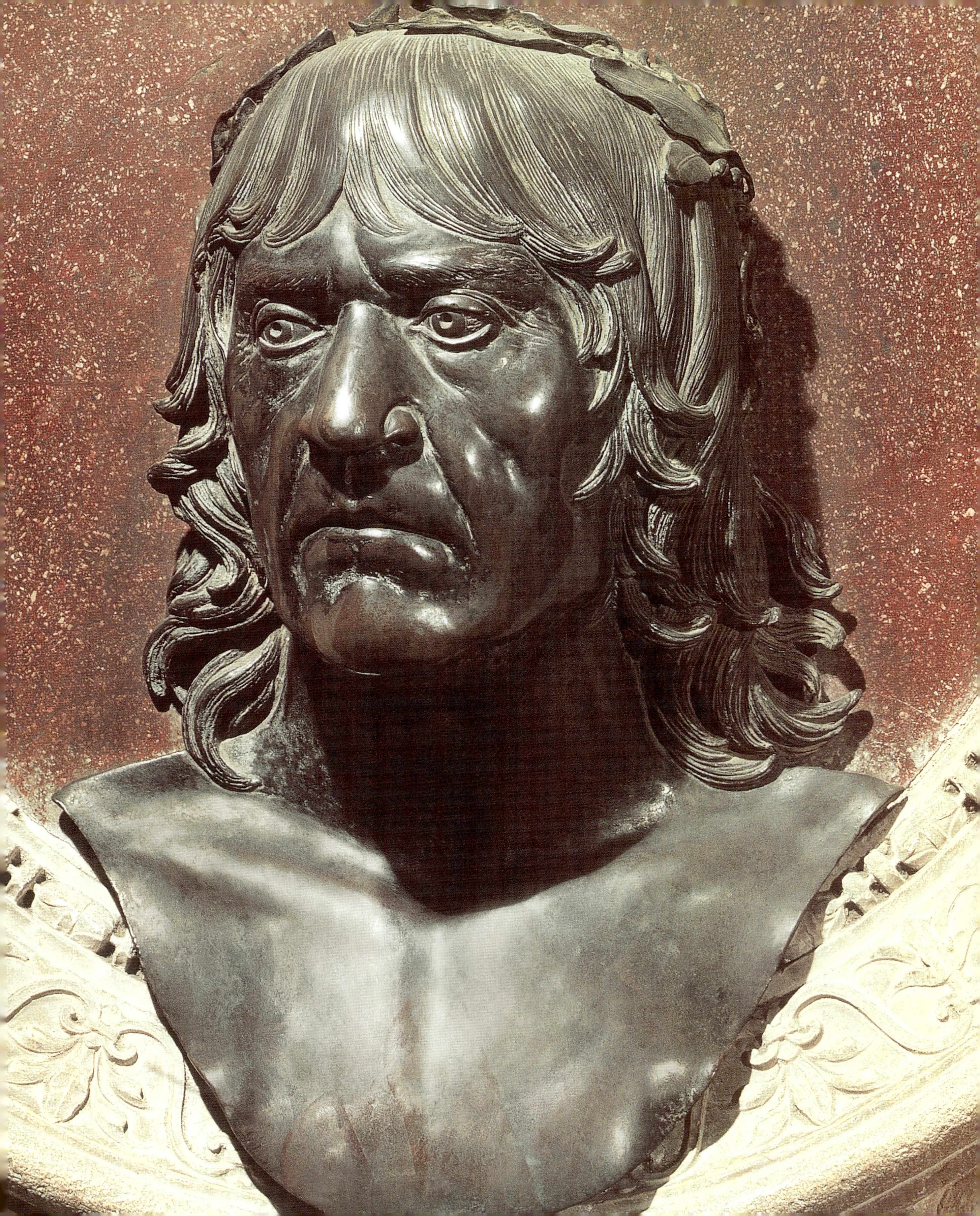

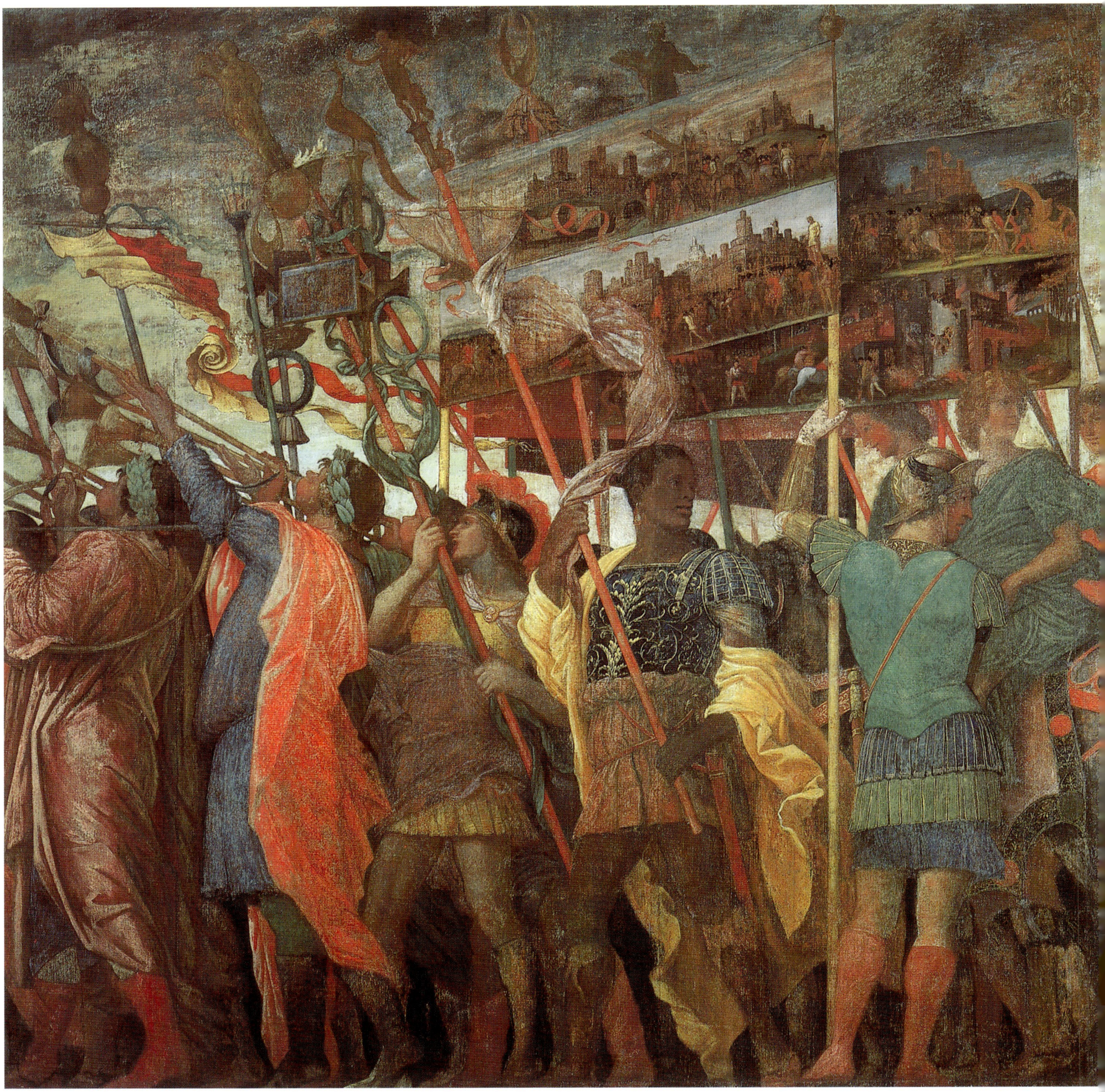

The "Triumphs of Caesar" and Other Visions of Antiquity

Mantegna's deep attachment to classical antiquity and his close relationship to contemporary humanists are illustrated in a remarkable record written in 1464 telling of his presence in a boating party on Lake Garda, near Mantua. The members of the party were on a field trip to study classical antiquities which lay in ruin on the islands and the nearby shores and fields. The author of the account, Felice Feliciano, was a humanist and loved in particular to transcribe and study Roman inscriptions, an activity he engaged in while visiting the shores of Lake Garda. Also on the trip were two others, Samuele da Tradate, who was a painter active in Mantua and a dilettante in humanistic learning, and Giovanni from Padua, an engineer and a contributor to Ludovico Gonzaga's building efforts in Mantua. Felice wrote:

> "Starting out together, with Andrea Mantegna the Paduan, incomparable friend, Samuel de Tradate, and myself Felicano of Verona, for the sake of relaxing our thoughts, we came from a field by way of Lake Garda to greenswards like heavenly gardens in the most delicious dwelling places of the Muses... There we saw a number of remains of antiquity, and first, on the island of the monks, one with highly ornamental letters on a marble pillar."[11]

On the following day, the company set out for farther sites on the shores of the lake, the trip taking on more and more of a festive mood:

> "Under the rule of the merry man Samuel de Tradate, the consuls being the distinguished Andrea Mantegna of Padua and John the Antenorian, with myself in charge with the bright troop following, through dark laurels taking our ease. Having crowned Samuel with myrtle, periwinkle, ivy, and a variety of leaves, with his own participation, and entering the ancient precincts of Saint Dominic, we found a most worthy memorial of Antoninus Pius Germanicus surnamed Sarmaticus. Steering then toward the house of the holy protomartyr [Saint Stephen], not far from the said precincts we found in the portico an excellent memorial of Antoninus Pius the God, nephew of Hadrian the God, resident of that region. Going on then to the house of the first pontiff nearby, we found a huge memorial of Marcus Aurelius the Emperor... Having seen all these things, we circled Lake Garda, the field of Neptune, in a skiff properly packed with carpets and all kinds of comforts, which we strewed with laurels and other noble leaves, while our ruler Samuel played the zither, and celebrated all the while."[12]

Felice then tells us Mantegna and the others thanked the Virgin Mary for having given them good weather and the opportunity to see such splendid antiquities.

No other record of the time demonstrates the high spirits, the devotion, and the romantic attachment of Renaissance men to the Roman past. Mantegna, wearing a crown of laurels, and pretending to be a Roman consul offers an insight into his playful participation in this humanistic field trip, while the

82. *Triumphs of Caesar I*, called *The Standard Bearers*, c. 1484-1499. Tempera on canvas, 266 x 278 cm. Royal collection, Hampton Court Palace, Hampton Court.

study of decaying monuments reveals the genuinely scholarly and serious nature of this outing. Felice nods to Christianity in his mention of the Virgin Mary, but this was a celebration of the classical past, and the pagan god Neptune and the Muses were also happily evoked. For Mantegna and his humanist friends, the ancient past was not something cold, distant, and abstract, but was familiar and part of their everyday lives. Feliciano entitled this brief record "*Jubilatio*," or Jubilation, marking it as an explicitly joyous occasion. It is perhaps difficult for us today to understand this blithe enthusiasm for Roman antiquity. Yet the novelty of the rediscovery of the classical past, the near proximity of the artistic and architectural remains, and the sense of renewal felt during the fifteenth century fired the imagination of those who would bring about a rebirth of classical culture.

This account gives some insight into what it was Mantegna and his friends found most exciting about antiquity. The hedonistic mood of the boating party is most striking; the world of antiquity opened up a realm of pleasures Christian culture had long frowned upon. The mood of joy in Felice's account is the result of this epicurean search for the good life, and the participants thought it appropriate to embellish their journey with richly woven carpets, musical instruments, and "all kinds of comforts." There was also an appreciation shown for the beauties of Nature, recalling the idyllic descriptions of the countryside in Roman pastoral poetry. During this outing, the members of the party also seemed to relish the sense of majesty and power that was embodied in the Roman Imperial inscriptions and memorials to their rulers. All of this for Mantegna and his friends harkened back to a time when the Italian peninsula was the centre of great empire; Italians of the fifteenth century could looked back on classical times as a kind of Golden Age of peace and prosperity. Indeed, as descendants of those who ruled on the Italian peninsula, they were aware the very blood of the ancient Romans flowed in their veins, thus adding to the enthusiasm of their rediscovery of ancient culture. There was more to this connection than ethnic heritage, and Felice's account stresses the rewarding intellectual challenges the classical world offered: inscriptions to copy, history to explore, and a pantheon of gods to worship in reverence that was only partly in mock. In short, the world of antiquity offered to Mantegna and his companions a delightful mixture of sensual and intellectual pleasure. The account of the boating party, which survives by chance and offers just one glimpse into such activity, illustrates in vivid terms Mantegna's life-long engagement with the world of classical culture.

Trips such as these contributed to Mantegna's expertise in classical antiquities. Already when he was studying under Squarcione in Padua, young Mantegna began this accumulation of knowledge about ancient art, copying the plaster casts and drawings after the antiques his master had gathered for the use of his pupils. Mantegna's self-education in this area continued for the rest of his life. Many artists kept copies of antiquities they had seen and studied, and Mantegna surely did the same, for his paintings indicate he had a large collection of drawings or other copies of classical sculptures he utilised in his finished paintings. Mantegna's interest in antiquities and knowledge of the classical past is further attested by Felice Feliciano's dedication of a book of Roman inscription to Mantegna in 1463. This scholar, whom he accompanied on the boating party to Lake Garda, praised Mantegna in his dedication as "a prince of painters, and their only light and comet and a man of great genius... most prompt and partial to the investigation of antiquities." Felice promised to help Mantegna learn even more, and this dedication – a great honour for a painter – indicates the painter's connectedness to the world of humanistic learning, even if Felice's offer to assist him in learning still more indicates the humanist's thought that even intelligent artists were in need of help from scholars of ancient literature.

83. *Arch of Constantine*, Rome, 312-315 A.D. Marble, 21 m. *In situ*.

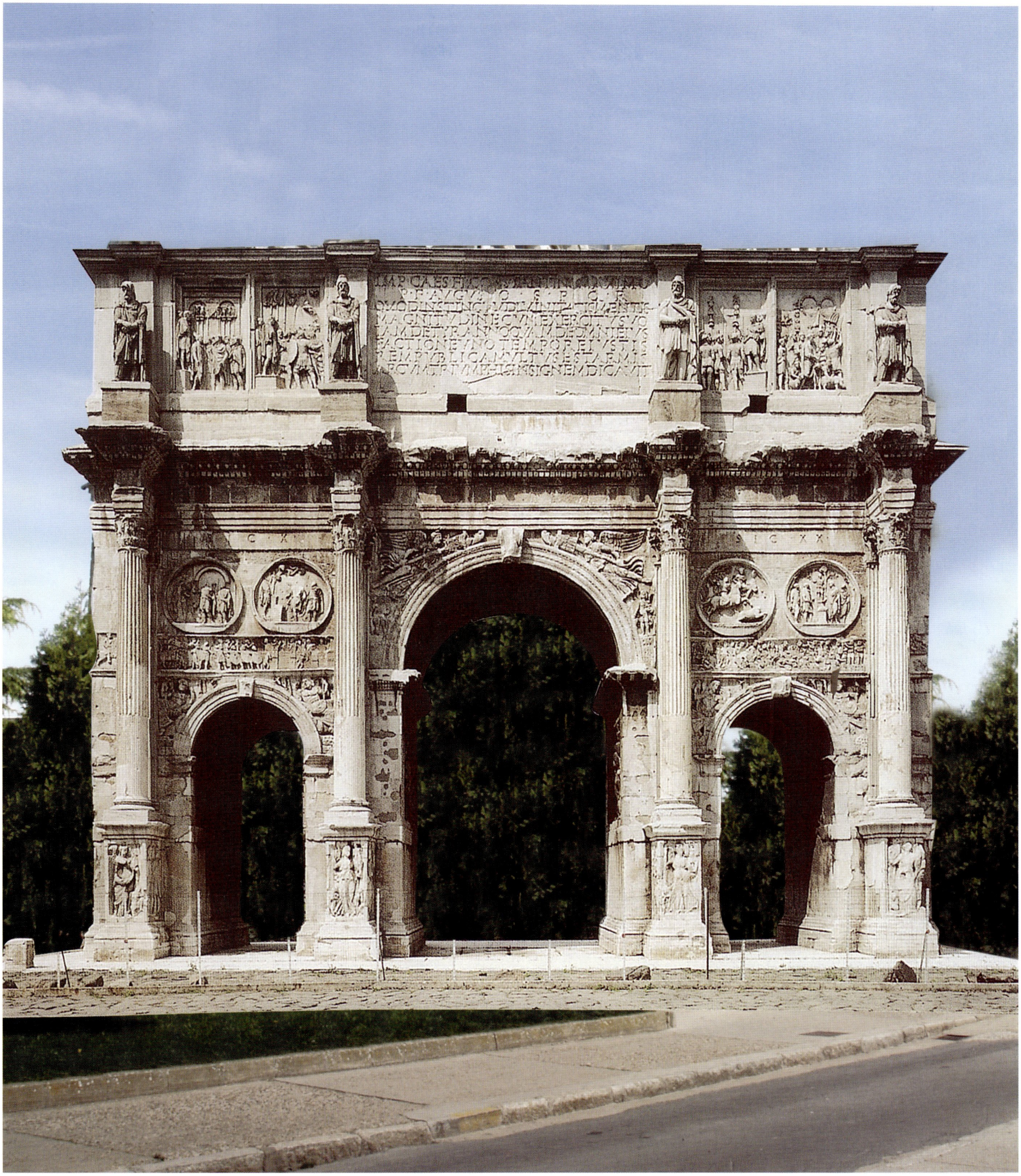

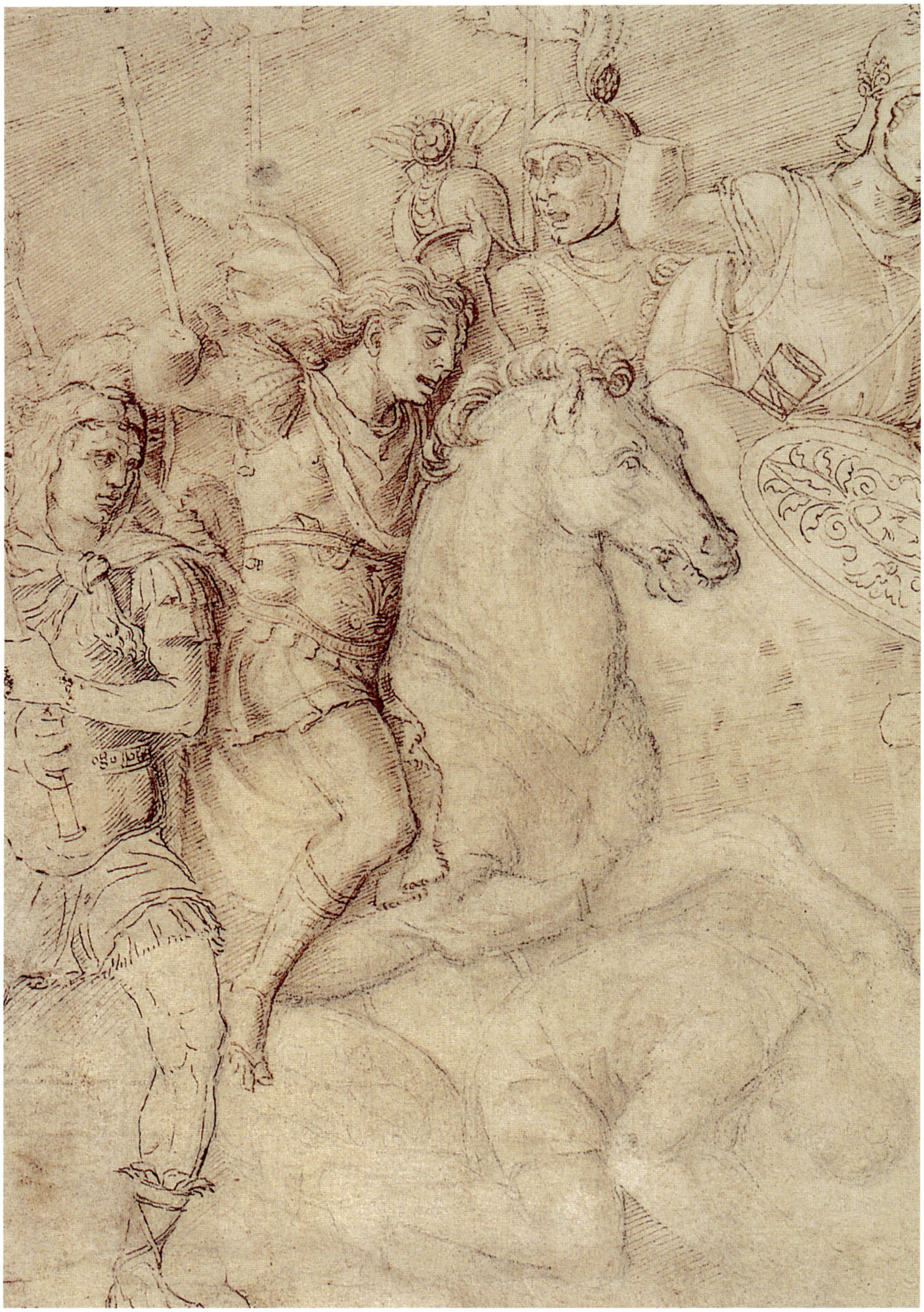

A recorded incident throws light on the mature Mantegna's visual access to antique designs. In 1476 a Florentine banker with artistic interests wrote to Ludovico Gonzaga and asked him if he could borrow a book of drawings containing copies made after classical sculptures of fauns, satyrs, centaurs, and battling men. Ludovico wrote back to the Florentine explaining the architect Luca Fancelli had lent it to Mantegna a while before, but Mantegna had since passed it on to another artist. This anecdote shows Mantegna in relationship to other artists who wanted to trade information on classical antiquities, which were often difficult to travel to see and which were frequently known to artists and laymen only via copies made by someone on the spot. It is this kind of exposure to antiquity, whether through originals or by way of Renaissance copies, that Mantegna maintained over the decades and nourished his own art.

As court painter in Mantua, Mantegna frequently exchanged views with his patrons about classical art. In 1472 the Cardinal Francesco Gonzaga invited Mantegna to join him in the town of Porretta, where there were restorative baths, to discuss with him some aspects of the Cardinal's collection of Roman bronze sculptures. Francesco wrote to his father, Ludovico Gonzaga, saying, "With Andrea I will have amusement showing him some of my cameos and bronze figures and other beautiful antiquities, on which we may study and confer in company."[13] Mantegna did some collecting of antiquities, acquiring a bust of the Empress Faustina, a work some identify as a bust now in Mantua. In February of 1483 the ruler of Florence, Lorenzo de' Medici, visited Mantegna's house during a brief stay in Mantua and the artist showed Lorenzo some of his paintings and his collection of sculptures from antiquity. In another display of his knowledge, at the end of his life Mantegna offered advice to the marquise of Mantua, Isabella d'Este, on whether or not to purchase classical pieces when they came on the art market. Mantegna owned an original classical bust of a woman, but since the Roman lady resembled Isabella d'Aragon, the widowed Duchess of Milan (and admired Isabella d'Este), the marquise asked Mantegna to sell it to her for her own collection. He was reluctant to do so, evidence of his attachment to collecting antiquities. In short, even in an age when knowledge of classical art was becoming widespread, Mantegna stood out as a connoisseur, capable of recognising quality and authenticity in ancient art.

Visual evidence of Mantegna's attention to antiquity is abundant, as his paintings and drawings are full of reflections and variant copies of existing Roman monuments of the time. A drawing in Vienna serves as valuable example of a copy made after the antique during Mantegna's stay in Rome in 1488-1490 (Fig. 84). (Note the soldier on the left and the shield on the right were added by a later hand). Mantegna went to Rome to work on a chapel for the Pope, as we have seen, but he took the opportunity to see as much as possible, including the very large and visible Arch of Constantine (Fig. 83). This well-preserved monument was built in the early fourth century C.E. by the Emperor Constantine, who had reliefs from earlier Roman art removed and mounted on the arched structure along with contemporary carvings. The reliefs made during Constantine's time were in a more schematic manner than those made before; Mantegna was attracted to the earlier, finer style as found in a battle relief dating from the time of Trajan (Fig. 85). His copy (Fig. 84) shows the left side of the composition; he has filled in some of the facial expressions and varied the poses slightly for greater effect (for example, the horse in the copy is not seen in such strict profile). He must have made other copies in his sketching walks about Rome, but this is a rare surviving record of his activity of that nature.

84. *Drawing after a Trajanic relief on the Arch of Constantine,*
1488-1490.
Quill and ink and black chalk on paper, 18.9 x 27.3 cm.
Albertina, Vienna.

Mantegna's own visions of antiquity were created for men like those who sailed on Lake Garda looking for Roman ruins on the shore. Still, like all great artists of the Renaissance, he transformed his classical sources, making original creations rather than slavish copies. Mantegna always mixed his particulars from antiquity – the inscriptions, costumes, sculptural reliefs, architecture – with elements of his own invention. Indeed, he knew no ancient paintings, so even had he wished to imitate classical art precisely he would have found this difficult. Yet his tough realism does evoke the spirit of Roman art, especially the kind of lively narrative sculpture found on ancient sarcophagi and public monuments (cf. Fig. 85). In borrowing from the classical past, Mantegna looked more at the vivid naturalism of Greco-Roman art rather than the more generalised and ideal kind of classicism which has inspired so many artists since the Renaissance period. Mantegna always sought to give a palpable presence to his painted scenes, and he succeeded by recreating a world based on his own observations of the real

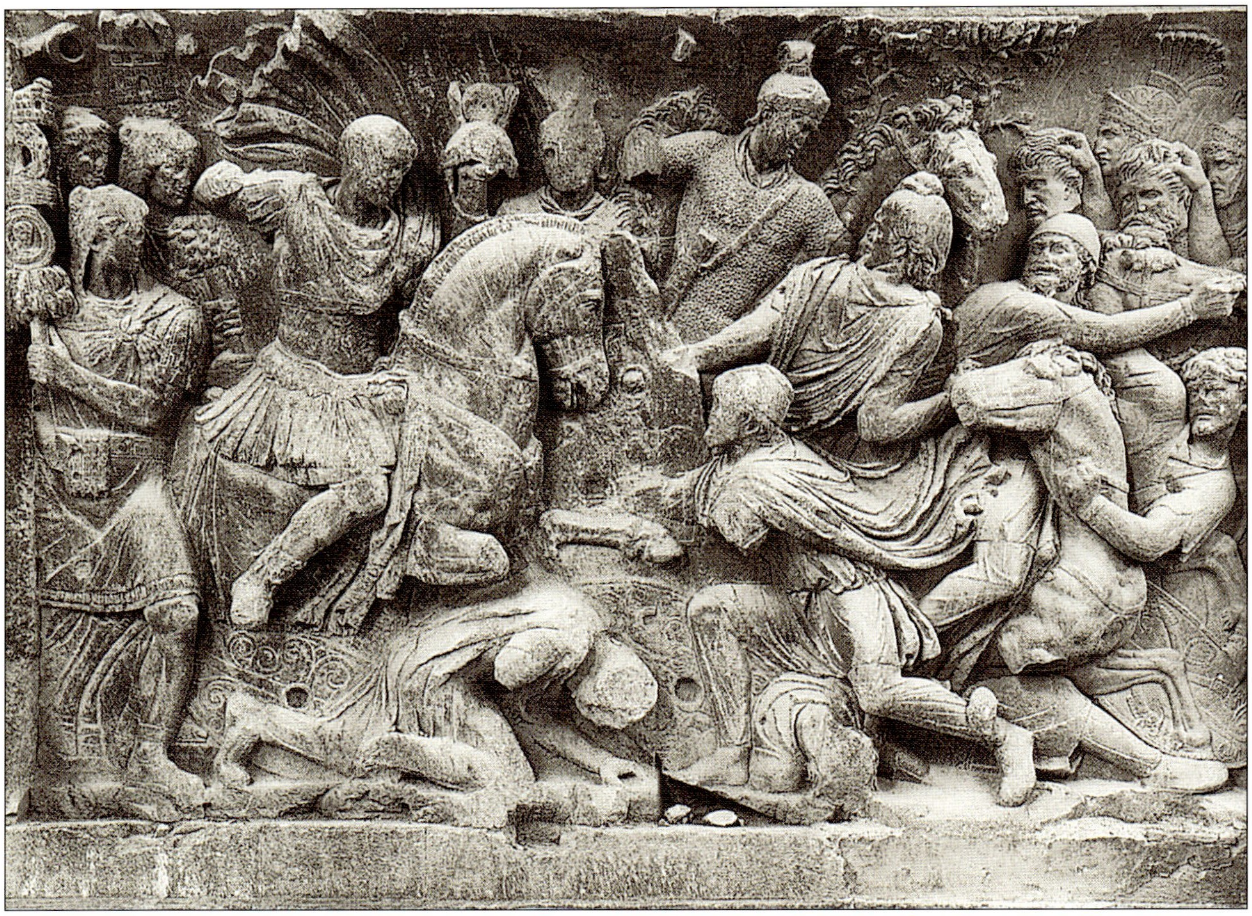

world as well as modelling his art on the more vivid kinds of ancient sculpture available to him. The largest and most important of the artist's recreations of antiquity is formed by his *Triumphs of Caesar*, nine large canvases having found their way to Hampton Court Palace (Figs. 4-6 to 4-14). These have endured as Mantegna's most famous works over the centuries, striking in their size, complexity, and the grand, symphonic presentation. Although there is no sure record of the patron, and there is some possibility they were commenced for Marquis Federico Gonzaga, or even originally conceived by Ludovico Gonzaga, it is most likely Mantegna made the *Triumphs* for Francesco Gonzaga. He was the ultimate recipient, and referred to them in one document as "our paintings." Mantegna was in his employment during the creation of the pictures, so the series must be considered to be the commission of Francesco. It is possible there were more than nine canvases, although it remains uncertain, and the nine works of the ensemble offer a sense of completeness as they are.

85. *Trajan Conquering the Dacians*, Arch of Constantine, Rome, second century A.D. Marble. *In situ*.

The paintings were begun about 1484-1486 and finished in the late 1490s, or perhaps as late as 1505. Their original intended location is not certain, but they were probably meant for a long corridor in a Gonzaga palace or castle in Mantua. It is appropriate that the *Triumphs of Caesar* has ended up in a setting not so different from its likely original one; the canvases are now kept in a large, long room that is part of a great ruler's palace. The present noble setting of the *Triumphs* helps to evoke the original site. If one aspect mars the *Triumphs*, it is their deplorable condition. They have undergone every imaginable form of damage, although a restoration (1962-1975) helped to return them closer to their original appearance. Still, they are greatly overpainted and abraded at the same time, and one of them is in such poor condition that no restoration at all was undertaken, accounting for its darkened surface. A "triumph" (*triumphus* in Latin; *trionfo* in Italian) for the ancient Romans was not primarily a victory, in our sense of a triumph, but was the parade that happened

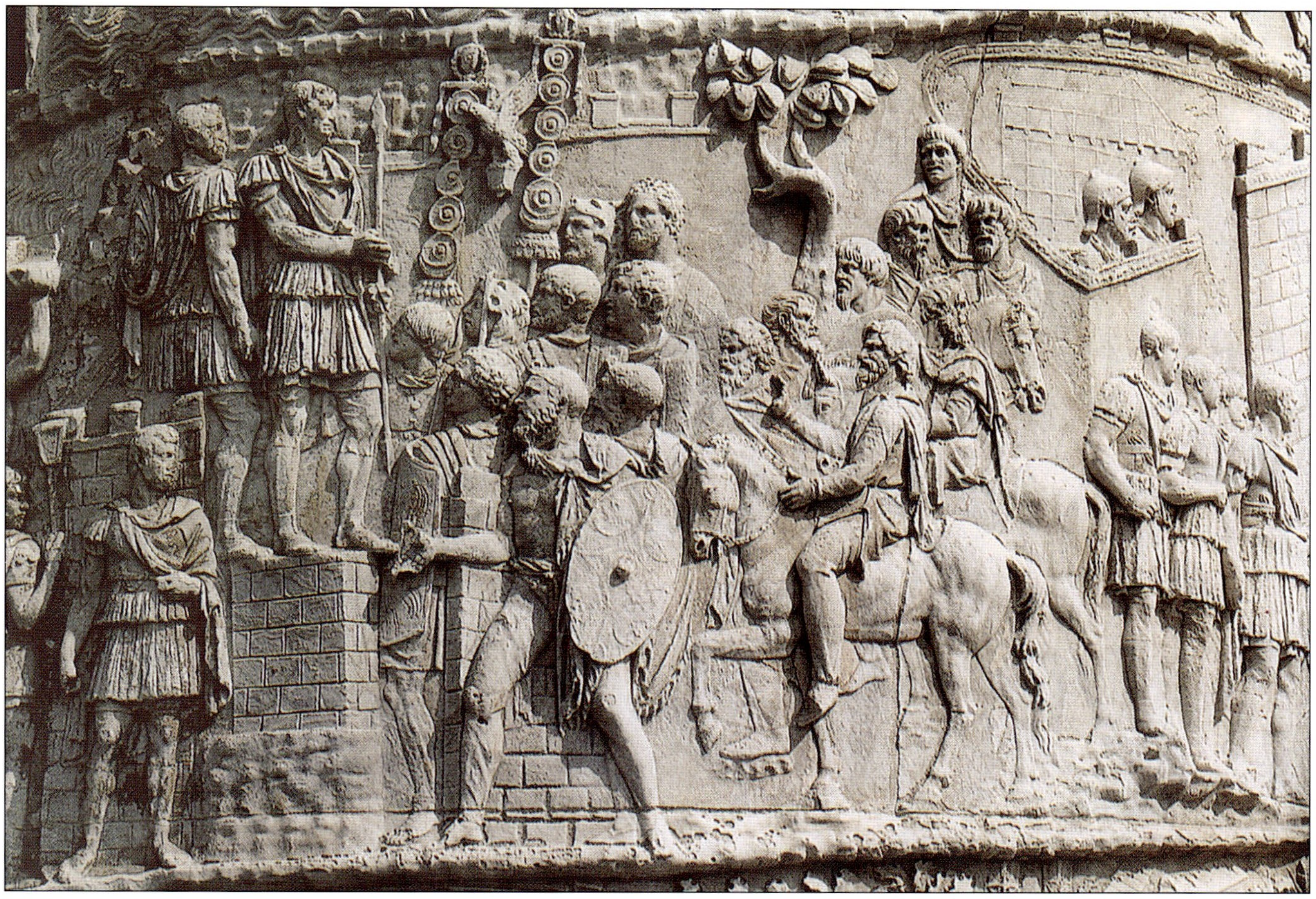

after a victorious battle or campaign. Several famous Roman writers described in detail the events of a triumph, which involved the display of captured men, weapons, and valued spoils of war before the cheering crowds of Rome. The conquering leader would ride in a chariot in the long procession, which wound its way around the city and finished its course on the Capitoline Hill at the great temple of Jupiter. The Roman Empire was built on a series of military victories, and the *triumphus* was an important aspect of Roman culture, a celebration of martial success.

In order to further mark their victories, Romans erected triumphal arches to commemorate specific victories. These monuments, a hybrid of architecture and sculpture, resemble free standing city gates, and were replete with images of victory and with representations of the triumphal processions held after the successful military campaigns. There were several such triumphal arches

86. *Battle Scene*,
Column of Trajan, Rome, 110-113 A.D. Marble. *In situ*.

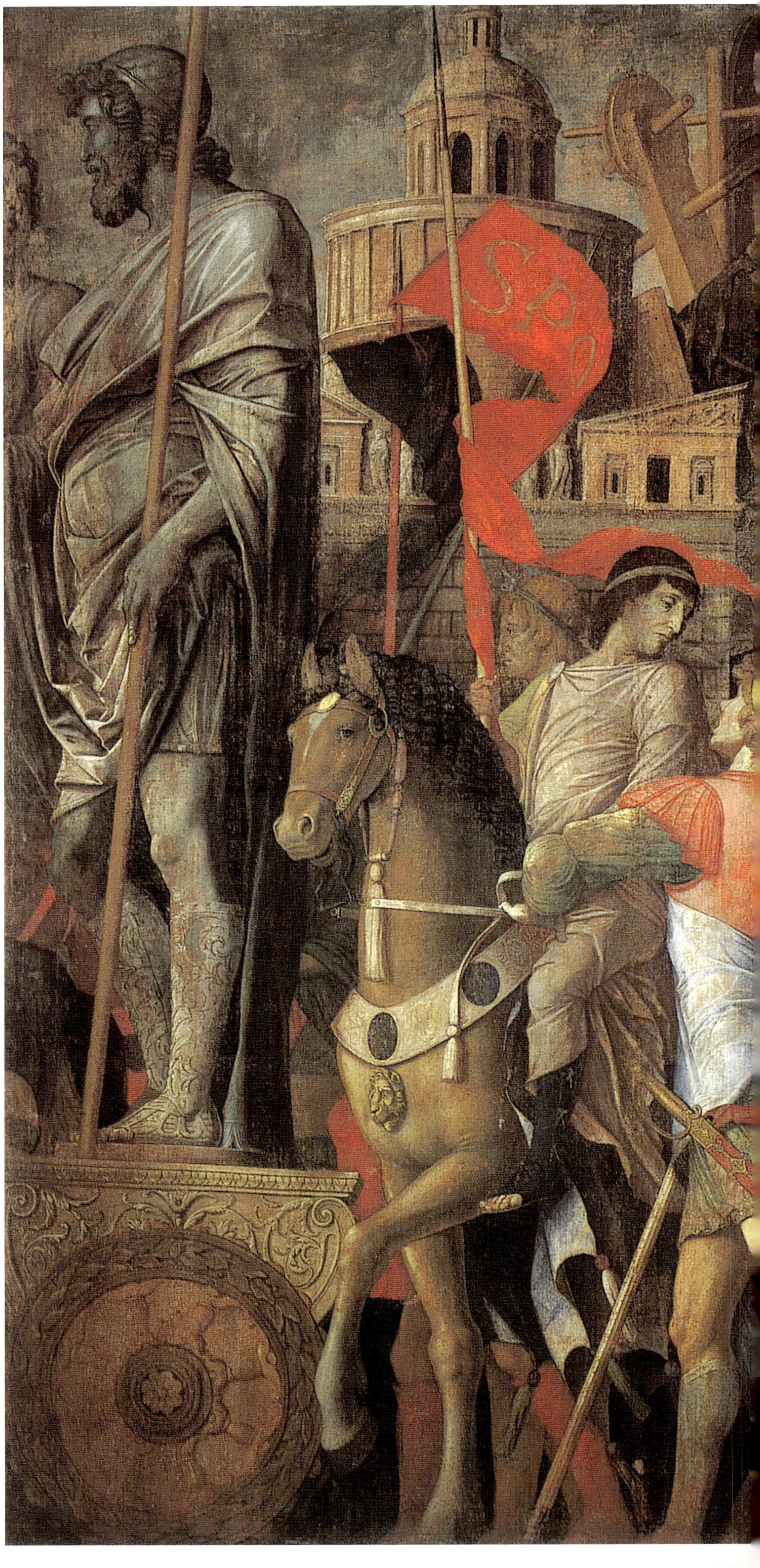

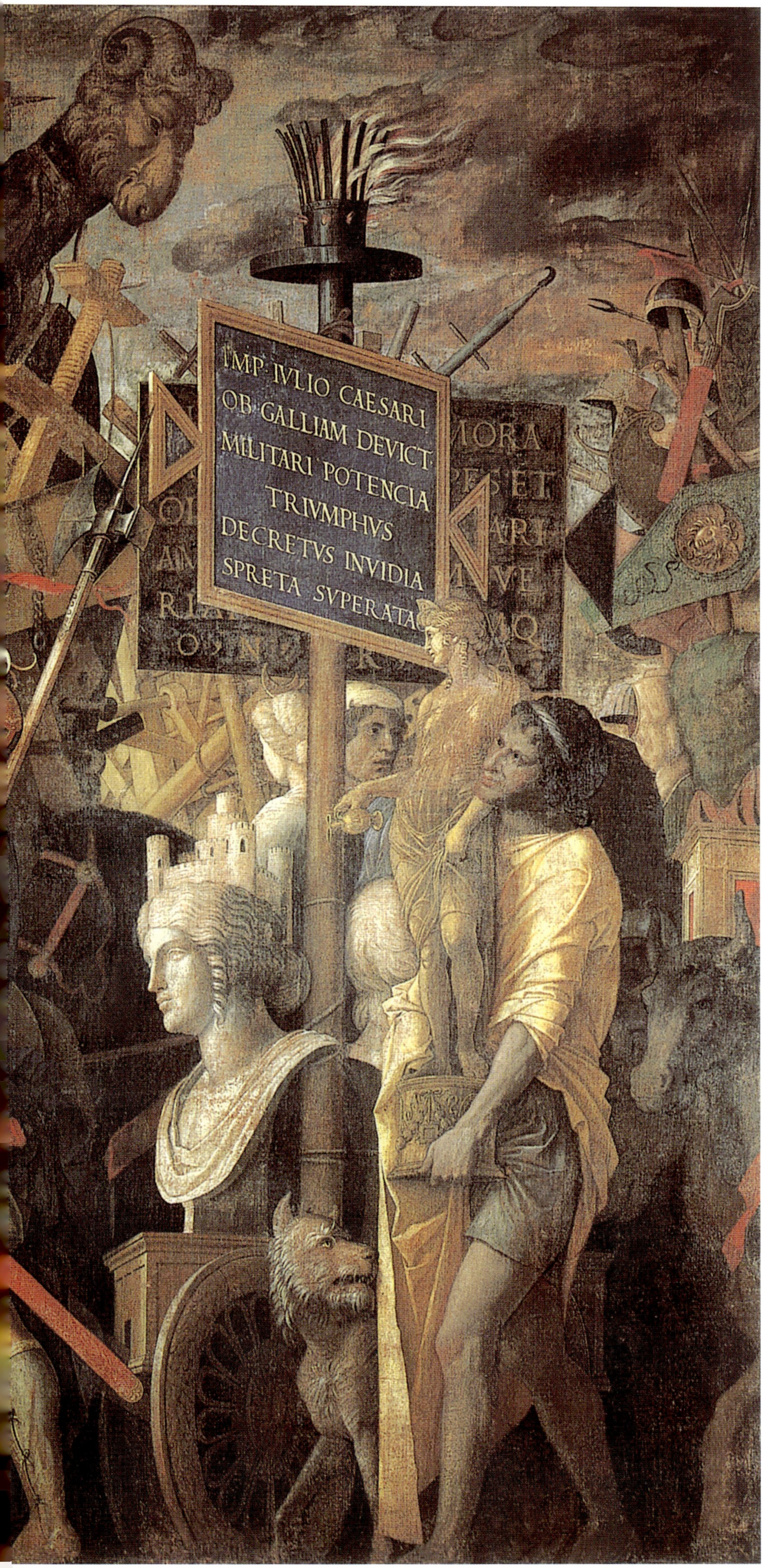

87. *Triumphs of Caesar II,* called *Bearers of Statues of Gods,*
c. 1490,
Tempera on canvas, 266 x 278 cm.
Royal collection, Hampton Court Palace, Hampton Court.

in Italy Mantegna could have known, at least from copies. He was certainly influenced by the famous reliefs on the Arch of Titus (built in 79 C.E.) illustrating in realistic and striking detail the triumphal procession led by Titus to commemorate the Roman victory over the rebellious Jews (Fig. 94). Plunder from the temple in Jerusalem is displayed in one of the reliefs, and in his *Triumph of Caesar*, Mantegna imitated the sense of movement and military vigour displayed in the Arch of Titus. Other extant reliefs in Rome, including those of the Arch of Constantine (Fig. 85) and military scenes on the columns of Trajan and Marcus Aurelius included details of Roman costume and military gear that would have served Mantegna well in his recreation of antiquity in the *Triumphs of Caesar* (Fig. 86). The design of these classical reliefs was widely known by artists across Italy via copies, and Mantegna undoubtedly had access to their appearance even before he went to Rome in 1488-1490. The painter drew on a number of sources, visual and literary, for his *Triumphs of Caesar*. Among written sources for Roman triumphs, he turned to Plutarch, Appian, Livy, and Pliny the Elder, probably with the help of scholarly advisers. There was also an Italian text from the 1460s, Flavio Biondo's *Roma Triumphans*, that Mantegna had access to for information about Roman triumphs in general. Biondo was interested in seeing his Italian contemporaries, in particular the Popes, relive the glory of ancient Rome, and he included a considerable amount of information about practices in Roman triumphs, stressing their colourful variety and describing in detail the processional route through Rome taken by the victors and their train. His book, which was available in the Gonzaga library, was the kind of text an artist of the time could use with great profit.

The *Triumphs of Caesar* were commissioned about a decade after Mantegna's completion of the *Camera Picta*. During his time at the Mantuan court, the main patrons of Mantegna were Ludovico, for whom he worked for nineteen years, and his grandson Francesco, whom the artist served for twenty-two years. Francesco, the likely original patron of the *Triumphs*, took over power in 1484 from his father, Federico, who reigned for only five years. We saw Francesco portrayed as a child in the *Camera Picta*; in the intervening years he had learned the necessary military skills to become a respected soldier and field leader, ready to become marquis although he was still only a teenager. In Renaissance Italy, the rulers of city-states dominated by single families had to take matters in their own hands and become proficient military generals. As is indicated by the circumstances surrounding the *Madonna of Victory* (Fig. 67), Francesco earned a good reputation as a commander, and he would remain known for his skill as a military leader. His services as a *condottiere*, or hired military leader, brought him and his regime great wealth, and helped to sustain his position as ruler of the Mantuan city-state. He later broadened his outlook somewhat, but he remained to the end a military man, with related interests in hunting, hawking, and – above all – the breeding and riding of fine horses, for which Mantua was becoming famous around the world.

Francesco, a general and political leader, rather optimistically chose Julius Caesar as his ideal model. Caesar was highly regarded by Renaissance rulers with humanistic pretensions because of his skill as a general as well as his literary talents, which he displayed most notably in his *Commentary on the Gallic Wars*, a description of his string of victories over the Gauls. This text served to fire the imagination of fifteenth-century Italians, as it was standard reading for someone like Francesco Gonzaga, who had been given a classical education. It is fitting that – like Caesar, who has been reputed as perhaps the greatest general the world has ever known – Francesco Gonzaga would achieve a military victory over the descendants of the Gauls, the French, in an event celebrated in Mantegna's own altarpiece in the Louvre. One contemporary called Francesco a "*novo Cesare*," a new

88. *Triumphs of Caesar III*, called *Bearers of Trophies of Arms and Booty*, c. 1490.
Tempera on canvas, 268 x 278 cm.
Royal collection, Hampton Court Palace, Hampton Court.

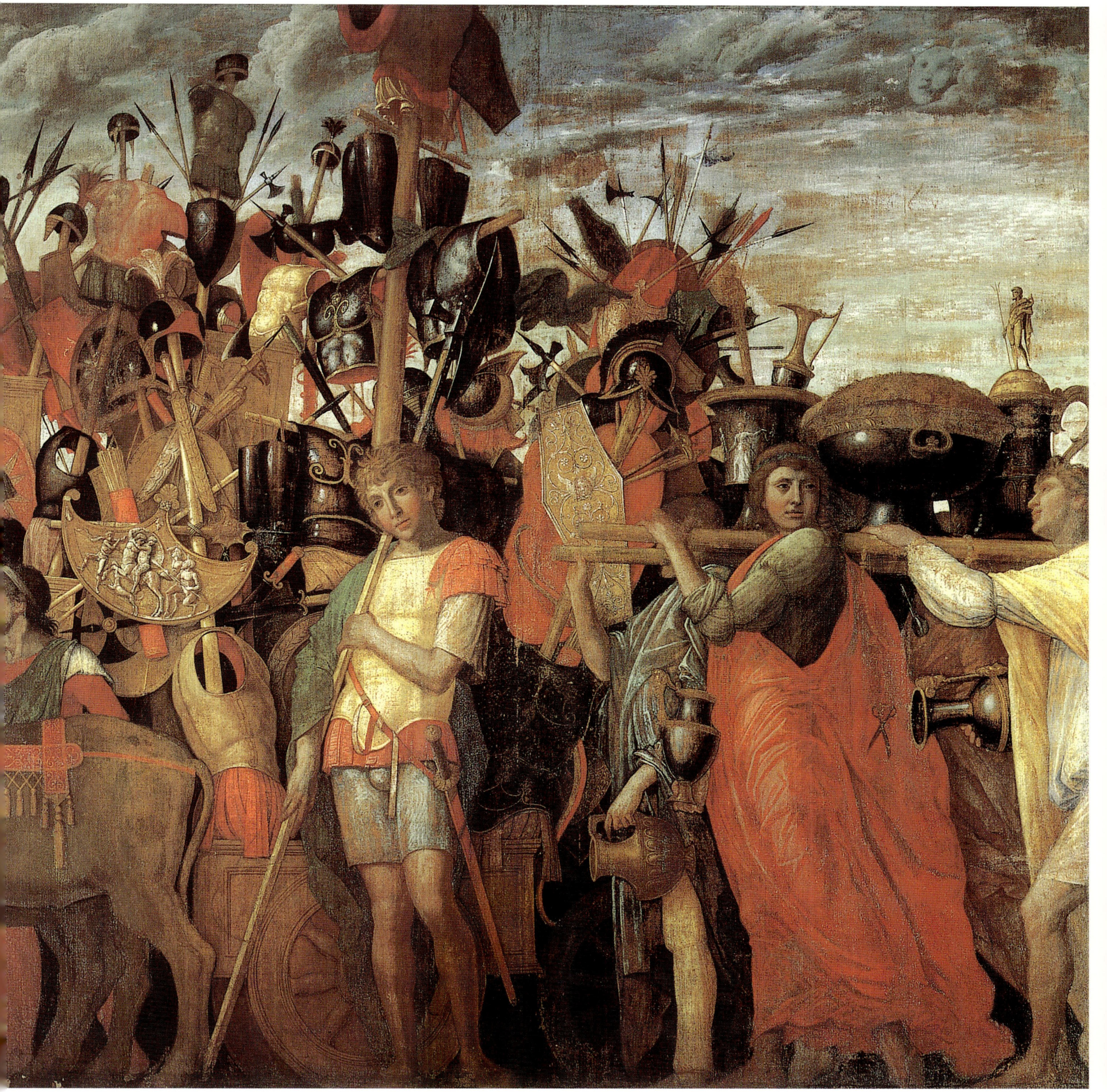

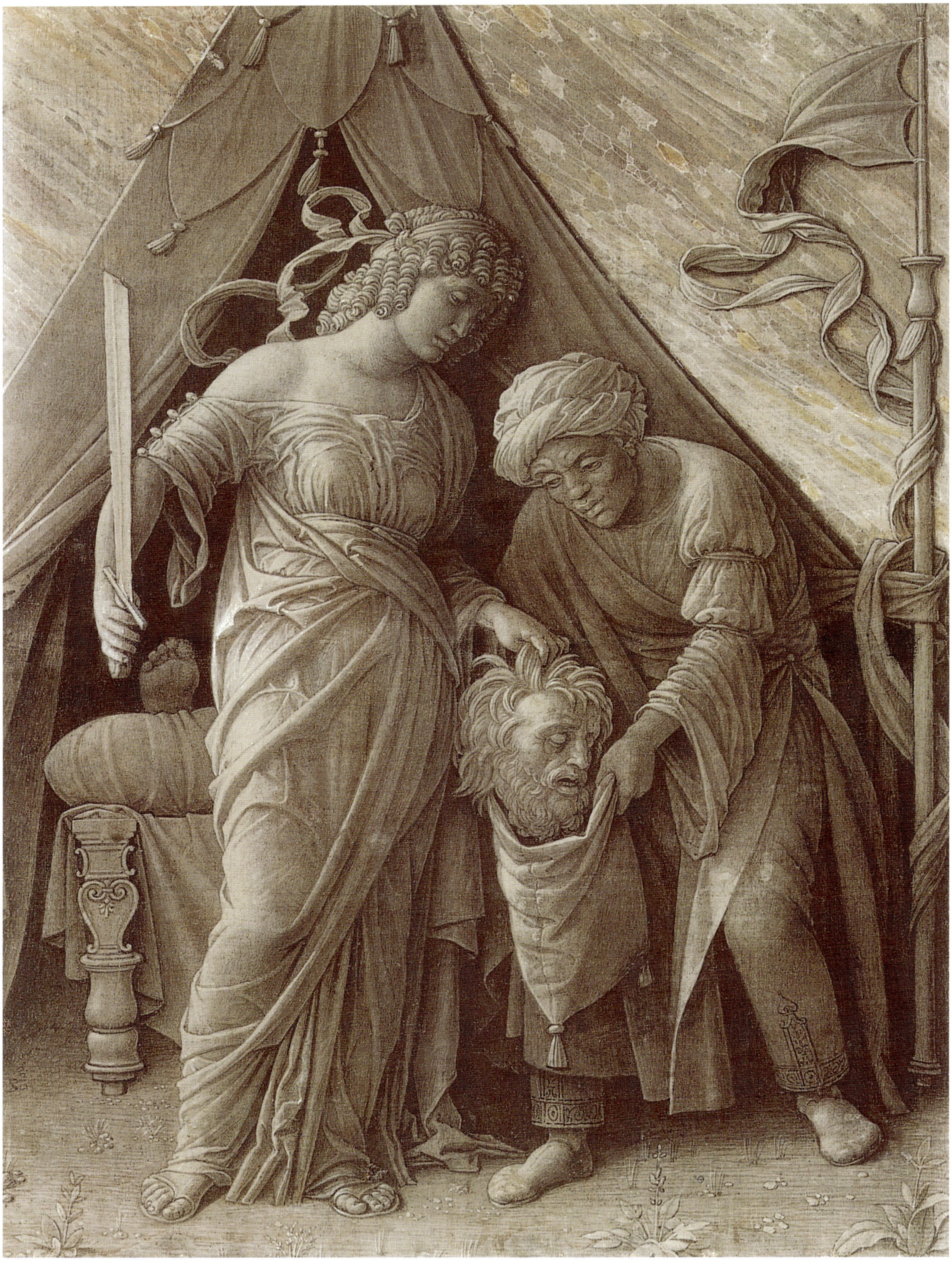

Caesar, and Mantegna's pictures were to provide Francesco with vivid representations of the *marchese's* hero. Mantegna's paintings represent the conflation of at least two triumphal parades held by Julius Caesar, thus the pictures are usually referred to in the plural as *Triumphs*, although most of the imagery refers to the Gallic triumph of Caesar, celebrating his conquest of Gaul. Mantegna's canvases were hardly the first fifteenth-century paintings of a triumph. Indeed, it can be said the Renaissance was the age of the *trionfo*. Triumphant parades were celebrated in a number of ways: some occurred at aristocratic weddings, others were allegorical parades for special occasions, and a few were genuine military triumphs. All these *trionfi* were represented in literature and in the visual arts, so Italians were accustomed to them. Mantegna's works were the greatest artistic expression of a form of celebration that coloured the cultural life of Renaissance Italy.

The revival of the Roman notion of a *triumphus* first occurred in literature in the fourteenth century. Dante Alighieri described as the climax of the *Purgatory* of his *Divine Comedy* the triumph of the heroine Beatrice. Drawn on a chariot pulled by a fantastic gryphon, Beatrice rides in triumph as a symbol of Christian purity. Petrarch, another Italian writer of the fourteenth century, wrote a *Triumph of Scipio Africanus*, evoking the visual magnificence of a secular, ancient triumph. More importantly for shaping the artistic tradition, he penned various triumphs – including the triumphs of Love, Chastity, Death, Fame, Time, and Divinity – imagined as the victorious parades of allegorical figures who were seated on cars. His memorable descriptions were widely represented by artists in the fifteenth century, especially on furniture paintings meant to celebrate marriages. For example, the fifteenth-century Florentine painter Jacopo del Sellaio painted a *Triumph of Love* following Petrarch's description, representing pairs of lovers obediently following the chariot-borne Cupid. The *Triumph of Time* had an old man with a scythe standing on a car, with a mournful crowd looking on. Typically, a *Triumph of Chastity*, following Petrarch, would be represented by showing a white-robed virgin attended by a gathering of virtuous maidens. These scenes seem at times quaint, but even so they were recognised as transformations and embodiments of the classical ideal of the victorious triumph.

The *trionfi* that took place on the streets and piazzas of Italian cities were even more elaborate than painted triumphs. When the bride or daughter of a ruler was married, or when a duke or duchess entered a friendly city on a ceremonial occasion there was often a splendid and elaborate *trionfo*. Brides were taken through the city on special triumphal cars, and they passed through ephemeral triumphal arches; along the way they were greeted by people dressed as planets, divinities, or angels. Often the car of the bride would stop and one of these actors would read a lengthy poem in praise of her beauty or virtue. Francesco Gonzaga's own wife, Isabella, rode through Mantua after their wedding in her own triumphal car, an event that took place, fittingly, about half-way through Mantegna's monumental labours on the *Triumphs of Caesar*.

Political rulers in Renaissance Italy often rode in triumph. Borso d'Este, ruler of Ferrara and the uncle of Isabella d'Este, was received in triumph in Reggio in 1453, being greeted at various points in the city by figures representing virtues such as Charity and Justice, and another man dressed as Julius Caesar met Borso and exhorted him to virtue. Religious holidays were also sometimes celebrated in this way, with allegories of Death or the Virtues shown as triumphant. The street triumph, like the artistic ones, were widespread and marked important occasions, but were not particularly classical in their subject matter, being a mixture of medieval allegory and ancient ideas. Even the well-publicised triumph of King Alfonso of Aragon in Naples in 1443, an event celebrated

89. *Judith with the Head of Holofernes*, c. 1495-1500. Tempera on canvas, 48.1 x 36.7 cm. The National Gallery of Ireland, Dublin.

by the erection of a triumphal arch in the Roman tradition, was not particularly classical in its details (lacking the full array of features of a classical *triumphus*), and the staging included a number of Christian, medieval themes. Similarly, paintings of the mid-fifteenth century attempted to represent ancient triumphs, such as those by the Florentine Apollonio di Giovanni, appear rather decorative in style and late medieval in spirit, with an abundance of gold leaf and unhistorical costumes and weaponry. What was lacking before Mantegna was a sense of historical accuracy, a convincing recreation of the classical past.

This is what Mantegna provided; the importance of his *Triumphs of Caesar* was its archaeological plausibility, the very scale of the staging, and the boldness of the narrative. Accustomed as they were to seeing *trionfi* that were quaint conflations of medieval allegory and popular festival traditions, Mantegna's viewers had never seen a representation on the impressive scale of a Roman *triumphus*. It is true his images are not historically accurate in all their details; for example, the chariots in the *Triumphs of Caesar* resemble Renaissance parade carts, not authentic ancient specimens. Moreover, the armour displayed is Roman, not Gallic as it should be, and even the topography and architecture is only generally reminiscent of ancient Rome, and does not attempt to reproduce the genuine parade route the processions took.

Still, his pictures are much closer to being archaeologically accurate than were the early works of this type by other Italian artists. Previous painters had represented triumphs less historically, and Renaissance festival directors had taken up the idea of the triumph and adapted it to a contemporary event using certain allegorical ideas, but Mantegna boldly recreated the splendour and the historical detail of a classical military parade. As usual, Mantegna did not dryly and pedantically reproduce Roman art, but instead created a lively and spirited painting evoking the antique past, the large canvases constituting his most complicated and varied pictures. Many contemporaries must have agreed with the assessment of the sixteenth-century writer Giorgio Vasari, who said the *Triumphs* were Mantegna's "best work ever"[14]

Mantegna depicted Caesar's triumph in nine canvases. They essentially form one work of art, but each section has a somewhat different character and we can view them from start to finish, seeing them as if they formed a parade passing before us. The first section of the *Triumphs* highlights the standard bearers (Fig. 82). The painting sets the keynote for the rest of the series, with its crowds of figures and great variety of poses and actions. The ancient Roman writer Appian described a triumph with trumpeters crowned in garlands of ivy, a remark that inspired Mantegna here. As in the other pictures for the series, he painted the figures closer to the viewer as appearing higher up than those behind, indicating the pictures were intended to hang somewhat above eye level.

The arrangement of people and objects is aggressively dense, and one can almost hear the blasting of the trumpets. One dark-skinned soldier indicates Mantegna's attempt to portray the extent and cosmopolitan character of the Roman Empire. No fifteenth-century viewer had ever seen such a well-studied picture, replete with the figural types, sculptural details, and costumes of antiquity. The second painting of the series brings in a literary element, a plaque with the inscription declaring Julius Caesar to be the victor over the Gauls (Fig. 87). On the cart on the left is a statue of a god, a reminder that the Romans removed artworks *en masse* from their vanquished cities and brought them back to beautify their own. On the right, a man carries a beautiful statue of a goddess; a dog

90. *Triumphs of Caesar V,* called *The Elephants,* c. 1500-1506. Tempera on canvas, 267 x 277 cm. Royal collection, Hampton Court Palace, Hampton Court.

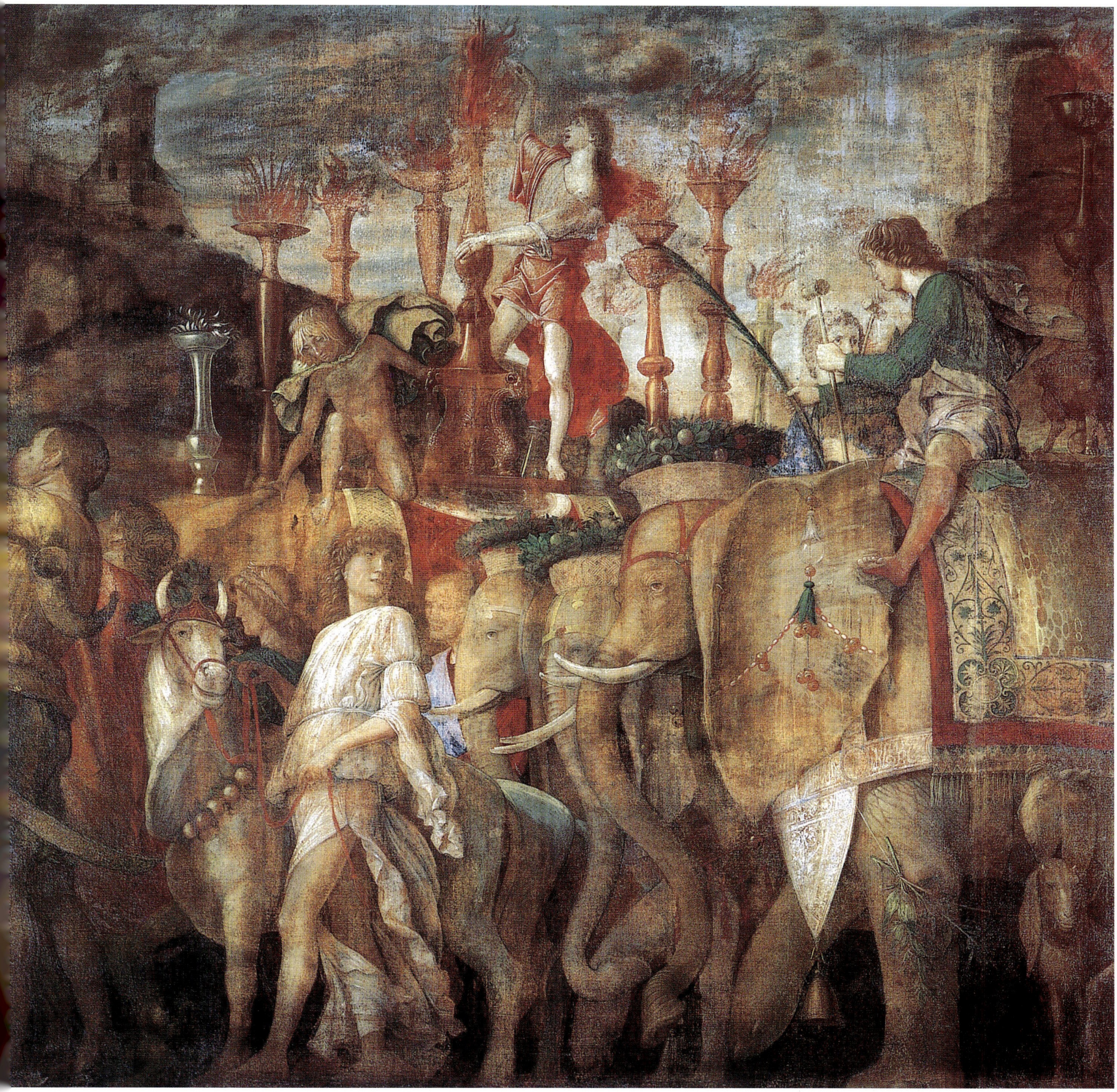

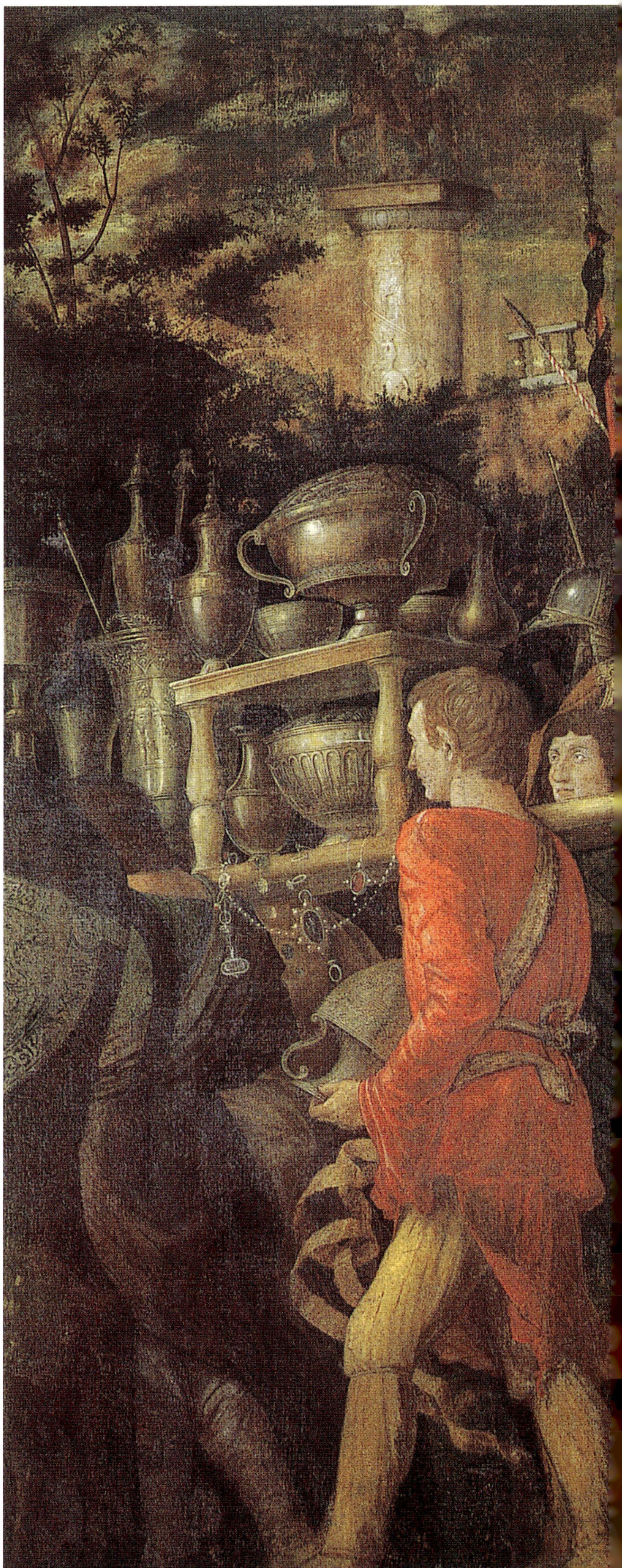

91. *Triumphs of Caesar VI,* called *Bearers of Golden Vessels and Crowns,* c. 1500-1506.
Tempera on canvas,
268 x 278 cm.
Royal collection, Hampton Court Palace, Hampton Court.

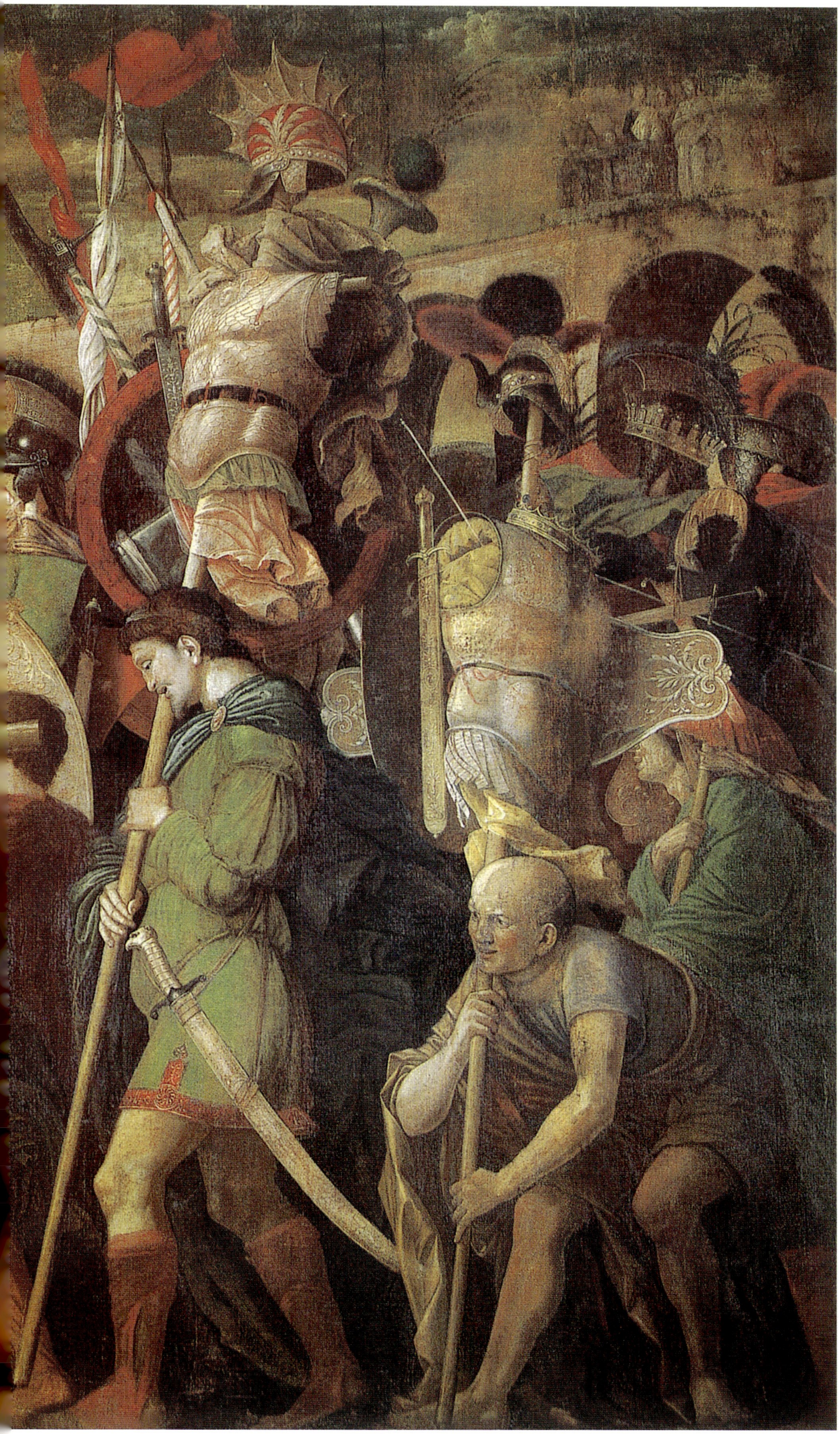

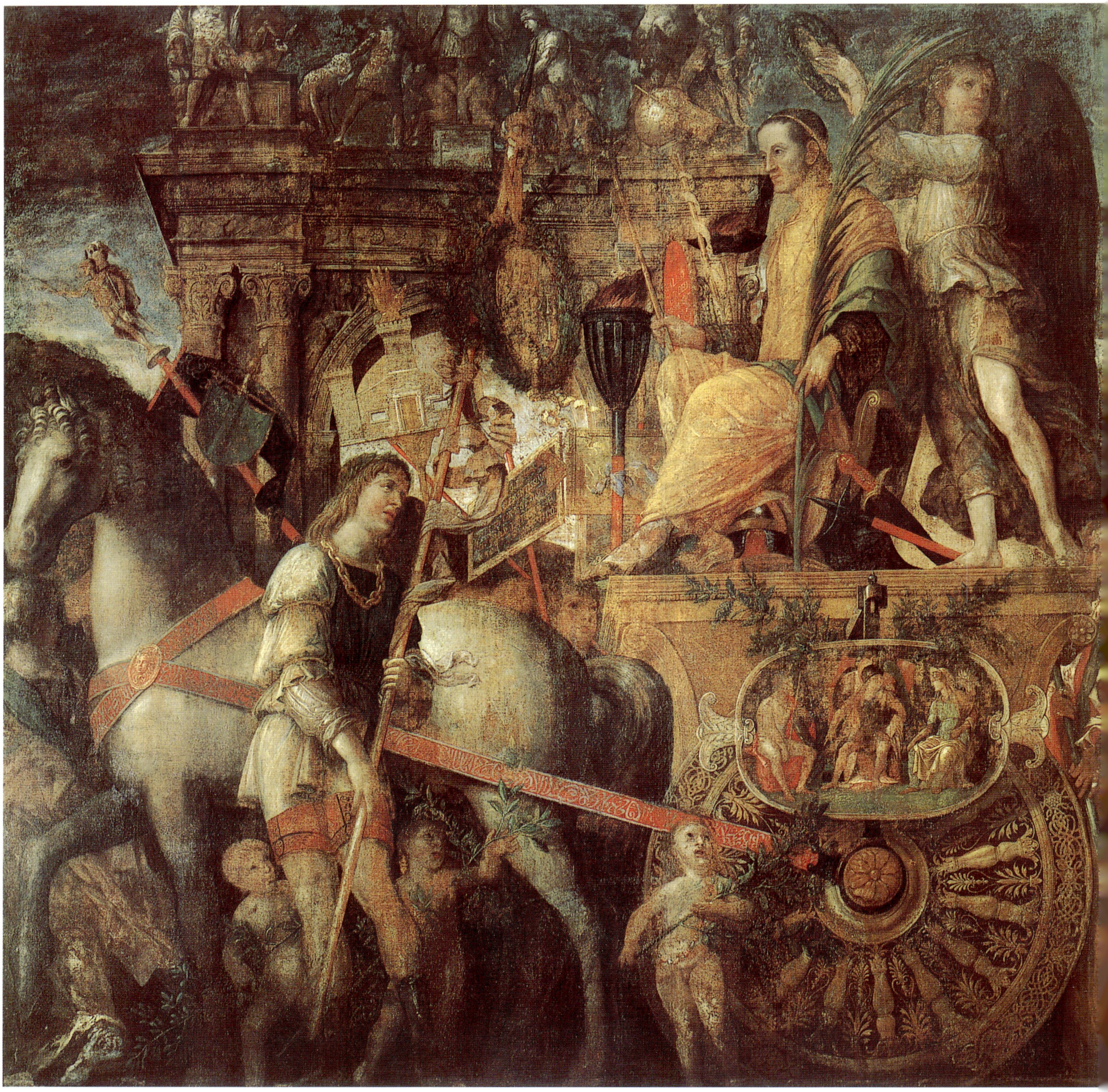

suspiciously eyes the sculpture, perhaps deceived by its lifelikeness, referring to a widespread kind of anecdote told in antiquity of animals that were tricked by the verisimilitude of art. The background gives the first glimpse in this parade of classical architecture, the round structures echoing the wheels and other rounded forms in the picture. The third and fourth paintings (Fig. 88), representing the carrying of military trophies and silver and gold vessels, recall the reliefs on the Arch of Titus in Rome (Fig. 94); instead of the famous Jewish Menorah that appears in the Arch of Titus, Mantegna shows a glittering collection of precious objects and weapons.

The landscape setting in these paintings has little to do with the city of Rome, and is another example of Mantegna's characteristic backdrop formed of rounded hills and scattered, classical structures. It is especially curious the buildings Mantegna represents are often shown as if in ruin, or a state of disrepair, with bricks used to support collapsed walls, as were many ancient structures in the fifteenth century. This is a romantic vision of antiquity, a mixture of past and present; his rendering evokes the spirit of the boating party with his humanist friends, who delighted in the discovery of crumbled, ancient building and monuments. Mantegna's classical edifices are archaeologically studied, but their presentation resonated to his contemporaries by showing them in a familiar fashion, namely, in disrepair. He was thus willing to sacrifice some accuracy in order to reach out to his spectators. Mantegna's efforts recall the sham ruins found in England in the eighteenth and nineteenth centuries, which similarly catered to a particularly learned group of connoisseurs who knew classical and Gothic buildings first-hand in varying states of preservation. Perhaps the most striking of the pictures in the *Triumphs of Caesar* is the fifth one, representing elephants, which Mantegna seems to have based on memory or from some other source, since they are depicted with some discrepancy from natural appearances (Fig. 90). Again taking care to have the background buildings echo foreground elements, Mantegna places a tower on the distant hill, similar to the vertical thrust of the torches. A lithe youth lights a flame, his graceful, dynamic turn standing in contrast to the massive, pensive elephants. The sixth canvas shows more trophies and crowns (Fig. 91). The seventh contains a particularly moving motif: it depicts male captives, whom Mantegna shows proceeding with great dignity and sadness, an emotional state visible to us even through the damaged paint surface. The artist endows these enemies of the Romans with stoic gravity and melancholy, but lightens the scene with the presence of a jeering buffoon on the right, probably based more on contemporary rather than ancient jesters. Behind the captives, spectators view the scene from behind bars, their enclosure adumbrating the captive status of the involuntary paraders.

The eighth canvas illustrates musicians, important elements for conveying the sound and the rhythm of the celebration. Trumpets and plunder are held in the air so as to form a musical, contrapuntal arrangement, and fruit on the upper left adds to the festive aspect of the composition. Finally, the ninth painting (Fig. 92) represents Julius Caesar atop his chariot, a triumphal arch looms in the background, but not based on one from Rome; it is a variant on an arch located on the Dalmatian coast mainland not far from Venice, an arch Mantegna could have known from drawn copies in circulation. Caesar is being crowned by a youth who places the victory wreath on his head. Street *trionfi* in Italy often had youths dressed up as allegories, and this crowning figure in the painting echoes that practice more than it does any ancient Roman custom. On the wheel of the cart is an image of Neptune, Mars, and Peace seated together, signalling the successful end of Caesar's martial activities. Mantegna's great achievement in the *Triumphs of Caesar* was recognised

92. *Triumphs of Caesar IX*, called *The Triumphal Chariot*, c. 1484-1492. Tempera on canvas, 268 x 279 cm. Royal collection, Hampton Court Palace, Hampton Court.

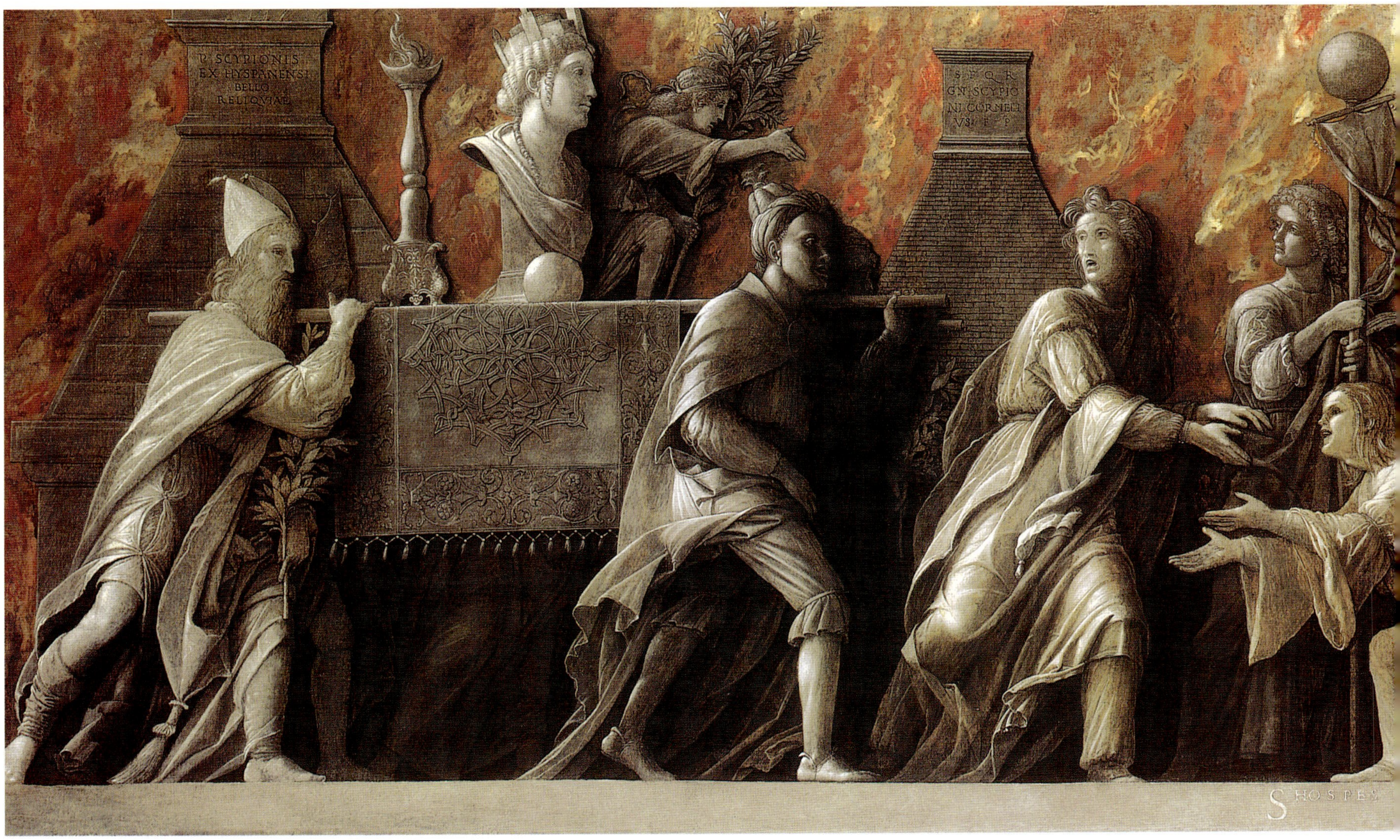

during his lifetime. In 1489, the artist wrote in conventionally modest manner to Francesco that he was not ashamed of the works painted thus far on the *Triumphs*. The paintings were well received by the rulers of Mantua. Some striking testimony was provided by Francesco Gonzaga. In 1492 he gave a grant of land to Mantegna and praised his abilities as a painter, saying he was excellent in his craft and citing the "*Triumph of Caesar* that he is now painting for us with figures that almost live and breathe." The patron appreciated the realism of the details, the skill with which they were carried out, as well as the historical approach of the artist. There was positive reception from humanists, too. A friar in Mantua who was also a Latin poet, Battista Spagnoli, wrote verses praising the *Triumphs*, saying Mantegna's series "shines brighter than the stars;" Spagnoli wrote that Andrea rivalled the great painters and sculptors of classical antiquity in his skill and mimetic power, making him "the glory of our century."

The effect of the *Triumphs of Caesar* can also be gauged by the reaction of the marquise, Isabella d'Este. She bought a biography of Julius Caesar while travelling in Venice in 1491, and in 1496 she was attempting to purchase a copy of Caesar's *Commentaries on the Gallic War*. In 1507, Isabella noted in a letter she would like to visit Rome to see the ruins of antiquity and to "contemplate what it must have been like when a victorious general was celebrating his triumph." Mantegna's paintings helped to whet her appetite for further study and enjoyment of classical art and history. We also know her father, Duke Ercole d'Este of Ferrara, was taken by his son-in-law Francesco in 1486 to see the first paintings done by Mantegna for the series, and the Ferrarese duke was "greatly pleased." Vasari's

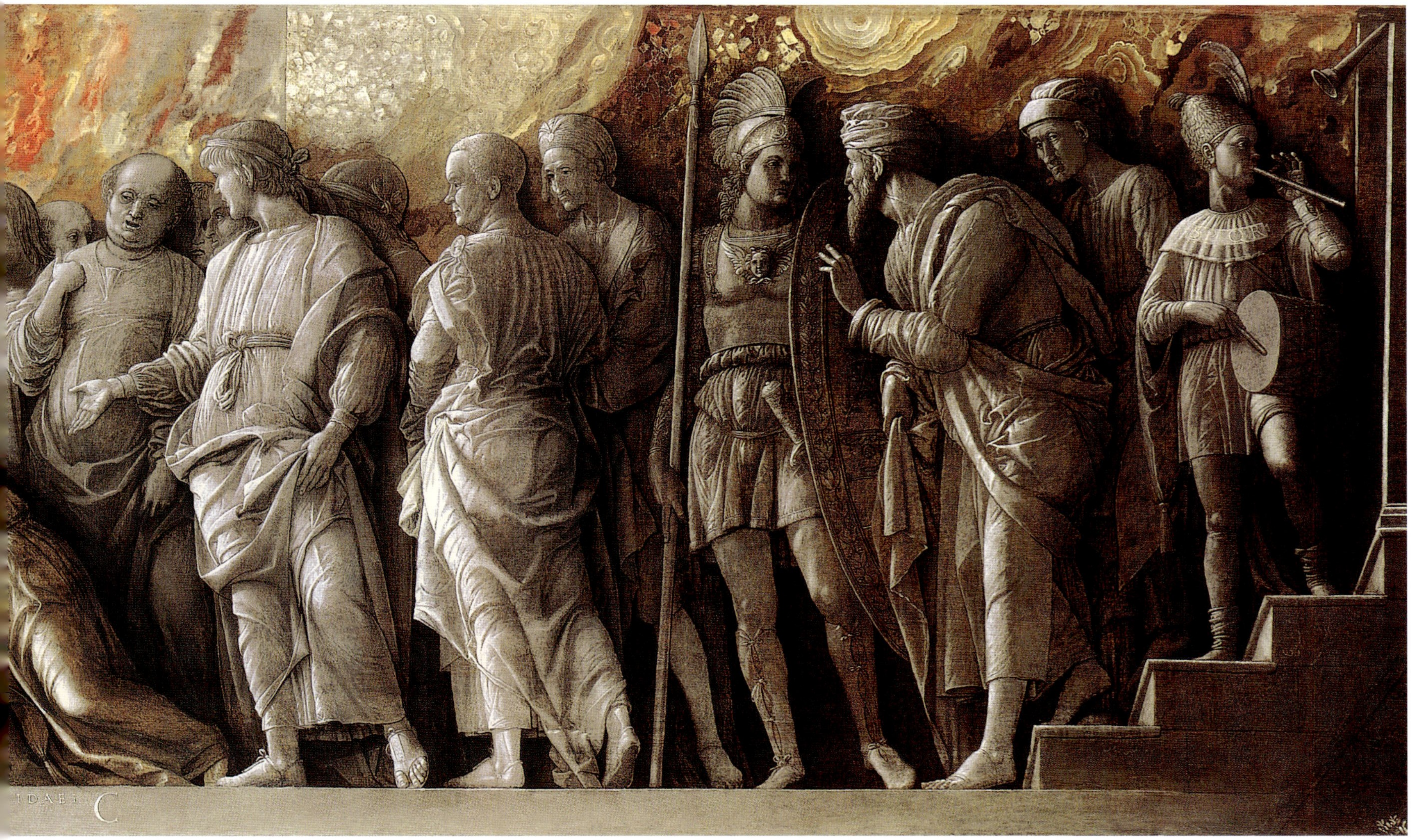

designation of them as "the best thing that Mantegna ever painted" is echoed by the great number of copies that have been made since their completion, beginning early on (cf. Fig. 114). Over the coming decades and centuries a stream of visitors to the court in Mantua admired them, not the least of which was the great seventeenth-century painter Peter Paul Rubens from Flanders, who painted a copy based on two of the sections. Rubens, with his Baroque penchant for colour, movement, and complexity, was powerfully drawn to these fifteenth-century paintings. Mantegna's paintings are extraordinarily complex, and form a bridge between the antiquity and the High Baroque.

The pictures were undoubtedly meant for some permanent site (by the early sixteenth century they were in the Palazzo di San Sebastiano in Mantua), yet they were on occasion brought out and used for temporary purposes, their transportation facilitated by their being on canvas. In 1497 they were used at a festival held in a courtyard of the Ducal Palace. In 1501, six of the *Triumphs of Caesar* served to adorn a theatrical hall at the palace, and they possibly served the same purpose in 1507. In the Renaissance, "theatre" was practically synonymous with classical drama, and the plays held in courts such as Mantua were either Roman plays by authors such as Plautus or Terence, or were modern imitations based on classical themes and dramatic styles. Mantegna's paintings of the triumph of Julius Caesar already have a festive, theatrical appearance to them, and would have served to establish a splendid, antique ambiance for a theatrical production held at the Gonzaga court. The *Triumphs of Caesar* constituted a grandiose project; most of Mantegna's other works made in the spirit or style of antiquity are far more modest in scale. Many of them are also done in an inventive new style.

93. *Introduction of the Cult of Cybèle at Rome,* 1505-1506.
Tempera on canvas,
73.5 x 268 cm.
The National Gallery, London.

Mantegna perfected a way of painting figures in *grisaille*, placing them against a fictive marble background. By doing so, he created the illusion that the figures are of white marble or bronze, set before a background of swirling, coloured marble. He had already included fictive sculpture in several works, such as in the *Camera Picta*, but here the *grisaille* paintings were independent works.

These paintings served as clever and less expensive means to produce the appearance of Greek and Roman marble sculpture. Ancient Roman paintings were still unknown at this time, but sculptures were widely collected and visible; Mantegna endowed these *grisaille* paintings with the appearance of classical sculpture, appealing to the contemporary desire to imitate classical art. The Early Renaissance theorist Leon Battista Alberti had said good painted figures should look hard like sculpture; Mantegna went one step further, and painted some of his actors as if they were indeed carved figures. It is as if Mantegna deliberately rebelled against the admonition of his own teacher Squarcione, who said his earliest works looked too much like sculpture. Mantegna made a virtue of this fault, and created a clever kind of painting, one that embraced

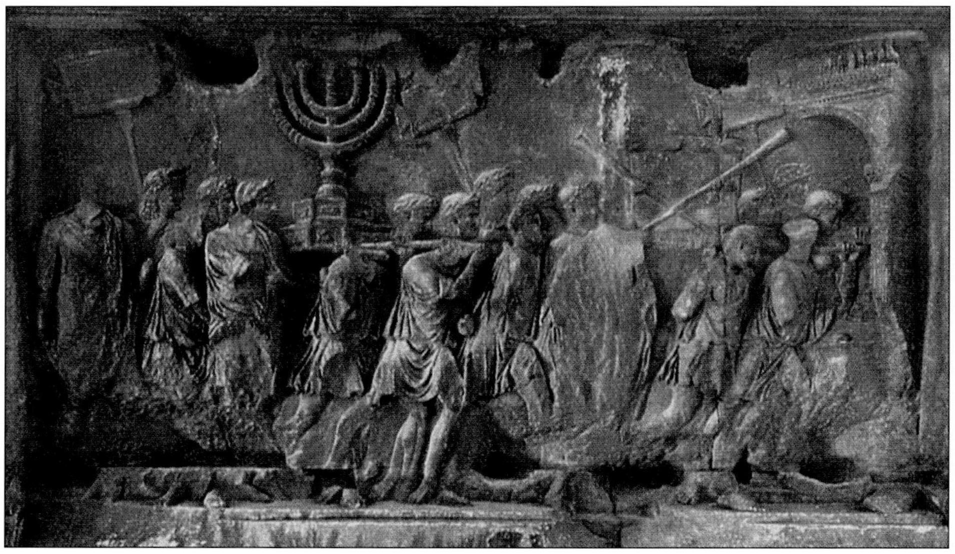

the arts of both painting and sculpture and successfully evoked antiquity, and appealed to a contemporary penchant for *trompe l'oeil* artistry. In the fifteenth century, as today, original classical sculpture was difficult to obtain; when the Gonzaga were not turning to Mantegna for his fictive sculptures in paint, they sought the services of sculptors who could provide them with variant close copies of classical compositions, rendered without the imperfections and damage that marred the original sculptures from antiquity. The leading artist in Mantua for this genre was Pier Jacopo Alari-Bonacolsi, who was called Antico because his work was reminiscent of the antique ("*antico*" in Italian), Greco-Roman style. He was trained as a goldsmith, and his work is always beautifully detailed and crafted. Much of his work constitutes copies, or variant copies, of original works from antiquity. A typical sculpture by him is his *Apollo* (Fig. 95), made of bronze and gilding making it appear the young god has blond hair and a golden robe and sandals. This statuette is closely based on the famous Greek *Apollo Belvedere* now in the Vatican collection. Such small, bronze works as Antico's were avidly collected and commissioned by Francesco Gonzaga and his wife Isabella. Mantegna's *grisaille* paintings for the same patrons should be seen in this context, his *grisaille* pictures similarly serving as lively, well-formed imitations of both the style and content of classical art.

94. *Spoils from the Temple of Solomon in Jerusalem*, Arch of Titus, Rome, 81 A.D. Marble. *In situ.*

The largest and most impressive of his paintings made with fictive sculptural figures in the antique manner is the *Introduction of the Cult of Cybele at Rome*, which is now in the National Gallery, London (Fig. 93). Mantegna painted it in 1505-1506 for Francesco Cornaro, a wealthy Venetian, who ordered four paintings from Mantegna (but the artist died before he could paint any others). Venice was not an ancient city (it was founded in the chaos during the dissolution of the Roman Empire), but the spirit of humanism had permeated Venetian culture during the *Quattrocento*, and many citizens there were anxious to own works in imitation of classical art in both style and subject matter. In an act of devotion to antiquity, the members of the Cornaro family insisted they were descended from the Cornelia family, which included the Roman hero Publius Cornelius Scipio, known as Scipio Africanus because of his military victories in Africa. Mantegna's paintings for Cornaro were to illustrate scenes from the life of a cousin of Scipio Africanus, called Scipio Nasica. It is a sign of Mantegna's fame that he was asked by a Venetian patron to carry out this project and, although he felt he was being underpaid, Mantegna finally continued with the project, which was interrupted by his death in 1506. The painting was meant to be placed over a door, and that accounts for the low point of view of the perspective.

The painting embodies a strong moral content, illustrating virtue and its reward. Mantegna derived his narrative from accounts given by the Roman writers Juvenal, Valerius Maximus, Appian, and Livy. The cult of the earth goddess Cybele, who was celebrated in Asia Minor, was to be introduced into Rome on the recommendation of a female seer (sibyl). Carried on a litter is Cybele's cult statue and a sacred stone from her temple, but since there was as yet no temple in Rome devoted to her, the statue had to be kept in a private home. The young Scipio, because of his personal qualities and moral reputation, was chosen by the Roman Senate as the worthiest man in the Roman state to keep the statue in his house, which is shown on the right. There is some dispute among scholars concerning which figure is the main protagonist, but the middle position, the forcible, emotional gesture, the less interested reactions of the others, and the slightly yellow colouring distinguishing him from the more uniformly grey of the other figures all indicate the youth in the centre is Scipio. The young man kneels fervently in the centre and reaches out toward the holy litter, which is carried forward by priests of the cult of Cybele. The archaeological attention of Mantegna appears vividly in the exotic costumes, evoking the world of Asia Minor during Roman antiquity. Renaissance viewers and humanistic scholars were not just interested in a cold, academic representation of classicism; they delighted in such details as the exotic eastern priest on the far left and the strange cap of the Moor who holds up the forward right part of the litter.

As well as illustrating the patron's purported ancestor in action, Mantegna depicts the tombs of other ancient ancestors of Francesco Cornaro on the left of the painting, identifiable from the classical inscriptions. Mantegna died before he could finish other paintings for the series, but his brother-in-law, Giovanni Bellini, painted *The Continence of Scipio* as a companion piece. Bellini followed Mantegna's lead in making the work with fictive stone figures and coloured marble background. It is likely Mantegna would have painted this subject had he lived, another illustration of virtue in the Cornaro clan, this time representing Scipio Africanus giving back a captive maiden to her fiancée and family, even though he could have kept her as a slave. Bellini's painting echoes the style and format of Mantegna's work, while the moral content is also similar. These works are classical in all their aspects, including the style, apparent medium (made as if marble), subject matter, and the moralising nature, which conveyed the ancient, philosophical emphasis on personal virtue.

The idea of painting fictive sculptures illustrating stories from antiquity caught on fast, and Mantegna painted a number of such works for eager patrons. He was surely motivated also by the desire to demonstrate the superiority of painting over sculpture. The *paragone*, or comparison, of the arts was on the minds of Renaissance thinkers, and as a painter Mantegna took the opportunity to show the potentiality of painting; and it is notable that his apparently sculptural figures have an unusual lifelikeness as if they were paintings, in addition to the successful illusion that these are three-dimensional creations. One of these *grisaille* pictures was his *Dido* (Figs. 4-26). The painting, illustrating the Queen of Carthage, was painted for an unknown patron, perhaps for a woman, for it is in the tradition of representation of virtuous and famous women so popular in the Renaissance; works of this type decorated many bedrooms and other private chambers for aristocratic ladies of the Renaissance. This picture, which had as a companion piece an image of *Judith with the Head of Holofernes* (Montreal Museum of Fine Arts), and perhaps other works in the series that are now lost, would have served as an *exemplum virtutis*, an "example of virtue," in an age when moral lessons as illustrated by particular lives were carefully studied. Dido was a notable ruler of antiquity, and this indicates the painting would have been appropriate for a ruler's wife, perhaps Isabella d'Este. Mantegna painted Dido in a grave, classical style, and the apparent material of the figures is also redolent of classical art. The technique is especially intriguing, because the figure of Dido is rendered in a golden fashion as if in gilded bronze. Some now-lost works by Mantegna are recorded as having been done "*finto di bronzo*", in fictive bronze, and the *Dido* is in that mode. It was even rarer (and, consequently, more expensive) to find a bronze sculpture from antiquity than a marble one, so Mantegna's paintings would have served the purpose of providing bronze works done in a classical style on noble, virtuous subjects. Another fictive bronze painting is Mantegna's *Prophet and Sibyl*, the latter a pagan poetess from classical antiquity who foretold future Christian events (Fig. 97). The two seem to be in an animated discussion, and although they are meant to be regarded as sculptural, their supple liveliness gives them the appearance of painted figures; their lively realism also encompasses the idealising beauty of classical sculpture. Unlike the more artificial *grisaille* figures set

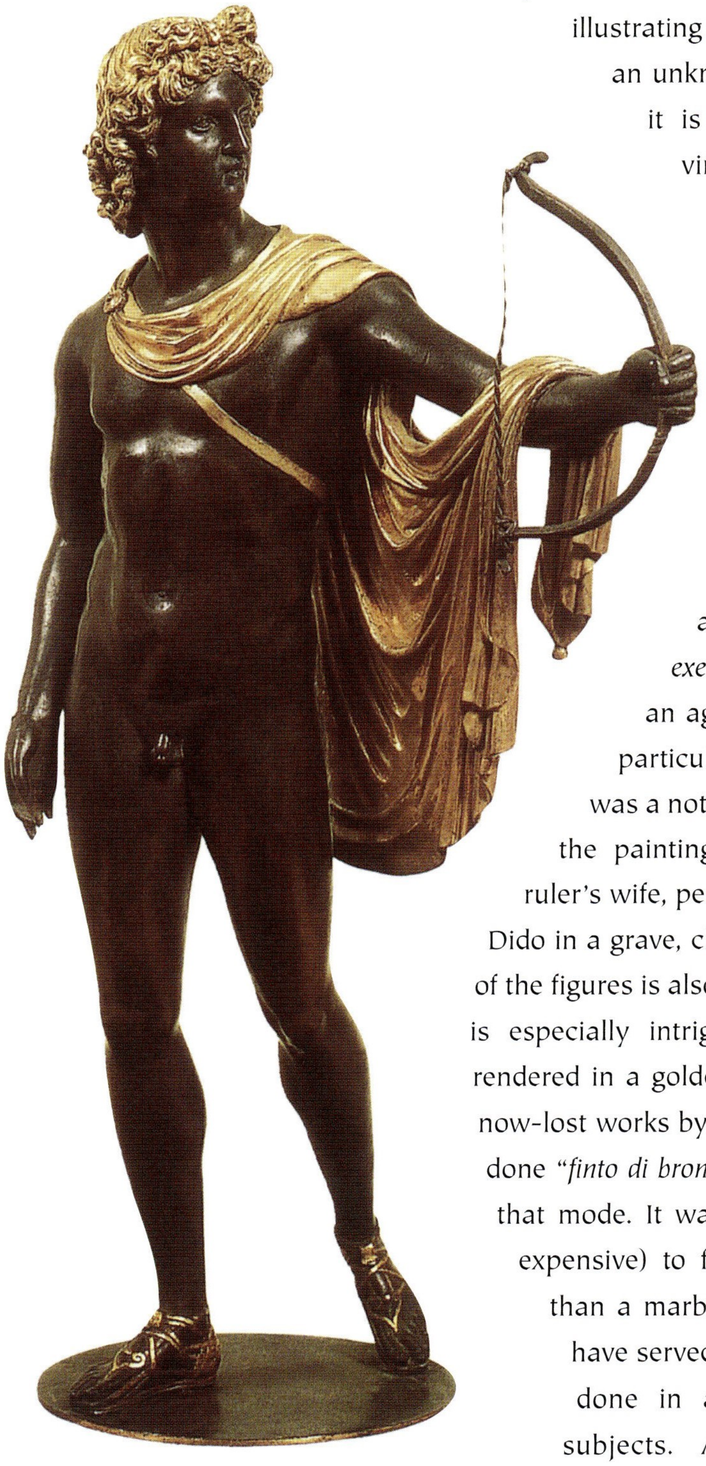

95. Pier Jacopo Alari-Bonacolsi, called Antico, *Apollo*, late fifteenth century. Bronze with gilding and silver, h: 40 cm. Ca' d'Oro, Venice.

96. *Dido*, c. 1500. Tempera on canvas, 65.3 x 31.4 cm. Museum of Fine Arts, Montreal.

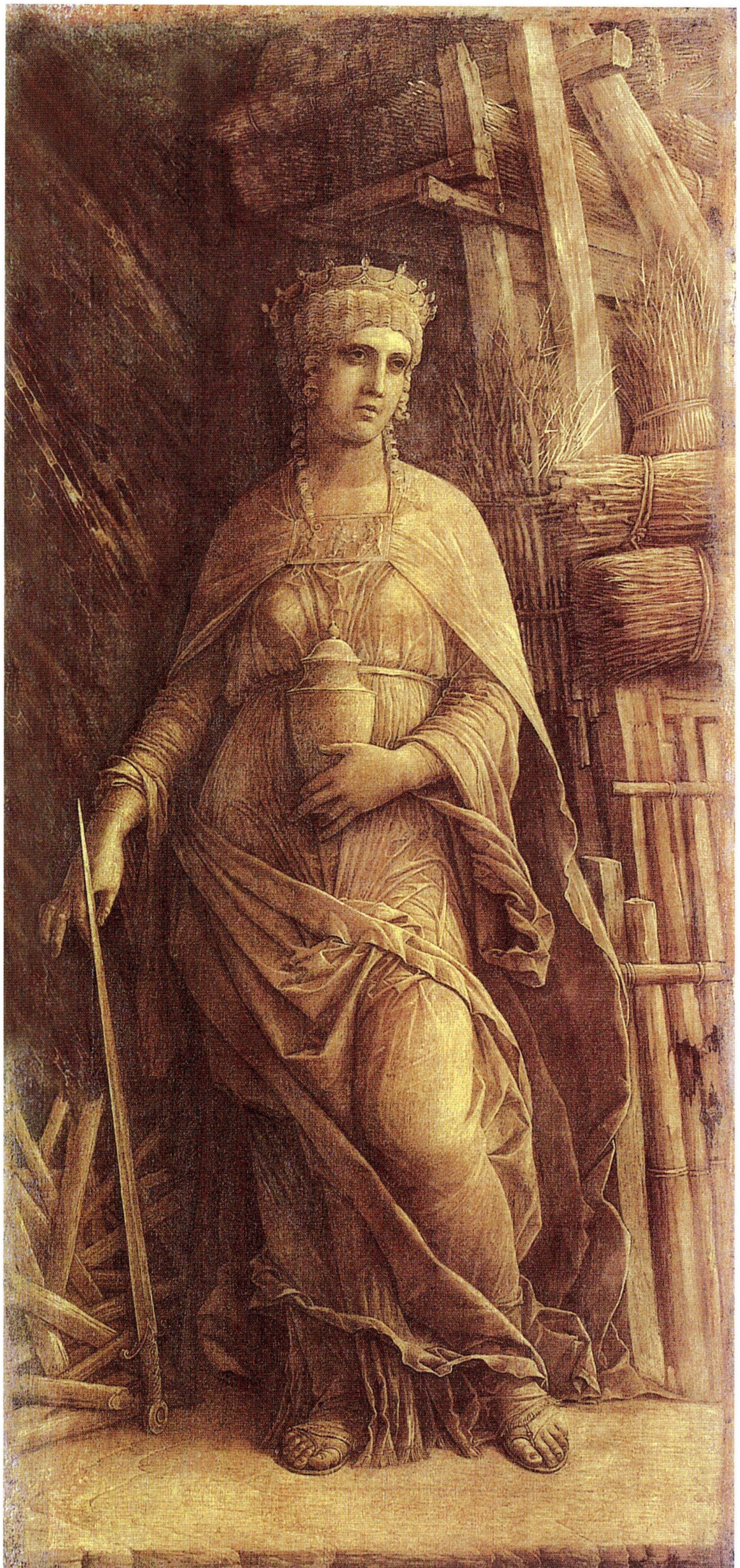

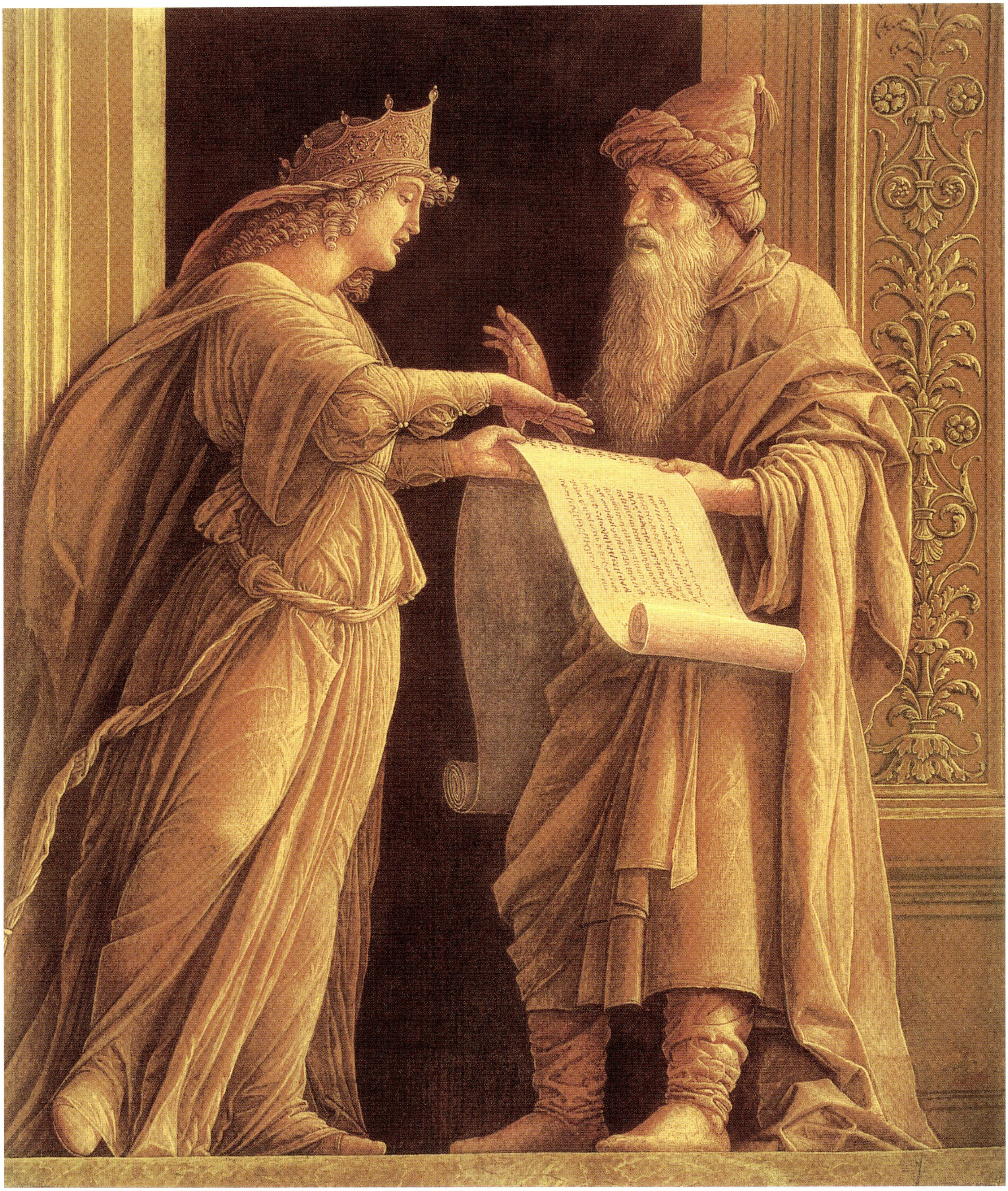

against swirled, coloured marble slabs, here a more plausibly real backdrop is used; the result is a clever conflation of the modes of painting and fictive relief. The classical relief form was utilised also for Biblical subjects, such as the *Judith with the Head of Holofernes* (Fig. 89), in fictive off-white marble and a swirling marble background that reinforces the character of the work as one of apparent sculpture rather than as painting. Mantegna specialised in illustrating classical ideas and themes popular among Renaissance writers. This is most clearly seen in a drawing, perhaps in preparation for a painting or a print, of *The Calumny of Apelles*. The story, told by several ancient authors, is of a youth who has been falsely brought forward to judgment; Fraud and Deceit accompany him along with Calumny and Envy, and he is supported in spirit only by Penitence, an old woman who stands off to the side. Mantegna's drawing shows, characteristically, both his originality and his dependence on literary sources. Leon Battista Alberti, in his treatise *On Painting* of 1435, had suggested this subject for fifteenth-century artists to paint because of its roots in antiquity and its possibilities for lively narrative. Alberti recommended it as a good subject, describing the scene and noting, "if this 'historia' seizes the imagination when described in words, how much beauty and pleasure do you think it presented in the actual painting of that excellent artist [Apelles]," referring to the famous Greek painter of the fifth century B.C.E.[15]

Mantegna's drawing is a good example of his adherence to a program set out by a contemporary writer, both wishing to see the forms and subjects of classical antiquity brought to life. But Mantegna changed the young man to a girl, a symbol of Innocence, and he has her not imploring the Heavens as the written sources specify, but instead she beseeches Truth, who is shown pointing upwards. The drawing seems to be conceived as relief in fictive sculpture, so perhaps it is instead a study for a *grisaille* painting or a print conceived as a classical relief. In any case, the drawing further demonstrates Mantegna's attraction to antiquity, and shows his reading of Alberti's treatise *On Painting*. Most importantly, it shows his independence before his sources, which he was always willing to alter for iconographic or stylistic reasons. Mantegna's known visions of antiquity were in two-dimensional works, either paintings, drawings, or engraving. Yet on one occasion he had an opportunity to design a classicising statue of the poet Virgil. The sculpture was to be set up in a city square in Mantua, the poet's hometown. The commission shows the interaction between patron, advisers, and artists. Isabella d'Este, the Marquise of Mantua, asked the Neapolitan humanist Giovanni Pontano in 1499 for advice about how Mantegna should make the work. Pontano wrote to Isabella that it would be best to make the work out of marble because if it were made out of a metal such as bronze it might be melted down in the future to make artillery pieces or something else. Pontano had further advice about the dress and pose of Virgil, which he recommended be simple and noble, the figure wearing a laurel crown and donning a toga or a senatorial dress and mantle, but not carrying a book. Mantegna never completed this sculptural project, but a clumsy drawing exists that is a rough copy of his ideas, showing he generally took the humanist's advice. Although this project never came to fruition, the documentation serves as an illustration of Mantegna's collaboration with a learned adviser and a cultured, interested patron.

The range of Mantegna's classical vision was broad, and we will see more evidence of Mantegna's work on antique themes and style in the next two chapters. Another way for Mantegna to explore the world of ancient artistic style and thought was through the medium of engravings. And his paintings for the Isabella d'Este – like the statue of Virgil she commissioned from him – evoke the philosophy, artistic themes, and style of Greco-Roman culture.

97. *Prophet and Sibyl*, c. 1490-1500.
Tempera on canvas,
48.5 x 48.4 cm.
Cincinnati Art Museum, Cincinnati.

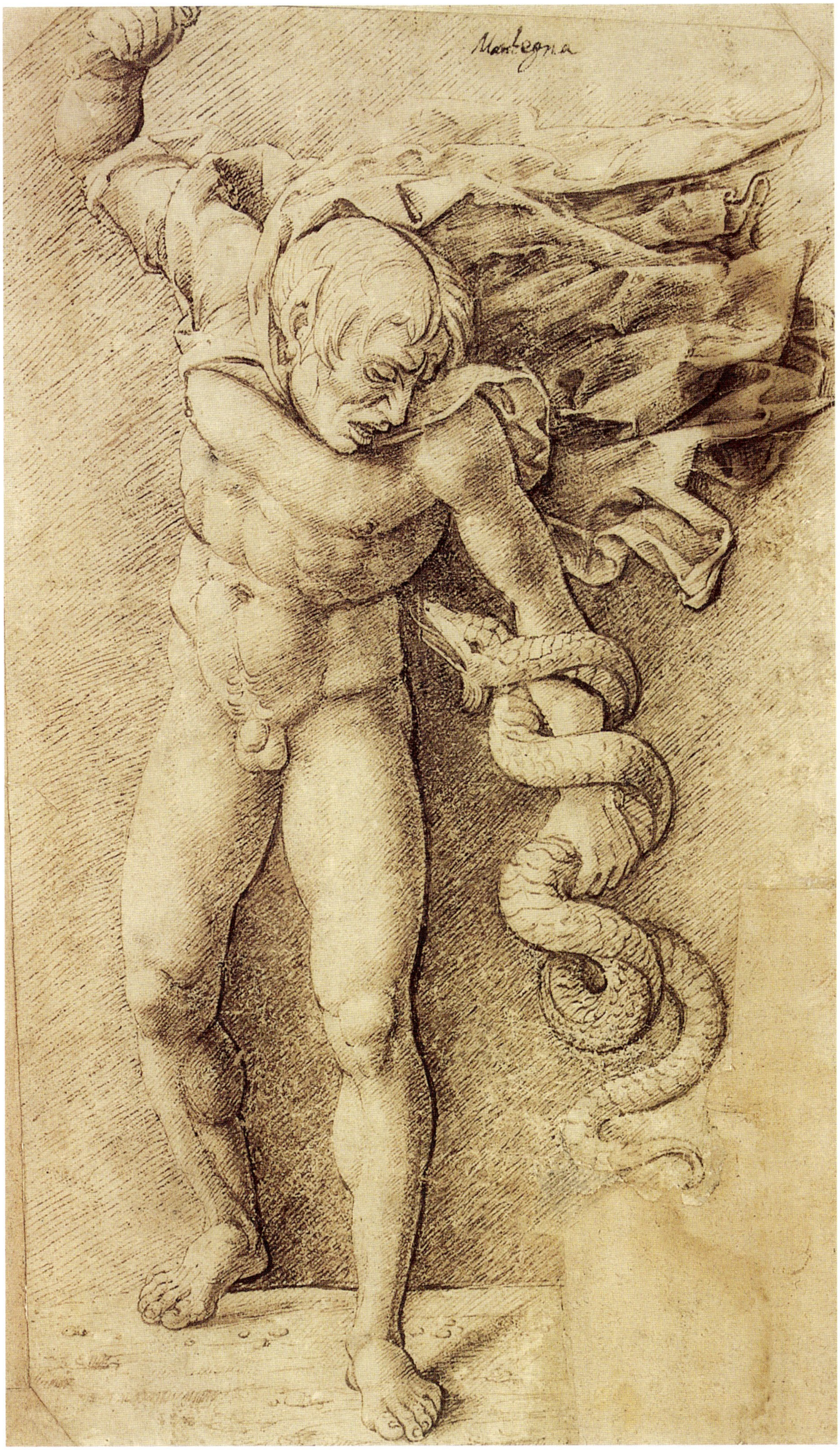
Mantegna

Mantegna and the Art of Printmaking

Mantegna was the first great artist of the Italian Renaissance to invent his own compositions and reproduce them in multiple copies by printing the designs on paper. Mantegna spread his fame through what at the time was modern technology. Long known in China, designs reproduced on paper had been made in the West since about 1400. The earliest prints in Europe were woodcuts, which were produced initially in countries north of the Alps, especially in Germany. In these early woodcuts, a block was cut so the part to appear in white would be removed and the areas left in relief would print as black when inked and pressed onto paper. This is the same principle behind the printing of letters in books, or as in a modern typewriter. Indeed, both woodcuts and printing were most widespread in the north of Europe: Johann Gutenberg's Bible and other major printing projects were produced at about the same time woodcuts were beginning to flourish north of the Alps. This development was aided by the growing abundance of paper, which could be produced in mass quantities because of improved manufacturing techniques. More important was the growing market, with the demand fuelled by a new group of middle-class buyers eager to acquire prints and printed books, many of them liberally illustrated with woodcuts. Aided by burgeoning demand, more abundant paper, and technological advances, the production of books and prints mushroomed in the late fifteenth century.

Mantegna was a central figure in the transformation of printmaking in Italy into a high art. Most prints of the early fifteenth century were not what we call great artworks; the process of elevating the field of printmaking from a craft to a fine art had already commenced in Germany and the Low Countries soon after mid-century. In the north of Europe, woodcuts produced before about 1450 were generally for popular consumption. Often containing images of simple religious scenes or individual saints, they were sold at fairs, purchased by pilgrims of all social classes en route to their destinations, or given out for free by religious confraternities. The creators of these inexpensive images were sometimes called "saint makers," designers of simple devotional figures for a broad market. Folded into one's pocket, glued on to walls with melted wax, or set into cheap frames, these early prints were inexpensive works of art produced by artisans, not by the most revered artists. This situation began to change in the middle and late fifteenth century, when artists such as the German painter Martin Schongauer began to produce superb prints of the highest quality (Fig. 99). Mantegna was well aware of the potentialities of printmaking, and he joined those northern European artists who turned printmaking into a fine art. With the fine style of his prints, their large size format, and the broad range of sacred and secular subject matter, Mantegna advanced the art form to a new and higher level.

Mantegna is not known to have designed any woodcuts; he preferred to make finer and more subtle prints than printing from a panel of wood which, by its nature, cannot be cut into so many fine lines without the exposed ridges breaking off during the printing process. Mantegna was like the northern European masters who turned from woodcuts to prints from metal sheets called engravings. Of course, some masters, such as Albrecht Dürer, have demonstrated it is indeed possible to produce beautiful and subtle woodcuts (Fig. 100), but even Dürer turned to making works by printing from copper plates when he sought an even more intricate and fine effect. Mantegna, like a growing number of European artists, wanted the results only printing on metal can produce.

98. *Faun Attacking a Snake,* c. 1480.
Pen and ink on paper,
29.3 x 17.3 cm.
British Museum, London.

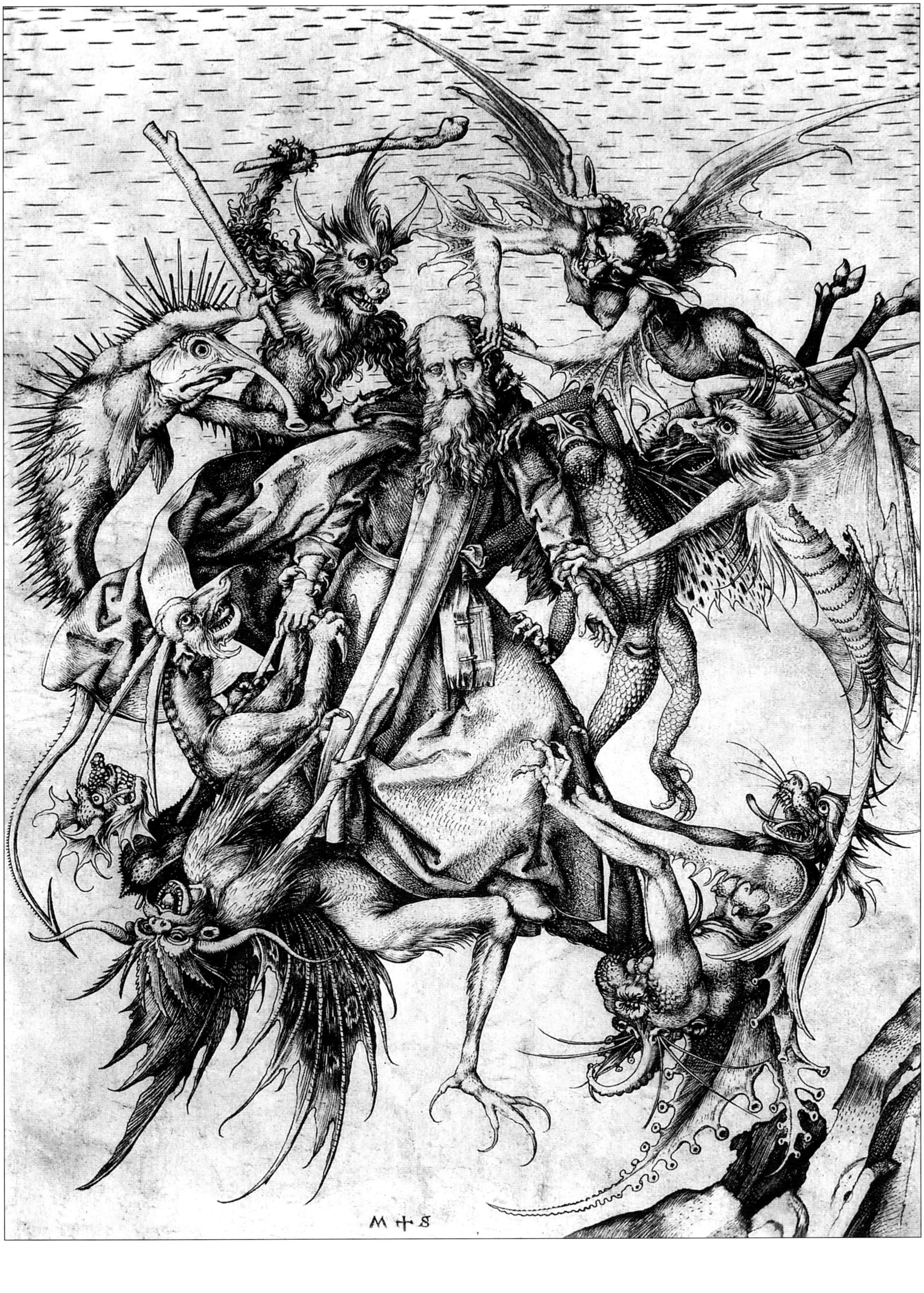
M+S

The making of engravings began in the sphere of goldsmiths. Some early prints from metal plates originated in works known as *nielli*, which result from the incising of designs onto silver plates. The grooves are then tinted in a black substance called *nigellum* in Latin (hence *niello* in Italian). These were not intended as printing plates, but it was discovered these plates or casts of them could, when inked, produced a printed image. Goldsmiths and other metalworkers produced *niello* prints in the fifteenth century, and several Florentine artists specialised in such images. This craft, and the art of engraving proper, remained in the hands of artists of skilled but relatively limited talents, as the necessary abilities to work the metal remained with professional goldsmiths, and not with trained painters. Before Mantegna, the best Italian painters stayed with their own craft, and left the working of metal to professional metalworkers. These specialists, such as the Florentine Francesco Rosselli, made engravings of great interest to the history of art because of the subject matter, technique, and charming narrative style.

Although Mantegna was the earliest Italian master of the first rank to produce fine engravings systematically in many different subjects and over the course of many years, there was one great Italian artist near Mantegna's time who turned his hand to the production of an engraving: the Florentine painter Antonio del Pollaiuolo designed one spectacular engraving representing battling, naked men (Fig. 101). This enigmatic work, made in about 1465-1470, was the only known work of this type by Pollaiuolo, and Mantegna may in any case have preceded him, if his earliest efforts do date to the 1460s, as is often believed. Whether Pollaiuolo preceded Mantegna or not with his famous and elaborate engraving, the Mantuan artist was in debt to the Florentines in the field of printmaking, as he was in some other aspects of his art-making. Mantegna was in Florence in 1466, and would have been exposed to numerous examples of printmaking, and he could have met the metalworkers who were making *nielli* and engravings. With this exposure, and with some knowledge of the craft as being carried out in the north of Europe, he entered in spectacular fashion into the field of printmaking.

It was an important development that prints were at last designed by the best painters and designers of their times, including such leading lights as Pollaiuolo and Mantegna in Italy, and Martin Schongauer and Albrecht Dürer in the north. Finally, superb works by great artists could be produced in relatively large quantities and shipped easily across national borders. Ideas would henceforth travel quickly, and collectors could own a specimen of work of the best artists in Europe at reasonable prices. Today we are accustomed to having a wide range of reproductions available to us, but imagine when this was a new phenomenon, when artistic ideas could travel quickly and widely, and when art of the highest rank could be collected by a broad range of people.

Mantegna's level of participation in the art of printmaking is not documented and is highly debated among scholars. Preparing the copper plates, cutting them with a burin, inking the grooves, and running off the impressions to make an engraving is a difficult and tedious process. There is no certain evidence Mantegna cut and processed his own plates, and it is not impossible that in every instance he left the procedure to a trained professional, such as Giovanni Antonio da Brescia or Giulio Campagnola. If this were the case, then the hands of the collaborators would account for many of the details of the execution of texture, line, and shading. However, there is also some reason to think Mantegna did labour on some of his engravings from the beginning to the end of the process. There seems to be a growing application of skill and an improving technical perfection in a group of engravings as time went on; this would make it improbable that professional engravers were in every instance carrying out his designs,

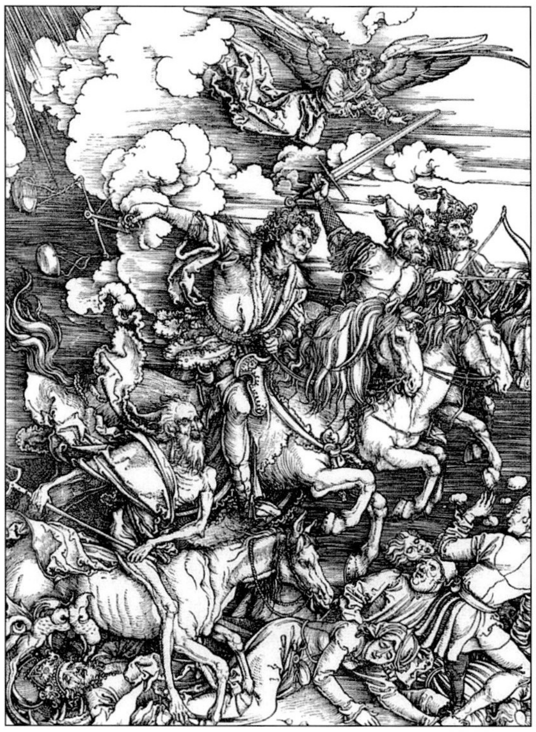

99. Martin Schongauer, *The Temptation of St Anthony*, c. 1475. Engraving, 31.5 x 22.9 cm. The Metropolitan Museum of Art, New York.

100. Albrecht Dürer, *Four Horsemen of the Apocalypse*, c. 1498. Woodcut, 39.4 x 28.1 cm. Galleria degli Uffizi, Florence.

because they would not have been learning in this way. Indeed, a number of Mantegna's engravings are unfinished to at least a small extent, indicating an experimental process. Mantegna also made his prints larger than was generally normal, some of these going badly because of the difficulties of printing evenly and clearly from such a large plate. His printmaking apparently involved a great deal of trial and error. It is plausible to believe Mantegna designed and produced from start to finish – cutting the plates as well – at least some of his engravings; a number of observers are convinced, for example, he personally worked on the plates for Figs. 71, 106, 108, 109, and 113. Still, even those who argue Mantegna produced his own engravings early on acknowledge that after about 1475 he hired professionals to produce the plates from his designs, and we can recognise the hands and special mark of his professional collaborators. In this study, we will leave aside in individual instances the thorny question of who actually worked on the metal plates, and regard them all at least as the product of Mantegna's artistic mind. The captions for engravings here, bearing the attribution to Mantegna, should be intended to indicate he designed the composition and he may well have also had a role (at whatever level) in the production of the print. The chronology of these prints is also difficult, and the dates offered here are approximate and offered tentatively, recognising again the scholarly debate in this area.

As an employee of the Gonzaga court, the artist was in a good position to make engravings. He could work on the prints during times when his official duties were not so onerous, perhaps between major commissions. Instead of taking months to make a painting, an engraving – even if Mantegna worked on the plates – might take days or weeks even for an elaborate composition. Since he received a regular salary, he did not have to worry about a market for his experiments in printmaking. The small number of surviving prints indicates he was not producing as many as possible, making not dozens but perhaps a dozen or fewer of each. Mantegna worked on engravings to produce stimulating ideas and to work out the intellectual problems of making engravings; his goal was not to mass-market his ideas and distribute as many as possible, as was the aim of so many other printmakers of the fifteenth century and later. Still, he did produce multiple copies of his inventions, and these certainly found a wider field of collectors than his paintings.

Although the production of engravings is usually a complicated and collaborative undertaking, we have remarkably few documents concerning Mantegna's relations with other artists and with patrons in this sphere of his activity. One document we do have is an extraordinary one, however, concerning the attempt by Mantegna to prevent his designs from being copied and reproduced by other engravers. In September 1475, an engraver named Simone da Reggio complained to Marquis Ludovico Gonzaga that Mantegna had had him and the artist Zoan Andrea assaulted by ruffians as well as officially accused of sodomy; Mantegna was irate because he feared Simone and Zoan had wronged him and violated his rights to his own inventions. The letter of complaint against Mantegna reads:

> "[To] the most illustrious and excellent lord, Lord Ludovico Marquis of Mantua, etc. my most especial lord: I make bold to inform your lordship of how I have been treated in your city, and to let you know my name is Simone di Ardizoni da Reggio, painter and engraver with the burin. When I came to Mantua, Andrea Mantegna made me grand offers, presenting himself as my friend. And since I have long since been a friend of Zoan Andrea, painter in Mantua, and he told me when we were talking that he had been robbed of *stampe* [= prints or metal plates for prints], drawings, and medals, he moved me to pity that he had been so badly treated. I said I would do these *stampe* over, and I worked for

him for about four months. When the devilish Andrea Mantegna found out I was doing these prints over, he sent a Florentine to threaten me, saying I would pay for it. And besides that, one evening I was assaulted by the nephew of Carlo de Moltone and more than ten armed men, Zoan Andrea and I, and left to die, and this I can prove. And again, to keep the work from continuing, A[ndrea] M[antegna] found some ruffians to do his bidding and they accused me to the criminal court of being a sodomite, and the one who accused me is named Zoano Luca of Novara, the notary who has the accusation is a relative of Carlo Moltone. Being a foreigner, I had perforce to flee, and I am now in Verona to finish these prints... I have gone to forty cities and nothing was ever said against my good name, only now Andrea Mantegna with his arrogance and rule of Mantua, and if your lordship does not restrain him he would be the cause of great scandals arising, and I humbly commend myself to your lordship. [Signed] Simone de Regio."[16]

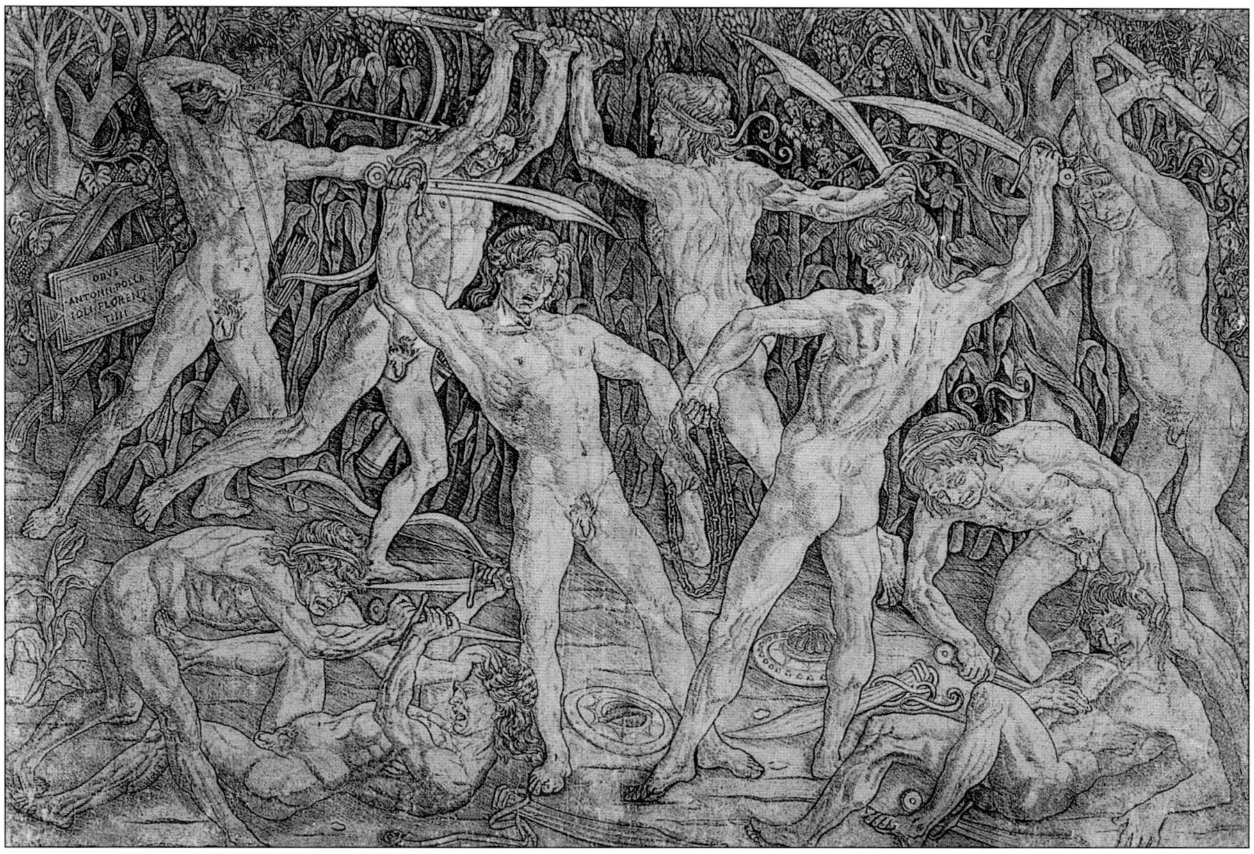

A plausible interpretation of this complaint is that Simone and Zoan were arranging to produce copies of Mantegna's designs based on the prints or plates they had produced or acquired. If this were the case, it is obvious why Mantegna was upset, for it would have resulted in the distribution of the master's compositions.

There were no standard copyright laws in the fifteenth century, and it was easy to borrow the designs of others by copying in painting or prints. Artists had long copied the works of others for study and to aid their own artistic growth, but to borrow ideas and produce engravings from them could be especially lucrative if the prints were sold widely. Mantegna wanted to be able to control the distribution of his own ideas. Simone da Reggio, in helping the painter Zoan Andrea to produce prints based on plates or designs Mantegna made, was violating what we would call intellectual

101. Antonio del Pollaiuolo, *Battle of Naked Men*, c. 1465. Engraving, 38.4 x 58.9 cm. The Metropolitan Museum of Art, New York.

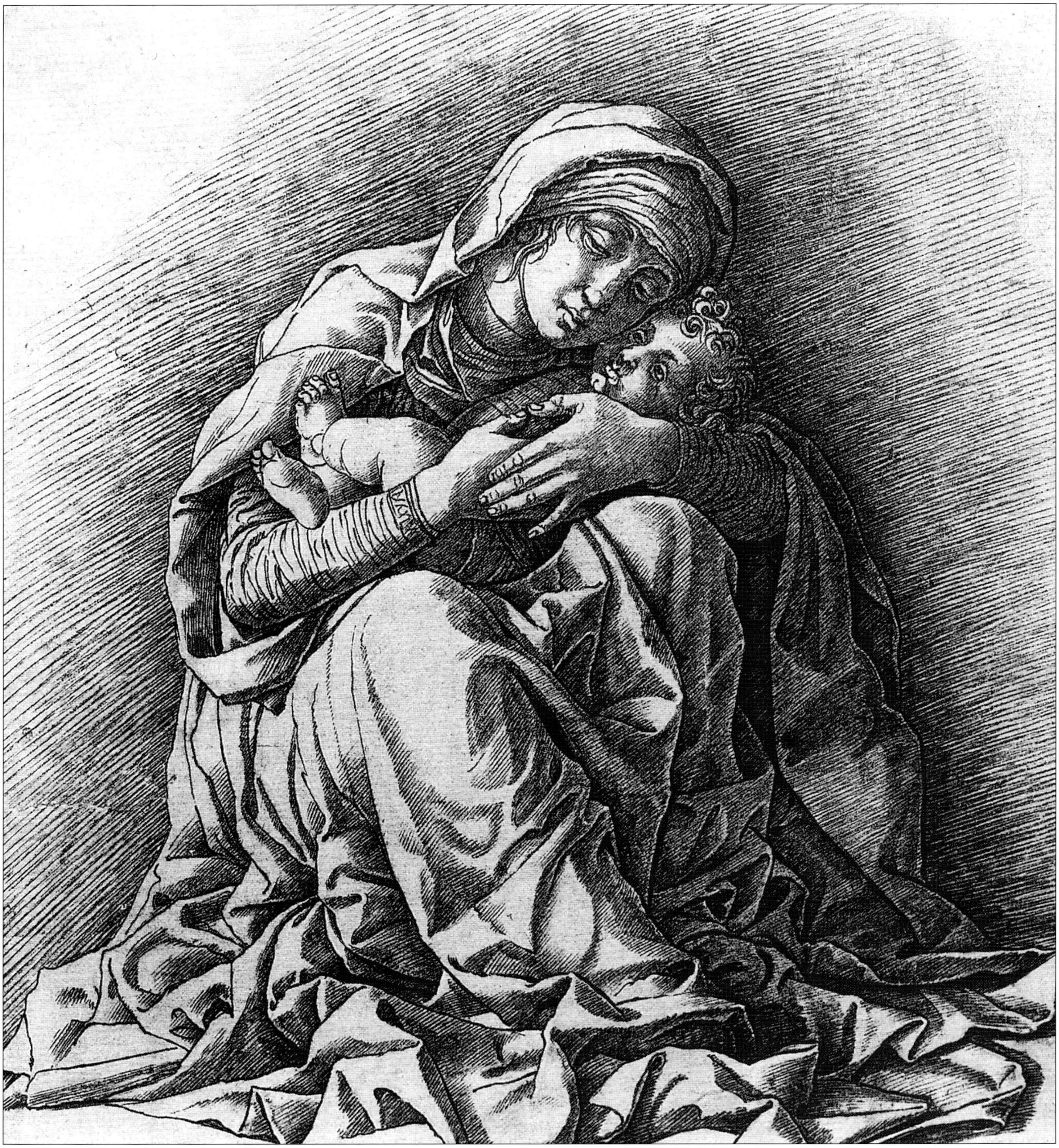

property rights, hence Mantegna's reaction. Mantegna was not the only one trying to protect his copyright privileges. In 1505, Albrecht Dürer denounced the Italian engraver Marcantonio Raimondi for copying his inventions, and soon thereafter the Venetian government passed a law forbidding anyone to use Dürer's signature monogram in prints. But Mantegna, impelled by his short temper and moral indignation, took matters into his own hands in this regard, not waiting for any legal authority to come to his aid. Even apart from any light Simone's letter throws on Mantegna's engravings, it contains a number of other striking elements. It states Mantegna had a general reputation of arrogance and over dominance in Mantua. As the Gonzaga's favoured court painter, he certainly must have felt justified in feeling secure in his position, and he apparently felt free to punish the upstart who was helping to reproduce his designs. Yet the *marchese* did invite Simone to come to Mantua to tell his story (he never showed up), so Mantegna's position was not so secure that he could commit the crime of hiring thugs to beat up a fellow artist. Mantegna also went to the

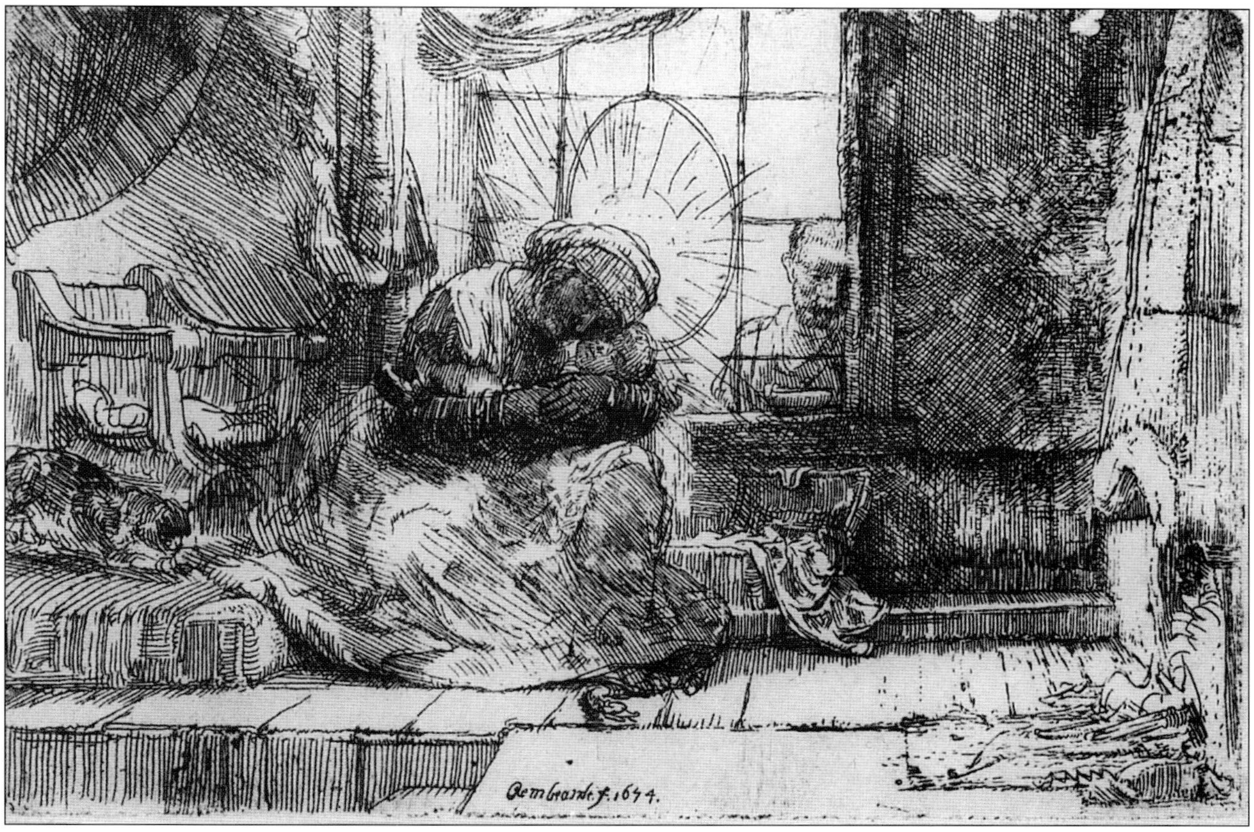

trouble of having the fellow accused of sodomy (essentially, homosexuality), which, although it was often overlooked by the law, was in Renaissance times punishable by fines, dismemberment, or even death. Accusations of sodomy were frequent in the Middle Ages and Renaissance period, as it was an easy way to eliminate a rival or frighten a competitor. Leonardo da Vinci was accused of sodomy while he lived in Florence, and the painter Alessandro Botticelli came under official suspicion for the same offence. Mantegna's attempt to have the supposed copyist punished for sodomy was a serious step, and indicates he felt deeply threatened by the appropriation of his artistic ideas.

Turning to Mantegna's prints, we find the application in a new medium of the ideas he conveyed in his paintings, with similarities in composition, style, and subject matter. One advantage of prints was whereas only one patron could receive his tender painting of the *Madonna and Child* (Fig. 71), more collectors could obtain a specimen of his finely wrought and equally maternal engraving of

102. *Madonna and Child*, c. 1480-1490. Engraving, 21 x 22.2 cm. Albertina, Vienna.

103. Rembrandt van Rijn, *Virgin and Child*, 1674. Etching, 9.4 x 14.3 cm. The Metropolitan Museum of Art, New York.

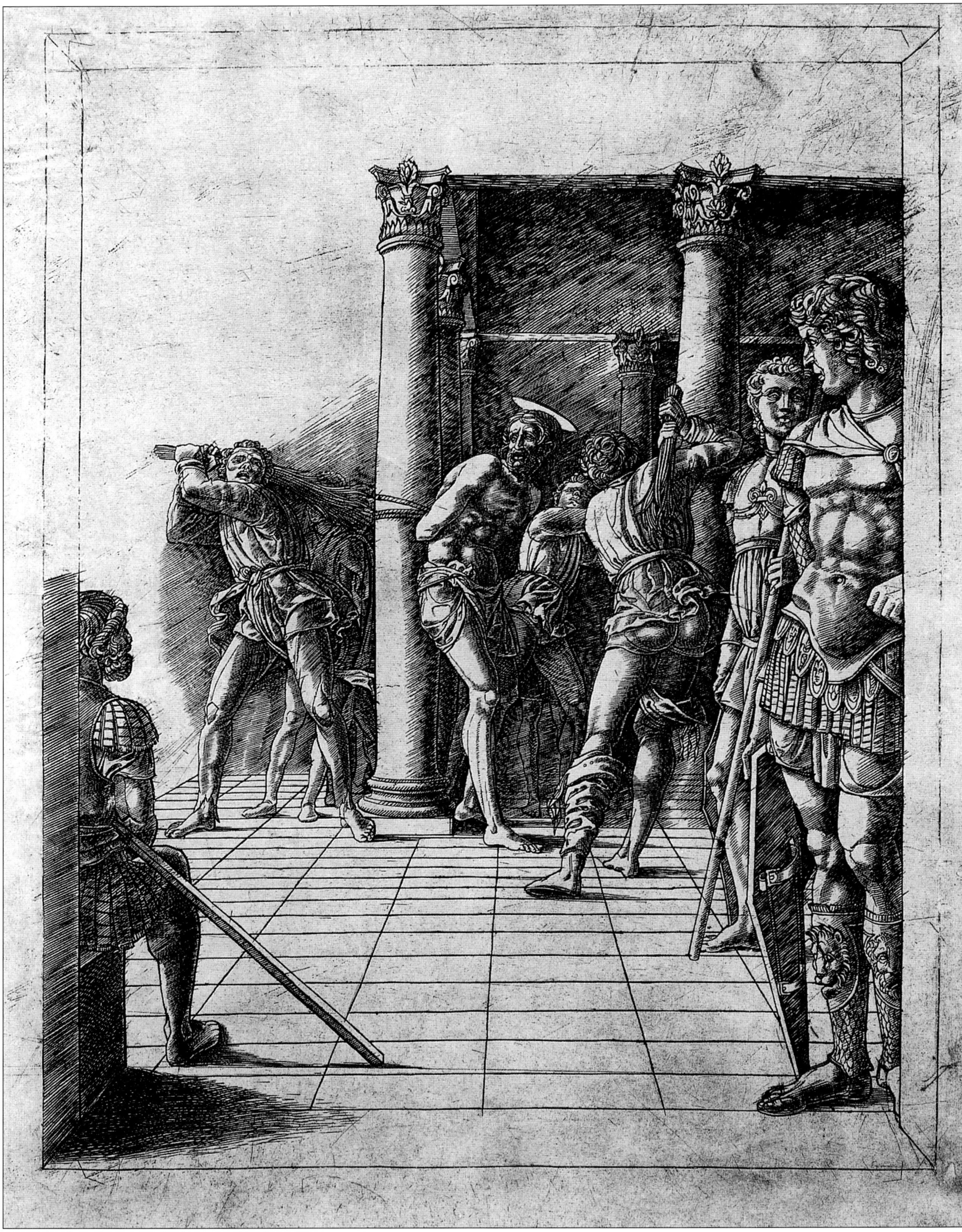

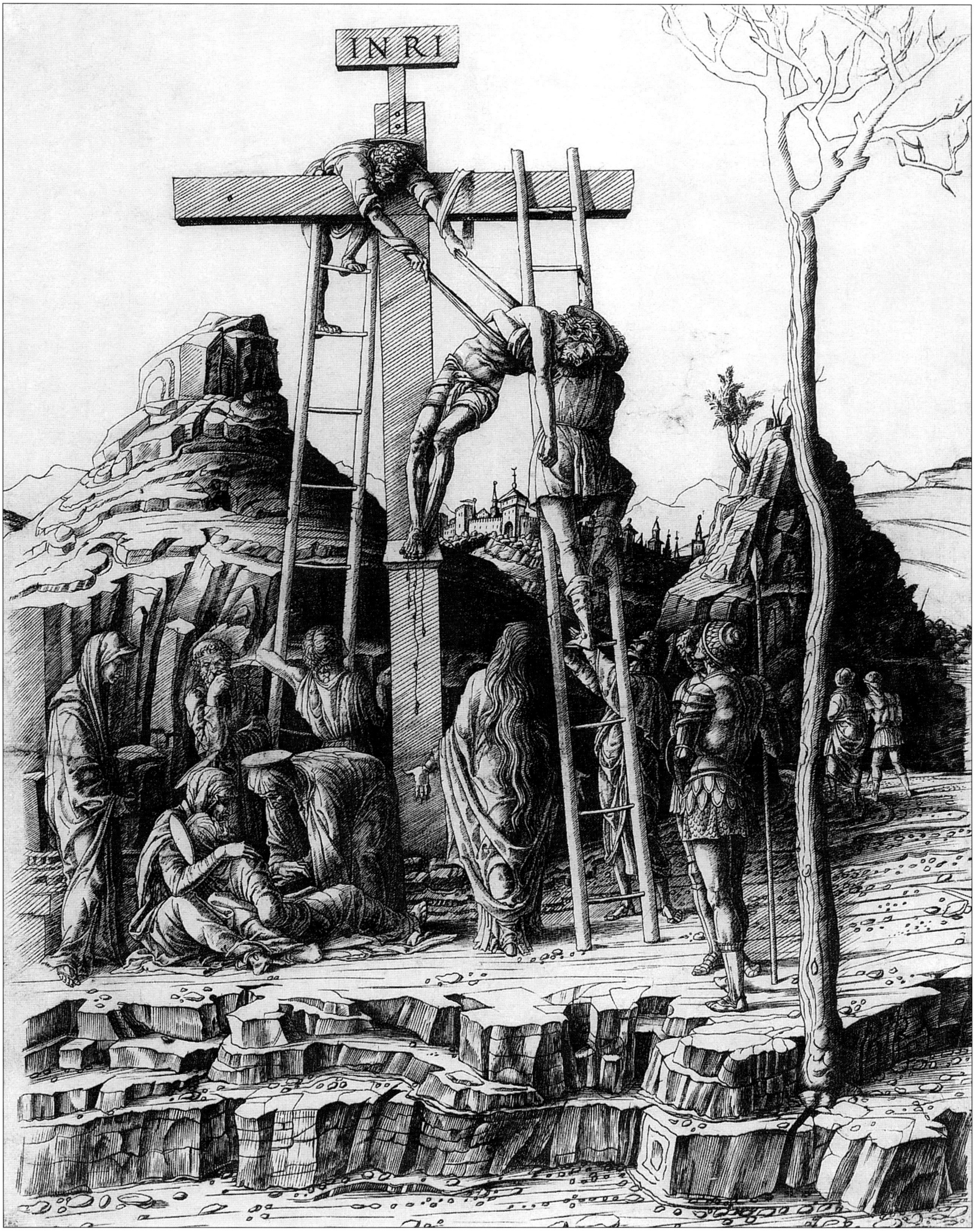
INRI

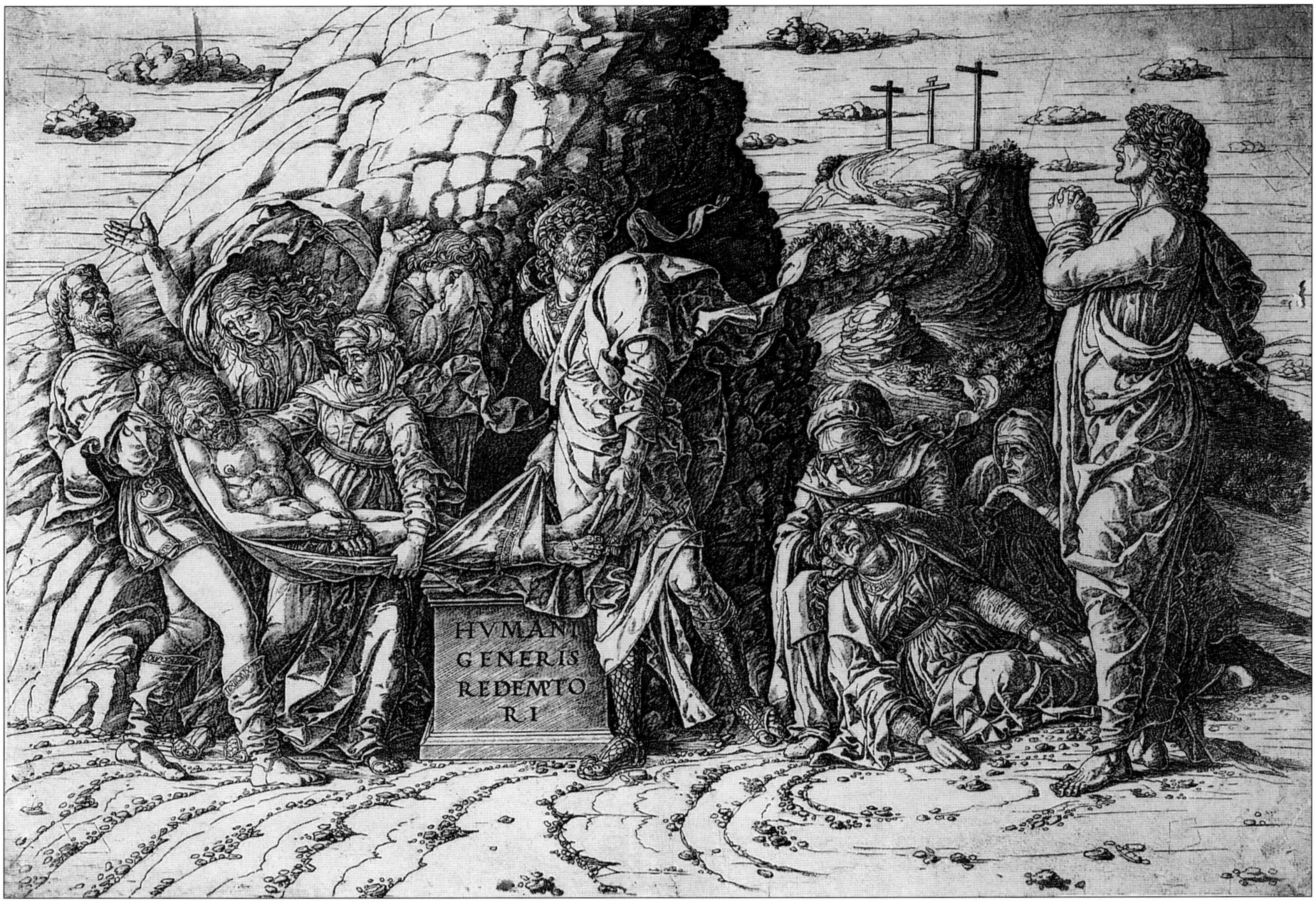

the same subject (Fig. 102). Mary holds Christ snugly in her arms. She is seated as a Madonna of Humility, and looks away from him in knowing thought. Her garments dominate the lower portion of the composition, and form a sea of drapery folds and linear cross-movements. The atmosphere around them is indicated by the parallel lines hovering as a backdrop. This engraving serves as an example of the unique qualities separating the art of printmaking from painting, for the former involves a whole new range of specific artistic features. The print of the *Madonna and Child* is one of Mantegna's richest engravings, with stunning transitions of light and dark and warm texture to the surface. In typical Italian fashion, Mantegna used parallel lines (not cross-hatching) to achieve a rich, tonal effect of light and dark. In this particular print, the texture is particularly striking partly because of the use of dry point. The technique of dry point is the incising of the copper plate with an instrument which throws up shavings of copper onto the edge of the lines, which then print as slightly fuzzy, giving an attractive, warm texture to the print. (Most of the engraving attributed to Mantegna here includes at least some use of dry point.) Either Mantegna was achieving this effect himself or he was, in consultation with his hired engraver, making sure this was happening. The result of this technique and the tender composition make the *Madonna and Child* one of Mantegna's masterpieces. Even the Baroque master Rembrandt, whose own technique as a printmaker was unsurpassed in its richness and subtlety, was moved to copy Mantegna's engraving in a print of his own (Fig. 103).

104. *Flagellation of Christ,* c. 1465-1470.
Engraving, 44.2 x 34.3 cm.
Kupferstichkabinett, Berlin.

105. *Deposition from the Cross,* c. 1465.
Engraving, 45.2 x 36.2 cm.
British Museum, London.

106. *Entombment,* c. 1465-1470.
Engraving, 29.9 x 44.2 cm.
The National Gallery of Art, Washington, D.C.

In addition to seeking an attractive surface texture in his printmaking, Mantegna achieved a striking three-dimensionality in his engravings. His paintings and drawings too are very convincing in their modelling, which gives a rounded look to the objects in his picture space. These effects are easier to achieve in painting and drawing, because one can use brushstrokes or washes of shading and colour to give a complete and continuous surface that appears rounded. In engravings, though, one uses only lines against the blank paper; it is no wonder so many woodcuts and engravings of the fifteenth-century appear stiff and flat. Mantegna took the art of engraving to a new level, representing a world that appears tangible, deep, and subtle. He also endowed his engravings with the kind of lively linearity and sharp design that characterises his paintings.

Mantegna's engravings are related to his drawings and paintings in subject matter as in style. A large percentage of his engravings have to do with the death and suffering of Jesus, appealing to the same need for close communion with the Passion of Christ to which his pictures also catered. Well before Mantegna's time there was already a rich history of the production of Passion imagery in woodcuts and other engravings. In the north of Europe, prints of the torture and death of Christ were widespread, as people collected these images, often gluing or attaching them to walls or keeping them in scrapbooks. The medium of printmaking is particularly suitable to scenes of the Passion of Christ because the sharp, liney quality of the prints helps to convey emotional suffering and pain (cf. Fig. 99).

One of Mantegna's earlier images of Christ's death, from the 1460s, is an elaborate *Deposition from the Cross*, with a detailed and rocky landscape illustrating the empty and stark feeling of death (Fig. 105). Even the clouds and foliage appear hard as stone, underscoring the mood of mourning. His unfinished *Flagellation of Christ* (Fig. 104; note the incomplete areas on the left) dramatically shows the torturing of Christ, the cruel action taking place while idle, pitiless Roman soldiers stand passively by. One of his greatest religious engravings is *The Entombment* (Fig. 106), characterised by strong and vivid emotional reactions of the actors. An engraving of *The Risen Christ with Saint Andrew and Longinus* serves as a startling vision of the resurrected Christ, whose presence before us is mediated by two holy men who share the spectators's piety (Fig. 108). These engravings, although lacking in colour, would have served the same function as paintings, suitable as objects of devotion, moving works by a great master. Beyond the specific subject, this was an age when the importance of the artist's name was becoming a chief factor in collecting, when not just a certain scene was sought, but a specimen of a master's work. One could thus own "a Mantegna" in receiving one of his prints, a work of great beauty and fine technique.

Whether or not Mantegna was cutting his own plates, there is evidence that he took care to provide rich, tonal drawings, for his own use or to help to ensure the final prints would embody his special artistic style if the designs were to be taken up by professional metal workers. In the *Faun Attacking a Snake* (Fig. 98) and *The Risen Christ with Saint Andrew and Longinus* (Fig. 108), Mantegna produced carefully wrought and subtle drawings, using washes of various colours (Figs. 98 and 107; cf. also Fig. 110). In these cases, the drawings by Mantegna were transcribed literally onto the plate in some fashion, for the engravings and drawings by Andrea are the same size. Thus, he managed to control the invention, the texture and shading, and the size of the print.

What did fifteenth-century collectors do with Mantegna's engravings? Certainly the works were treated differently from popular prints of the time. Lower levels of prints in the fifteenth century were pasted into books or on walls, or kept in a less formal way on one's person during trips. In other words, cheap woodcuts and engravings of the fifteenth century were sometimes collected and treasured, and sometimes used as ephemeral objects, like postcards or Christmas cards today.

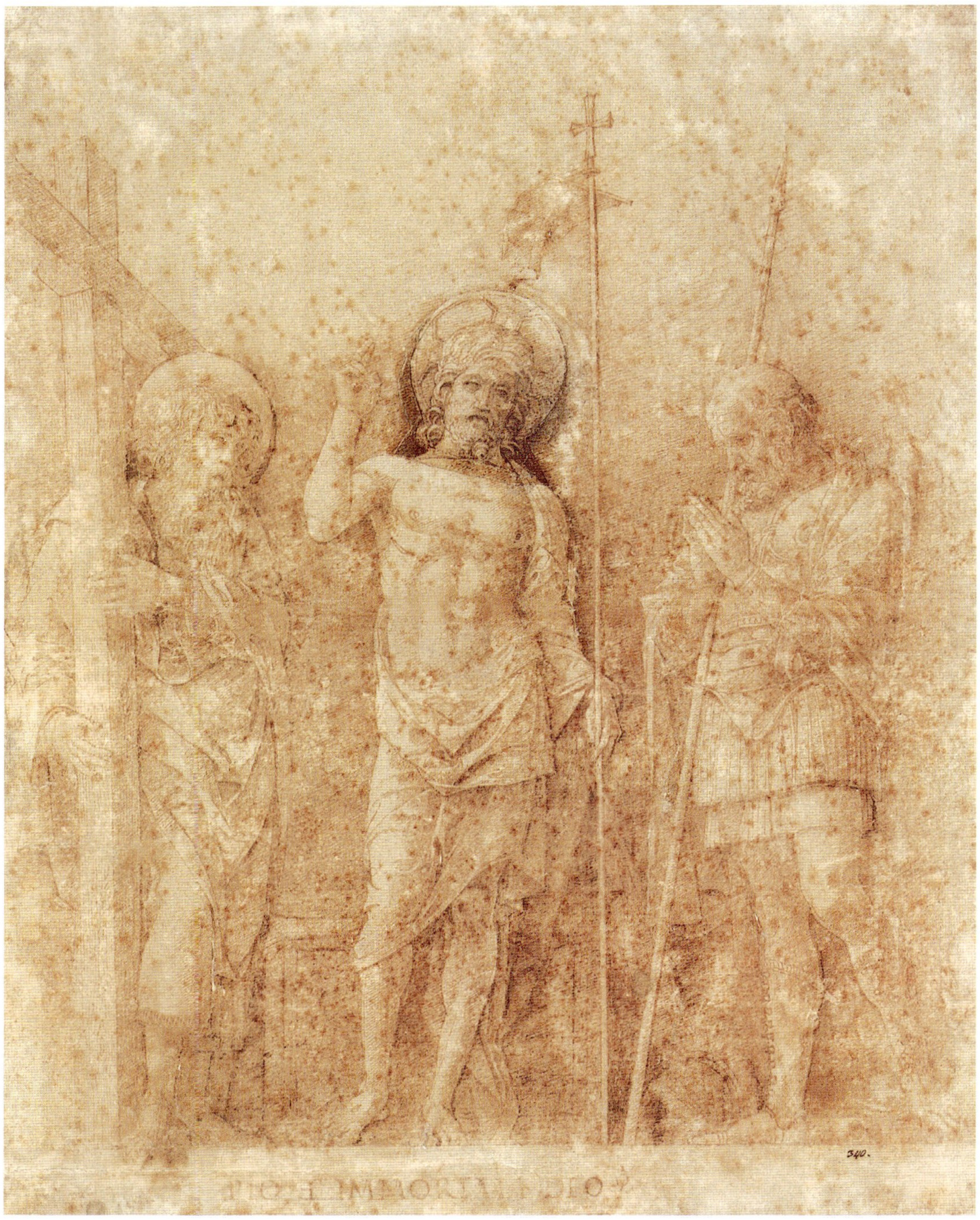

Yet, the size of most of Mantegna's engravings and their high quality meant they were probably kept as loose sheets in what we would call portfolios, perhaps stored in chest drawers. In addition some of them were applied to canvas and treated as portable pictures. Mantegna's prints were works of art, not popular religious objects. When they were attached to canvas and hung on walls, they competed with paintings, forming more accessible examples to Mantegna's artistry.

We have only scant evidence as to how Mantegna's engravings were distributed, and who acquired them, although documentation from the time for other artists aids us. Although we have records of sales of his prints, and we lack any firm evidence about the price of Mantegna's engravings in his lifetime; if he was selling them, they certainly would have cost far less than any of his paintings.

Certainly, the existence of multiple copies meant a wider spectatorship was able to acquire them, so courtiers and merchants in Mantua and elsewhere in Italy could own one even if a painting was out of their grasp. In addition to perhaps selling engravings, Mantegna gave some away, a practice conducted by other artists of his stature.

A German contemporary of Mantegna, Martin Schongauer, carried his own engravings with him on travels and gave them as gifts to his hosts and benefactors along the way. Later, Albrecht Dürer also gave his works away liberally as gifts to patrons, friends, and other artists. Mantegna gave a small painting of Christ as a gift (Fig. 70), and documentary evidence indicates he made similar use of his engravings. One series of letters from the court of Mantua offers insight into how contemporaries kept and carried engravings, and how Mantegna

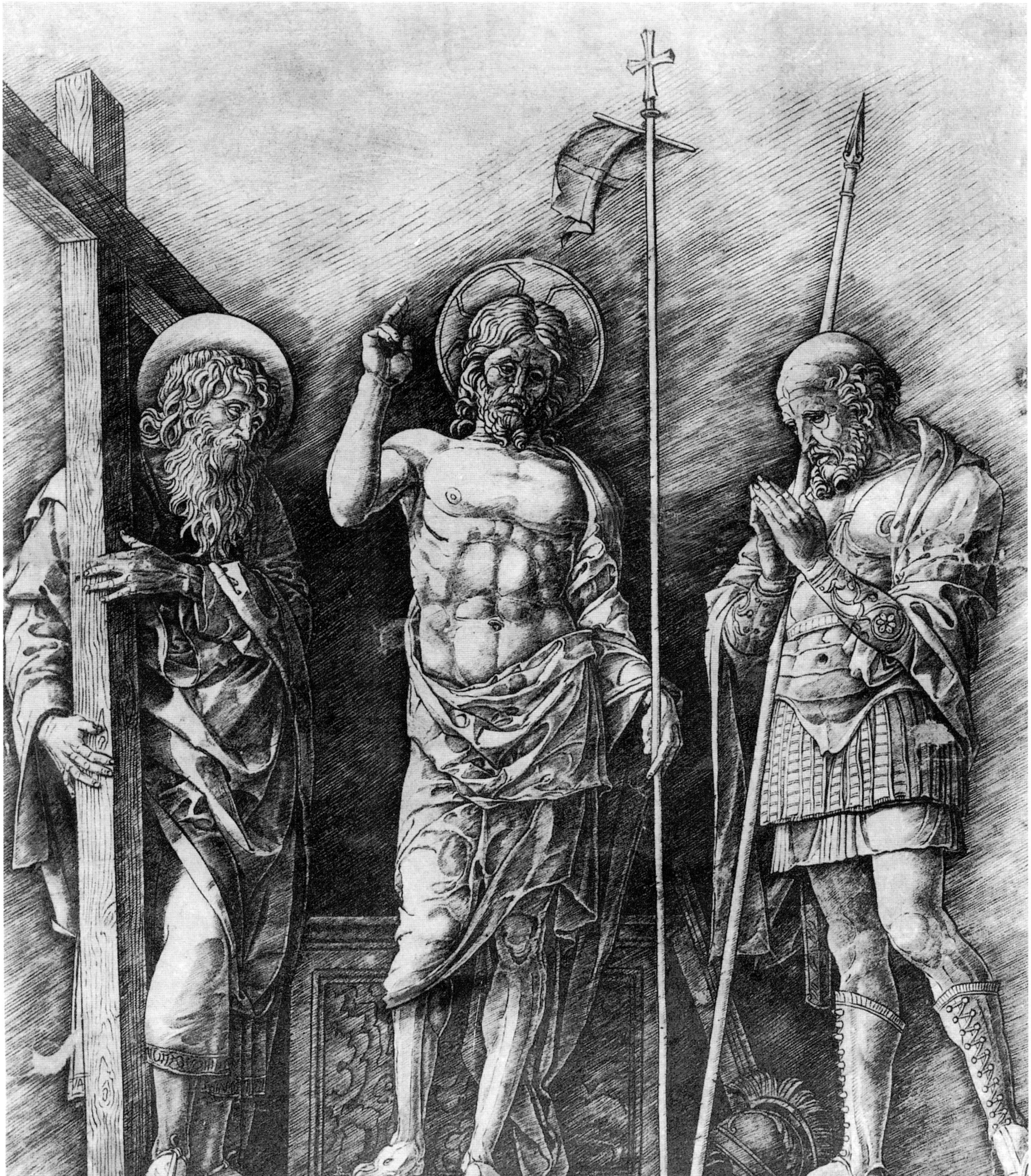

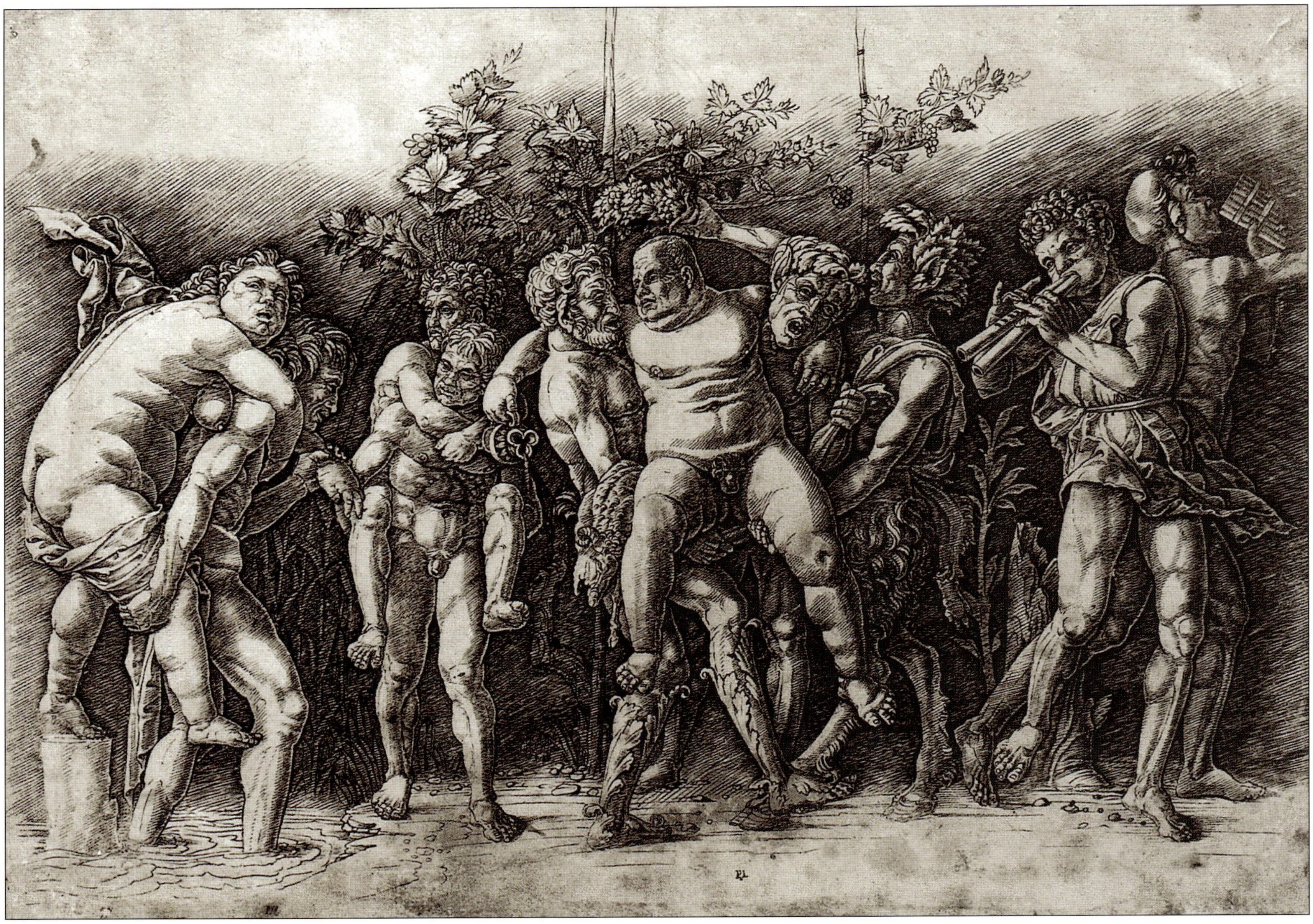

presented them as gifts. In 1491, Mantegna mentioned a certain *quadretino* ("little picture") he gave as a gift to the marquis, Francesco Gonzaga. A later document reveals this *quadretino* was an engraving; it is most likely one designed by Mantegna, although this is not absolutely certain. It was then given as a gift by the *marchese* to someone in Milan. The Mantuan courier who travelled to Milan kept it in a soft cover so as not to damage it, keeping it suspended in a box. Mantegna then promised to give Francesco another one to replace the engraving the marquis had given away, noting he had the metal plate and could easily make another one. Thus, we see the artist, his patron, and the friends of his patron in a small circle of gift giving, the print used by the ruler to honour someone in a foreign court, and two different impressions of the print used by Mantegna to please and flatter the patron. He kept the plate in reserve, running off copies when he needed them.

Since Mantegna was a court employee, the marquis and the rest of the Gonzaga family had opportunities to obtain his prints. Yet, they found a wider circle of artists than that. Indeed, a major group of potential collectors or viewers of Mantegna's prints consisted of other artists. This included not just artists in Italy but those living all across Europe; prints, so easily transported, were the chief means during this period of making one's style known beyond the Alps and across the Italian peninsula. Michelangelo made a painted copy (now lost) of Schongauer's beautiful engraving of the

Temptation of Saint Anthony (Fig. 99). Raphael pinned up prints by Albrecht Dürer on the walls of his studio so his students could learn the German artist's designs and compositions. Similarly, Dürer copied part of Mantegna's engraving of a *Battle of Sea Gods* (Fig. 113), in addition to copying his *Bacchanal with Silenus* (Fig. 109). Mantegna's prints were a way for many northern European artists to learn about the Italian Renaissance.

Closer to home, there is abundant evidence the designs from Mantegna's prints were copied, directly or in variant form, into prints, paintings, and drawings of other Italian artists, especially in other northern Italian cities such as Ferrara, Venice, and Milan, where Mantegna's own personal reputation was most high. Even though he did not produce numerous copies of his engravings, they found their way into the hands of others, and were copied, as Dürer did, so his designs eventually found a wide audience.

The information about the stealing of Mantegna's designs by Zoan Andrea tells us that in Verona (which was in Venetian territory) Mantegna's ideas were to be reproduced and distributed to a wide market, even if he had planned only a more limited edition of engravings for those compositions. Prints helped Mantegna's style to spread throughout Italy and beyond.

In addition to noble patrons and other artists, there was another potential audience for Mantegna's printmaking at the time, and that was among humanists. Prints were a way for Mantegna to illustrate edifying subject matter in a high style. Mantegna produced a large number of engravings on humanistic topics; indeed, some of his secular prints are quite complex, and could only be understood by an erudite viewer. As a painter Mantegna worked for the court, and his portraits, murals, and easel pictures – unique and time-consuming to produce – were meant for his patrons; but his engravings could more easily achieve a wider spectatorship by being sold or given to humanist-collectors.

Alternatively, if scholars never had the opportunity to collect Mantegna's engravings, many of these prints were acquired by aristocratic patrons with interests in classical themes and ancient, pagan subject matter. These works, even if never owned by the less wealthy intellectuals, could have been lent to and enjoyed by humanistic scholars and dilettantes interested in antiquity.

The secular engravings of the Renaissance were similar in subject matter to the many small bronzes produced in northern Italy during the time, works widely collected by humanists who used these small representations of classical satyrs and other creatures as inkwells and candlesticks. These bronze pieces, which were produced in great numbers in Padua and Mantua during the later fifteenth century, included plaquettes of Greco-Roman scenes, and served as affordable but beautiful and inspiring specimens of classical style and subject matter.

Both these classicising bronzes and the engravings of Mantegna could be kept in a study or library, acting to spur the intellect and helping to revive the kinds of subjects and styles humanists knew flourished in antiquity. In one instance, he used a small bronze of this type as a model for a child in one of his engravings, or the sculptor made the figure in response to the engraving, evidence of the kind of exchange and interdependence these two forms – engravings and bronze figurines or plaquettes – had for viewers and artists during Mantegna's time.

107. *The Risen Christ with St Andrew and Longinus,* c. 1475-1480. Pen and ink and brown wash on paper, 35 x 28.5 cm. Staatliche Graphische Sammlung, Munich.

108. *The Risen Christ with St Andrew and Longinus,* c. 1475-1480. Engraving, 31.9 x 27 cm. Bibliothèque nationale de France, Paris.

109. *Bacchanal with Silenus,* c. 1470-1475. Engraving, 29.9 x 43.7 cm. Private collection of the Duke of Devonshire, Chatsworth.

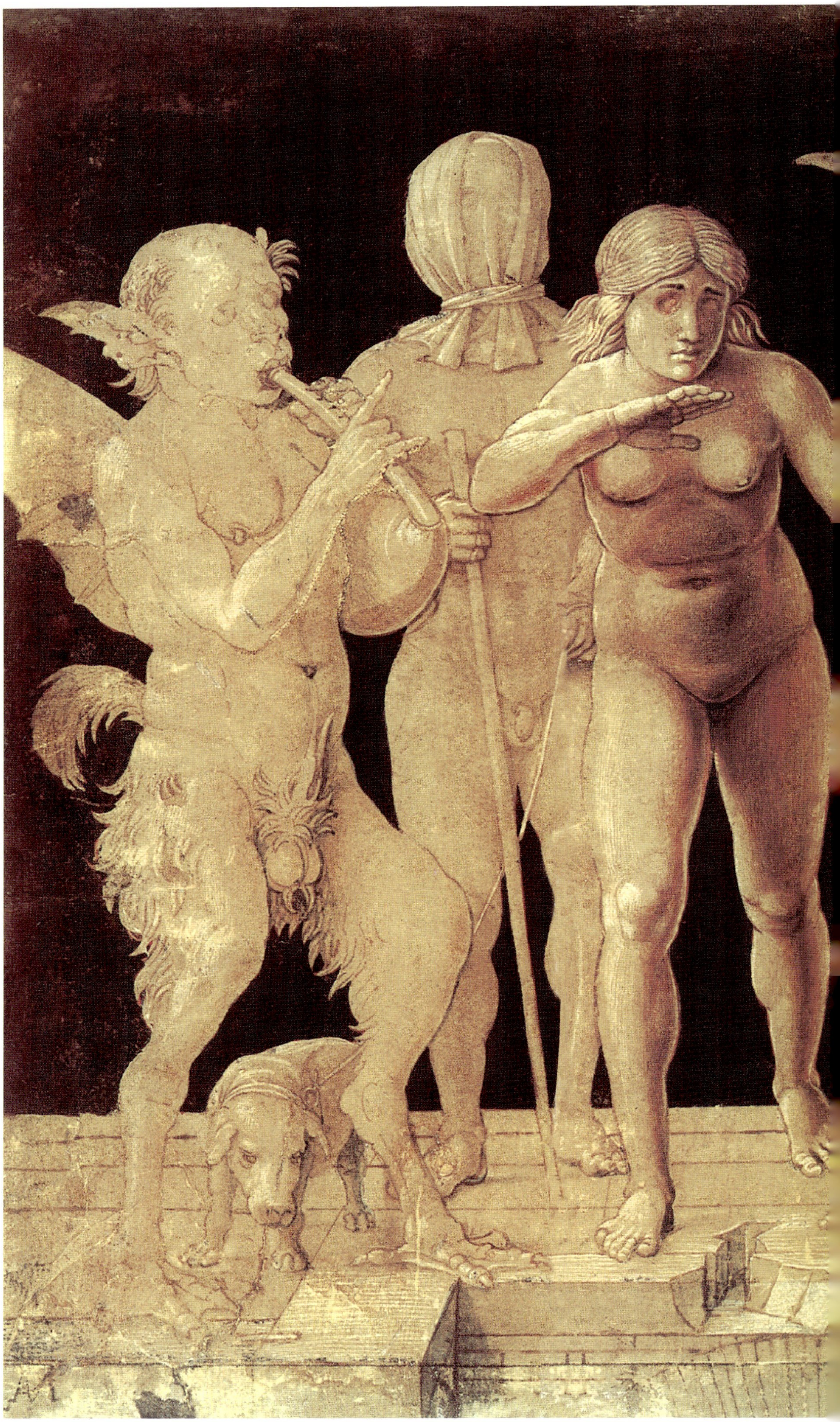

110. *The Fall and Rescue of Ignorant Humanity*, c. 1490-1500.
Pen and ink, heightened with white, with additions of black and red, on paper,
28.7 x 43.3 cm.
British Museum, London.

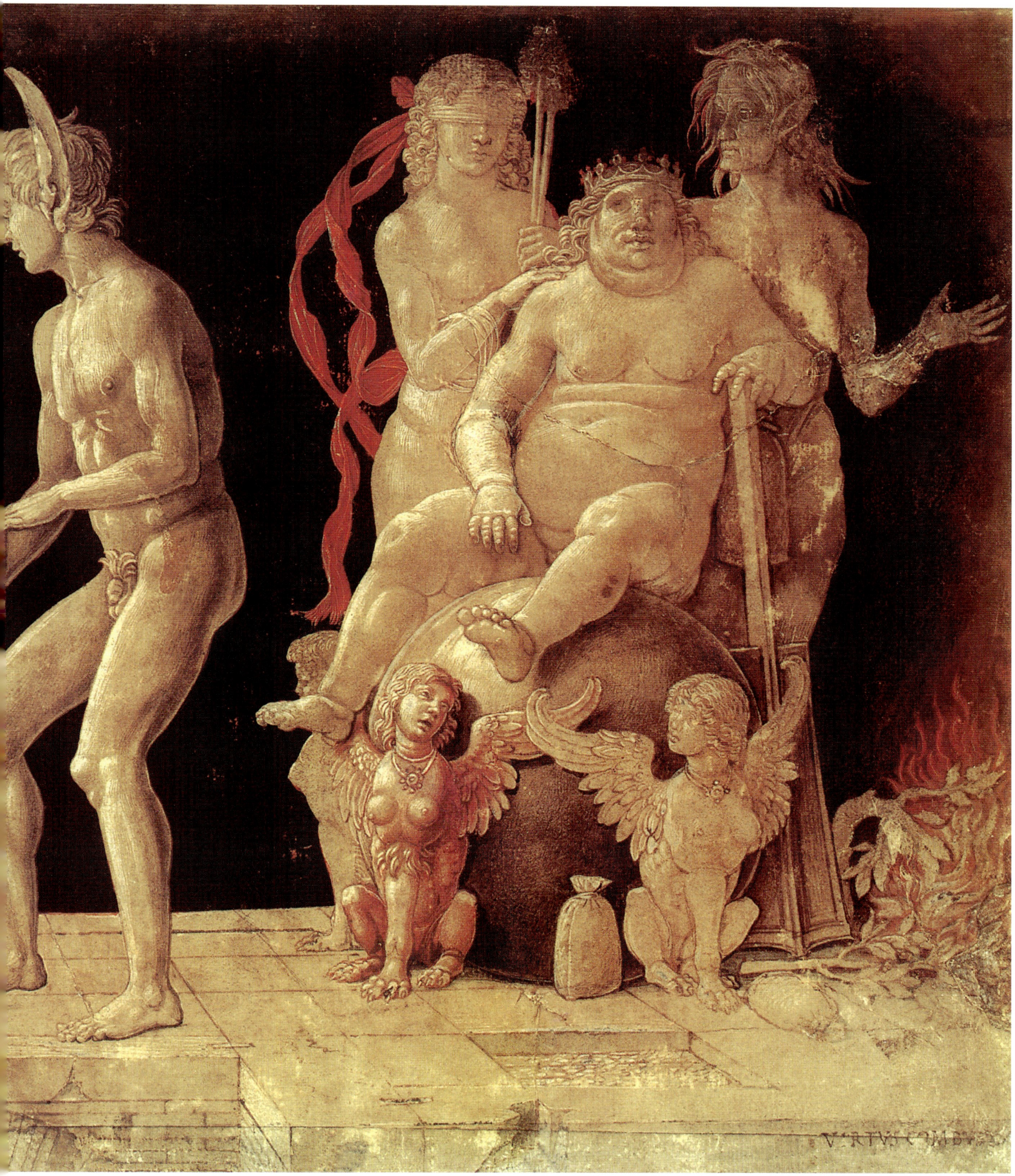
V·RTVS·COMB

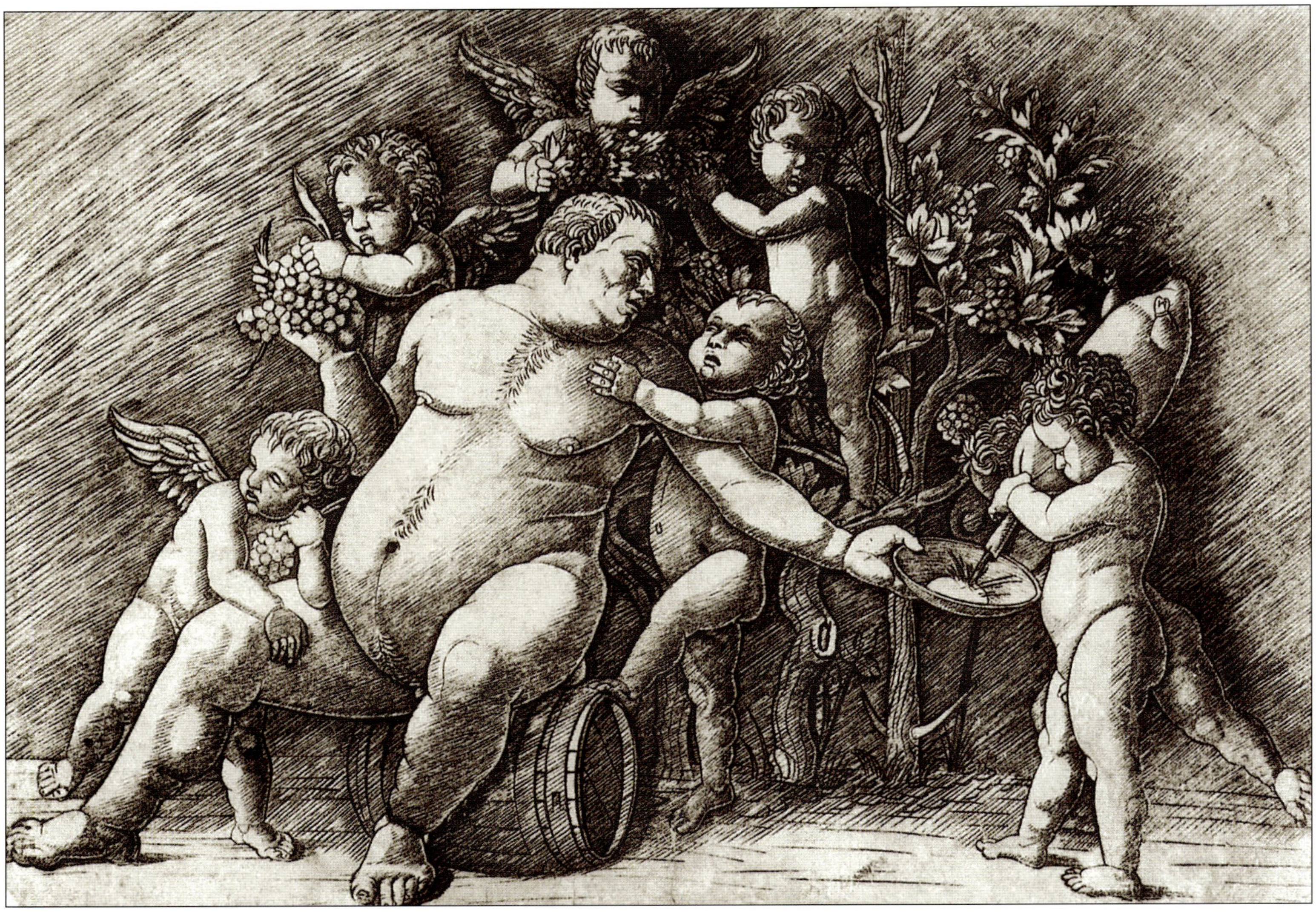

In order to appeal to erudite viewers – whether learned patrons or professional humanists – several of Mantegna's prints consisted of frankly pagan and secular subject matter intended to instruct as well as to amuse the spectator and evoke the spirit and the artistic style of antiquity. An example of this is his pair of engravings, pendants meant to be looked at together, of a *Bacchanal with a Wine Vat* and a *Bacchanal with Silenus* (Fig. 109). On the right of the latter is Silenus, a principal follower of Bacchus, whose weighty figure is a burden to the two humans and a satyr who support him. Bacchus was a god of wine and revelry, and all these figures are enjoying wine, which causes one to become prey to various passions.

In antiquity, stringed instruments symbolised order and reason, as opposed to the passionate wind instruments, played on the far right. The drunkenness here is a symbol of passion out of control, and Mantegna's representation of these fat, melancholy and inebriated figures would have appealed to those acquainted with classical ethical systems, which consistently warned against allowing oneself to become sway to desire and unreason. In that sense, Mantegna's work, no matter how amusing, is moralising, and would have appealed to learned spectators, for whom the essential contrast of good and bad/evil is not between the holy and the demonic (as in Christianity), but between reason and passion.

111. *Silenus Aided by a Group of Children*, c. 1480-1500. Engraving, 26.3 x 23.6 cm. British Museum, London.

112. *Hercules and Antaeus*, c. 1490-1500. Engraving, 19.9 x 14 cm. British Museum, London.

Mantegna expressed this classical ethical warning with actors and attributes drawn from antiquity, including satyrs, followers of Bacchus, Silenus, and wind instruments. This engraving seems to have

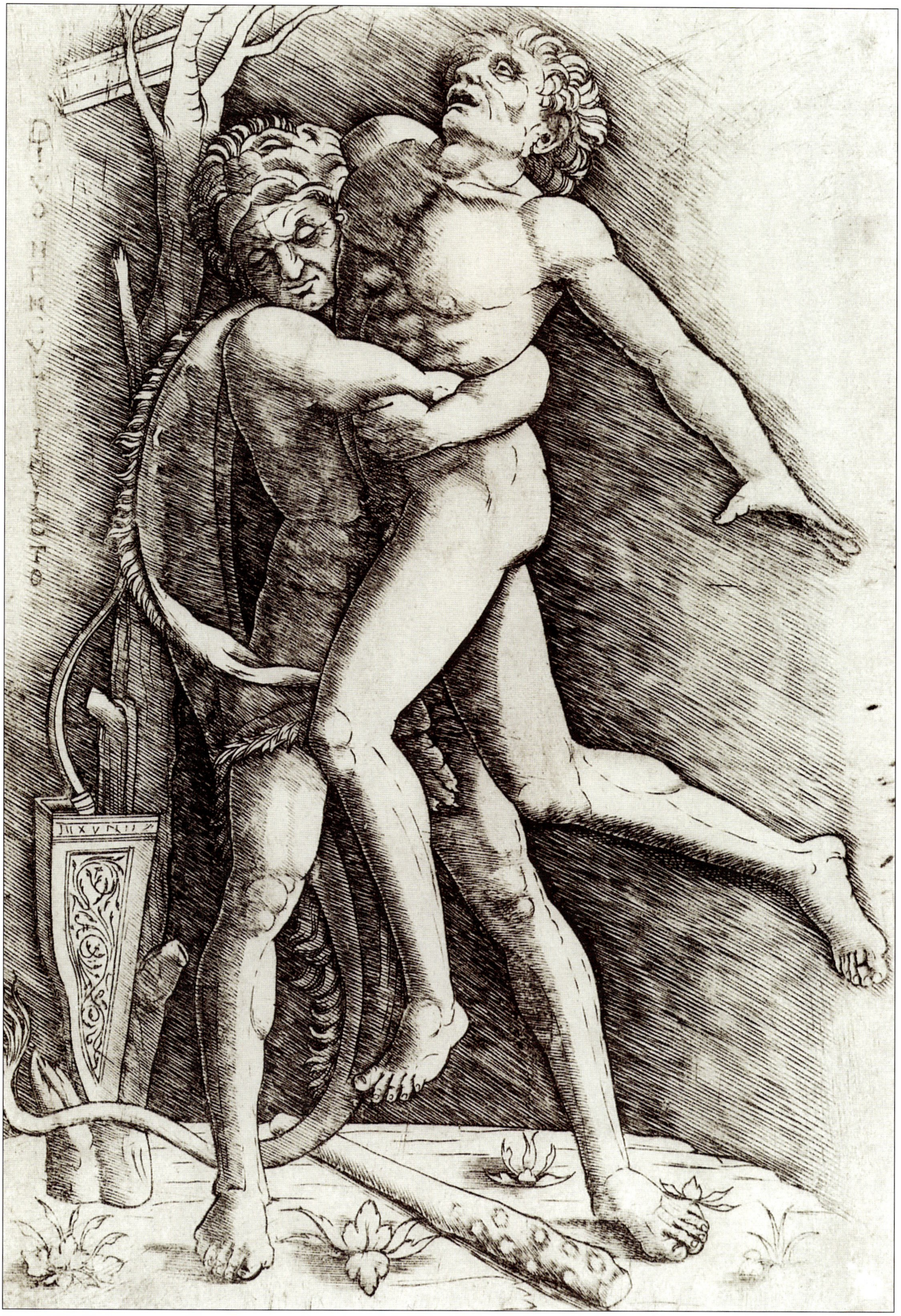

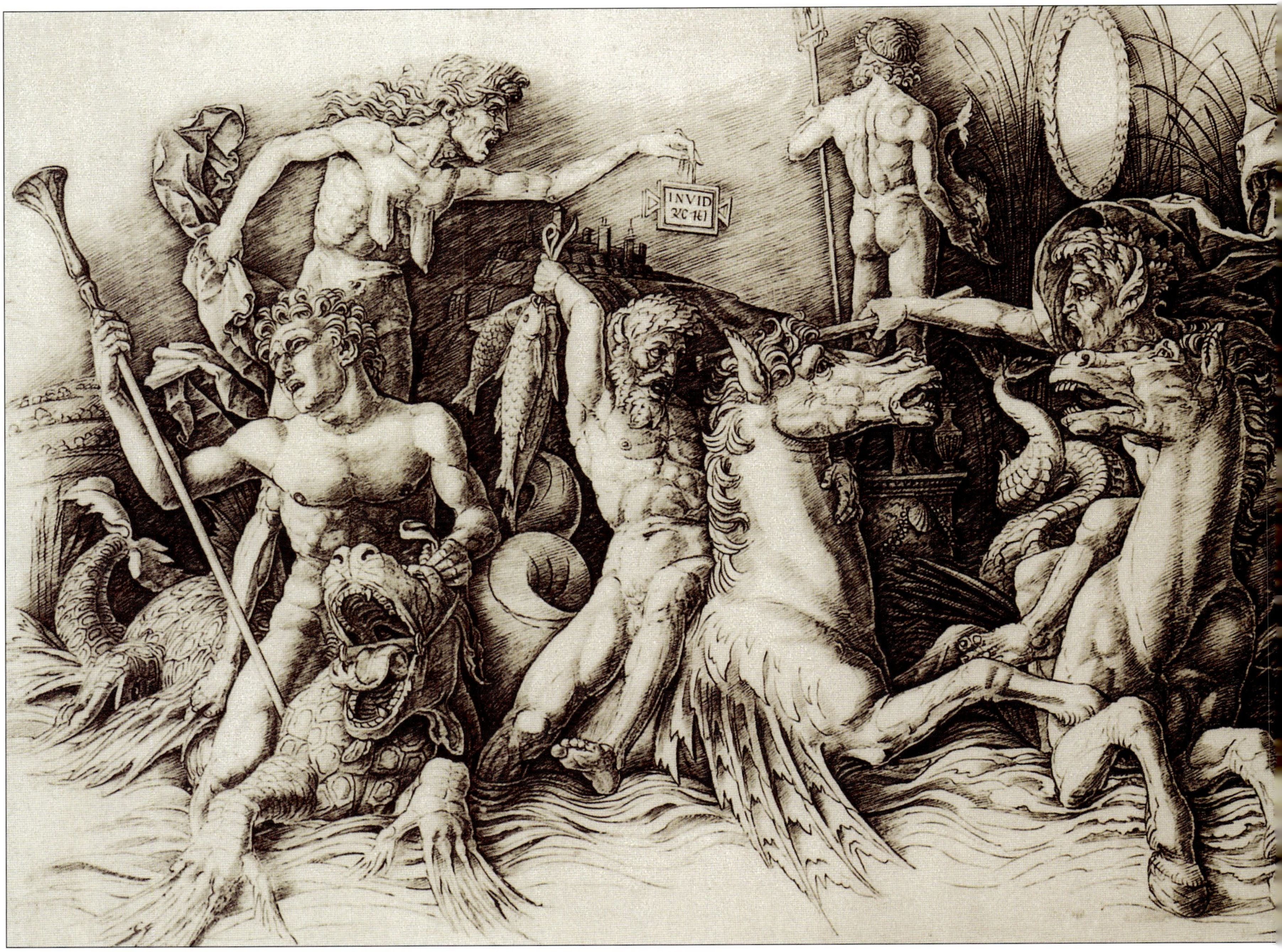

evoked great interest at the time, for there are different copies and versions by other artists. Mantegna produced a work on a related, moralising subject, showing the bloated Silenus aided by little *putti*, who are feeding his insatiable lust for wine (Fig. 111).

Along similar lines is Mantegna's spectacular engraving of a *Battle of the Sea Gods*, a work thoroughly in the spirit of antiquity (Fig. 113). It is hardly surprising given Mantegna's characteristic originality, that he was the first Italian artist to use two plates in one composition. One metal plate can only be so large and still be successfully pressed for the impression, so he designed this monumental engraving on a pair of plates, which must be exactly aligned with each other to make the long, frieze-like composition. This scene is replete with classical gods of various descriptions who are battling with weapons appropriate for ocean dwellers. The motivating figure is *Invidia*, or Envy, who is identified by an inscription. Classical moral philosophers regularly identified envy (a particularly pernicious form of desire) as a leading cause of moral perturbation; it was denounced as an enemy of personal tranquillity, which was

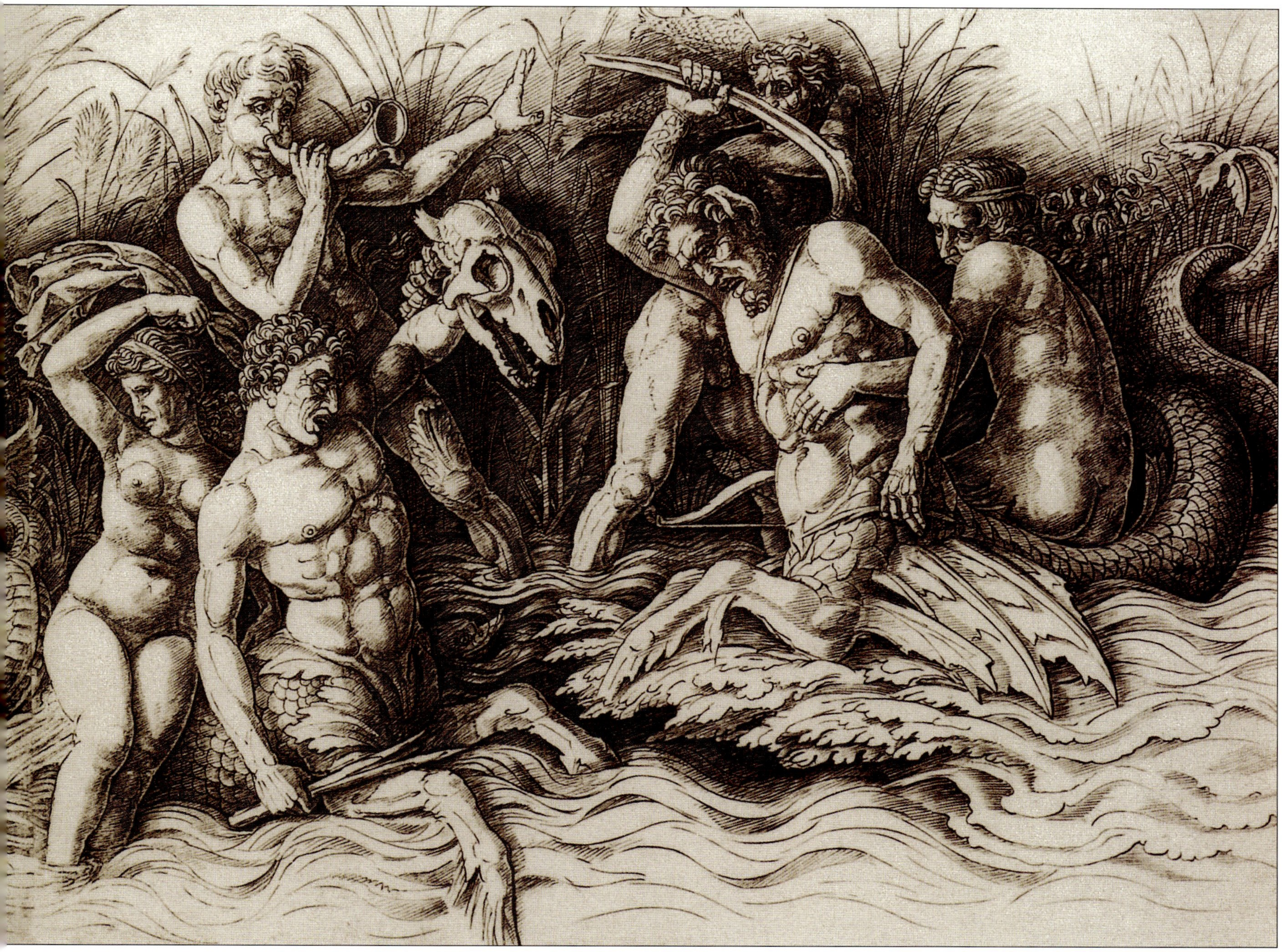

the ideal of ancient philosophers. As in the *Bacchanal* engravings (Fig. 109), this work represents the language, moral ideals, and personages of classical antiquity. Some of the sea gods are part creature, to further indicate they are subject to the throes of passion, the same proclivities implicitly condemned in Mantegna's *Bacchanal* engravings.

In the *Battle of the Sea Gods*, his composition is remarkably similar to a Roman relief of sea creatures, a damaged piece best seen in Renaissance drawn copies. It is characteristic of Mantegna that he did not slavishly copy this ancient sculpture; he varied the composition, and used it only as a beginning for his own inventive idea for the engraving, which has a relief-like composition which, like the subject matter, is redolent of antiquity.

Mantegna's most elaborate print, *The Fall and Rescue of Ignorant Humanity*, continues this humanistic moralisation (Fig. 110). In letters to Francesco Gonzaga in 1489 and 1491 Mantegna took the opportunity to note, "Ignorance is always opposed to virtue."

113. *Battle of the Sea Gods*, c. 1470-1475. Engraving, 28.3 x 82.6 cm. Private collection of the Duke of Devonshire, Chatsworth.

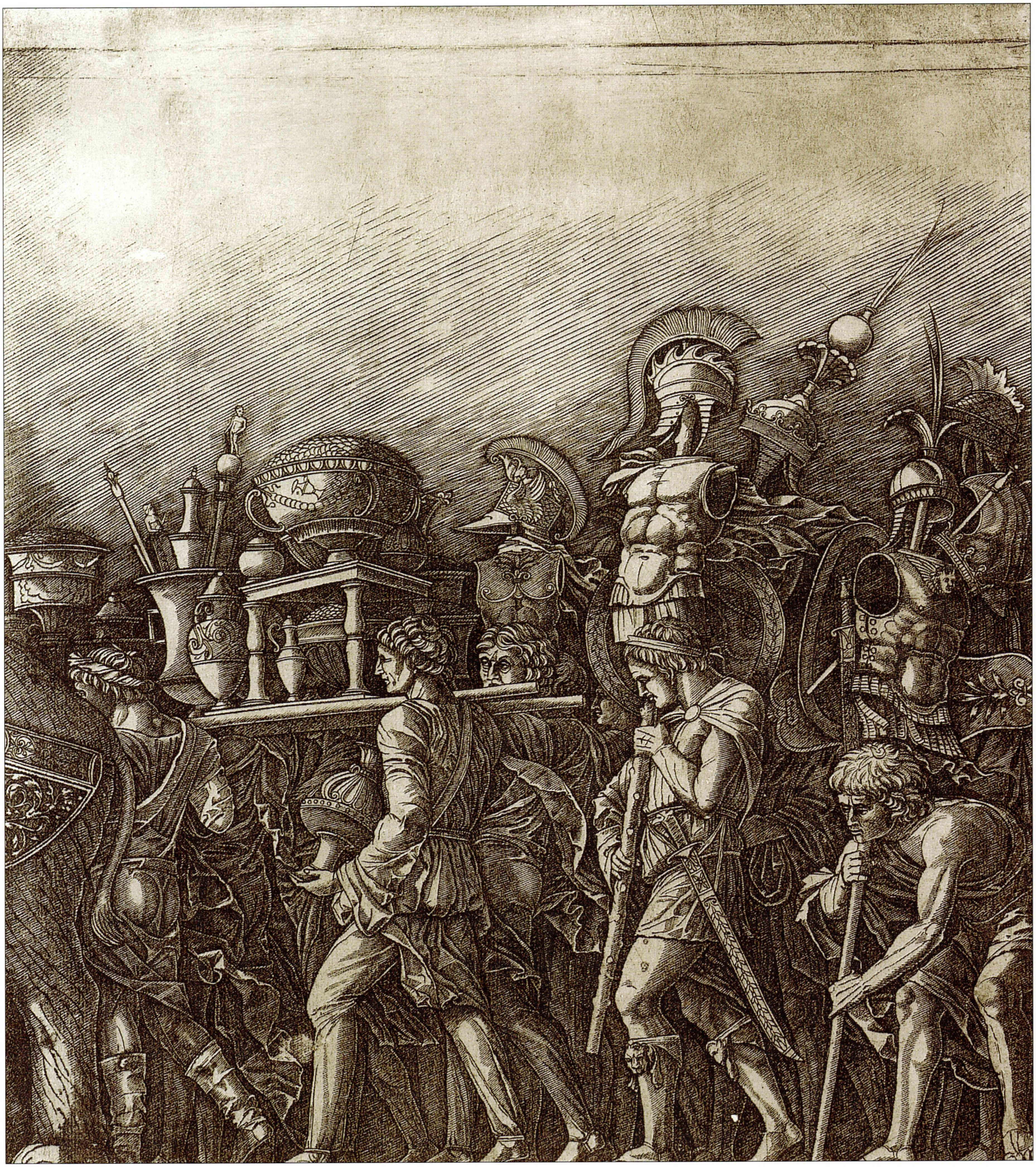

This idea, which contradicts the popular notion that child-like simplicity and naiveté are conducive to virtue, finds expression in a print designed by Mantegna. We can assume Mantegna intended this print chiefly to appeal to the sentiments of his patrons and employers, and it is noteworthy that the print reflects themes which, as we will see in the next chapter, formed an integral part of Mantegna's work for Francesco's wife, Isabella d'Este.

In a two-stage setting, Ignorance, a fat, nude woman, sits on the upper right. She is counselled by Ingratitude (who is blindfolded) and the hag Avarice. Ignorance sits on a ball, which symbolises instability, and has little control of the rudder she grips. Since she is figuratively blind to truth, Mantegna represents Ignorance without eyeballs. Two sphinxes, symbols of deceit because of their riddles, hold up the ball. Riches are disparaged here, too, as Ignorance has near her a sack of coins, and loose coins rest in a shallow pit before her.

Farther to the left, Error, a man with long ears, is pulling a woman down and about to throw her into a pit. A satyr, playing a wind instrument, symbol of lust and passion, stands nearby; he appears to be sexually excited, a characteristic condition of satyrs. Another figure, probably symbolising Fraud or Deceit, has a bag over his head. For the woman in the grip of these Vices, there is little chance for salvation, and she will soon end up in the heap of bodies below.

This complex image – which was best appreciated by a viewer with a love of pictorial complexity and philosophical reflection – continues in the lower part of the sheet, and there we get a glimmer of hope for mankind. On the lower left, a tree symbolises *"Virtus Deserta"* ("Deserted Virtue"), identifiable from the inscription and because the virtuous Daphne in Ovid's *Metamorphoses* was turned into a tree so she might escape the clutches of a sexual attack. In front of her are the letters *"Virtuti S.A.I."* in Latin standing for "virtue is always opposed to ignorance," or *"Virtuti Semper Adversatur Ignorantia."*

The carnage of bodies does not bode well for virtue, but the hope of redemption is evidenced by Mercury's intervention; this god, who symbolises peace, concord, progress, logic, and science, is helping one man to escape from the pile of bodies. As we will see, many of these figures, such as the satyr, Mercury, the tree of deserted virtue, and an allegory of Ignorance, will reappear in Mantegna's paintings for the marquise, Isabella d'Este (cf. Figs. 120 and 122).

Still, these ideas were in the air of the time, and more generally would have found partisans at the time among those embracing the classical ideal of the superiority of reason and logic to ignorance and passion. The wealth of allusions to specific classical ethical ideas indicates a humanist at the Gonzaga court was counselling Mantegna. This work, complex in style and subject matter and meant for elite spectators, is worlds apart from the simple prints of the "saint makers" who produced popular woodcuts.

Still in this humanistic vein are Mantegna's engravings showing labours of the god *Hercules*. One work (Fig. 112) shows the heroic actions of Hercules as he crushes Antaeus, a giant who had been terrorising people. He gained his strength from being connected to the ground, so Hercules is lifting him up before killing him, an episode Mantegna had painted decades before in the *Camera Picta* (cf. Fig. 43). Another engraving by Mantegna illustrates Hercules conquering the Nemean lion. These

114. Giovanni Antonio da Brescia, *Copy after Mantegna's Triumphs of Caesar VI*, called *Bearers of Golden Vessels and Crowns*, c. 1500.
Engraving, 29.3 x 25.6 cm.
Kupferstichkabinett, Berlin.

are classical and inspirational images, revealing the heroic side of Hercules, a god who had chosen in his youth to favour virtue over vice and good deeds to a life of enjoyment. It happened at times, if one were named after a god, one might commission images of that god in a work of art. No one prominent at the court of Mantua was called Ercole, but the father of Mantegna's employer, Isabella d'Este, was named Ercole (Hercules): Ercole d'Este, Duke of Ferrara.

Thus, it is possible these engravings were meant as flattery to the Ferrarese duke. Another print by Mantegna, the *Faun Attacking a Snake* (Fig. 98), also includes an inscription mentioning Hercules, even though it has nothing to do with the god Hercules, so it is possible Isabella's father was the recipient of this print as well.

Perhaps Mantegna hoped to curry favour with neighbouring rulers, as well as honour the father of his employer, and it would not be surprising if he indeed planned this beautiful image for Ercole I. Other impressions would have been run off the press, though, and the series would have had a wider distribution than just to a single person. Hercules remained a favourite god of virtue during the Renaissance period and later.

So far we have been looking at the engravings Mantegna most likely intended from the beginning to be prints, either working the copper plates on his own or in collaboration with a master metalworker. There was another important development in printmaking during this period, though, the rise of reproductive engraving, which greatly helped to spread Mantegna's fame and provide copies of his ideas for a broad, international market.

A reproductive engraving is one not designed from the beginning to be reproduced as a print, but is a copy of an independent work, be it a painting, drawing, or sculpture. Reproductive engravings were important means for artists' works to become known. Today we are awash in a sea of imagery, but in the Renaissance copies of famous paintings were harder to come by, and the making of reproductive engravings served an important function, as viewers did not have to travel to experience the compositions of great works of art.

This spread of ideas occurred early on with Mantegna's works. For example, in the last years of the fifteenth century and in the early sixteenth century his *Triumphs of Caesar* was reproduced in more than one series of engravings (cf. Fig. 114). The engraver of the works shown here was working from preparatory drawings (not the paintings, from which they differ in details). These should not be confused with Andrea's own engravings, intended from the beginning to be prints. Similarly, another master copied part of Mantegna's Uffizi *Adoration of the Magi* (Fig. 115), a copy made over a generation later than the original for sale to those who would enjoy Mantegna's design. There were many more reproductive engravings made of Mantegna's works during and after his life time.

Even though he was not necessarily encouraging such copies, reproductive engravings helped to spread the artist's fame, another example of the revolutionary effect printmaking had on European art and society during the Renaissance period. Whether from his own engravings or from reproductive engravings that copied his designs, Mantegna was at the centre of the new art of printmaking of his period.

115. After Mantegna, *Virgin and Child in a Grotto*, c. 1500. Engraving, 39 x 28.2 cm. Rijksmuseum, Amsterdam.

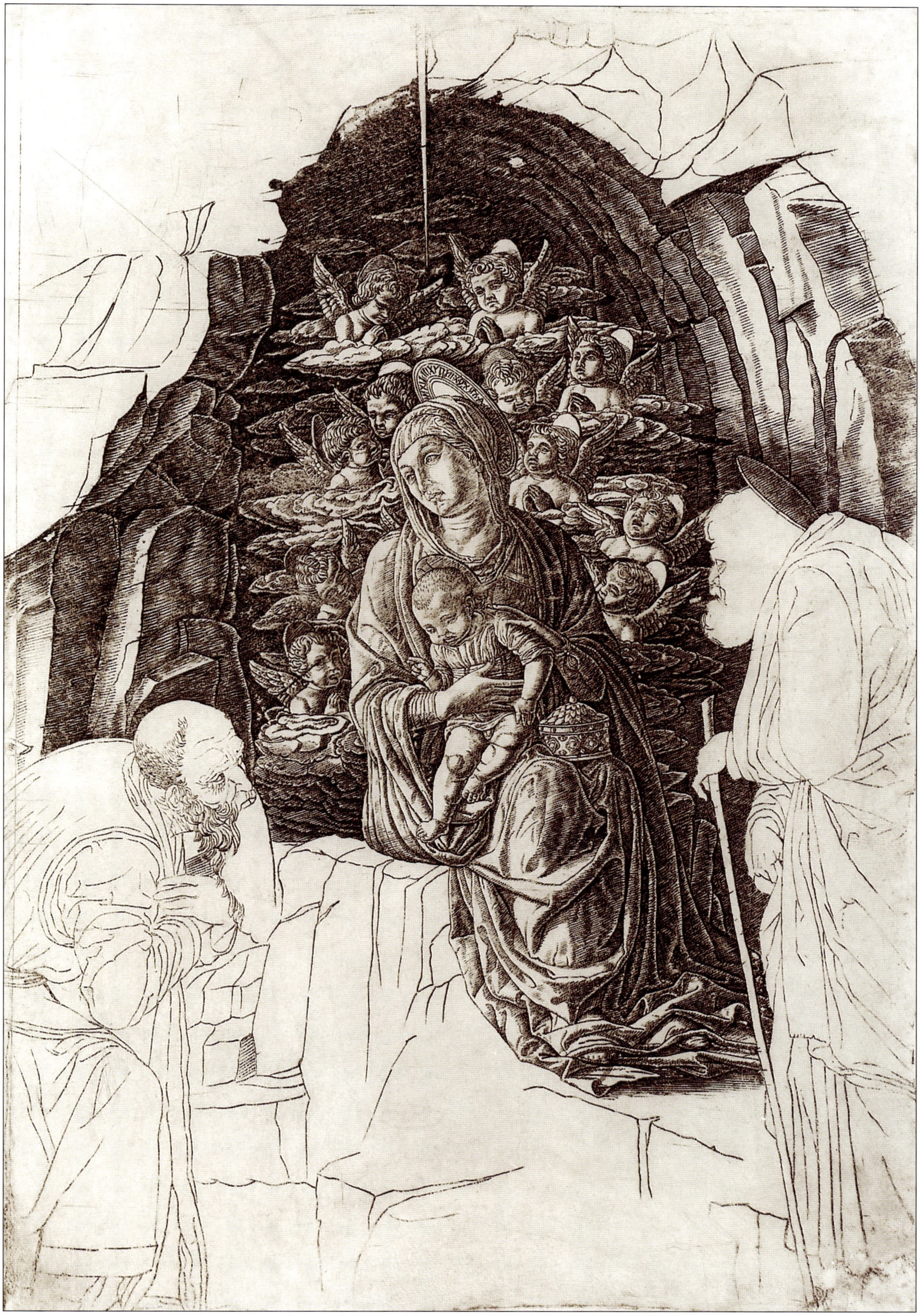

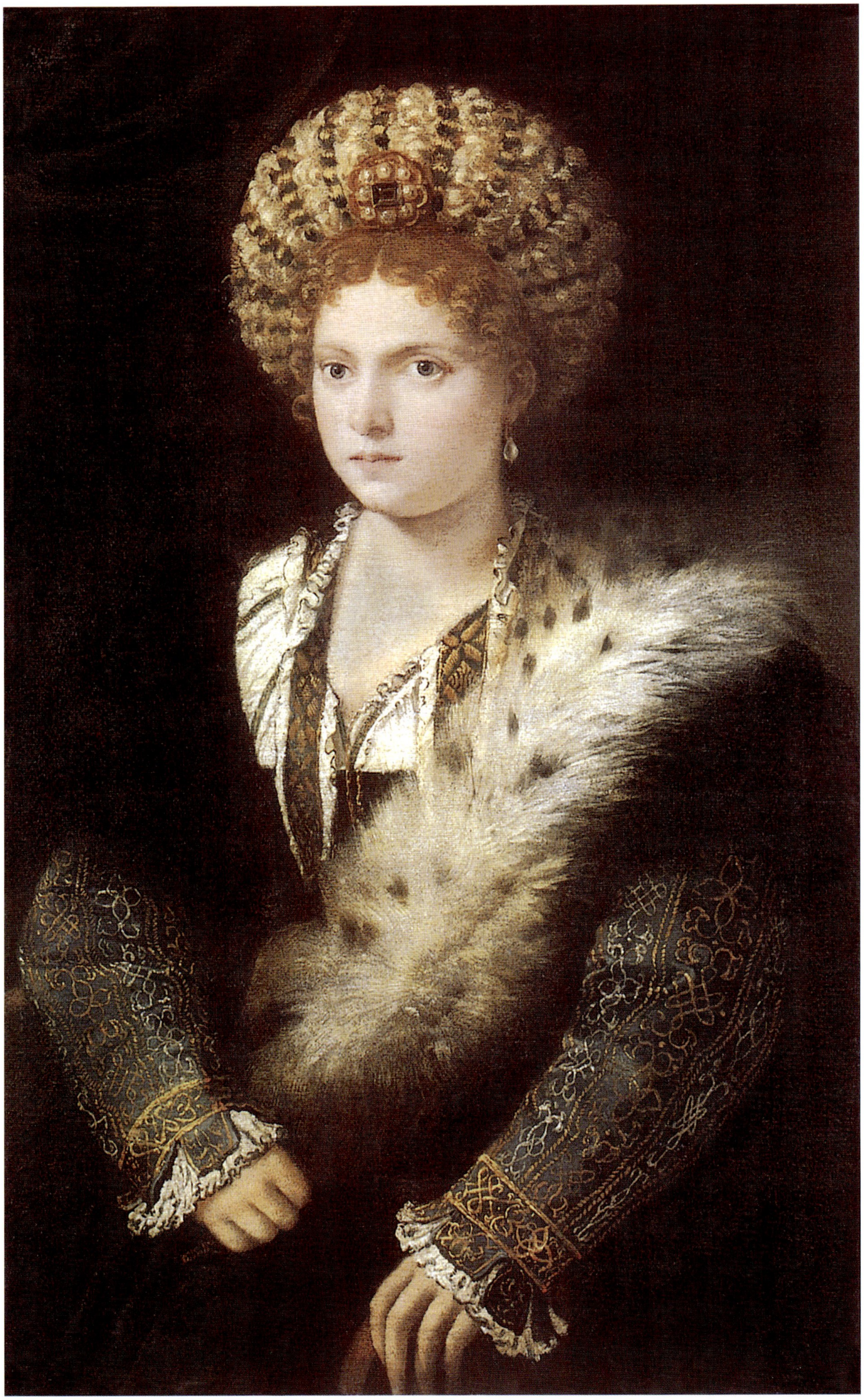

Patroness and Painter: The "Studiolo" of Isabella d'Este

In his activity as an engraver, Mantegna most likely had a free hand to invent his own designs. How different it was for him to labour for Isabella d'Este, the *marchesa* of Mantua! This remarkable woman was one of the great patrons and collectors of art during the Italian Renaissance, and she was an exacting master indeed. Her life forms an important episode in Renaissance history, and Mantegna's work for her constitutes one of the high points in his own career as a painter. Many of the finest artists of the Renaissance worked for her, including Leonardo da Vinci and Giovanni Bellini. A sense of her refinement and intelligence is conveyed in a portrait of her by the sixteenth-century Venetian master Titian (Fig. 116).

A word about her background will help to put Mantegna's great patroness in historical context. Isabella, born in 1474, was raised in court of the nearby city-state of Ferrara, and was betrothed to the fourteen-year-old Francesco Gonzaga in 1480, the match forming a strong link between two great ruling houses. Isabella showed signs of lively intelligence at an early age. When a Mantuan envoy interviewed her at the time of her betrothal, he reported of the young princess:

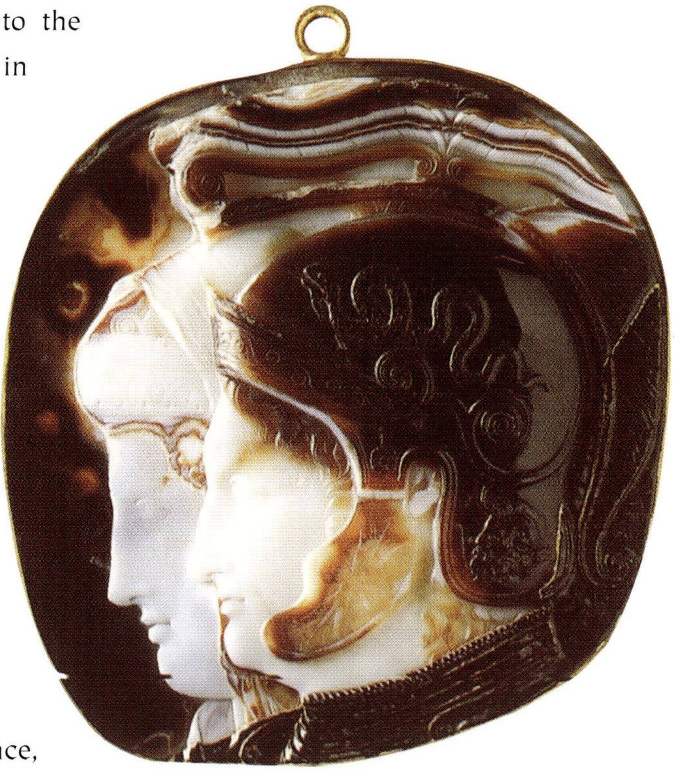

> "I questioned her on many subjects, to all of which she replied with rare good sense and quickness. Her answers seemed truly miraculous in a child of six, and although I had already heard much of her singular intelligence, I could never have imagined such a thing to be possible."[17]

116. Tiziano Vecellio, called Titian, *Portrait of Isabella d'Este*, 1534-1536. Oil on canvas, 102 x 64 cm. Kunsthistorisches Museum, Vienna.

Other contemporaries praised the girl's easy grace and the elegance of her movements. Her education included rigorous tutoring in Latin, and she earned a reputation early on for reading and reciting it with some facility, a rare feat in an age when girls were provided with far less education than were boys.

117. *Portrait of a Ptolemaic Royal Couple*, 3rd Century B.C. Cameo, 11.5 cm. Kunsthistorisches Museum, Vienna.

When Isabella arrived in Mantua as a young bride in 1490 she brought with her the refined taste for art, literature, music, and dance she had developed growing up at the Este court at Ferrara, where there was a great flowering of culture in the fifteenth century. As a girl, Isabella learned to play the lute and to sing, and always maintained a good reputation as a skilful musical performer. Young Isabella witnessed the first performances since antiquity of secular theatre; comedies from ancient Roman times were enacted in Ferrara in a great courtyard of the Ducal Palace. She especially loved the comic dancing that took place between the acts. Isabella heard chivalric tales read aloud by Ferrarese poets, and she watched the court painters execute large mural projects on sacred and secular subjects for her father, Duke Ercole I d'Este. All this gave her a taste for art and literature that she would bring with her to the court at Mantua.

Mantegna's best-known works for Isabella were for her *Studiolo* ("Little Study"), a place of retreat in which to write letters and enjoy literature, art, music, and conversation. Such *studioli* were multiplying in the fifteenth century among noble patrons in northern Italy. These refined chambers epitomised the finest Italian Renaissance culture had to offer. Isabella became famous for being the first woman to have a *studiolo*. Although Isabella's mother did not have a *studiolo*, she did have her own decorated suite of rooms, painted loggias, and gardens in Ferrara in the castle, so once again Isabella would have gained inspiration from her patroness mother. Isabella's father, Ercole I d'Este, did have a *studiolo* containing images of what the documents call "nude females," perhaps symbolic figures of Virtues. Isabella's uncle, Borso d'Este, who ruled Ferrara from 1451 until 1471, had a famous *studiolo* with images of the Muses, some of which survive, including Michele Pannonio's *Muse*, now in Budapest (Fig. 118). This cycle for Isabella's uncle surely served as a catalyst for her desire to have a painting that included the Muses, whom Mantegna beautifully depicted in his *Mars and Venus* (Fig. 122). In short, Isabella learned in her noble surroundings in Ferrara that a great person ought to commission paintings by leading artists on lofty subjects, the works to be kept in a small chamber serving as a place of retreat, contemplation, and refreshment. No kind of interior space better indicates the highest aspirations of the Italian Renaissance, as these chambers linked the present to the ancient past, served as proto-museums and as libraries, and permitted at least temporary retreat from society.

Isabella was fortunate to find a painter of the calibre of Mantegna already in place at the court of Mantua, ready to carry out her wishes. The marquise, celebrated in her lifetime as a "Tenth Muse," was an eager and demanding patron. She described herself as *"appetitosa"* (hungry) for art, and she was always eager to acquire the best and most beautiful objects she could. Her collecting interests included Greek and Roman statues, ancient cameos, such as one portraying Hellenistic rulers (Fig. 117), rare and beautiful gems, elaborately embroidered clothing, and contemporary sculpture. Her interests were broad, but one specialisation is historically most important: she was the first woman of the post-classical world seriously and systematically to collect Greek and Roman antiquities.

Mantegna was working in Rome for the Pope in 1490 when Isabella became the *marchesa*. In order that Isabella would receive him favourably upon his return to Mantua, he asked Battista Guarino, her old tutor from Ferrara, to write a letter of recommendation to her. The letter, dated to October 1490, said:

> "Gifted and virtuous men like [Messer Andrea Mantegna] have no need of recommendation to Your Excellency, for of yourself you are exceedingly inclined to love and favour those whose are deserving, but yet that I would do so, and thus I pray you to entertain him lovingly and hold him in good esteem, for in truth besides his excellence in his art, wherein he has no equal, he is all courtesy and kindness, and Your Ladyship will get from him a thousand good conceits in designs and other things that will befall."[18]

The part about Mantegna being "all courtesy and kindness" was a bit of an exaggeration, for we know the painter could be quite troublesome, but doubtless he was guaranteed to treat the marquise kindly. As it turns out, Isabella did receive Mantegna warmly and employed him frequently.

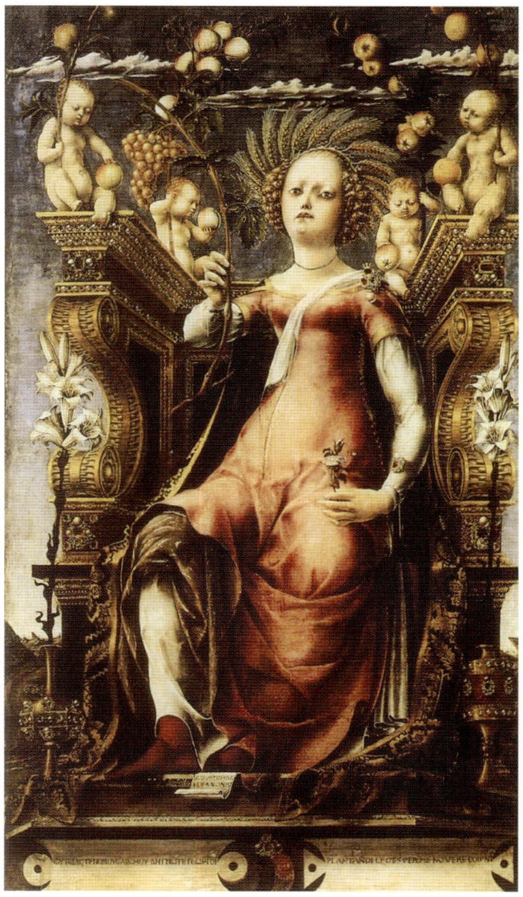

We know Isabella thought highly of Mantegna. There was at least one known time when Isabella was displeased by one of his artworks: in 1493 Mantegna made a now-lost portrait of Isabella to send to a nearby court, but she thought it did not resemble her and she refused to send it. But in this same period Isabella thought two real-life girls of the Gonzaga family were "so beautiful that Messer Andrea Mantegna could paint them no finer." Letters indicate Isabella clearly preferred Mantegna's style to other artists who also provided works for her *Studiolo*, and she thought his works superior even to those of Pietro Perugino, regarded by some as the leading painter in Italy. Isabella and Andrea exchanged friendly letters and notes on many occasions, and there was a warm understanding and respect between them.

Isabella's most significant project as a patron of the arts was the above-mentioned series of paintings for her *Studiolo*, located in the Castle of Saint George at Mantua near Mantegna's magnificent *Camera Picta* (see Fig. 35). This little study, which she affectionately called *"camerino nostro"* (our little chamber) was near to her heart, and the task of decorating it with pictures by the best painters in Italy consumed her interest for years. Next to the *Studiolo* was another room called the *Grotta*, or "Cave," which contained antique sculpture, cameos, manuscripts, musical instruments, and other curiosities and objects of beauty. (Both these rooms changed location in 1519, after the death of Isabella's husband). The *Studiolo*, which displayed a number of different small objects, and included other decoration as well, such as painted and gilded woodwork, was most importantly devoted to the display of a coherent cycle of pictures on loftily classical subject matter. These two rooms, the *Grotta* and the *Studiolo*, formed a famous and splendid pair. One sixteenth-century writer described the chambers as follows, noting Mantegna's contribution to her famous rooms:

> "Here are hidden the rarest treasures of Italy. Here is the suite of fine rooms that the magnanimous Isabella d'Este built and richly adorned. Two of these contain works of art which fill mortals with joy and wonder. They are decorated with rich gilding, with exquisite designs and intricate carving. Here Mantegna and other masters display their genius in sublime painting."[19]

Although the works are now scattered from these two rooms in collections around the world, some of the rich carving and gilding of the original *Grotta* and a second *Grotta* of Isabella still exist in the castle and Ducal Palace.

Isabella commissioned paintings for the *Studiolo* from Andrea Mantegna, who was her own court artist, as well as other pictures by the Bolognese artist Lorenzo Costa, Pietro Perugino (the teacher of Raphael), and later the famous High Renaissance painter Antonio Allegri, called Correggio. All these paintings have ended up in the Louvre Museum in Paris. Mantegna painted two *grisaille* paintings in fictive bronze to be placed over the doors, but these unfortunately do not survive and their subjects are uncertain. The description indicates they were to evoke bronze antique figures, classical visions perhaps like his *Dido* (Fig. 96) or his *Introduction of the Cult of Cybele at Rome* (Fig. 93), a fictive marble work also meant to be placed over a door.

118. Michele Pannonio, *Muse*, c. 1450-1460.
Tempera and oil on panel, 136.5 x 82 cm.
Szépmüvészeti Múzeum, Budapest.

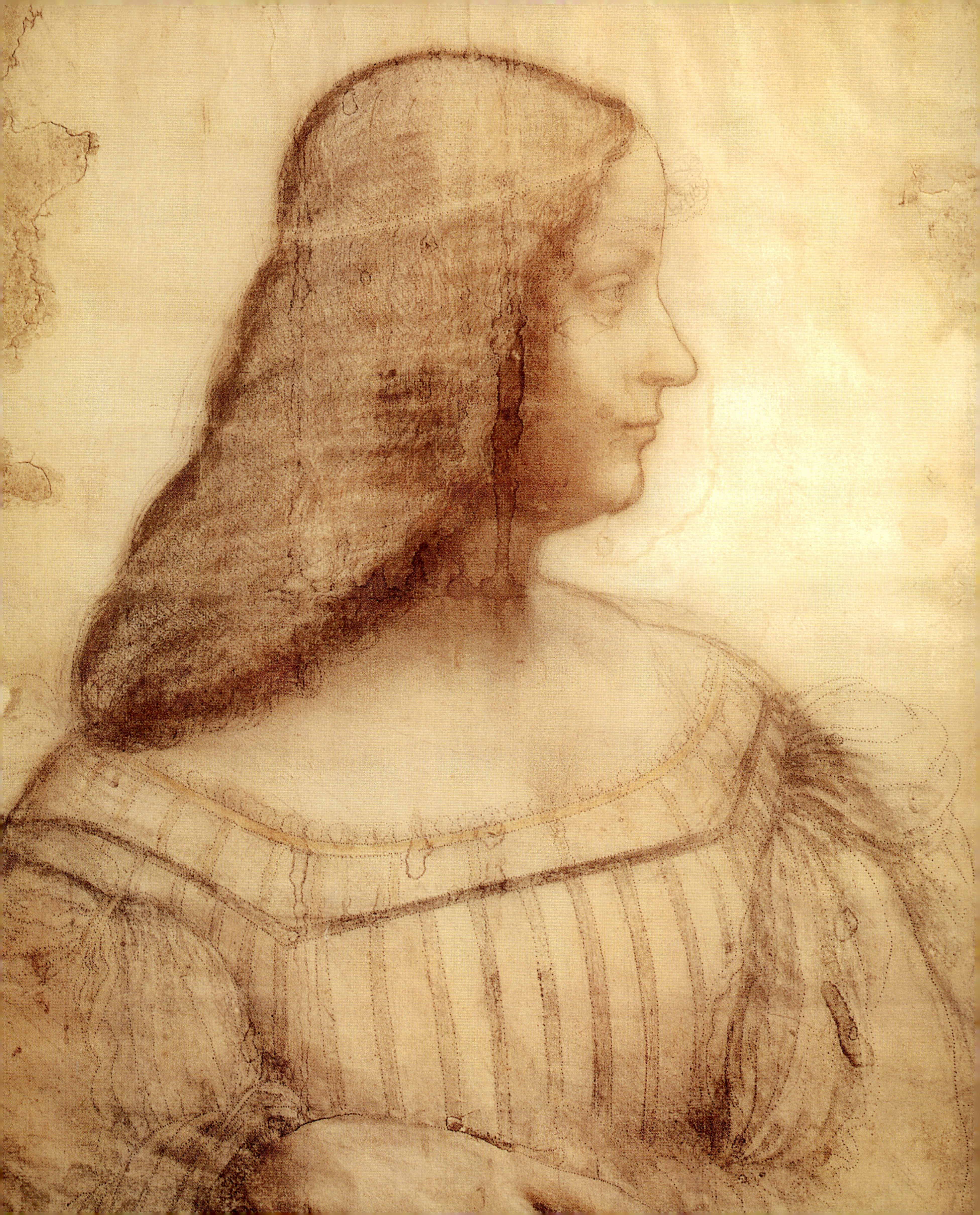

Mantegna worked on his paintings for Isabella's little chamber between 1497 and 1502, when he was an old man, yet eager to please his young patroness. We know Perugino was not allowed to deviate from the stipulated program, and it is unlikely Mantegna was encouraged to do so either. Andrea, like his fellow painters, presumably had to adhere to a strict program of subject matter dictated by Isabella, who worked out the details in consultation with a humanist adviser at the Gonzaga court in Mantua, a wealthy aristocrat, learned scholar, and lawyer named Paride da Ceresara, who could read Latin, Greek, and Hebrew. He must have helped to provide details of classical literature and philosophy for Isabella, but it was likely she who invented the overall scheme of the room's pictures, which were to celebrate such notions as Wisdom, Celestial Love, Chastity, and the conquest of Vice. Mantegna added numerous embellishments of colour, gesture, and composition to the program, contributing an artistic aspect the patron and adviser could not have been able to imagine. Mantegna's paintings are quite complicated in form and meaning, and we will have to explain some of the particulars of these extraordinary works.

The more openly dramatic of Mantegna's two pictures is his *Minerva Expelling the Vices from the Garden of Virtue* (Fig. 120). This work, with its rich foliage backdrop, numerous figures, and elegantly flowing draperies is the most lush and elaborate of Mantegna's smaller easel paintings. The painting is bursting with deep greens, and populated by a strange gathering of figures, both good and evil. The picture is allegorical, the ideas conveyed through figures who stand for various moral, philosophical concepts. On the left, Minerva (called Pallas Athena in Greek) – the goddess of Reason, Wisdom, and the arts – enters and gives fright to various personifications of Vices. These evil figures have invaded the very Garden of Virtue. In the sky, three women representing the virtues of Fortitude, Temperance, and Justice ride a heavenly cloud and encourage Minerva to achieve victory.

Fortitude, identifiable from her column and club (attributes of the strong god Hercules), looks down sympathetically towards Minerva, while the other cloud-borne virtues look upwards and silently implore other gods to join the battle, two of whom appear in profile in the clouds on the upper left. The most important of the Virtues is the "Mother of all Virtues," Prudence, who is hidden from our sight, imprisoned behind the wall on the right. On the wall is a small inscription on a piece of paper, a message from the invisible Prudence, begging for assistance: "And you, O gods, help me, the Mother of Virtues." Minerva's immediate goal in the picture is to save Prudence, whose ethical importance is that she provides man with the balance and moderation needed to live the perfectly moral life. The viewer can be certain Minerva will win out. In all, Mantegna depicts a clear message in the picture: Wisdom and Reason, aided especially by Fortitude, will triumph over Vice and lead to the attainment of moral virtue.

The Vices are among the most colourful and rich elements in any of Mantegna's paintings, striking in their ugliness and invention. Renaissance writers and artists propounded the notion that beauty indicates moral goodness and ugliness connotes vice and moral corruption. The reverse of Leonardo da Vinci's *Portrait of Ginevra de' Benci* (National Gallery of Art, Washington) bears an inscription saying "Beauty adorns Virtue," and this idea exactly expresses the distinction made by Mantegna, who shows the heroine Minerva as comely and the Vices as horrid, even subhuman. To Minerva's left is a female satyr, a half-human half-goat, who carries young satyrs with her as she flees. She is accompanied by airborne cupids, their butterfly wings symbolising moral inconstancy.

119. Leonardo da Vinci, *Portrait of Isabella d'Este*, c. 1499-1500. Black stone with touches of red chalk in hair and skin and highlights in yellow pastel in the dress, 61 x 46.5 cm. Musée du Louvre, Paris.

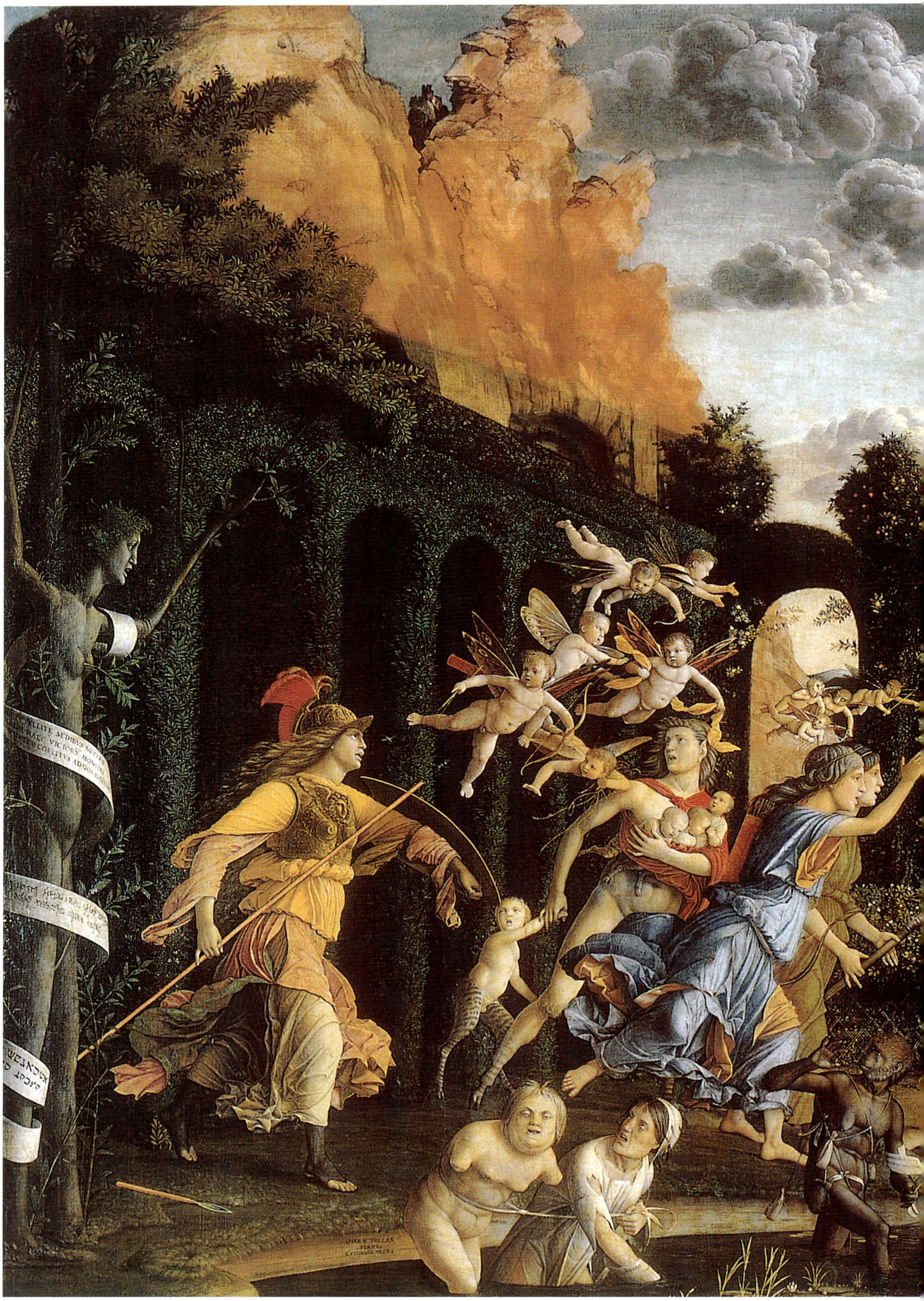

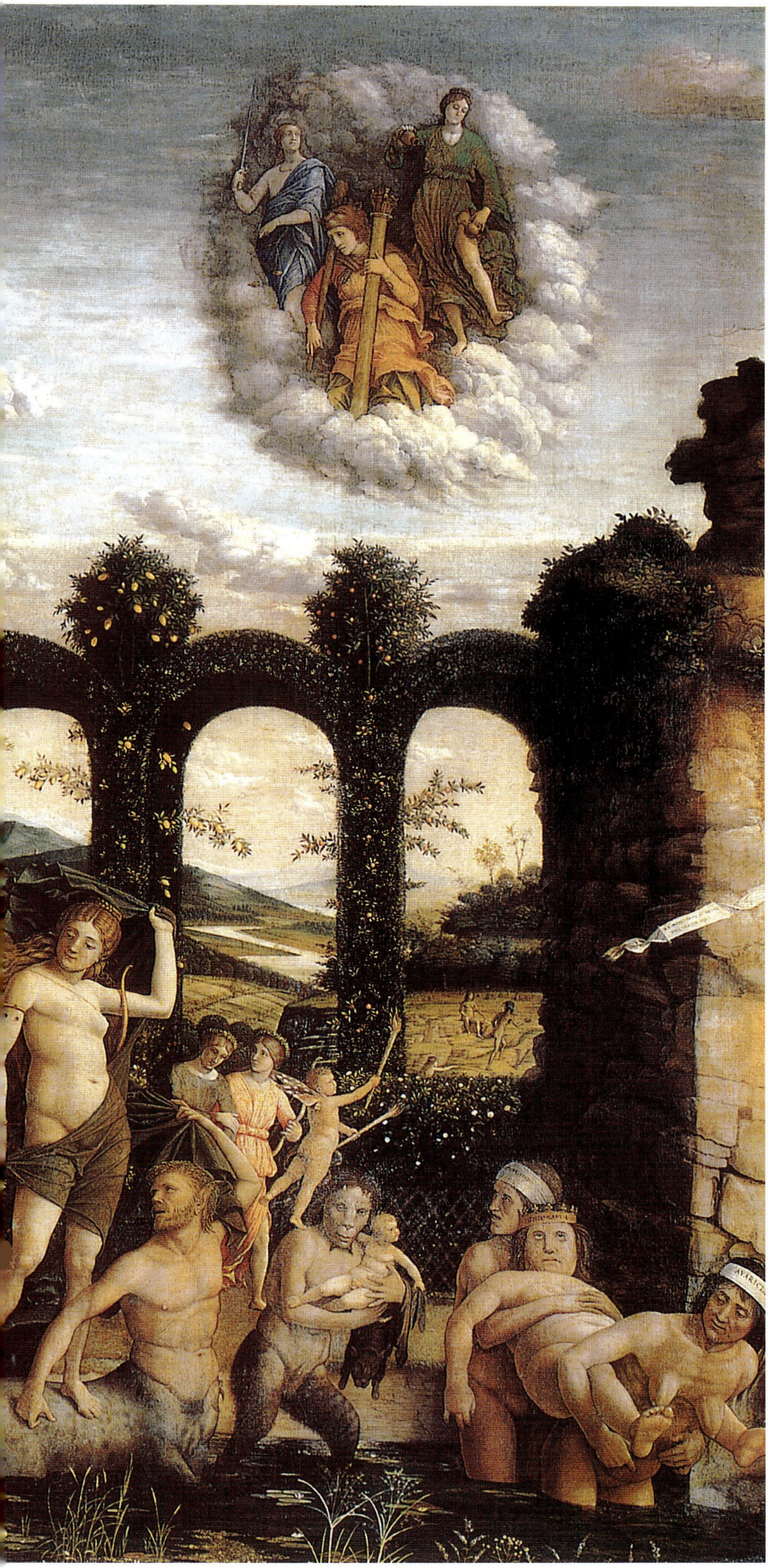

120. *Minerva Expelling the Vices from the Garden of Virtue,*
c. 1497-1502.
Tempera on canvas,
160 x 192 cm.
Musée du Louvre, Paris.

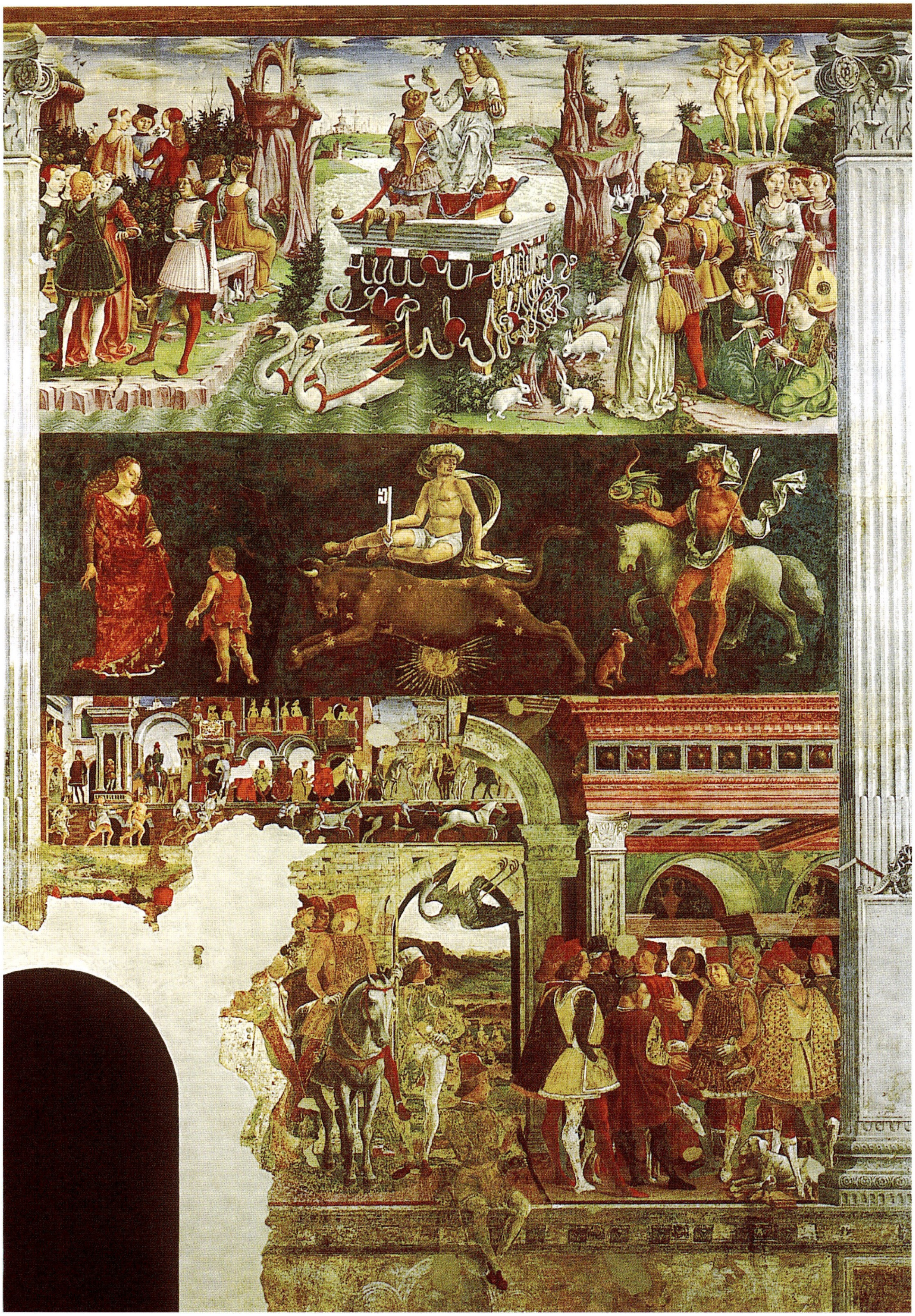

They have fanciful faces, one with that of an owl, a symbol of sin because owls are nocturnal and see well in the darkness, and another like that of a monkey, who symbolised vice. These haunting figures show Mantegna's inventiveness at its best.

Several of the Vices are wading knee-deep through swampy water, which they are further befouling by their very presence. On the left is Sloth, identified by the inscription *"Otium"*. Bloated, misshapen, and armless, she has a haggard and lazy expression, and her ugly, naked body stands in contrast to those of the beautiful nude maidens who appear in other paintings for the *Studiolo*. Sloth is so lazy she needs no arms, and has to be aided along. Pulling Sloth is her spiritual sister Inertia, whose name is inscribed on her right sleeve. Her clothes are torn, and her hair is strangely growing in bunches through her tattered headpiece. Just to the left of centre in this swamp is one of Mantegna's most striking figures, a simian creature with dark fur and one dangling breast who defends itself from Minerva. Neither man nor woman, animal nor human, this figure, as identified by the numerous inscriptions written on pieces of paper on its body and parcels, personifies Immortal Hatred, Fraud, and Malice. The monster bears little bags containing seeds of Evil and Suspicion.

Mantegna depicts to the right of this furry Vice stock symbols of moral corruption: a centaur, recognised as debased by passion because it is part animal, and a hideous satyr with a face striped like a cat's and a wolf or fox skin over its shoulder to indicate its predatory nature. Like most satyrs, he is shown with an erect, animal-like phallus. This creature is bearing a little child, who symbolises Earthly Desire (Cupid). Cupid is the son of Earthly Venus, who rides atop the centaur and, despite the partially concealing garment, displays herself provocatively. Finally, on the far right are two ugly women, Avarice and Ingratitude, who carry off Ignorance, the last absurdly wearing a crown and, more appropriately, bearing an insipid expression.

The goddess Minerva is the protagonist of the painting, and Mantegna has paid special attention to her appearance. With her beautifully formed face and lovely, flowing hair, she bears a serious and war-like expression and seems to cry out. She is very embodiment of ideal beauty and of the dynamic equilibrium of movement that characterises classicism. She is fully armed with helmet and shield, and wears a breast-plate adorned with an apotropaic image of Medusa.

Minerva's spear is broken and part of it is lying on the ground. Renaissance contemporaries associated a broken spear with success in jousting, indicating the target has been struck, so the broken weapon stands for Minerva's prowess in battle. She is preceded in her efforts by two goddesses, one of whom is Diana, the virgin huntress of antiquity (she has a quiver of arrows) and another unidentifiable goddess who bears a torch. Like Minerva, they race towards the wall to save imprisoned Prudence from the hands of the vicious creatures who surround them.

Mantegna might have been overwhelmed by having to include these details in the painting, yet he managed not to make the picture look dry and pedantic. He even succeeds in including a considerable number of inscriptions in the painting without disturbing the narrative flow. On the very far left, an anthropomorphic tree is sympathetic to Minerva's cause, and bears an inscription conveying a message to the sky-borne Virtues: "Come divine companions of the Virtues who are returned to us from heaven, banish these foul monsters of Vices from our seats." This is an olive

121. Master of the Sforza Altarpiece, *Madonna Enthroned, 1494.* Tempera and oil on panel, 230 x 165 cm. Pinacoteca di Brera, Milan.

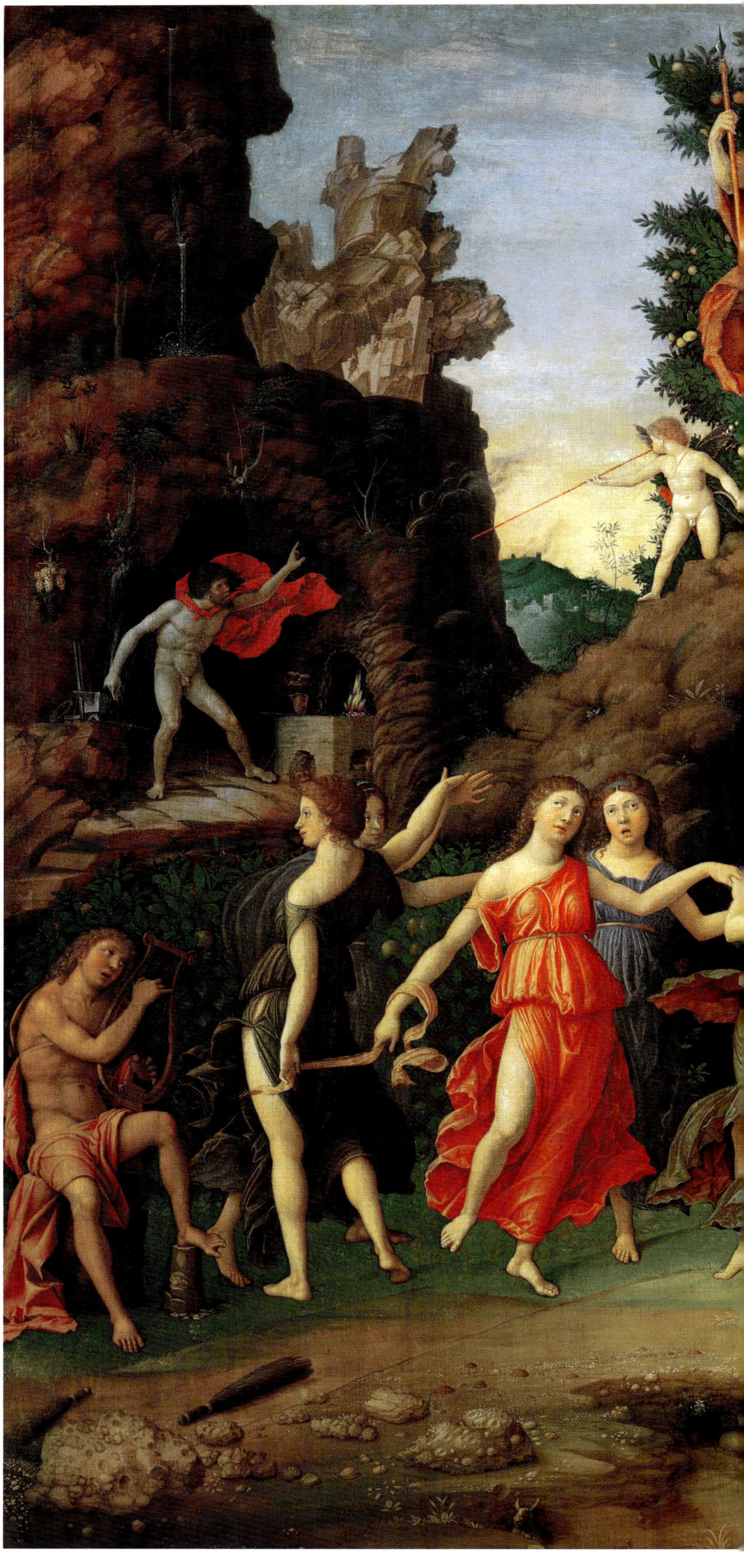

122. *Parnassus*, called *Mars and Venus*, c. 1497-1502.
Tempera on canvas,
150 x 192 cm.
Musée du Louvre, Paris.

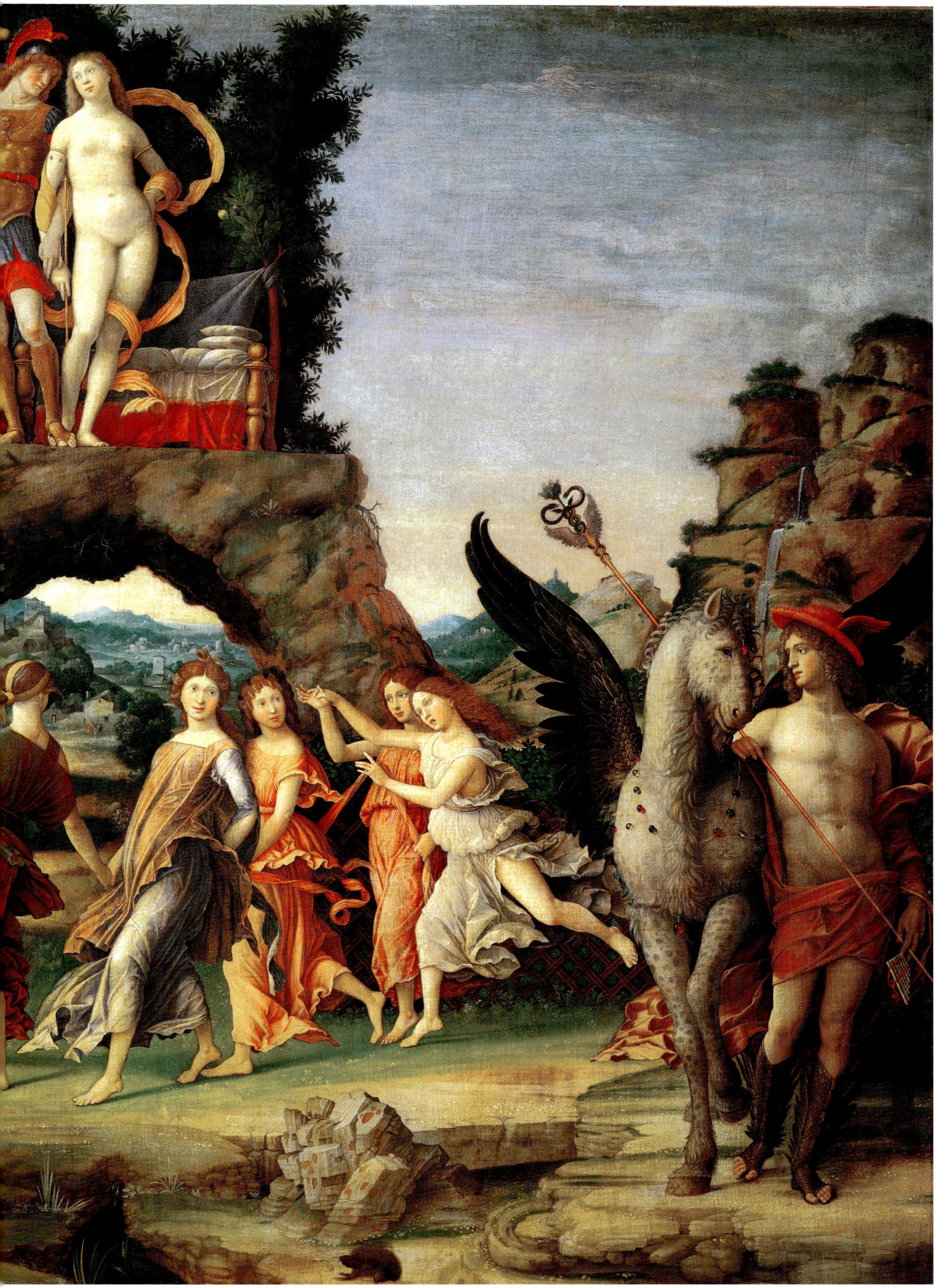

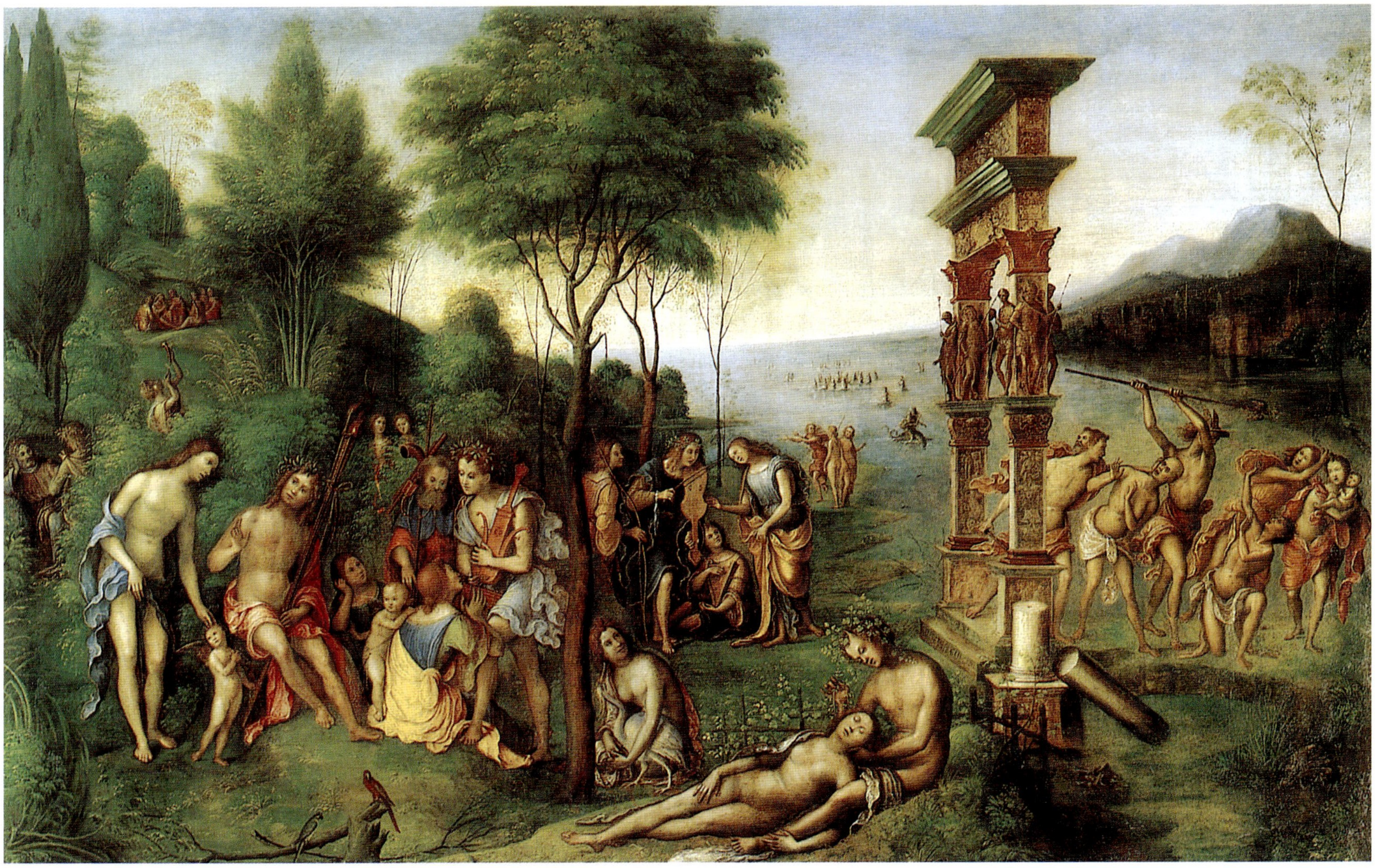

tree, the leaves of which constitute an attribute of Minerva and which therefore symbolises learning, wisdom, and peace. The half-tree, half-woman form is a reference to the story of Daphne, a nymph who was chased by Apollo and whose father turned her into a tree in order to help her escape from Apollo's sexual advances and thereby preserve her virginity. Although reminiscent of the metamorphosis of Daphne, this tree is probably meant to be an allegory of "Deserted Virtue." A similar figure appears in an engraving by Mantegna, as we saw earlier (Fig. 110).

The *Minerva* is full of allusions to Isabella's own interests and philosophical idealism. Isabella surely identified herself with Minerva, the very symbol of learning and the arts. Even the setting reminds one of the role of gardens in Isabella's life. Gardens for aristocratic patrons were places of retreat, a haven from the worlds of social intercourse, commerce, noise, and other disturbances to living the good, philosophical life. The castles and palaces in Ferrara and Mantua had their fruit-laden, verdant gardens, which were thought to be moral places where the soul could develop toward philosophical ideals. Isabella had available to her several such private sanctuaries, including her own so-called Secret Garden, the space of which still exists in the Ducal Palace in Mantua. She is documented as having spent many hours in similar gardens, alone or with companions, and she regarded these as noble havens from the common herd and from the distraction of rulership. Thus, the presence of Vices in the garden depicted by Mantegna would have been seen as a horrifying invasion of an aristocratic retreat that was established to allow intellectual and spiritual development.

The Latin quotations around the picture reflect Isabella's interests in ancient philosophy and moral epigrams. Next to Otium (Sloth), Mantegna painted the inscription, *"Otia si tollas periere cupidinis arcus"*, "Take away leisure and Cupid's bow is broken." This remark, reminiscent of "idle hands are tools of the devil", expresses well Isabella's cultural pretensions, as the Latin tongue, the reference to the ancient figure of Cupid, and the thought itself are rooted in classical culture and philosophy. The same moralism and erudition are displayed by the inclusion of the classical goddesses Minerva and Daphne. The disparaging of satyrs and centaurs, which were well-known symbols of ethical corruption to the Greeks and Romans, also put Isabella in company of those who embraced classical attitudes. In one part of the picture, though, only a pseudo-intellectualism is present. The inscription on the tree on the left is seemingly written in three languages, but while the first is Latin, the second has Greek lettering but spells out the same message in Latin, and the "Hebrew" is written in false lettering and is total nonsense! Isabella could read neither Greek nor Hebrew, and she was content to have a façade of erudition displayed here.

Mantegna's other learned painting for Isabella's philosophical program for the *Studiolo* is his *Mars and Venus* (Fig. 122). The agitation and complexity of the *Minerva* gives way here to a balanced, harmonious composition reflecting the ideal moral perfection of the subject matter. The work is not as crowded with allegorical figures and inscriptions as is the *Minerva*. The place is Mount Helicon, which is visited by Apollo and the Muses, who dwell on nearby Mount Parnassus. Apollo was the god of artistic inspiration, and he is shown on the far lower left playing his lyre. His music moves the Muses to sing and to dance in measured, elegant steps. The nine Muses, like Apollo, inspired song, dance, and poetry, and their lovely forms and sweeping garments constitute one of the most beautiful gatherings in any of Mantegna's paintings. This painting is a forcible reminder that one of the chief functions of the *Studiolo* was to form a place of retreat for the study and practise of the arts of poetry and music. In the Renaissance, these arts were not mere idle entertainment; it was deemed morally uplifting to dance and sing to music that is harmonious and noble. Similarly, poetry was thought to be a rational and elevating literary form. Isabella liked to dance, and she occasionally wrote some poetry. She was skilled on the lute and clavichord, and was widely praised for her beautiful voice. One contemporary noted, with perhaps a bit of hyperbole, "When she moves her lips in song, such sweetness rains from heaven that the air rejoices and the wind pauses, intent on such sweet harmony." Isabella preferred to sing and play in private or before a very few selected friends. She also took the trouble to have craftsmen produce elaborate musical instruments for her use, made of the best woods and finest inlaid materials. Her *Studiolo* was such a place where, retreating from the cares of the world, she might have practised her musical skills, and Mantegna's Apollo and Muses echoed her interests in music and poetry.

The main protagonists of the painting are Mars and Venus, who stand in front of a bed atop a small, rocky bridge (Fig. 122). We have seen Venus in the Mantegna's *Minerva*, but this is not the same goddess. Echoing sentiment found among certain ancient writers, Renaissance writers thought there were two Venuses, twin sisters. One was the lascivious, earthly Venus, who appears in Mantegna's *Minerva*, but this one is the celestial, divine Venus. This latter induces not mundane sexuality, procreation, and eroticism, but divine love – celestial longings and a pure, heavenly kind of desire. Since Heavenly Venus is pure, she is nude (as were Adam and Even before they sinned), and she shows herself to the viewer not in a shameful or provocative way, but more in a state of innocence and divine perfection. In the *Minerva*, Earthly Venus strides atop a centaur, but here Divine Venus

123. Lorenzo Costa, *Comus*, c. 1505-1510. Tempera on canvas, 152.5 x 238.5 cm. Musée du Louvre, Paris.

is standing on high with the heavens behind, as she and Mars are literally elevated close to the celestial realm. Their bodies are gracefully inclined towards each other, indicating their souls too are in a blissful harmony.

One of the accomplishments of the Divine Venus was that she caused Mars, the god of war, to lay down his arms and join her in lovemaking. This action was symbolic of the power of love, especially divine love, to avert war and destruction. This conceit was well established in Renaissance art, but it is surely significant that Isabella's husband was noted for his martial skills, while her own reputation was that of a civilising, cultural beacon in the Gonzagan realm. Just as Isabella could identify herself with Minerva in the companion painting, so too was Divine Venus an ideal expression of her and her place in the Mantuan city-state. This identification was made in the fifteenth century, when the humanist Battista Fiera, reflecting on Mantegna's painting, compared Mars and Venus to Francesco and Isabella.

Mantegna did not set out here to condemn the marital infidelity engaged in by Mars and Venus. Renaissance viewers seem to have had no great qualm with the fact that Venus, at the time of her union with Mars, was married to the god Vulcan. This act of adultery with Mars was not necessarily admirable, but it was overshadowed by positive aspects of the story, including her divine nature and the chief benefits of her action, namely, the taming of war and the production of a child, Anteros. Just as there were two Venuses in Renaissance mythology, there were two Cupids. The first is Cupid (or Eros in Greek), son of Earthly Venus and Vulcan; he incites men and women to engage in indulgent sexuality, and he justly appears in the arms of a satyr in Mantegna's *Minerva* (Fig. 120). His half-brother, a kind of anti-Cupid – Anteros in Greek – incites a holier form of desire or love. He is shown in the *Mars and Venus* to the left of Mars. Anteros carries a bow but not the famous gold-tipped arrows, indicating he has no power to incite earthly passion. Clearly, here as in other paintings in the *Studiolo*, carnal sensuality is singled out as a central vice, recalling the important place Earthly Venus and Cupid play in Mantegna's *Minerva*.

The love of Mars for Heavenly Venus in this painting is pure. The opposite of divine love – carnal lust – is symbolised in the *Mars and Venus* by Vulcan, Venus's husband, who is jealously standing off to the left and gesturing angrily. In a brilliantly humorous invention, Mantegna represents the triumph of higher love over base desire: Anteros is shooting a dart from a blow gun, and – as indicated by a thin line drawn by the artist into the paint surface – the weapon is striking Vulcan in the genitals. There were frequent jokes in the Renaissance about cuckolded husbands and about frustrated male sexual passion in general, so contemporary viewers would have regarded Vulcan as laughable indeed, especially with the slap-stick motif of the well-aimed blow dart. There is also some reference to contemporary social stratification here, for Vulcan was a forger of metals and was therefore a base mechanic. He belonged, therefore, to a lower social class than the other gods in the picture, and his sexual desires also placed him on a lesser moral scale than the other figures. The rage and ignobility of Vulcan are expressed not just by his physical actions and gesture, but by one of Mantegna's characteristically clever and poignant pictorial motifs – the jagged, light-coloured rocks overhead – which in their quartz-like shape and irregular eruption seem to explode from the mountainside like the anger and jealousy of Vulcan himself. This adds piquancy to the scene, and echoes the rocks dramatically erupting on the left side of the *Minerva Expelling the Vices*.

124. Lorenzo Costa, *Coronation of a Lady*, c. 1505-1510.
Tempera and oil on canvas,
165 x 198 cm.
Musée du Louvre, Paris.

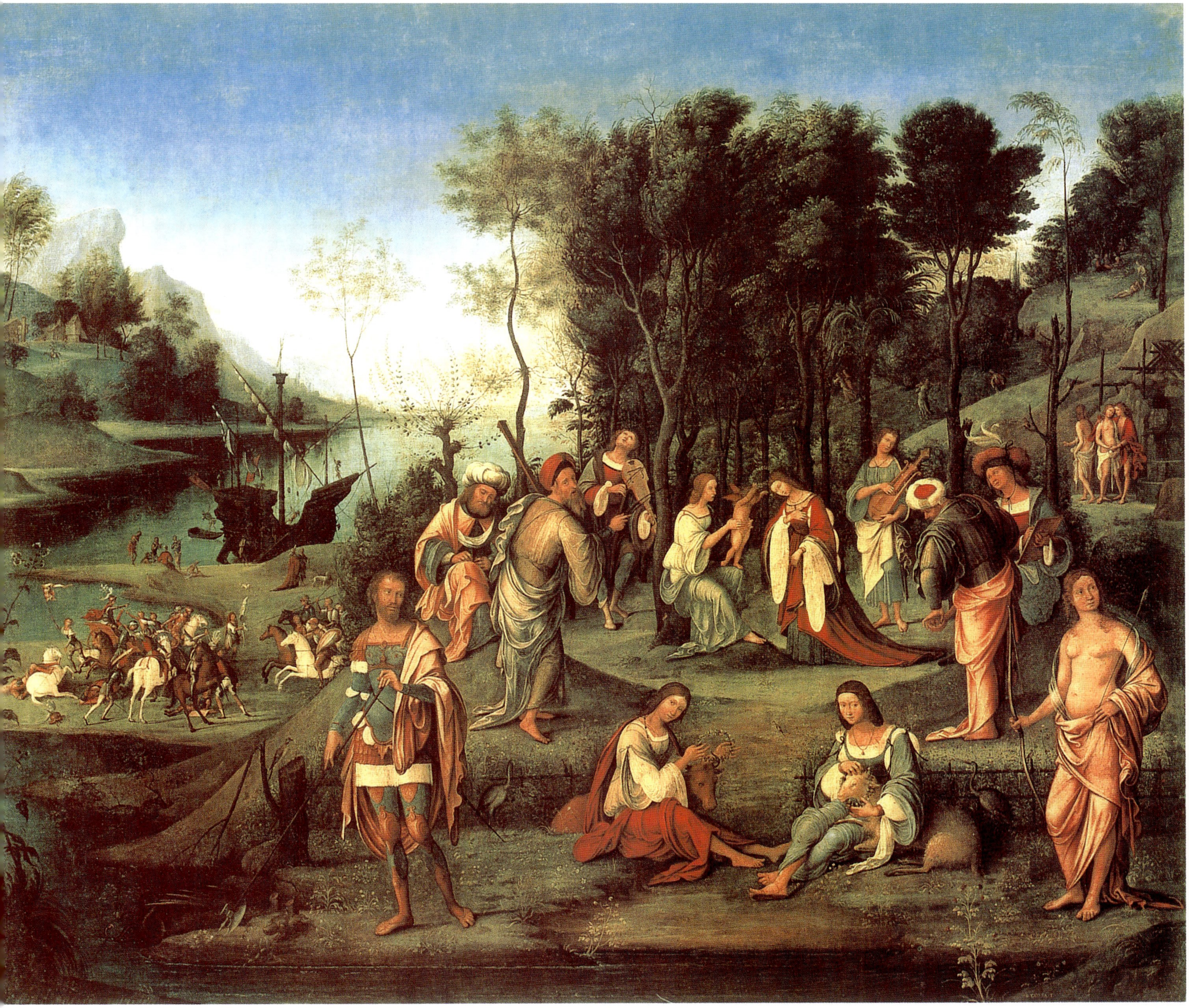

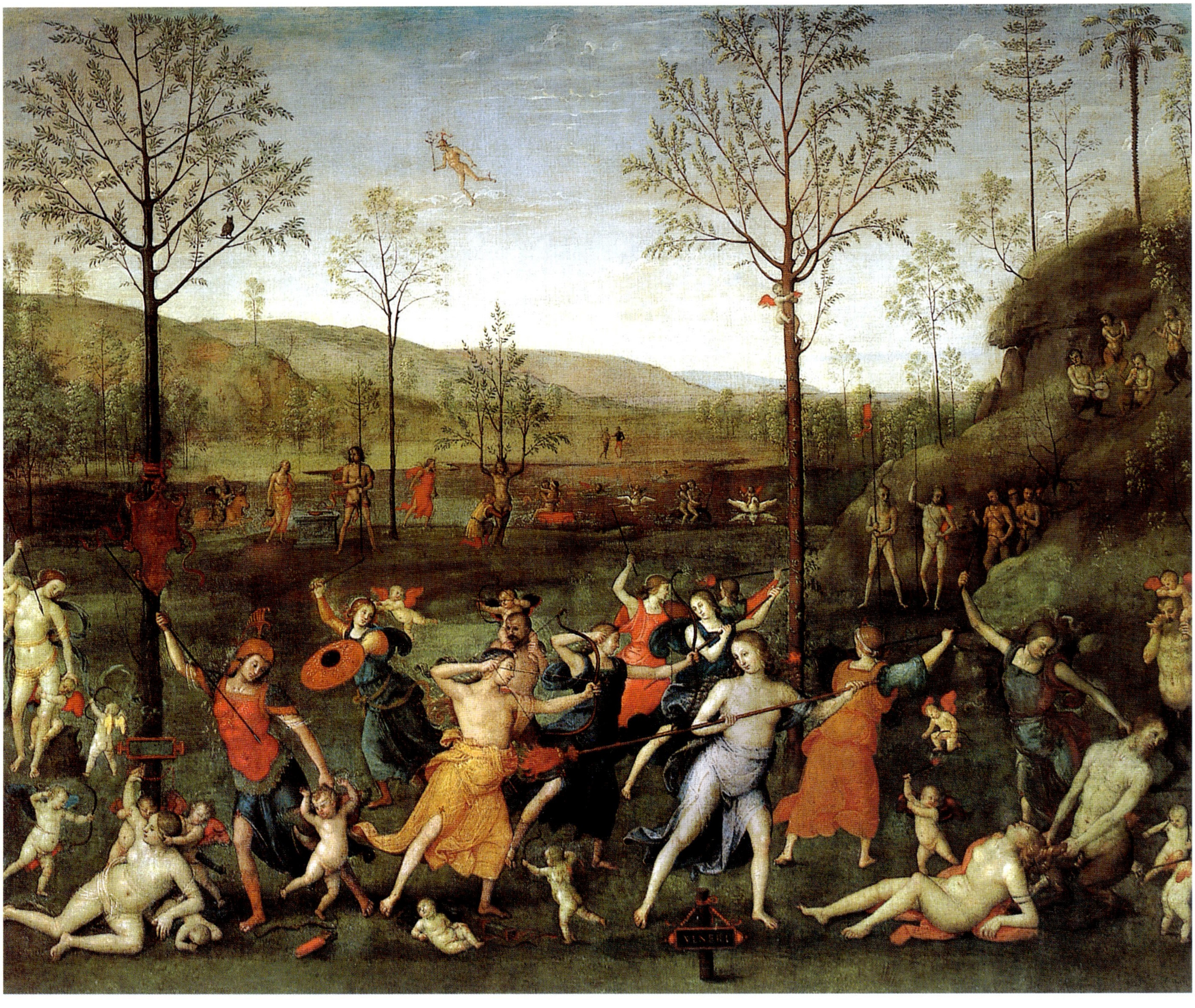

There are other significant figures and creatures in the *Mars and Venus*. On the right is Mercury, the messenger god, who was also a god of eloquence and science. The snake-entwined caduceus he carries was a symbol of peace and concord. He is a civilising god, and his winged horse Pegasus was thought in the Renaissance to be a symbol of Fame and therefore of moral achievement. Pegasus is conspicuously gentle and relaxed, indicating this is not a time for struggle or striving. The highest forms of cultural life are being celebrated at that moment; this is a peaceable kingdom, and Mercury and Pegasus can rest. Some smaller creatures in the foreground, including a squirrel and a rabbit, also seem at ease. The presence of the rabbits is perhaps explicable by their association with Venus, because of their reputation as quick and prodigious procreators, but it is also possible Mantegna meant to indicate that gentle, timorous, animals such as squirrels and rabbits can inhabit this placid world of music, dance, and Divine Love.

An interest in astrology perhaps lies behind Mantegna's *Mars and Venus*. Most Renaissance people took astrology very seriously, and Isabella was no exception, as she believed strongly in this occult science. One of the most famous fresco cycles of the fifteenth century, the Hall of the Months in the Palazzo Schifanoia, was made in Ferrara just before Isabella's birth, and as a youth she would have seen its representation of astrological symbols and seasonal activities. For births, marriages, and battles the astrological positions were deemed important and significant. In the portrait of baby Isabella, the manuscript album in which her likeness appears includes exact information about the hour and minute of her birth. The figures in Mantegna's *Mars and Venus* make sense together as emblems of art and civilisation, but it is surely also significant that when Isabella married Francesco Gonzaga in February l490 the planets Mars, Venus, and Mercury and the brightest star of the constellation Pegasus all stood under the sign of Aquarius. It was certainly a splendid coincidence that Mantegna was able to include gods who symbolised Isabella's philosophical ideals and who also, through their astrological associations, were relevant for her marriage to a martial husband. This coincidence must also have pleased Paride da Ceresara, Isabella's humanist advisor, because he was not only interested in astrology but later in life devoted himself to a study of this and other arcane sciences.

It is important not to underestimate Mantegna's artistic achievement in his *Minerva* and *Mars and Venus*. Many Renaissance art theorists, such as the humanist writer Leon Battista Alberti, recommended painters rely on poets and other writers for their ideas, and the ideal of *ut pictura poesis*, painting should be like poetry, was widely supported. Still, then as now painters often did best when they relied on their own inventions and were not forced to illustrate written, programmed instructions. Indeed, the Venetian painter Giovanni Bellini declined to paint a picture for Isabella because, as a go-between stated, he liked to "let his will wander freely" when designing pictures. But Mantegna fully met the challenge posed to him by Isabella and her adviser. His idyllic landscapes, dramatic narratives, flowing garments, lovely flesh and hair, and other delightful pictorial details are fully enjoyable in an aesthetic sense. His works are infused with an idealised naturalism, and contain a balance of levity and gravity. In short, in his paintings for Isabella, Mantegna met the highest challenge for any Renaissance artist: to create paintings that are artistically beautiful and also express an intelligent and detailed program of philosophical ideas. The meaning and context of Mantegna's two paintings for Isabella become clearer when they are seen in the light of the other works Isabella commissioned for the chamber. The best documented is the one by Pietro Perugino, whose fame caused Isabella to seek a work from him and wait, although impatiently, for years before

125. Pietro Perugino, *The Battle between Chastity and Love*, c. 1503-1505. Tempera on canvas, 158 x 180 cm. Musée du Louvre, Paris.

its delivery from his workshop in central Italy. We know a great deal about the commission because the detailed literary program for the work is recorded in a letter written by Isabella to the artist:

> "My poetic invention, which I wish to see you paint, is the Battle of Love and Chastity – that is to say, Pallas [Minerva] and Diana fighting against Venus and Love. Pallas must appear to have almost vanquished Cupid... The issue of the conflict between Diana and Venus must appear more doubtful.... Behind these four divinities, the chaste nymphs in the train of Pallas and Diana will be seen engaged in a fierce conflict, in such ways as you can best imagine, with the lascivious troop of fauns, satyrs, and thousands of little Loves."[20]

No such instructions for Mantegna's pictures survive, but extant documentation implies such a detailed program was indeed given to him. For his part, Perugino followed this program rather closely, as Diana, the virgin huntress who appears in Mantegna's *Minerva*, shoots an arrow at Earthly Venus (Fig. 125). Her son, the love-provoking Cupid, is seized and is about to be killed by Minerva. The general theme is the same as that tackled by Mantegna in his pair of paintings, but Isabella was happier with Andrea's works than with Perugino's, as she preferred his detailed manner to Perugino's broader handling. She wrote to Perugino in June 1505 after the picture was delivered to her in Mantua, "[it] pleases me, as it is well designed and well coloured, but if it had been finished with greater diligence it would have been more to your honour and our satisfaction, since it has to hang near those of Mantegna, which are painted with the greatest clarity and distinctness [*son summamente netti*]."[21] This is an important record. In general, High Renaissance painting – of which Perguino's style was a prelude – is more broadly painted and indeed less "carefully finished" than most Early Renaissance painting, such as Mantegna's. Isabella's judgment is an indication that she still found the hard, detailed, searching manner of the Early Renaissance attractive, not necessarily thinking the artistic evolution toward the new High Renaissance manner to be an improvement.

Mantegna started one of the other paintings for the *Studiolo*, but he died before it was finished. Lorenzo Costa, who succeeded Mantegna as court painter in Mantua after l506, perhaps used some ideas and compositional solutions drawn by Mantegna (Fig. 123). The meaning of the *Comus* seems at first to be unclear, but it resolves itself into a number of recognisable incidents. The god Comus sits on the left, holding a torch, a weapon he has apparently seized from Earthly Venus (she held it in Perugino's painting). Divine Venus stands there with Cupid, who is holding a wreath instead of a bow and arrow. Thus, Earthly Venus and Cupid have been conquered, and they have been overtaken by higher longings, symbolised by Apollo, who stands nearby with a musical instrument. On the right Vices try to enter this area, but they are expelled by Janus and Mercury, the latter of whom was in attendance in Mantegna's *Mars and Venus*. In Mantegna's painting Mercury was posed elegantly, but here he dramatically defends the Garden of Virtue by using his caduceus as a weapon. The work helps to flesh out the full context of Mantegna's two completed works for the project, although this painting is somewhat disjointed and not fully successful. It makes one appreciate how Mantegna's known pictures for the *Studiolo* followed complicated programs and still resulted in unified compositions.

126. Antonio Allegri, called Correggio, *Allegory of Virtue*, c.1530. Tempera on canvas, 141 x 86 cm. Musée du Louvre, Paris.

A more coherent composition by Costa for the *Studiolo* and a key work for understanding the project is his *Coronation of a Lady*. The lady in question is an idealised portrait of Isabella, and she is crowned by Cupid, who has given up his amorous ways and is rewarding the philosophical Isabella with a

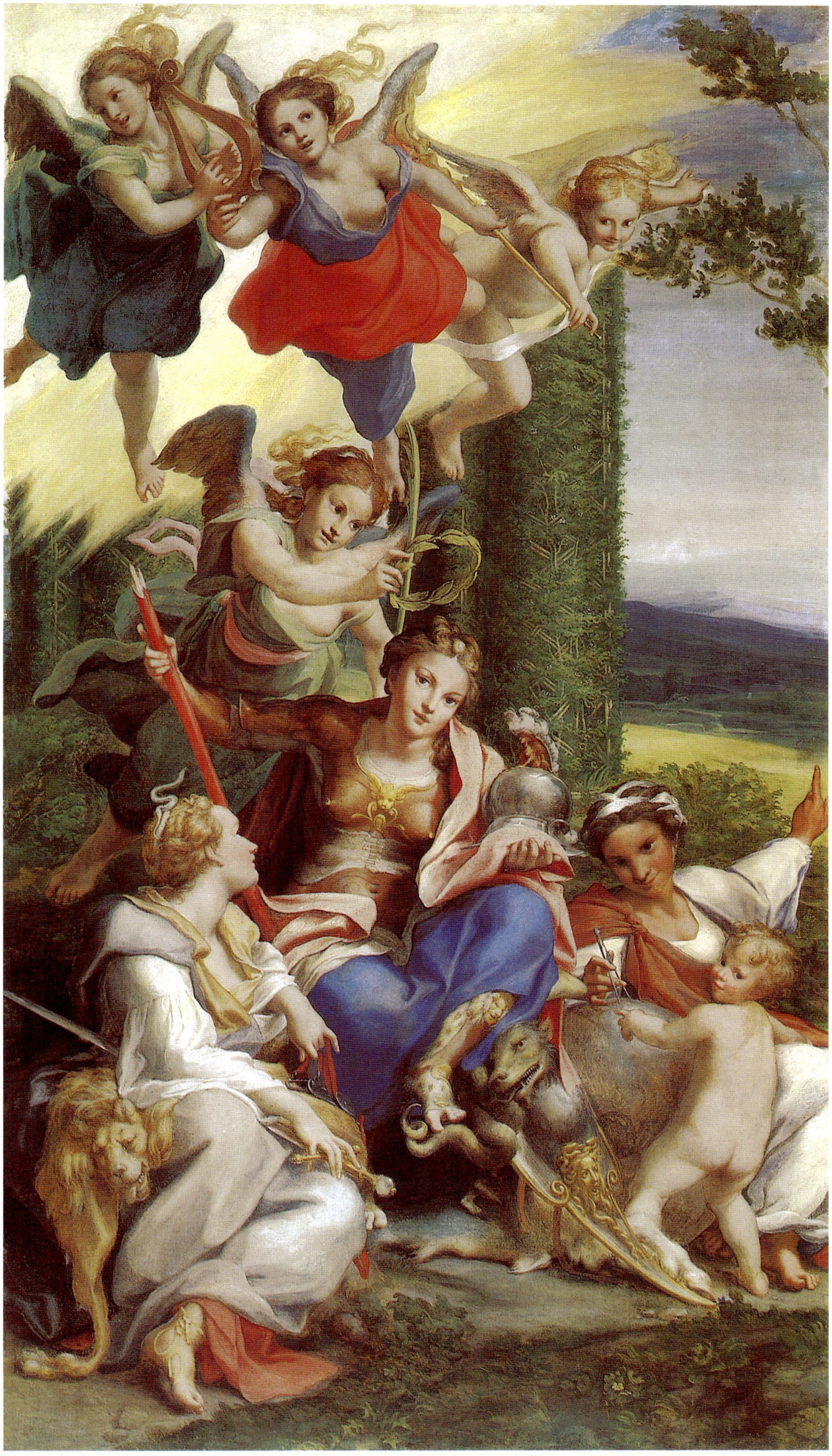

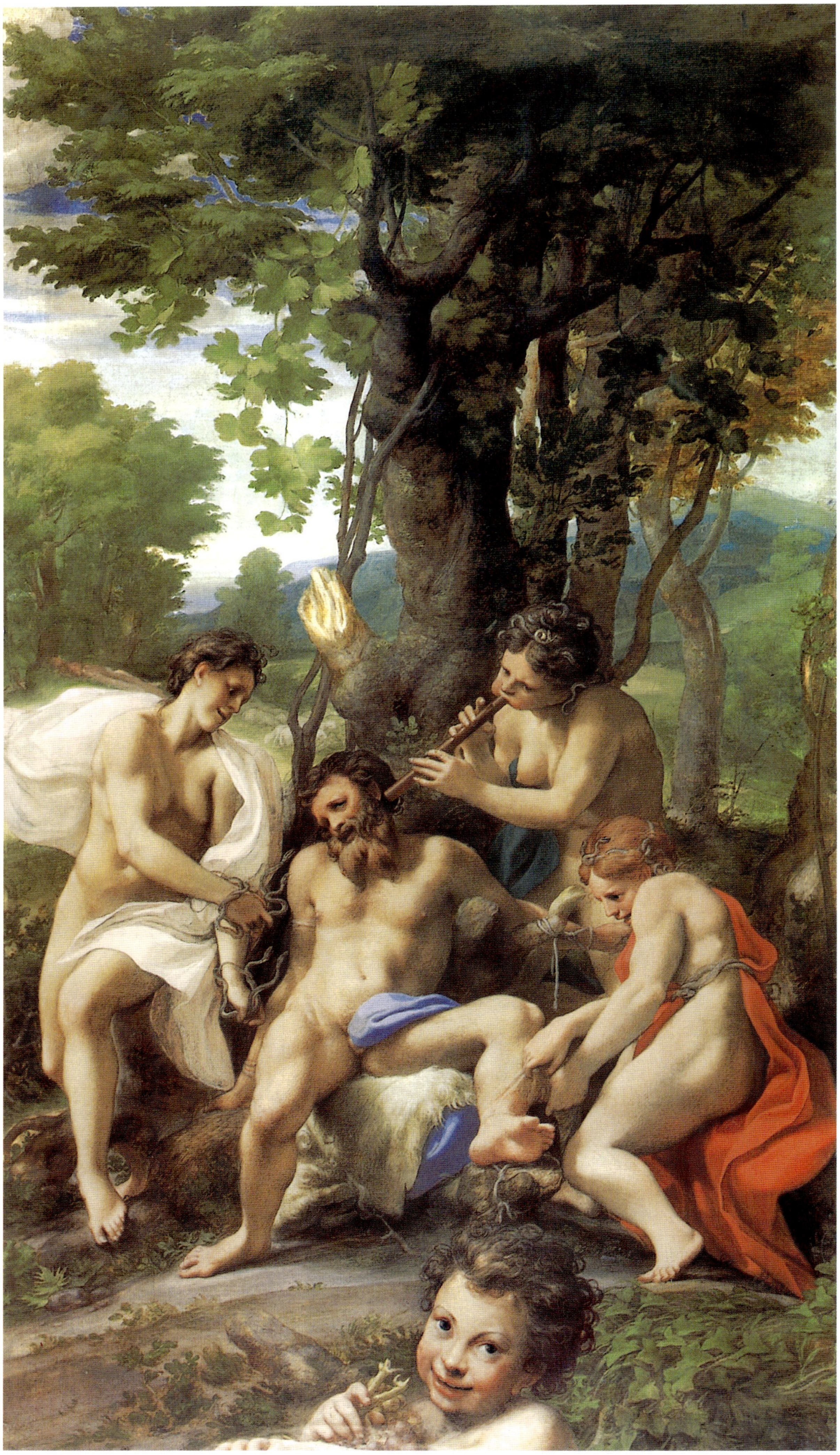

crown of laurel leaves, attributes of Apollo and the Muses. Some other figures in Costa's painting are less specifically referential than this idealised image of Isabella. Several play music, the civilised, harmonious art beloved by the *marchesa*. The most important other figures for a consideration of Mantegna's contribution to the chamber are Diana, the virgin huntress, and Cadmus, the dragon-slayer (and therefore defender of Good), because they look up to the right towards Mars and Venus in his painting, which was adjacent to it in the placement of the pictures in about 1510. These glances link two of the great paintings for the project and the picture's chief incident shows the crowning of Isabella, the great patroness of this learned and beautiful series.

Long after Mantegna was dead, Isabella added to the cycle two paintings by Antonio Allegri, called Correggio, who created his pictures for the room in about 1530. Isabella moved her *Grotta* and *Studiolo* from the Castle to the Ducal Palace in 1522, and eight years later she added Correggio's paintings to the series. The *Allegory of Virtue* (Fig. 126) includes Minerva at the centre; as in Mantegna's painting, she holds a broken spear, symbolic of her victorious strike against Vice. She is being crowned with laurel leaves, which were symbolic of poetry, and is surrounded by Virtues. The *Allegory of Vice* by Correggio (Fig. 127) shows a nude man who is tortured by various Vices. He is being bound and a lascivious woman is playing a wind instrument close to his ear. The wind instrument was often associated with eroticism because of its wild sounds and woodland connotations (Pan played one), and the "torture" is having its effect because the man is clearly having an erection, which is cleverly disguised by a piece of garment. Correggio illustrates an important concept Mantegna had expressed years earlier in his two paintings: sexuality is a kind of torture, and should be avoided in favour of higher, more satisfying intellectual pursuits.

These works by Correggio, like those by Mantegna, Perugino, and Costa, embody Isabella's philosophical attitude. She endeavoured to have her artists express her moral ideals in a gracious and perfect style. The ideas as expressed in the *Studiolo* are far more than the Christian ideals of chastity and purity embraced by the Church. Instead, Isabella's thinking was essential classical rather than medieval. Numerous Greek and Roman writers stressed one should avoid sensual pleasure, practicing instead philosophical thinking, bringing one the lasting value of moral virtue. In order to see other evidence of Isabella's attraction to classical ideas, one need have looked no further than the original ceiling of the *Studiolo*. Although the paintings of Mantegna and others are long gone from the chamber, part of the ceiling and some original decoration survives, including inscriptions with Isabella's name and the motto *"Nec spe nec metu,"* which means "Neither hope nor fear." This was the slogan of the Stoics of antiquity, and indicates one should not hope in transient things such as love, fame, or fortune, but should count on the certain and permanent good derived from developing one's virtues. The Greco-Roman gods, allegorical figures, and classical philosophical ideals in her little study inform one of the most splendid and important series of paintings of the Renaissance, which got its name from the rebirth of antiquity as embodied in projects like Isabella's *Studiolo*.

There were no surviving ancient pictures Isabella could purchase, so she turned to contemporaries like Mantegna to evoke in pictures the spirit of the classical past. It should be remembered, though, Isabella was greatly interested in acquiring ancient works of art, and this afforded even more opportunity for collaboration between Isabella and Mantegna. He acted repeatedly as an adviser when she was offered antiquities for purchase. For example, in 1505 an agent presented to her an ancient statue in ivory, but she turned it down saying Andrea Mantegna and a second appraiser

127. Antonio Allegri, called Correggio, *Allegory of Vice*, c. 1530. Tempera on canvas, 141 x 86 cm. Musée du Louvre, Paris.

thought it was of poor quality and possibly a fake. Another agent, writing in 1507 (and not knowing the painter was dead), offered a Greek sculpture to Isabella and optimistically wrote in his letter that Mantegna was sure to approve her acquiring it. It is no wonder, as we have seen earlier, Isabella wanted him to design the public statue of Virgil for the city of Mantua, because she esteemed his expertise of antique form and style. Both patron and artist were passionate in their love of classical antiquity, and Mantegna was instrumental in helping Isabella to turn both her *Studiolo*, with its modern paintings, and the adjacent *Grotta*, with its ancient original sculpture, into little museum galleries that were admired for decades by visitors to the Gonzaga court. Before leaving her, we might ask what role her husband played in the matters of erudite patronage. The striking answer is that, in an age when few women – even those of noble birth and high station – acted independently, Isabella both as a young bride and later as a mature woman happily pursued her activity as a patron and collector essentially alone, without interference from her husband, Francesco Gonzaga. Indeed, he acknowledged he lacked Isabella's knowledge and interest in collecting art and objects of beauty, noting he "understands horses and weapons better than engraved gems." Their marriage was essentially dynastic, political rather than loving, and they pursued most of their personal and cultural interests separately.

One final episode continues the interaction between Isabella and Mantegna, but hardly shows the marquise in the best light. In 1505 Mantegna fell gravely ill, and it made matters considerably worse that the Gonzaga court went several months without paying his salary. By early 1506 the painter was in some financial difficulty, having a short-term need for cash. Mantegna said to Isabella in a pathetic letter, "For many months I have not been able to secure a penny. I find myself in need especially at present, since I was hoping things would not be thus I find myself overwhelmed." His pleas to receive this back payment went unheeded, so Mantegna was forced to offer to sell Isabella a prized possession from his own collection, a bust of the Roman Empress Faustina, possibly identifiable with a surviving work. Although his difficulties were caused by the court's debt to him, Isabella haggled with the artist to lower the price to 25 ducats from the 100 ducats Mantegna wanted. Eventually Isabella paid the sum he asked, but after taking possession of the piece she could not come up with all the money originally promised. Isabella was genuinely short of funds and perhaps she was not at fault, but this episode soured the relations between the two in the last year of his life, and during the bargaining period Mantegna told a go-between Isabella was acting "shamefully." Mantegna's personal, emotional attachment to the antique past is shown by an account of his giving over of the bust of Faustina. An intermediary in the exchange wrote: "He handed it over to me with great ceremony and commended it to me with great insistence, not without strong jealousy appearing, in such a manner that I am almost sure he will die, unless he may have it given back to him." Finally, Isabella won, and ended up with Mantegna's prize.

Whether or not Isabella treated Mantegna unfairly in this last episode, the successful collaboration between them as patroness and painter remains the most important feature of their relationship. To the end, Isabella maintained great respect for Mantegna, and when he died later in 1506 she lamented, "A great light has gone out." The Marquise of Mantua was fortunate to have Mantegna serve her, but he too was lucky to have so involved and thoughtful a patroness, who challenged him to create erudite and beautiful paintings that evoke the spirit of classical antiquity. Her ideas for the series of paintings in the *Studiolo* helped Mantegna to elevate his art and produce elaborate compositions that are artistically pleasing and that illustrate the highest philosophical ideals of Italian Renaissance culture.

128. *The Penitence of St Jerome*, c. 1448-1449. Tempera on panel, 48 x 36 cm. Museo de Arte, Sao Paolo.

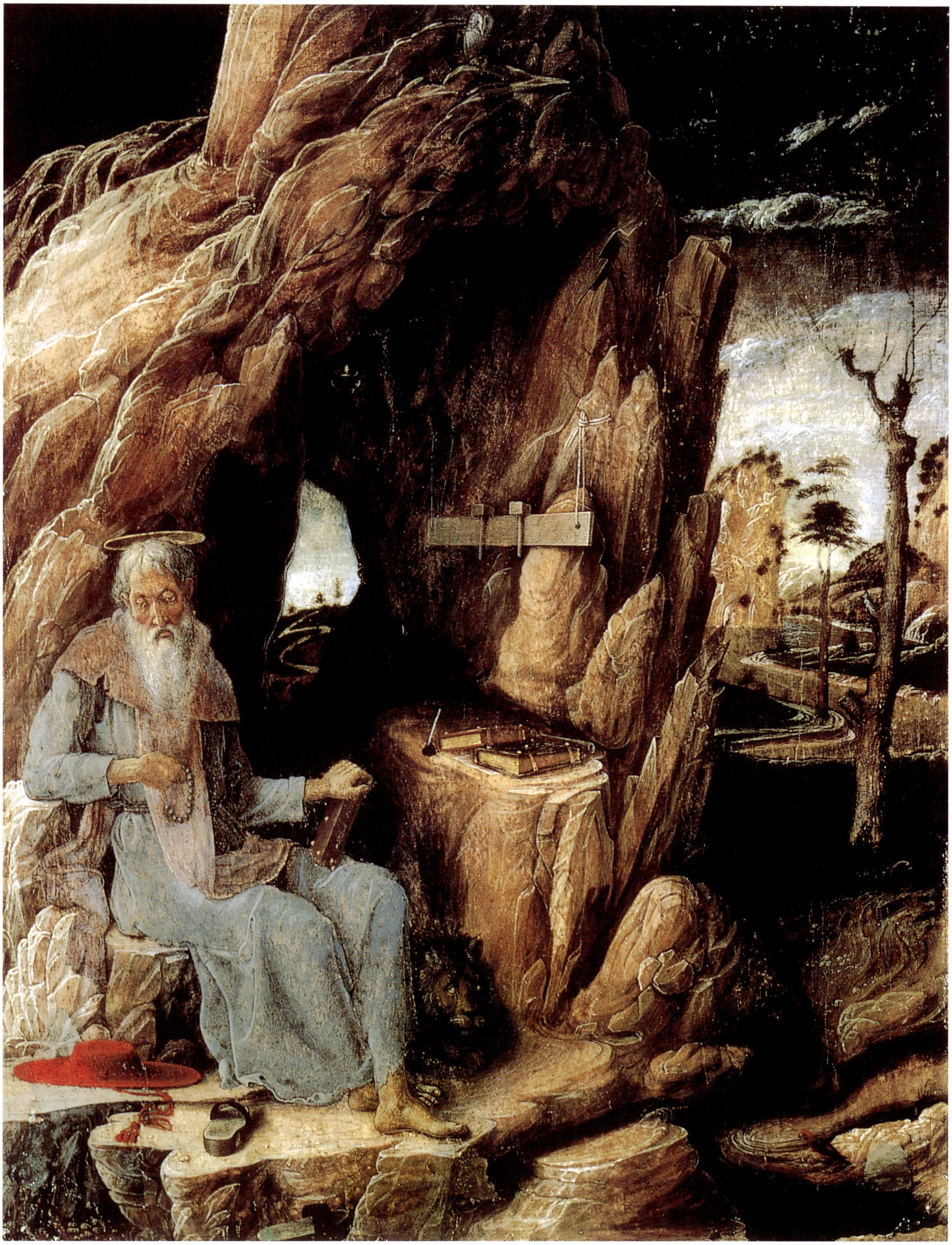

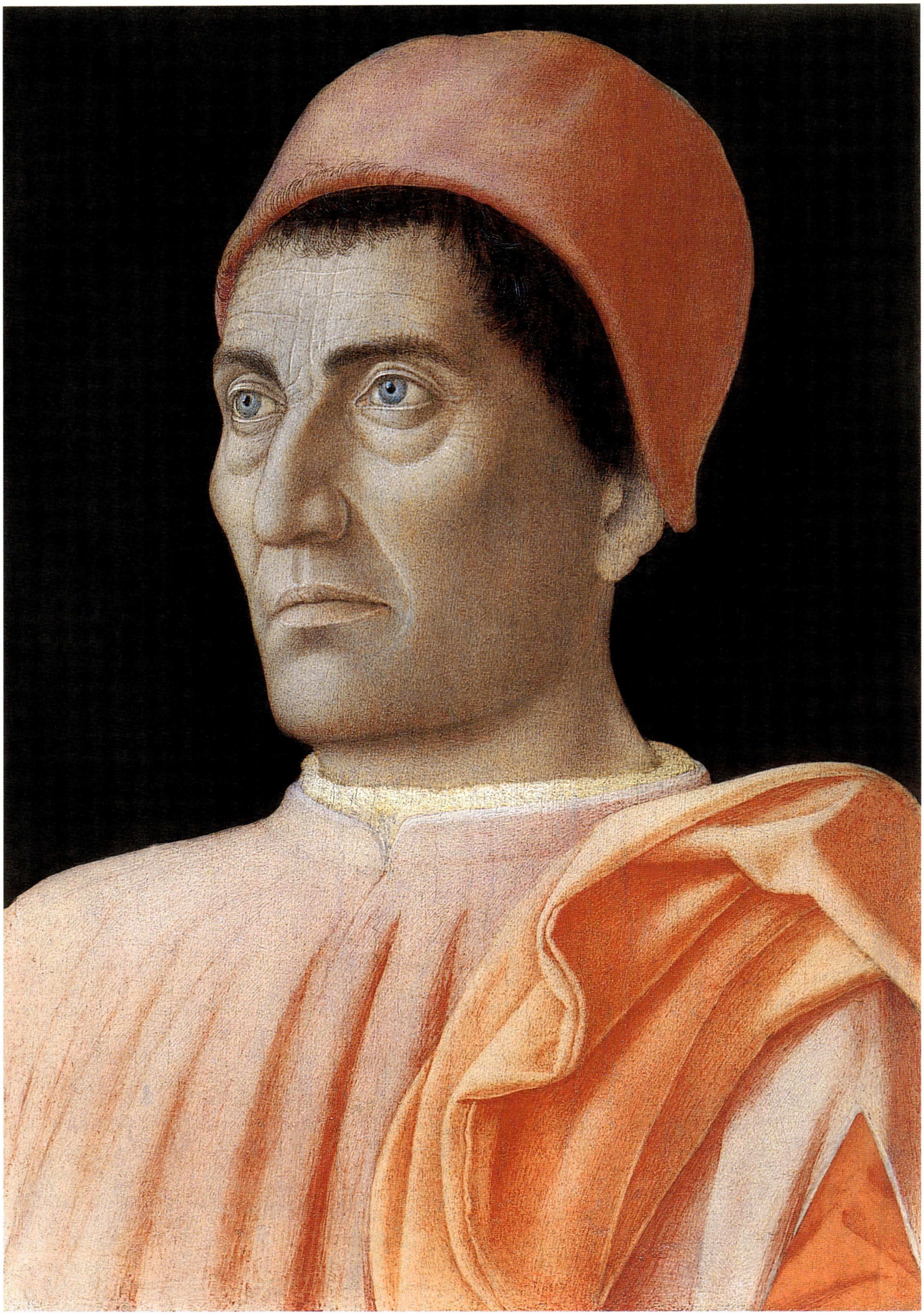

Mantegna's Place in History

Mantegna served Isabella d'Este as a painter of humanistic themes, an adviser for the acquisition of antiquities, and a designer of sculpture. His dealings with her, like similar aspects of his life and work, epitomise the change that had occurred in the status of painting during the Renaissance. In medieval times, an artist was valued as a craftsman who worked marvels with his hands. While Mantegna did impress contemporaries with his manual dexterity, he brought other intellectual elements to his work, especially his knowledge of classical culture, and in so doing he helped to elevate the profession of painting by advancing the rise in the status of being an artist. He was among a group of *Quattrocento* artists, including Leon Battista Alberti and Leonardo da Vinci, whom we recognise today as leading representatives of this new type of artist-thinker.

In his treatise *On Painting* of 1435, Alberti advised painters to "be learned in all the liberal arts... Next it will be of advantage if they take pleasure in poets and orators, for these have many ornaments in common with the painter. Literary men, who are full of information about many subjects, will be of great assistance in preparing the composition of a 'historia', and the great virtue of this consists primarily in its invention."[22]

Alberti dedicated the Latin version of his treatise in 1435 to Gianfrancesco Gonzaga, father of Ludovico, and it is fitting that it was in Mantua that an artist – Andrea Mantegna – flourished who so fully embodied the new ideas Alberti promulgated. The learning evinced in Mantegna's works from the beginning to the end of his career is the fruit of his association with men of letters, and the result of his own research into classical antiquity. Mantegna allied his art with the world of philosophy, history, and literature, and in this way he helped turn painting into a branch of humanistic thinking.

Accompanying the gain in the intellectual estimation of painters during the Renaissance was a rise in their social standing, and Mantegna was an early example of a painter who improved his position in the social hierarchy. The importance of this rise – going from being the son of a country carpenter to being an honoured courtier and a lesser nobleman – was recognised already in the Renaissance period. The sixteenth-century writer Giorgio Vasari regarded Mantegna's success as a product of genius and talent rewarded by sympathetic patrons, and he saw Mantegna's rise from working class circumstances to court artist as an act of justice. Vasari's message to his contemporary patrons was that they should reward talent whenever possible, as had happened to Mantegna:

> "As is known by every ambitious and reasonably successful artist, generosity is a powerful spur to talent. Craftsmen work all the harder, ignoring fatigue and discomfort, when they can hope for the rewards and honours which foster their talents and make them better known. It is certainly true that genius is not always recognised and rewarded as it was in the case of Andrea Mantegna, an artist who was born of very humble stock in the Mantua district, working in the fields as a boy and yet (as I shall describe) rising to the rank of knight through his own efforts and good fortune."[23]

129. *Portrait of a Man,* c. 1470-1475.
Tempera on panel,
41.3 x 29.5 cm.
Galleria degli Uffizi, Florence.

Here Vasari expresses the optimistic notion that merit, when rewarded, will achieve great things, and he notes Mantegna's entrance into the ranks of the lower nobility.

Since titles still meant something in Italian society, Mantegna was honoured to attain the titles of knight and count, using these titles in letters and signatures on paintings. Among fifteenth-century Italian painters only the Venetian Gentile Bellini, Mantegna's brother-in-law, achieved an equal status, becoming a count in 1469. Later in history other artists, most notably the sixteenth-century artist Titian and the seventeenth-century Spanish painter Diego Velázquez, also gained titles, bringing lustre to the profession of painter. Mantegna stood at the beginning of this process, when worldly success was the reward of talent and craftsmanship.

Mantegna's extraordinary contributions were recognised by contemporaries, and he was respected to the end of his life and beyond for his artistic endeavours. Mantegna was one of the most lauded artists of the Renaissance, and he had begun to receive encomiastic praise when he was still a teenager. Already in the 1440s the Venetian poet Ulisse degli Aleotti admired a highly realistic portrait of a nun by the seventeen-year-old Mantegna (a work now lost). Others, such as the Hungarian poet and humanistic Janus Pannonius, praised the lifelikeness of Mantegna's painting; Pannonius compared Mantegna to the Roman historian Livy, a compliment that gauged the high level of achievement found in his pictures. Verses of the nobleman Filippo Nuvoloni (1441-1478) compare Mantegna to the greatest painters of all time, describing him as one who is knowledgeable as well as being skilful with his hands. When Mantegna died, an instrument-maker for Isabella d'Este, Lorenzo da Pavia, said "I can never hope to meet a finer draftsman or a more original artist." We have seen Isabella preferred Mantegna's style to Perugino's, who was rated by many as the leading artist in Italy.

The greatest encomium devoted to Mantegna and his art comes from the hand of Giovanni Santi, who was the father of the High Renaissance painter Raphael. Giovanni, an artist of modest merit, wrote some verses in about 1494 in which he stated Mantegna was the greatest painter of his time, excelling in drawing style, compositional invention, perspective, grace, beautiful colouring, and three-dimensionality. As part of this paean, Santi described a visit to Mantua by the Duke of Urbino, who saw Mantegna's work:

> He had the greatest pleasure in admiring
> The marvellous painting and the exalted art
> Of Andrea Mantegna's high and famous genius
> To whom Heaven opened wide its gates
> With gifts in excellent and worthy painting
> Which flourishes in our outstanding age.
> Far more than others, Andrea bears the banner
> Of its great authority.
> Wherefore the Duke, as a distinguished master
> Giving his attention to these paintings
> Of the fine arts, with their great distinction,
> Praised them roundly, and again extolled them
> With words and praises splendidly.

130. After Mantegna, *Judith with the Head of Holofernes*, c.1500. Tempera on panel, 30.1 x 18.1 cm. The National Gallery of Art, Washington, D.C.

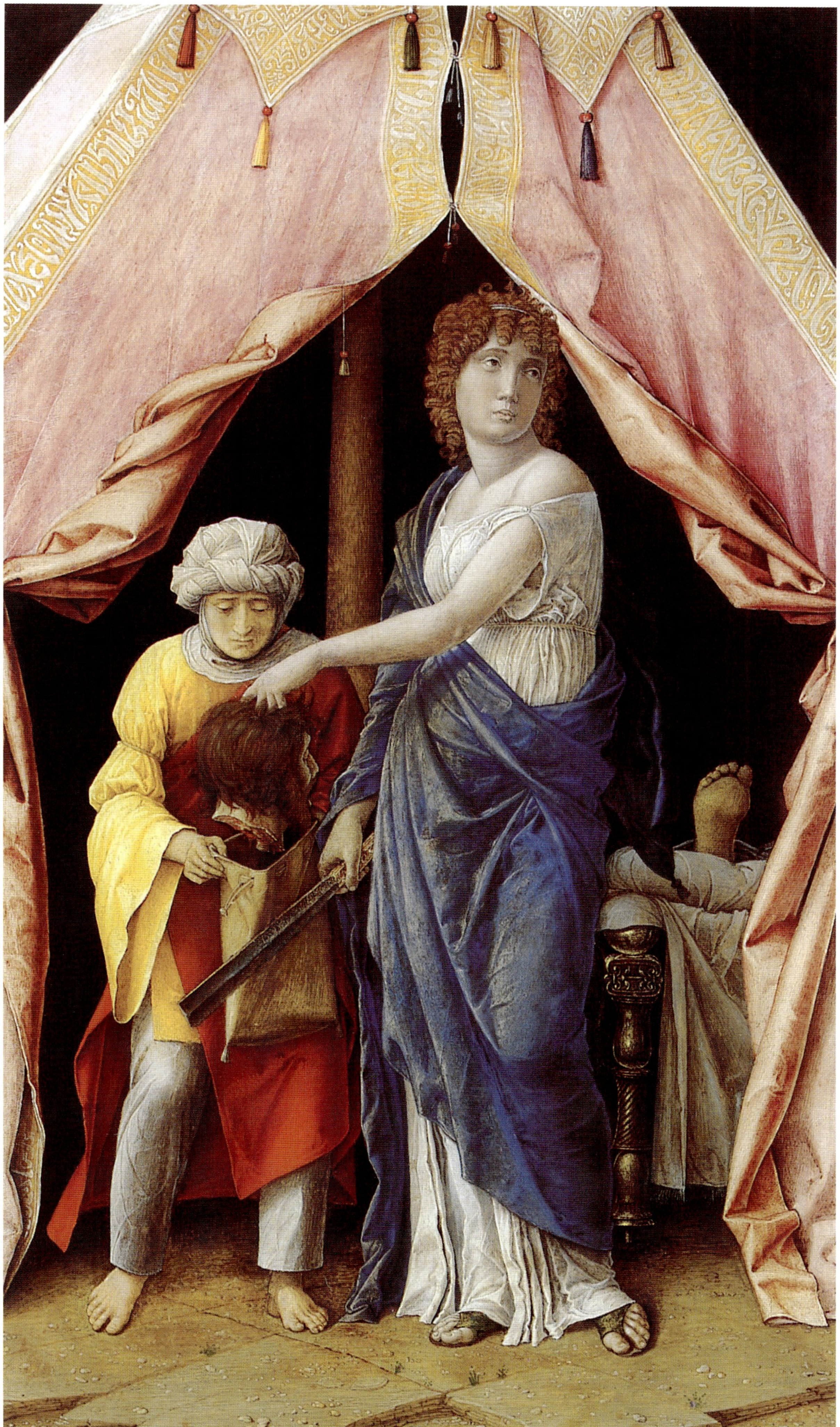

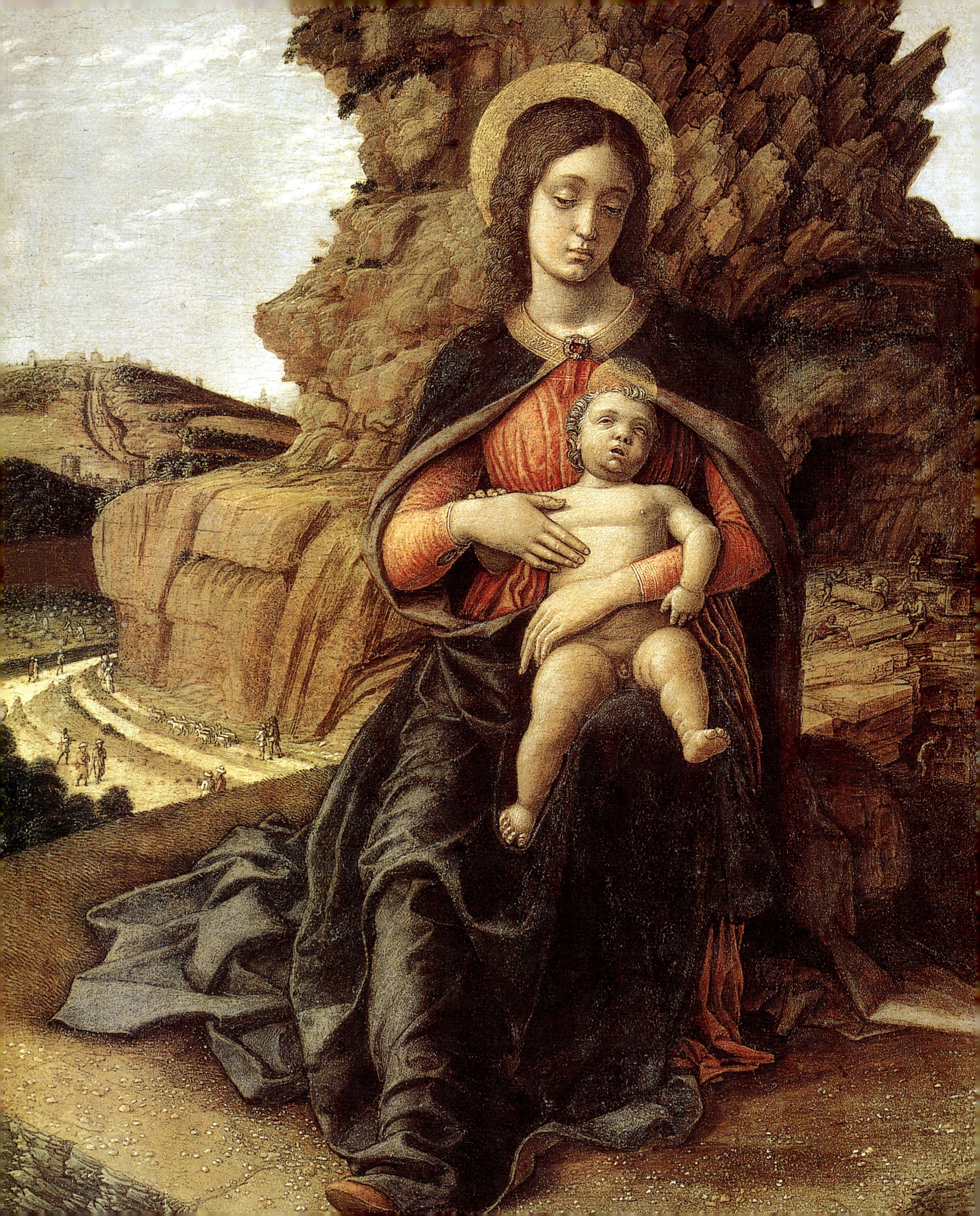

Santi goes on to praise specific features of Mantegna's style, and he adds the duke was stupefied when he first saw Mantegna's "sweet paintings and exceptional art."[24] Santi emphasised Andrea was made a knight solely on account of his painting.

Appreciation for Mantegna continued well into the sixteenth century. For example, the noted Ferrarese poet Ludovico Ariosto, in his epic *Orlando furioso*, (published a decade after the painter's death), lists Mantegna as one the greatest painters of all time. Baldassare Castiglione, author of the *Book of the Courtier* (written in the early sixteenth century), ranked Mantegna among the five great painters of the age. Later in the century, the Tuscan writer and artist Giorgio Vasari, although putting Mantegna together with some of the "dry" painters of the fifteenth century, had a sensitive appreciation for Mantegna's realistic details, and he provides an appreciative description of several of his pictures.

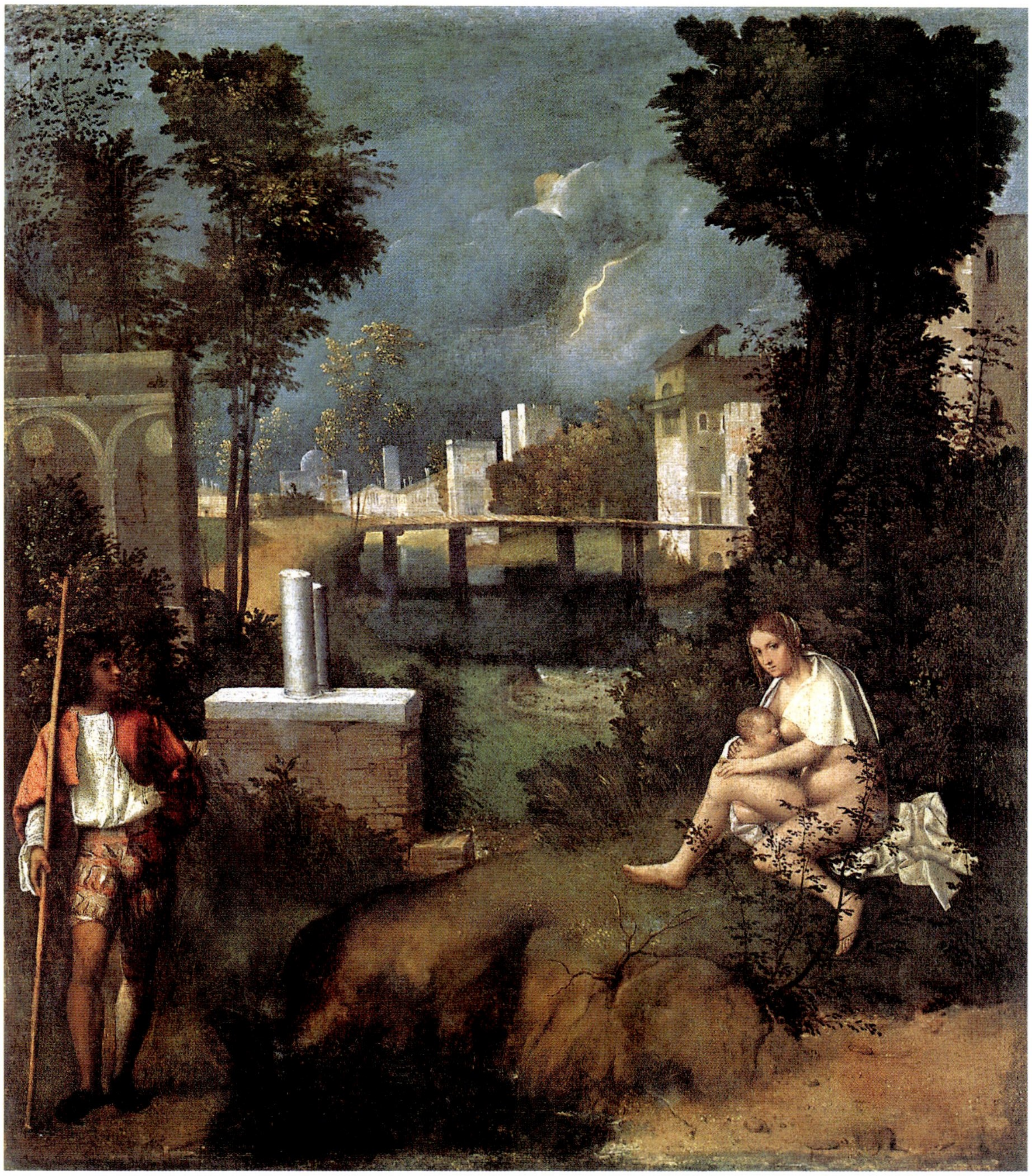

Mantegna's art was influential in his own time, and it was widely copied, serving as a model for other artists. We have seen Albrecht Dürer copied Mantegna's engravings, and a number of other artists, especially in northern Italy, borrowed ideas from his paintings and prints, finding inspiration in their taut linearity, dramatic narrative, and archaeological sensibility.

So many painters attempted to work in Mantegna's manner that it is sometimes difficult to separate the work of first-rate imitators from those of the master. A *Judith with the Head of Holofernes* and a drawing of *Putti Playing with Masks* serve as two instances of contemporary artists borrowing the style or designs of Mantegna (Fig. 130).

Despite the importance of Mantegna's art in his own time, the spread of his influence was hindered by the great change in style occurring near and after his death; a new artistic revolution made his style seem outmoded. It is sometimes asserted that Mantegna's artistry – based on idealised naturalism and antique inspiration – stands at the beginning of the classical taste that came to prevail in the coming centuries. Some arrive at this conclusion because of the classical roots of his style, others by citing the more pure idealism appearing in some of his later works, as attested, for example, by the figures in the *Madonna of Victory* (Fig. 67).

Although in historical retrospect we can see some connection between Mantegna's art and that of classicists from the sixteenth century on, later painters and theorists saw the matter differently, and the question of Mantegna's influence has to be framed within the art-historical context of succeeding generations.

Despite the admiration his art continued to attract, it was the style which flourished during the generation after Mantegna's death which came to have the greatest effect on the development of later painting, including the classicism promulgated in the studios and art academies of Europe from the sixteenth until the nineteenth century.

One important aspect of the style of the sixteenth century was technical, involving a different kind of paint and a new way of applying it. In the last years of Mantegna's life a novel manner came into prominence based on relatively free brushwork and carried out increasingly with a rich application of oil paints. Artists of the sixteenth century moved away from the pasty technique practised by Mantegna and other *Quattrocento* painters.

To the end, Mantegna made almost exclusive use of egg-based tempera and animal-glue distemper in his easel paintings, which are more opaque and less fluid in handling than the new method, with oil potentially producing a more luminous result. Oil painting is especially successful when applied to the representation of subtle shadowing, soft textures, and sensuous flesh.

Although Mantegna's style ameliorated somewhat later in life, it never approached the new soft manner of the Venetian painter Giorgione (Fig. 132) or the smoky shadowing of Leonardo da Vinci. In contrast to the portraits of Leonardo, those of Mantegna appear linear and unmodelled (Fig. 129).

131. *Madonna of the Stonecutters*, c. 1490.
Tempera on panel, 32 x 29.6 cm.
Galleria degli Uffizi, Florence.

132. Giorgione da Castelfranco, *The Tempest*, c. 1506.
Oil on canvas, 82 x 73 cm.
Accademia, Venice.

133. Leonardo da Vinci, *The Virgin of the Rock*, 1483-1486.
Oil on panel, 199 x 122 cm.
Musée du Louvre, Paris.

Today we appreciate the lively design and colour of Mantegna's style, but over the coming centuries the practice of applying oil-bound pigment to canvas in order to achieve a graceful, suggestive effect became the pictorial ideal.

Related to the technical changes occurring in the early sixteenth century was a broader, more generalised approach to painting, leading away from the detailed practice of Mantegna. The classical canon of painting taking root in the sixteenth century and which flourished for centuries called for the avoidance of particulars, and the making of pictures that are simple, stately, and slow in rhythm. The easy grace and theatrical artificiality of the High Renaissance replaced the intensity and the particularised realism of Mantegna and his contemporaries.

Compared to the works of the High Renaissance, Mantegna's are brittle, liney, and dry. Mantegna's diligent technique and taut, dramatic style gave way all across Italy to a broad handling of paint, a more generalised narrative approach, and a simpler, more imposing compositional method.

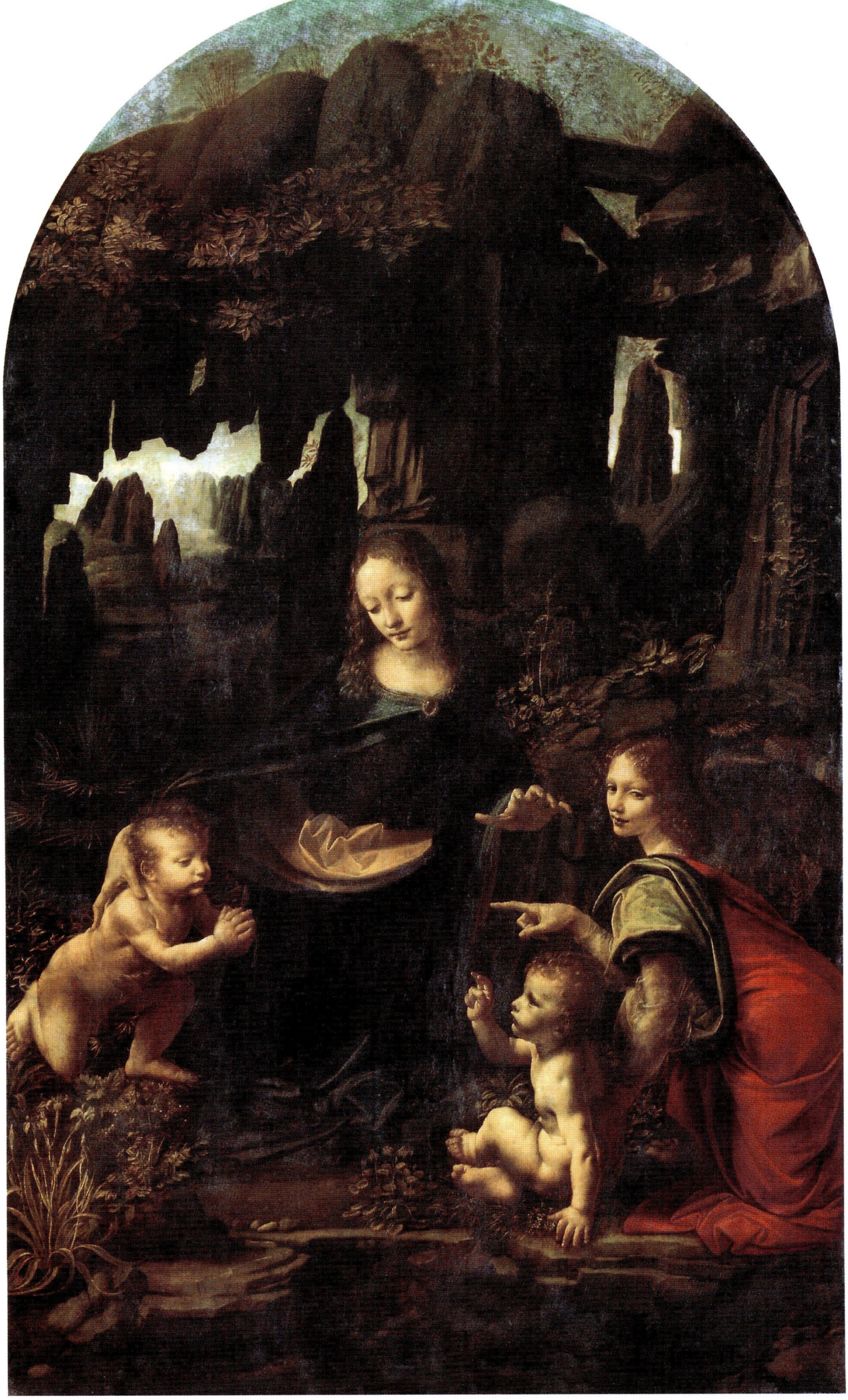

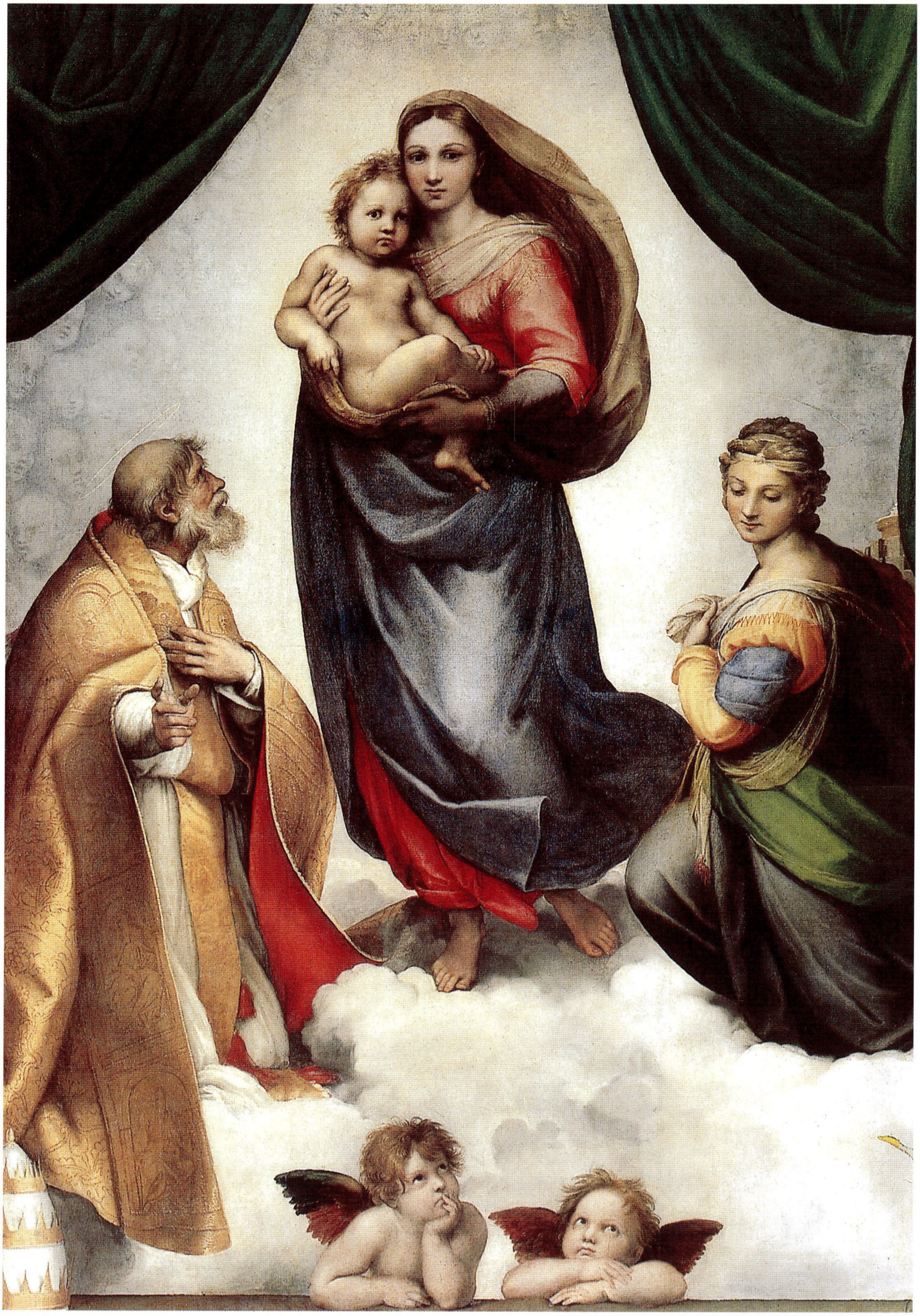

By the end of the first decade of the *Cinquecento* (1500s), at least one of Mantegna's patrons seemed to favour the new art sweeping Italy. In 1508, Francesco Gonzaga promised to provide another noble collector with a painting done "by a hand softer and sweeter than Mantegna's was."

This is the kind of attitude that would favour the move toward a style such as Correggio's, whose works indeed had the sweetness and painterly handling the more brittle and heroic paintings by fifteenth-century masters lacked (cf. Figs. 126 and 127).

By the time of Giorgio Vasari, the artist and early art historian writing in the middle of the sixteenth century, Mantegna's style was typical for its age in that is was "dry, hard, and harsh." Unlike the sixteenth-century painters, whose works were "exquisitely graceful," Vasari thought Mantegna belonged with the group of *Quattrocento* painters whose work lacked liveliness and a harmonious blending of colours, the earlier works seeming to be the product of overexertion. Vasari preferred what he called the "effortless intensity" of Michelangelo and the grace and charm of Leonardo and Giorgione.

These changes in artistic style are echoed in the page of Baldassare Castiglione's early-sixteenth-century *Book of the Courtier*, in which he calls for effortless grace in human actions. Mantegna's style seems to fit an older moral ideal, one of brisk heroic action rather than staid *gravitas* and philosophical calm.

The lesser value placed on the fifteenth-century manner, including the art of Mantegna, continued for the next several centuries. It is true there was a periodic appreciation of Mantegna's paintings in later times. For example, among art collectors, as famous a patron as Charles I eagerly sought to acquire the *Triumphs of Caesar* in the seventeenth century.

Mantegna's paintings were not widely copied before modern times, but the great Flemish master Peter Paul Rubens made a sensitive and complementary variant copy of two of Mantegna's paintings of the *Triumphs of Caesar*. We have also seen Rembrandt copied an engraving by Mantegna, and he owned the print (Fig. 103). These two Baroque artists, who were often denounced by classical theorists for their "low" realism, were attracted to Mantegna for his vivid lifelikeness, the Flemish painter to the lively triumphal parade, the Dutchman to an intimate domestic scene. At any rate, these copies were anomalies; the general practice in Baroque times was to ignore the *Quattrocento*.

Seventeenth-century critics, theorists, and painters in Italy and France fell into two camps, those who favoured a sensuous colouristic style and painterly brushwork, and those who championed a more balanced compositional approach and an emphasis less on colouring than on good design. They framed the argument in terms of Florence versus Venice, design (*disegno*) versus colouring (*colorito*), and Titian and Rubens versus Michelangelo and Poussin.

This was not merely a theoretical matter; classical artists such as Nicolas Poussin, Carlo Maratta, and Charles Le Brun indeed looked to the central Italian High Renaissance, especially Raphael (Fig. 135) for their inspiration. For their part, painterly artists turned to the sixteenth-century Venetian masters, including Titian, Paolo Veronese, and Jacopo Tintoretto, for guidance. For the

134. Raffaello Sanzio, called Raphael, *Sistine Madonna*, 1512-1513. Oil on canvas, 269 x 201 cm. Gemäldegalerie Alte Meister, Dresden.

most part, Mantegna and painters of his time were left out of this discussion. They were often admired as forerunners of the sixteenth-century styles, but they were not thought to be suitable models for imitation.

Among later painters, the great Neoclassicists, such as Jacques-Louis-David and Jean-Auguste-Dominique Ingres, paid homage to the High Renaissance and antiquity in words and in their reverent artistic imitation. Compared to the sweeping gestures, nonchalance, and grand generalisations in Raphael's works, Mantegna's must have seemed to them laboured and dry, too bogged down in particulars. Neoclassical theorists also prized the *Cinquecento* above all, ignoring the "Primitives" of the *Quattrocento* and instead elevating the sixteenth-century masters to semi-divine status.

It is not surprising the eighteenth-century painter and academician Sir Joshua Reynolds ignored Mantegna in his famous *Discourses*. Reynolds was interested in the sublime qualities of Michelangelo and the grandeur and decorum of Raphael, so the "barbarous state of the Arts" before Raphael's time held little interest for him.

With the coming of modern times and a more broad-ranging acceptance of different styles, Mantegna's paintings, along with those of his fellows of the Early Renaissance, have come back into fashion. Among the first of the major writers to appreciate Mantegna was the poet, dramatist, and essayist Johann Wolfgang von Goethe. Writing in 1786 in his *Flight to Italy*, he revealed he was smitten by the frescoes of the Ovetari Chapel, saying, "I've seen pictures by Mantegna, one of the older masters, that I'm amazed by! Words can't express the clear, confident present those pictures contain."[25]

This sensitive appreciation of Mantegna's realism was echoed by the growing number of authors of art history texts in the nineteenth century, and Mantegna achieved a place in the Pantheon of painters after a more catholic and historical approach to art history held sway. Today, Mantegna's critical star is very high indeed.

Even the notion he was a cold antiquarian has largely fallen out of favour. The sweetness of his Madonnas, his sparkling wit, and his attractive landscapes, dotted with romantic ruins, give lie to the idea that his pictures are little more than unemotional illustrations of an antiquarian dogma.

Even so, there remained objectors, such as the English critic and moralist John Ruskin (1819-1900), who judged Mantegna's paintings to be based too heavily on classical models and not enough on Nature.

Ruskin complained Mantegna was obsessed with science instead of matters of the spirit, to such an extent the painter was paralysed by the study of anatomy so even his best works, such as his allegories for Isabella d'Este (Figs. 120 and 122) are revolting; in general, Ruskin found a "viciousness" and vulgarity in Mantegna's works, and a hardness in his figures.[26]

The critic Bernard Berenson, writing in 1907, found more good to say about Mantegna, but also lamented his uncritical attitude toward the Antique, and accused Mantegna of borrowing from

135. Raffaello Sanzio, called Raphael, *The Transfiguration of Christ*, c. 1517. Oil on panel, 400 x 279 cm. Pinacoteca, Vatican.

poor Roman examples: "Englamoured and undiscriminating only as an Italian Humanist could be, Mantegna was blinded to the fact that his models were, in everything but conception, inferior to the work of his own peers and contemporaries."[27]

The notion of Mantegna as an overly devoted antiquarian appears from time to time in later literature, although not all authors find this kind of reverence to be a fault.

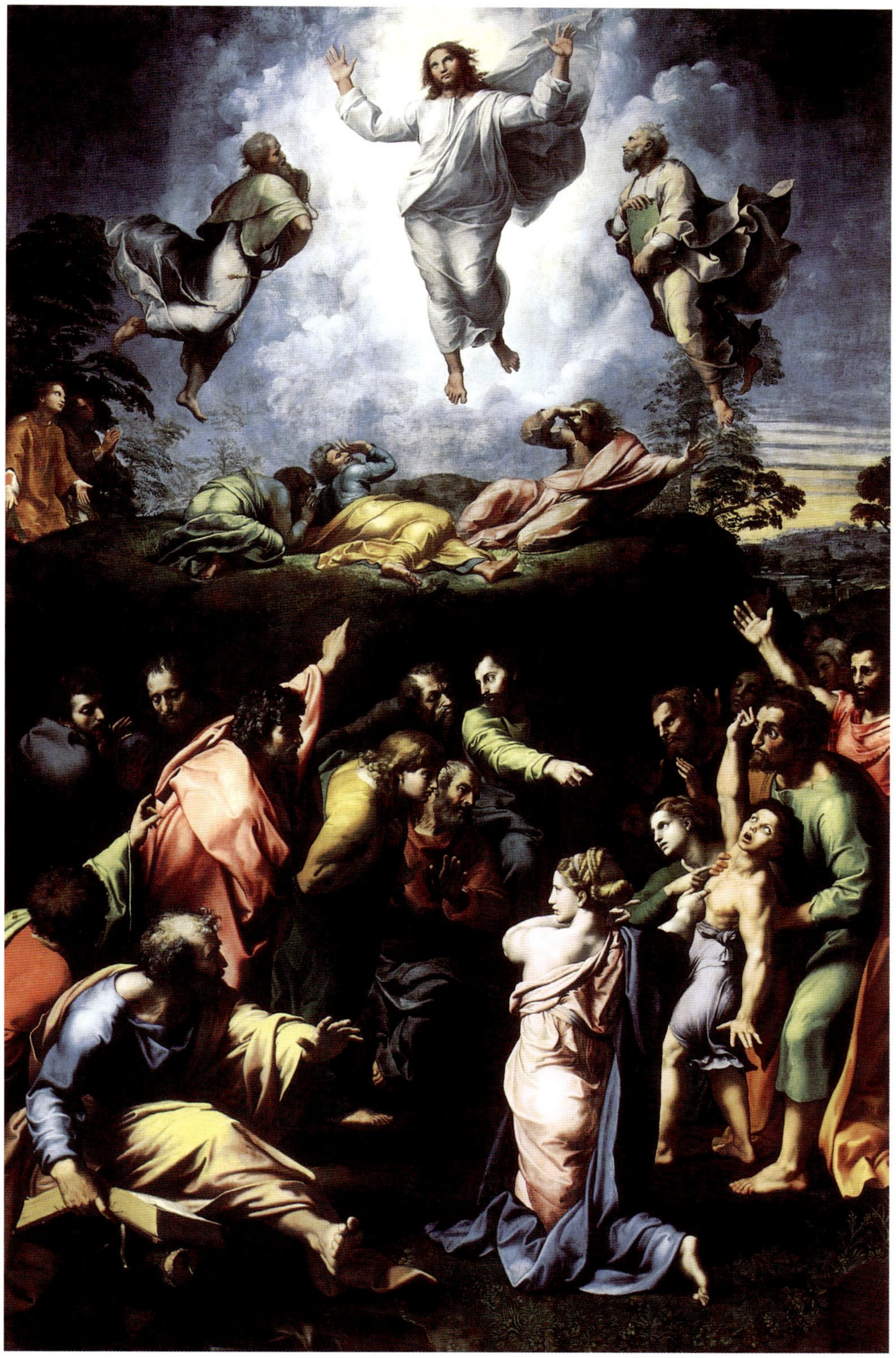

The criticisms of Ruskin and Berenson are enough to remind us that Mantegna's paintings are not for everybody. The connoisseur Roberto Longhi shared with Berenson the opinion that Mantegna's surfaces are insufficiently naturalistic and overly sculptural, a criticism which found expression already in the testimony of Francesco Squarcione, Mantegna's own teacher. The psychologist William James divided the world into tough-minded and tender-minded people; there is no doubt Mantegna works are best enjoyed by tough-minded viewers.

Despite the human sympathy and his occasional flashes of humour, Mantegna's pictures sometimes lack elegance, and they do indeed often come across as pedantically archaeological.

But his art has to be appreciated in the context of his time, when humanist scholars and learned patrons enjoyed a certain archaeological pedantry, and when the stridency of his works conveyed the heroic, sharp realism of classical Roman art.

With Mantegna, the elegant, pleasant world of Gothic painting gave way to a bitter naturalism and dramatic intensity. The medieval dream was ending, and it was time to engage directly the real world and to re-examine the pre-Christian civilisations in Greece and Rome.

Born near the end of the waning, Gothic world, Mantegna set out to fabricate a new universe. This was his great achievement, and his critical fortunes are so high today because we can appreciate the skill, devotion, and enthusiasm he put into fostering the cultural rebirth that occurred in the fifteenth century.

Notes

1. Giovanni Santi, quoted from Creighton Gilbert, *Italian Art, 1400-1500: Sources and Documents* (Englewood-Cliffs, 1980), p. 96.
2. Giorgio Vasari, *The Lives of the Artists*, selection and translated by George Bull (Harmondsworth, 1965), p. 241.
3. Vasari, *The Lives of the Artists*, p. 242.
4. Filarete, *Treatise on Architecture, Being the Treatise by Antonio di Piero Averlino, Known as Filarete*, 2 vols., translation, introduction, and notes by John R. Spencer (New Haven and London, 1965), I, p. 175.
5. See Caroline Elam, "Mantegna at Mantua," in *Splendours of the Gonzaga*, ed. David Chambers and Jane Martineau (Milan, 1981), p. 18.
6. Elam, "Mantegna at Mantua," p. 19.
7. Gilbert, *Italian Art*, p. 12.
8. Ronald Lightbown, *Mantegna* (Oxford, 1986), p. 178.
9. Gilbert, *Italian Art*, p. 134.
10. Gilbert, *Italian Art*, pp. 135-136.
11. Gilbert, *Italian Art*, pp. 179-180.
12. Gilbert, *Italian Art*, 180.
13. Gilbert, *Italian Art* p. 129.
14. Vasari, *Lives of the Artists*, p. 244.
15. Leon Battista Alberti, *On Painting and On Sculpture*, edited with translations and notes by Cecil Grayson (London, 1972), p. 97.
16. Gilbert, *Italian Art*, p.100.
17. Julia Cartwright, *Isabella d'Este, Marchioness of Mantua, 1474-1539: A Study of the Renaissance*, 2 vols. (New York, 1903; second edition), I, p. 4.
18. Lightbown, *Mantegna*, p. 188.
19. For overviews of the history of the Studiolo and Grotta, see Caroline Elam, Isabella d'Este's *studioli* and *grotte*: Introduction, in *Splendours of the Gonzaga*, pp. 164-165, and Egon Verheyen, *The Paintings in the* Studiolo *of Isabella d'Este at Mantua* (New York, 1971), pp. 7-21.
20. Verheyen, *The Paintings in the* Studiolo *of Isabella d'Este*, p. 26.
21. Translation from original text in Fiorenzo Canuti, *Il Perugino*, 2 vols. (Siena, 1983), p. 236.
22. Alberti, *On Painting*, p. 95.
23. Giorgio Vasari, *The Lives of the Artists*, p. 241.
24. See Gilbert, *Italian Art*, p. 96.
25. Johann Wolfgang von Goethe, *The Flight to Italy: Diary and Selected Letters*, edited and translated with an Introduction by T.J. Reed (Oxford, 1999), p. 58.
26. John Ruskin, *RÉSUMÉ of Italian Art and Architecture* (1845), ed. Paul Tucker (Pisa, 2003), pp. 50 and 109.
27. Bernard Berenson, *The North Italian Painters of the Renaissance* (New York and London, 1907), p. 43.

Bibliography

Monographs and Exhibition Catalogues on Mantegna:
- Nike Batzner, *Mantegna* (Cologne, 1998).
- Maud Cruttwell, *Andrea Mantegna* (London, 1902).
- Giuseppe Fiocco, *L'arte di Andrea Mantegna* (Bologna, 1927).
- Paul Kristeller, *Andrea Mantegna* (London, 1901).
- Ronald Lightbown, *Mantegna. With a Complete Catalogue of the Paintings, Drawings, and Prints* (London, 1986).
- Jane Martineau, ed., *Andrea Mantegna* (Milan, 1992). (Exhibition held at the Metropolitan Museum of Art in New York and the Royal Academy in London, Jan.-July 1992).
- Giovanni Paccagnini, with Amalia Mezzetti and Maria Figlioli, *Andrea Mantegna* (Venice, 1961). (Exhibition held at the Ducal Palace in Mantua, Sept.-Oct. 1961).
- Alberta De Nicolò Salmazo, *Andrea Mantegna* (Geneva, 2004).
- E. Tietze-Conrat, *Mantegna: Paintings, Drawings, Engravings* (London, 1955).

Documents:

A number of useful translations into English of original documents on Mantegna's life, including many of the longer quotes used here, are in:
- Creighton Gilbert, *Italian Art 1400-1500: Sources and Documents* (Englewood-Cliffs, NJ: 1980).

Mantegna and Printmaking:

Most of the literature cited above under monographs and exhibition catalogues deals in part with the issue of Mantegna and printmaking. The following consider the question further in more specific studies:
- Tancred Borenius, *Four Early Italian Engravers* (Boston, 1923).
- Suzanne Boorsch, "Letters: Mantegna and Prints," *Burlington Magazine*, 135 (Dec. 1993), pp. 826-827.
- Keith Christiansen, "The Case for Mantegna as Printmaker," *Burlington Magazine*, 135 (Sept. 1993), pp. 604-612.
- David Landau, "Letters: Mantegna and Prints," *Burlington Magazine*, 135 (Dec. 1993). pp. 827-828.
- Evelyn Lincoln, *The Invention of the Italian Renaissance Printmaker* (New Haven, 2000).
- David Landau and Peter Parshall, *The Renaissance Print, 1470-1550* (New Haven and London, 1994).
- Jay Levenson, Konrad Oberhuber, and Jaquelyn Sheehan, *Early Italian Engravings from the National Gallery of Art* (Washington, 1973).

The Camera Picta ("Camera degli Sposi"):
- Keith Christiansen, *Mantegna: Padua and Mantua* (New York, 1994).
- Michele Cordaro, ed., *Mantegna's Camera degli Sposi* (Milan, 1993).
- Rodolfo Signorini, *Opus hoc tenue: la Camera Dipinta di Andrea Mantegna* (Mantua, 1985).
- Rodolfo Signorini, *La più bella camera del mondo: La Camera Dipinta di Andrea Mantegna detta "degli Sposi"; The Most Beautiful Room in the World: The Painted Room by Andrea Mantegna called "degli Sposi"* (Milan, 1992).

Other literature on Mantegna:

Some of the following concentrates on Mantegna, in other works cited the artist is discussed as part of a larger context:
- Bernard Berenson, *The North Italian Painters of the Renaissance* (New York and London, 1907).
- Sergio Bettini and Leonello Puppi, *La Chiesa degli Eremitani di Padova* (Vicenza, 1970).
- I. Blum, *Andrea Mantegna und die Antike* (Strassbourg, 1936).
- Carla Cerati, *I Trionfi di Cesare di Andrea Mantegna e il Palazzo di San Sebastiano in Mantua* (Mantua, 1989).
- J.A. Crowe and G.B. Cavalcaselle, *A History of Painting in North Italy* (London, 1871), 2 vols. (Second edition: London, 1912, ed. Tancred Borenius, 3 vols.).
- Alberta De Nicolò Salmazo, *Il soggiorno padovano di Andrea Mantegna* (Padua, 1993).
- Giuseppe Fiocco, *The Frescoes of Mantegna in the Eremitani Church, Padua* (Oxford, 1978).
- Creighton Gilbert, *Italian Art 1400-1500: Sources and Documents* (Englewood Cliffs, 1980).
- Jack Greenstein, *Mantegna and Painting as Historical Narrative* (Chicago and London, 1992).
- Frederick Hartt, *History of Italian Renaissance Art* (New York, 1987).
- Phyllis Williams Lehmann and Karl Lehmann, *Samothracian Reflections: Aspects of the Revival of the Antique* (Princeton, 1973).
- Evelyn Lincoln, "Mantegna's Culture of Line," *Art History*, vol. 16, no. 1 (March 1993), pp. 33-59.
- Andrew Martindale, *The Triumphs of Caesar in the Collection of Her Majesty The Queen at Hampton Court* (London, 1979).
- Millard Meiss, *Andrea Mantegna as Illuminator: An Episode in Renaissance Art, Humanism, and Diplomacy* (New York, 1957).
- Giorgio Vasari, *Le vite de' più eccellenti pittori, scultori e architettori nelle redazioni del 1550 e 1568* (ed. P. Barocchi and Rosanna Bettarini, 1966-1987). 6 vols. (English translation of selections from Vasari's biographies by George Bull, *The Lives of the Artists* [London, 1965]).

The Gonzaga and Mantua:

The following publications contain background on the Gonzaga as rulers and patrons. Some of the studies include considerable discussion of Mantegna:
- Francis Ames-Lewis and Anka Bednarek, ed., *Mantegna and Fifteenth-Century Court Culture* (London, 1993).
- Franco Borsi, *Leon Battista Alberti* (Oxford, 1977), especially "The Works at Mantua," pp. 200-275.
- David Chambers and Jane Martineau, ed., *Splendours of the Gonzaga* (London, 1981). (Exh. cat., The Victoria and Albert Museum, London, 1981).
- Alison Cole, *Virtue and Magnificence: Art of the Italian Renaissance Courts* (New York, 1995).
- G. Coniglio, *I Gonzaga* (Varese, 1967).
- Giovanni Paccagnini, *Il Palazzo Ducale di Mantova* (Turin, 1969).
- Martin Warnke, *The Court Artist: On the Ancestry of the Modern Artist* (Cambridge, 1993).
- Joanna Woods-Marsden, *The Gonzaga of Mantua and Pisanello's Arthurian Frescoes* (Princeton, 1988).

Isabella d'Este as Patron and Collector:
- Clifford Brown, with Anna Maria Lorenzoni, "The Grotta of Isabella d'Este," *Gazette des Beaux-Arts*, ser. 6, vol. 89 (May-June 1977), pp. 155-171 and ser. 6, vol. 91 (Feb. 1978), pp. 72-82.
- Clifford Brown, with Anna Maria Lorenzoni, *Isabella d'Este and Lorenzo da Pavia: Documents for the History of Art and Culture in Renaissance Mantua* (Geneva, 1982).
- Julia Cartwright, *Isabella d'Este, Marchioness of Mantua, 1474-1539* (London, 1903). 2 vols.
- Sylvia Ferino-Pagden, *"La Prima Donna del Mondo": Isabella d'Este, Fürstin und Mäzentin der Renaissance* (Vienna, 1994). (Exh. cat., Kunsthistorisches Museum, Vienna, Feb-May 1994).
- Ernst Gombrich, "An Interpretation of Mantegna's *Parnassus*," *Journal of the Warburg and Courtauld Institutes*, 26 (1963), pp. 196-198.
- J. Lauts, *Isabella d'Este, Fürstin der Renaissance* (Hamburg, 1952).
- Egon Verheyen, *The Paintings in the* Studiolo *of Isabella d'Este at Mantua* (New York, 1971).

List of Illustrations